Islam in the modern world

A Christian perspective

Islam in the modern world

A Christian perspective

Norman Anderson
OBE, QC, LL.D, Hon.DD, FBA
Formerly Professor of Oriental Laws and Director of the Institute of Advanced Legal Studies in the University of London

APOLLOS

APOLLOS (an imprint of Inter-Varsity Press),
38 De Montfort Street, Leicester LE1 7GP, England

First published 1990
Reprinted 1992

British Library Cataloguing in Publication Data
Anderson, Norman, *1908–*
Islam in the modern world.
1. Christianity compared with Islam
2. Islam compared with Christianity
I. Title
200

ISBN 0–85111–414–8

Set in Baskerville 10 on 11 pt.
Typeset in Great Britain by Input Typesetting, London

Printed in England by Clays Ltd, St Ives plc

Contents

Preface

Part I Islam today

1 An introduction to Islam 3
2 The twin sciences of Islam: theology and the sacred law 43
3 Islamic mysticism: the most attractive face of Islam? 65
4 Islamic fundamentalism: 'Back to the Sharī'a!' 95

Part II The Christian response: the incarnation, cross and resurrection

Introduction to Part II 115
5 The incarnation: background to the contemporary debate 117
6 Christology down the centuries 137
7 The incarnation and other religions 161
8 The incarnation and personal faith today 181

Epilogue

Appendix: The so-called 'Gospel of Barnabas' 223
Notes 235
Glossary of Arabic terms 259
General index 271

Preface

The repeated reports in the media on the political repercussions of the publication of Mr Salman Rushdie's novel *The Satanic Verses*, together with the 'sentence of death' on the author (and repeated incitements to his assassination) voiced by Ayatollah Khomeini and other Islamic leaders, must have alerted everyone to the significance of Islam today. With its total population of little less than a billion, its solid dominance in many parts of the world and widespread dispersion elsewhere; with its sectarian, cultural and theological diversity and the growing power and extremism of its 'Islamic fundamentalists'; and with its basic, although much fragmented, cohesion, Islam demands the sympathetic, yet discerning, attention of us all.

My interest in Islam as a religion goes back to the latter part of my time at Cambridge, to fourteen years in Egypt and to repeated visits to most parts of the Muslim world. From soon after the Second World War, moreover, I became professionally involved in the study and teaching of Islamic law, on which I have written three books and scores of articles. While not a professional theologian, I have also been deeply concerned with the Christian faith and its interaction with other religions, especially Islam.

I have recently been encouraged by some friends, therefore, to bring together some of the more general (rather than strictly academic) articles about Islam that I have written over the years, revise them and round them off by adding new material – especially chapters on both Islamic mysticism and Islamic fundamentalism. Then came a subsequent suggestion that I should add a second part of the book devoted to the essence of the Christian answer – concentrating on three fundamental tenets of the Christian faith: the incarnation, atonement and resurrection. The fact that these three topics are those which our Muslim friends find the most difficult to understand and accept makes them, of course, particularly relevant in this context. The material concerned has been taken from four chapters from my book *The Mystery of the Incarnation* (now out of print for some years), after revision and a number of additions.

Finally, I have added an Epilogue which first summarizes the substance of the preceding chapters about both Islam and the Christian faith (any aspect of which *might* provide a basis for dialogue), and have then given an outline of those points on which I believe dialogue would be particularly relevant and rewarding.

I would suggest that readers should start with the Epilogue (pp. 205–7) ('A Look Back') as an introduction which might well have been included in this Preface; but that they should leave the remainder of the Epilogue to the end.

I am most grateful to those publishers who have given me permission to use material from books they have published: Hodder and Stoughton for much material from *The Mystery of the Incarnation* and a few extracts from *The Teaching of Jesus*; Collins for some material from *God's Law and God's Love*; IVP for the chapter on 'Islam' in *The World's Religions*; and *Arab Law Quarterly* for material from an article on 'Islamic Law Today'.

Norman Anderson

PART I
Islam Today

CHAPTER ONE

An introduction to Islam

The initial expansion of Islam

The early expansion of Islam[1] is one of the outstanding phenomena of history. Within ten years of the death of its founder, Muslim armies had burst out of Arabia and conquered the countries we now know as Jordan, Israel, Lebanon, Syria, Iraq, Iran and Egypt. Within a hundred years of his death, they had swept across North Africa, conquered Spain and penetrated Southern France; and during the same period they had swept east through Central Asia, poured into Northern India, reached the confines of China and built up an empire wider than that of Rome at her zenith.

Since then Islam has experienced several reverses, but has also made many significant gains. Its armies were defeated by Charles Martel of France, just one hundred years after the death of Muḥammad, and then, years later, had to abandon Spain. But in 1453 they conquered Constantinople and were subsequently twice halted only at the gates of Vienna. Otherwise, the history of Europe would have been radically different. Further east, they acquired a vast empire in the Indian subcontinent. It was primarily by trade and colonization, however, that Islam came to prevail in Malaysia, Indonesia and much of East and West Africa. So the influence of Islam now stretches from the Atlantic to the Philippines, from the Caucasus to Cape Town. More recently still, many Muslim immigrants have settled in Europe and North America.

Numbering some 900 million in all, Muslims now represent more than one in every six human beings, drawn from races as diverse as the European from the Hausa-Fulani, the Aryan Indian from the Philippine tribesmen. As Dr S. M. Zwemer wrote, more than half a century ago,

> A vertibrate and virile creed counteracts the centrifugal tendencies of nationality, race, climate and environment . . . The question of Zionism is front-page news in the Muslim press of India as well as in Egypt; it arouses the Muslims of Saʿudi Arabia, but also those of South Africa and Morocco. This unity and solidarity of the Muslim world through its religious creed, the pilgrimage to Mecca, the power of the press and the continued existence and power of the Sufi dervish orders cannot be denied.[2]

None the less, it is exceedingly difficult to summarize in one short chapter the history, faith and practice of Islam, since that religion has been, and is, very differently interpreted by a wide variety of sects and schools of thought which would all claim the name of Muslim. In the main, therefore, it will be necessary to confine our attention to what may be termed the central current of orthodox Muslim thought, with only brief and inadequate allusions to other and rival interpretations. If one excepts, however, the more extreme sects of the Shīʿa – and, of course, those communities such as the Druzes and the ʿAlawites which can no longer properly claim the name of Muslim[3] – it is to the person, life and revelations of Muḥammad that both the faith and the practice of all varieties of Muslims are usually traced. And while the greater part of the alleged sayings and doings of the Prophet must be regarded as fictions which mirror the history of the theology, politics and jurisprudence of early Islam, yet there is a real sense in which R. A. Nicholson is correct when he says: 'More than any other man who has ever lived, Muḥammad shaped the destinies of his people, and though they had left him far behind as they moved along the path of civilization, they still looked back to him for guidance and authority at each step.'[4]

The origins of Islam

Muḥammad's early life

Born about AD 570 at Mecca,[5] Muḥammad was the posthumous son of an almost unknown father, and his mother died when he was only six. He was brought up first by his grandfather and then by his uncle Abū Ṭālib, worthy members[6] of the family of Hāshim and the tribe of Quraysh. Little is known with any certainty of his early life. The Traditions tell us that his mother gave him to a Bedouin woman to suckle and that he passed his earliest years among nomad tents; that when twelve years old he went with his uncle to Syria, where he met a Christian monk named Baḥīra; and that he was later employed by a rich widow named Khadīja, who put him in charge of her caravans and finally rewarded his fidelity with her hand in marriage. All that can be regarded as certain, however, is that he grew up an orphan[7] and attained economic security only when, in early manhood, he married Khadīja, then (traditionally) a widow of forty. The marriage seems to have been remarkably successful, for Muḥammad took no second wife until Khadīja's death some twenty-five years later. A number of children were born to them, but only one daughter, Fāṭima, survived.

Whatever view may be taken about the Traditions concerning his boyhood, it is abundantly clear that the adult Muḥammad soon showed signs of a markedly religious dispositon. He would retire to caves for seclusion and meditation; he frequently practised fasting; and he was prone to dreams. Profoundly dissatisfied with the polytheism and crude superstitions of his native Mecca, he appears to have become passionately convinced of the existence and transcendence of one true God. How much of this conviction he owed to Christianity or Judaism it seems impossible to determine. Monophysite Christianity[8] was at that time widely spread in the Arab kingdom of Ghassan; the Byzantine church was represented by hermits dotted about the Hijāz with whom he may well have come into contact; the Nestorians were established in al-Ḥīra and in Persia; and the Jews were strongly represented in al-Madīna (Medina), the Yemen and elsewhere. There can be no manner of doubt, moreover, that at some period of his life he absorbed much teaching from Talmudic sources and had contact with some forms of Christianity; and it seems overwhelmingly probable that his early adoption of monotheism can be traced to one or both of these influences.[9]

His revelations

It was at the age of about forty that the first revelation of the Qur'ān (the 'Reading' or 'Recitation') is said to have come to him. It is recorded that a voice three times bade him 'Read (or recite) in the name of thy Lord . . .'[10] Thereafter no more revelations came for a considerable time; then suddenly, when passing through a period of deep spiritual depression, doubt and uncertainty, he is said to have seen a vision of the angel Gabriel which sent him home trembling to Khadīja for comfort and covering, only to hear the voice saying, 'O thou enwrapped in thy mantle, arise and warn . . .'[11]

There can be little doubt that these passages mark his assumption of the prophetic office, although many Western scholars consider that certain poetical passages in the Qur'ān which breathe the questioning spirit of the seeker rather than the authoritative pronouncement of the Prophet were composed at an even earlier date.[12] It seems, however, that Muḥammad himself was at first doubtful of the source of these revelations, fearing that he was possessed by one of the *jinn*, or genii, as was commonly believed to be the case with Arab poets and soothsayers. But Khadīja and others reassured him, and he soon began to propound divine revelations with increasing frequency. To the orthodox Muslim every verse in the Qur'ān is the *ipsissima verba* of God, communicated to the Prophet by the archangel Gabriel (whom Muḥammad seems to have identified with the Holy Spirit).

The earliest sūras[13] of the Qur'ān reveal a marked simplicity of concept. They urge the moral response of man created by Allāh, foretell the day of judgment, and graphically depict the tortures of the damned and the delights of what appears at first sight to be a very sensual paradise. Increasingly, however, the unity and transcendence of the one true God become the overriding theme. But the response was poor. His wife Khadīja, his cousin ʿAlī, his adopted son Zayd and a few more believed in his mission, but the leaders of the Quraysh tribe, influenced largely by their economic interest in the pagan rites and pilgrimage of the Kaʿba (a Meccan shrine containing a black meteorite) and by their opposition to his personal pretensions, ridiculed his claims. His preachings and revelations thereupon changed somewhat in tone. More and more he began to recount the histories of previous (mostly biblical) prophets, and to emphasize how they, too, had been mocked and ignored; sooner or later, however, judgment always fell on their traducers.

The Hijra

But the response in Mecca was still small, and in AD 622 Muḥammad took the decisive step of withdrawing with his followers (some 200 in all) to al-Madīna, to which he had been invited by a party of its inhabitants who had met him during the pilgrimage, had accepted his claims and had prepared their fellow-townsmen for his advent. This withdrawal (or Hijra) proved the turning-point in Muḥammad's career and has been appropriately chosen as the beginning of the Muslim era.[14] In Mecca he had been the rejected Prophet, pointing his countrymen to the one true God and warning them of judgment to come. In al-Madīna he soon became statesman, legislator and judge – the executive as well as the mouthpiece of the new theocracy.[15]

Into the detailed history of the next few years we have no space to enter, but the key to its understanding seems to lie in his attitude to the Jews. There can be little doubt that Muḥammad at first believed that he had only to proclaim his message to gain Jewish support – for was not his message the one, true religion preached by Abraham and all the patriarchs and prophets, ever-corrupted only to be proclaimed anew?[16] It was for this reason that his earlier references to the People of the Book (Jews and Christians) were almost uniformly favourable, and that he at first adopted several Jewish practices. At al-Madīna he was soon to find, however, that the Jews would not accept his claims. More, they ridiculed his sometimes inaccurate accounts of Old Testament incidents.[17] This was something he could not endure; for he had recounted these incidents as the direct revelation of God (introduced by such words as: 'This is one of the secret histories which We reveal unto thee. Thou wast not present when . . .'[18]) and had denied that he had learnt them from any human source. When it became apparent, therefore, that certain sūras of the Qur'ān did not agree with those Old Testament records of the same incidents which he had previously confirmed as authentic, he was driven to allege that the Jews had corrupted, or at least misquoted, their own scriptures.[19] From this time, therefore, date his strictures on the Jews, his banishment or massacre of Jewish tribes, and the decisive turn from things Jewish to Arabia and Mecca discernible in his teaching.[20] Henceforth it was to the Kaʿba rather than Jerusalem that the Muslim community must turn in prayer,[21] and the pagan rites of the pilgrimage were to be purified and incorporated into Islam.[22]

This, again, made it necessary for him to impose his will on Mecca and led to his struggle with the Quraysh – although it also paved the way for the latter's ultimate acceptance of Islam. For our present purpose the details are largely irrelevant. Suffice it to say that, after a somewhat chequered career, Muḥammad entered Mecca in triumph in 9 AH/AD 628, smashed the idols which surrounded the Kaʿba, and had established Islam, nominally at least, throughout the greater part of the Arabian peninsula before his death at al-Madīna in 11 AH/AD 630. It remains, however, to form some estimate of his character and of the source of his revelations; and to this we must now turn.

Muḥammad's character

The idea – once prevalent in Europe – that Muḥammad was an impostor from first to last has, happily, been abandoned, and of his initial sincerity, at least, there seems no doubt. Most Orientalists explain his earlier revelations in terms of wishful thinking. These depict the misery and frustrations of his early life; his deep conviction that the Arabs, like the Jews or Christians, needed a Messenger and a Book; his longing to be favoured with some revelation that would mark him as their Prophet; and his eventual conviction that words, thoughts and stories which various external or internal stimuli summoned from his subconscious mind constituted instalments of this revelation.[23] It is true that he has sometimes been regarded either as an epileptic, a subject of hysteria,[24] a 'pathological case,[25] or as heir to an 'Ebionitic-Manichaean' doctrine of revelation (which may be thought to have safeguarded his sincerity if not altogether his moral character).[26] Others have occasionally taken a highly critical view and have suggested that there is reason to believe that his symptoms of revelation were sometimes artificially produced.[27] Alternatively, of course, the phenomena may be explained as symptoms of intermittent spirit-possession, as claimed by modern spiritist mediums. The sharp, staccato style of the earlier sūras of the Qur'ān can be explained on any of these hypotheses. When we turn, however, to the long, rambling accounts of Jewish patriarchs and prophets which occupy so much space in the later Meccan and earlier Madinese sūras, we are confronted by the fact that Muḥammad sought (at this stage, at least) to satisfy the natural demand for some miraculous evidence of his Prophetic claims,[28] by ascribing exclusively to divine revelation his knowledge of stories which correspond in such detail with the Talmud that of their essentially Jewish origin there can be little doubt.[29] Thus R. Osborn felt compelled to conclude:

> To work (these stories) up into the form of rhymed Sūras . . . must have required time, thought and labour. It is not possible that a man who had done this could have forgotten all about it, and believed that these legends had been brought to him ready prepared by an angelic visitor.[30]

That it must have taken time is admitted by R. Bell, who substitutes 'suggestion' for the angelic messenger as the normal method of inspiration;[31] but this, as A. Jeffery points out, scarcely justifies Muḥammad's exclusive ascription to revelation of material he must have obtained from human sources.[32]

The same problem confronts us once more when we turn to the later Madinese sūras, which contain detailed regulations on all sorts of subjects which govern the lives of Muslims to this day. In these sūras, too, Muḥammad adopted the same form of rhymed prose, and represented the words as the direct utterance of God. There is considerable justification, therefore, for the conclusion of D. B. Macdonald:

> You cannot possibly imagine, in the case of long periods dealing with the law of inheritance or with the usages of marriage or

> with the quarrels of his followers, or emphasizing the position and dignity of the Prophet himself – you cannot possibly imagine how all these things rose to him from his subconscious, that he did not know very well what he was saying and had not his own distinct objects in the way in which he expressed himself.[33]

This conclusion may be thought to find support from the fact that personal (and other) problems were sometimes solved by a divine revelation of the most convenient kind: it was thus that he was granted the right, unlike other believers, to have more than four wives[34] and dispensed from the normal obligation to divide his time equally between them;[35] that he escaped criticism when, in defiance of Arab custom, he married the divorced wife of his adopted son;[36] that he was absolved from his oath to have nothing more to do with his concubine Mary and extricated from the trouble caused thereby among his several wives;[37] and that his wives were bidden to veil themselves,[38] were threatened with a double punishment for unchastity,[39] and were forbidden to remarry after his death.[40]

Other scholars are so profoundly convinced of Muḥammad's essential sincerity that they explain all these enigmas on hypotheses which avoid imputing to him any conscious imposture. I should myself regard it as at least possible that, in later life, he had become so convinced that he was the recipient of divine revelations, and so sure that he was the Prophet of God, that he genuinely mistook the pressure of circumstances and of his own inclinations for the divine voice that he believed he had so often heard. But this is primarily a problem for the psychologist, to which history can provide no solution.[41]

For the rest, his character seems, like that of many another, to have been a strange mixture. He was a poet rather than a theologian; a master improvisator rather than a systematic thinker. That he was in the main simple in his tastes and kindly in his disposition there can be no doubt; he was generous, resolute, genial and astute; a shrewd judge and a born leader of men. Occasionally, however, he could be cruel and vindictive; he could stoop to assassination; and he seems to have had a sensual streak. It is true that the size of his *ḥarīm* pales to insignificance beside that of Solomon and compares not altogether unfavourably with that of David; that his virtues outshone those of his contemporaries, while his failings can scarcely have provoked comment in his day and generation; and that he introduced a number of genuine reforms. If he had been taken by his followers at his own valuation, adverse comment on his character would have been largely out of place. For the Qur'ān, while it asserts his prophetic dignity in no uncertain terms, contains some express allusions to his mortality[42] and imperfection,[43] which seem quite incompatible with his semi-deification in some of those Traditions of his words and actions which soon assumed an importance second only in theory to the Qur'ān itself. In words which are either put into his own mouth or regarded as addressed to him by God he is depicted as pre-existent ('I was Prophet when Adam was still between clay and water'); as the purpose of all creation ('Had it not been for thee I had not created the world'); and as the Perfect Man, the impeccable model on which all should mould their lives.[44] Such Traditions are, of course, creations of a later date, invented by the Muslim community to put their Prophet on a par with the Christians' Christ. It is his misfortune rather than his fault, therefore, that it is with Christ rather than with David or Solomon that he is habitually compared – for in such company he cannot stand.

The Traditions

It is, moreover, one of the paradoxes of Islam that a religion whose founder expostulated against the veneration given to Christ, and who unequivocally asserted that he himself was a mere man, should have ended by advocating a slavish imitation of that founder's personal habits such as finds no parallel in Christianity or elsewhere. D. G. Hogarth justly remarks:

> Serious or trivial, his daily behaviour has instituted a Canon which millions observe to this day with conscious mimicry. No one regarded by any section of the human race as Perfect Man has been imitated so minutely.[45]

The well-known Traditionalist, Aḥmad ibn Ḥanbal (d. 241 AH/AD 854), is said never to have eaten water-melons because, although he knew the Prophet ate them, he could never ascertain whether he ate them with or without the rind, or whether he broke, bit or cut them.

In such circumstances it is no wonder that the collecting of Traditions as to what the Prophet had said or done soon became a profession, and that men travelled all over the Muslim world to hear them from those to whom his scattered Companions had allegedly confided them. They were regarded as the uninspired record[46] of inspired words and actions, and were handed down from mouth to mouth by a long chain of narrators whose names were always recorded in the first part of the Tradition (the *isnād*) as a guarantee of the veracity of the subsequent subject-matter (the *matn*). Very soon, however, fabricated Traditions began to flood the market, one man alone confessing before his death that he had invented some 4,000; and every vagary of political, philosophical or theological thought sought support in some alleged statement of the Prophet. At a later date the Traditions were collected and arranged by the great Traditionalists, some of whom made strenuous efforts to separate the true from the spurious. Unfortunately, however, they confined their criticism to scrutinizing the trustworthiness of the names in the *isnād* rather than the plausibility of the actual Tradition. Different collections are today accepted as authoritative by the different sects into which Islam has divided,[47] but in all cases such Traditions have taken their place beside the Qur'ān as the primary source of Muslim theology, law and practice.[48] In addition, cheap collections of stories of the Prophet, some of very questionable propriety, have until recently, at least, still provided the popular religious literature of thousands.

Muḥammad's view of Christianity

Of the tenets of Christianity Muḥammad seems to have had a very superficial, and in part wholly erroneous, knowledge. In his early life he was as favourably disposed to Christians as to Jews: and even in his later life they seem to have come under less severe strictures than the latter.[49] 'Īsā, the Quranic name for Jesus, was the Messiah, was born of a virgin and is called God's 'Word' and 'a spirit from God'.[50] He was a great miracle-worker and one of the greatest of the prophets.[51] But the Qur'ān depicts him as expressly disclaiming deity and seems to deny that he ever died on the cross:[52] instead, it says that 'it was made to appear so' (or 'he was counterfeited to them') and that God caught him up to himself. This has usually been interpreted by orthodox Muslims as meaning that someone else was crucified, by mistake, in his place.

It is interesting to speculate how Muḥammad may have come to hold such views. Whether he came into contact with a heretical Christian sect called the Collyridians who actually worshipped the virgin, or merely misinterpreted the excessive veneration given her by some contemporary Christian groups, we shall probably never know. But there can be little doubt that he believed the Christian Trinity to consist of the Father, the Virgin and their Child. (*C.f.* the Ash'arīte statement: 'God is One God, Single, One, Eternal. . . . He has taken to himself no wife nor child', and several verses in the Qur'ān.[53]) It is not surprising, then, that he not only denounced the doctrine strongly but also repudiated the whole idea of the Sonship of Christ, understanding it as he seems to have done in terms of physical generation. Instead, the Qur'ān depicts Christ as a prophet whose followers had deified both him and his mother against his will. Similarly, in his denial of the crucifixion, Muḥammad may have been influenced by Gnostic views;[54] by his hatred of the superstitious veneration, largely divorced from true theology or living experience, accorded to the symbol of the cross in seventh-century Arabia; or by his repugnance to believe that God would allow any prophet to come to such an end. He even believed that Christ had foretold the coming of another prophet, Aḥmad (a variant of Muḥammad); and Muslims frequently maintain that Christians have changed this reference into the predictions of the Paraclete in the later part of St John's Gospel.[55] Traditionally, most Muslims believe that Christ will come again to kill the Anti-christ and all swine, to break the symbol of the cross, and to acknowledge Islam. In Muslim eschatology the second coming of Christ and the advent of the Mahdī (the 'Guided One') are inextricably mingled. There is much truth in J. T. Addison's summary:

> If Muḥammad's knowledge of a decadent form of Christianity had been thorough, or if the Church which he knew so imperfectly had been stronger and sounder, the relations between the two religions might have been very different. As it was, however, what passed for Christianity in his confused mind was a distorted copy of fragments of a notably defective original.[56]

We have already seen that Muḥammad may well have been influenced by both Gnostic and Docetist views; in addition, the Church 'which he knew so imperfectly' was itself sadly divided in its Christology. The influence of Byzantine Christians (Orthodox), of Jacobites (Monophysites) and especially Nestorians was present in Arabia both before and after Muḥammad. See chapter 6 below.

The development of Islam

The scope of the present chapter allows no space for a summary of the history of Islam after its founder's death. It is impossible, however, to understand the present divisions of Islam – the different Shīʿī sects, the four Sunnī schools, the Ibāḍīs, *etc.* – without a passing reference to their origin, and to this we must now turn. It should always be remembered, however, that in Islam, as elsewhere, the adoption of sectarian views by ethnical and local groups has often been a mere expression in theological terms of an intense desire for freedom from foreign domination and for the preservation of exclusive traditions.

The Caliphate

Muḥammad died, according to the best-supported view, without having designated any successor (Khalīfa or Caliph). As the last and greatest of the prophets he could not, of course, be replaced. But the community he had founded was a theocracy with no distinction between church and state; and someone must clearly succeed, not to give but to enforce the law, to lead in war and to guide in peace. It was common ground, therefore, that a Caliph must be appointed; and in the event ʿUmar ibn al-Khaṭṭāb (himself the second Caliph) succeeded in rushing through the election of the aged Abū Bakr, one of the very first believers. But the question of the Caliphate was to cause more divisions and bloodshed than any other issue in Islam and almost from the first three rival parties, in embryo at least, can be discerned. There were the Companions of the Prophet, who believed in the eligibility of any suitable 'Early Believer' of the tribe of Quraysh; there was the aristocracy of Mecca, who wished to capture the Caliphate for the family of Umayya; and there were the 'legitimists', who believed that no election was needed, but that ʿAlī, the cousin and son-in-law of the Prophet, had been divinely designated as his successor.

Abū Bakr's short rule of two years was chiefly noted for the 'Wars of Secession' and (traditionally at least) for the first compilation of the Qur'ān. On the death of the Prophet many tribes had refused any longer to pay their dues, but Abū Bakr enforced obedience by the sword. It was, indeed, the death in battle of many of those who could recite the Qur'ān from memory which is alleged to have convinced the Caliph of the necessity of reducing it to writing. On his death, Arabia had been consolidated for Islam and the principle of 'fighting in the way of God', denounced by the Prophet at Mecca but adopted with such signal success at al-Madīna, had become the watchword of the young Muslim state.

Before his death Abū Bakr designated ʿUmar as his successor, and his election passed off without incident. He has been called the 'second founder of Islam', for in his Caliphate Syria, Mesopotamia, Persia and Egypt fell to the Muslim arms and many vital decisions were taken. He died without appointing a successor; and in the event ʿUthmān was elected, himself an aged and pious 'Early Believer', but a scion of the aristocratic house of Umayya which had opposed the Prophet almost to the last. It was under his orders that the present recension of the Qur'an was prepared in 30 AH/AD 649 and all variant versions were destroyed. But his family proved his undoing and he died by the assassin's knife.

The Khārijīs

The first actual schism, however, occurred during the Caliphate of ʿAlī, who succeeded ʿUthmān as the fourth and last of the 'Rightly-Guided' Caliphs. Two leading Companions, Ṭalḥa and al-Zubayr, supported by the Prophet's widow ʿĀʾisha, rose in revolt. They were beaten at the Battle of the Camel, where some 10,000 Muslims lost their lives – to the horror of the pious when they remembered that the Qurʾān condemned to eternal damnation those who killed a brother Muslim without just cause. Soon, however, ʿAlī had a much sterner foe to meet, for Muʿāwiya, the Governor of Syria, marched against him on the plea of avenging the assassination of his kinsman ʿUthmān, in whose death ʿAlī was accused of complicity. At first ʿAlī seemed again to be winning the day, but at the critical juncture of the battle Muʿāwiya cunningly succeeded in inducing ʿAlī to submit the question of the Caliphate to arbitration.

This deeply offended some of ʿAlī's own followers, who held that this question should never be debated on such human terms; by his agreement to such a course ʿAlī, they felt, had forfeited their allegiance. Still less, however, could they accord allegiance to Muʿāwiya: so they seceded (*kharajū*) and held themselves apart from the body of 'apostate' Islam (whence their name of Khārijīs). Thenceforward they drifted, split into rival sects, and constituted a perpetual thorn in the side of all authority;[57] to them the remainder of the Muslim community was far worse than the Jews or Christians, for the latter were people of a divine Book, while the former were apostates who should properly be killed at sight. They held that the Caliph should be elected on a basis of personal fitness, regardless of race or tribe; that the community should depose him if he went astray; that 'works' as well as 'faith' were necessary for salvation; and that one guilty of an unrepented sin ceased to be a believer. There were, however, many sub-sects. Eventually they divided into two main divisions, the one more, the other less, extreme; and the descendants of the moderate party, the Ibāḍīs, still survive in ʿUmān, in East Africa, and among the Berbers[58] of Algeria and Tripolitania, today distinguished by little more than minor points of theology and law from the main body of Sunnī (*i.e.* 'traditional' or orthodox) Islam.

The Shīʿa

The vexed question of the Caliphate soon led, however, to a far more important schism – that by which the whole body of the Shīʿa (the 'followers' or 'sect' of ʿAlī) broke off from Sunnī Islam. To the existence of a legitimist party who regarded ʿAlī as the divinely appointed successor of the Prophet we have already referred; and such were not deterred in their devotion when the ill-starred attempt at arbitration accomplished little, when ʿAlī continued to dispute the Caliphate with Muʿāwiya until he died under a Khārijī knife, or even when his elder son al-Ḥasan renounced his claim to succeed him in exchange for a princely stipend, and retired to end his life in dissipation at al-Madīna. Instead, they maintained that al-Ḥasan had been poisoned by order of Muʿāwiya, accorded him the title of 'Lord of Martyrs', and transferred their allegiance to his younger brother al-Ḥusayn.

The latter seems to have been made of somewhat better stuff; but when he rose in opposition to Muʿāwiya's son, Yazīd I, he was killed, with most of his family, at Karbala – a tragedy still commemorated each year throughout the Shīʿī world by the Passion Play of the 10th of Muḥarram. The horror of this butchery of the house of the Prophet rallied much support, however, to Shīʿī doctrines, and increasing numbers came to believe that God would never have left his people to impious rulers, or to the vagaries of human choice, but that there must always be some divinely chosen Imām, or Leader; that ʿAlī, so chosen, had been entrusted by the Prophet with esoteric teaching as to the real meaning of Islam which he had passed on to his descendants; and that after the death of al-Ḥusayn the office of Imām and infallible teacher had passed, as some held, to Muḥammad, son of ʿAlī by a wife of the Ḥanafiyya tribe, or, as the majority maintained, to ʿAlī Zayn al-ʿAbidīn, son of al-Ḥusayn and great-grandson of the Prophet.

After the four 'Rightly-Guided' Caliphs, the Caliphate became hereditary in the house of Umayya (41–132 AH/AD 660–748), and Muʿāwiya and his successors ruled for the most part as Arab kings of the old pattern, paying but scant allegiance to Islam. In such circumstances Shīʿī propaganda prospered exceedingly, especially among the Persian 'clients'[59] (*mawālī*), who saw therein a way to escape from Arab arrogance and a doctrine of the Imāmate more compatible with their pre-Islamic attitude to their kings. A number of insurrections were put down, but Shīʿī supporters eventually played a considerable part in the downfall of the Umayyad dynasty – only to find the throne seized, not for descendants of ʿAlī or the Prophet, but for those of the Prophet's uncle ʿAbbās.

Thus the Shīʿa continued under the ʿAbbāsid dynasty (132–656 AH/AD 748–1257) as a large and partly secret community, whose machinations came to the surface periodically in bloody rebellions, but who were continually weakened by their tendency to split into innumerable sub-sects. They split chiefly on the line of succession to the Imāmate. Some, like the Kaysānīs and Hāshimīs, held that it might pass to any child of ʿAlī (*e.g.* Muḥammad ibn al-Ḥanafiyya); others, like the Zaydīs, held that any descendant of al-Ḥasan or al-Ḥusayn might duly establish himself; but the more general view, shared by the 'Twelvers'[60] and the Ismāʿīlīs, was that the Imāmate passed from father to son in the line of al-Ḥusayn by a special form of transmission of a divine light-substance. But they differed, also, as to the nature of the Imāmate. To the Zaydīs the Imām was not supernatural, but could give authoritative teaching; the 'Twelvers' went further, and believed in the infusion of a divine light-substance in the person of the Imām which made him infallible and impeccable; while the Ismāʿīlīs went further still and, in their more extreme sub-sects, believed in a partial incarnation of the Deity either in one individual or, more commonly, in a succession of Imāms.

But this did not exhaust their differences. Another common cause of division was their concept of a 'hidden' Imām. Periodically, in most of the Shīʿī sects, men would become so attached to one Imām that they would refuse to believe that he had died; instead, he had only gone into hiding, whence he would one day re-emerge to bring in the Golden Age; others in the same sect, meanwhile, would transfer their allegiance to his successor. Sometimes the true explanation of this phenomenon seems to have been the intrigues of a series of adventurers who used the house of ʿAlī as tools and themselves acted in the name of the 'hidden' Imām; at others the prudence of the Holy Family, who frequently refused the danger of leading those insurrections for which their followers seem to have been always ready.

The chief branches of the Shīʿa found today are the Zaydīs of the Yemen, the 'Twelvers' of Iran, Iraq, India and the Lebanon and the Ismāʿīlīs (or 'Seveners') of India, Syria and East Africa. The Zaydīs, who are the most moderate of the Shīʿa, take their name from al-Ḥusayn's grandson Zayd, who rose against the Umayyad Caliph Hishām and was killed in 122 AH/AD 738. The Ismāʿīlīs and the 'Twelvers' trace the Imāmate not through Zayd, but his brother, Muḥammad al-Bāqir: the former to Ismāʿīl,[61] son of Jaʿfar al-Ṣādiq, and his son Muḥammad; and the latter through Mūsa'l-Kāẓim, brother of Ismāʿīl, to a certain Muḥammad ibn al-Ḥasan,[62] who vanished in about 260 AH/AD 873 but is regarded as still alive, as communicating his teaching to his leading divines (who, unlike the Sunnīs, still claim the right of *ijtihād*[63]), and as the Imām-Mahdī of the future. This is the state religion of Iran, where the leading canon lawyer (Āyatullāh) is today regarded as the final authority (al-Faqīh).

But the strangest story in Muslim history is that of the Ismāʿīlīs, among whom secret (*bāṭinī* or 'inner') teaching was carried to fantastic lengths. Emissaries were sent far and wide to make capital out of any anti-Government feeling, out of social and economic unrest, racial antipathies, or any form of scepticism. To the Khārijīs their teaching was represented as Khārijī, to the Shī'īs as Shī'ī, and to Persian nationalists as anti-Arab. Their technique seems to have been to excite doubt; to stress the need for an authoritative teacher; and to impose an oath of secrecy and implicit obedience. Initiates were passed, where suitable, through several grades, above the fourth of which, it seems, a mystic philosophy took the place of orthodox Islam. To this movement or conspiracy can ultimately be traced, through varying developments, the Qarmaṭians, who dominated Iraq at the end of the third century AH (ninth century AD), practised a form of communism, and scandalized the Muslim world by carrying off the black meteorite from the Ka'ba at Mecca; the Fāṭimid dynasty, which ruled Egypt for so long; the Druzes of the Lebanon, who still worship as God al-Ḥākim, one of the Fāṭimids of Egypt; the Assassins, who terrorized Syria and Iraq from their fortresses in the times of the Crusades and to whose last Grand Master of Alamūt the Āghā Khān traces his descent today; the Nuṣayrīs or 'Alawites of Northern Syria, who deify 'Alī; and those rather shadowy figures of history, the Ikhwān al-Ṣafā.[64]

Many of these sects are (or were) a law unto themselves and to their beliefs no further reference can be made. The great majority of the Shī'a, however, fully accept the Qur'ān though they often differ from the Sunnīs in its interpretation and even accuse the Caliph 'Uthmān of having suppressed a number of verses favourable to 'Alī. They also accept the authority of the Traditions, though they reject the Sunnī collections in favour of their own. In matters of faith and practice the differences between the two main divisions of Islam are considerable; but for the remainder of this chapter it will be necessary to confine our attention, in the main, to the Sunnīs, who not only greatly preponderate in numbers, but can also fairly be regarded as the more natural representatives of the central stream of Muslim thought.

The four Sunnī schools

It was not only about the Caliphate that controversy raged. The eternal conflict between the disciples of reason and of tradition has also been bitterly waged in Islam, both in law and in theology; and it is partly to this conflict that the development of the four orthodox schools of jurisprudence into which Sunnī Islam is now divided owe their origin in the early 'Abbāsid period. Such are the Ḥanafī (or Iraq) school, whose traditional founder was Abū Ḥanīfa (d. 150 AH/AD 766), which is followed today throughout most of the old Ottoman Empire and Northern India;[65] the Mālikī (or Hijāz) school, which derives its name from Mālik ibn Anas (d. 179 AH/AD, 795), which prevails in North and West Africa, Upper Egypt and the Sudan; the Shāfiʿī school, founded by al-Shāfiʿī, the 'father' of Muslim jurisprudence[66] (d. 204 AH/AD 817), which is followed in Lower Egypt, East Africa, Southern Arabia and South-East Asia; and the Ḥanbalī school, which is named after the great Traditionalist Aḥmad ibn Ḥanbal, and whose few modern followers are chiefly limited to the Wahhābīs of Central Arabia.

In course of time a bitter conflict developed between the speculative jurists, as their opponents considered the Ḥanafī school, and the traditionalists, a term claimed by all other schools – although they varied greatly in the degree to which they deserved it.[67] In reality the conflict had not developed in the time of Abū Ḥanīfa and Mālik, and the somewhat greater dependence of the latter on tradition and the former on speculation in constructing their systems can be adequately explained by the fact that Mālik lived in the very city and milieu of the Prophet, whereas Abū Ḥanīfa in Iraq had to deal with situations for which there was no prophetic precedent. Even so, however, Mālik (in company with all the earlier jurists) felt free to follow his own opinion or appreciation of public welfare when circumstances required. But this was just what the extreme traditionalists sought to exclude, for they held that human reason could not even deduce general rules from specific commands or prohibitions unless the revealed texts themselves indicated the underlying principle (*ʿilla*): man must not reason, but obey. It was the dominant influence of al-Shāfiʿī which secured the eventual triumph of a middle course, which recognized the overriding authority of 'authentic' Traditions from the Prophet but fully accepted the need for extending the divine texts by carefully defined rules of analogy to cover the ever-changing eventualities of daily life. In reality, of course, customary law, administrative practice and the early jurists' sense of equity, expediency and the 'spirit of the law' were major elements in the early development of the Sharīʿa (as the divinely authoritative law of Islam is called), however much later jurists sought to conceal this fact behind a façade of unhistorical Traditions or a convenient doctrine which grew up concerning the inerrancy and binding force of the 'agreement' of the Muslim community.[68] Eventually, however, all four schools came to accept the Qur'ān, the Sunna or practice of the Prophet (as preserved in the Traditions), the Ijmāʿ or agreement of the Muslim community, and Qiyās or analogical deduction from these three, as the four main sources of the law – although the Ḥanafīs in particular championed the right to depart on occasion from the conclusion to which a rigid application of analogy would lead, in favour of a different line of analogy which led to a solution they 'considered to be preferable'.[69]

All four surviving schools are now accepted as orthodox by Sunnī Islam and in theory any Muslim may adhere to whichever he likes,[70] although in practice his choice will largely depend on where he was born, or happens to live. Most authorities now consider, however, that he may elect to follow one school in one particular and another in another – which may be a matter of considerable convenience. For centuries, however, this right, if it existed, was seldom exercised, and for the most part a Muslim, having chosen his school, was bound by its tenets in all particulars. In no case, moreover, could he go back to the original sources of the law and re-interpret them: this right, known as *ijtihād*, was regarded as having lapsed for centuries, and its place had been taken by the duty of *taqlīd*, or accepting the rulings, down to the utmost minutiae, of a long series of successive jurists. Today, however, Muslim modernists are striving to free themselves from this bondage, and recent legislation in many Muslim countries concerning family law (in which alone the Sharīʿa is still widely applied) has been based on an eclectic principle of adopting whatever jurist's views seem, in each particular, most suited to modern needs.[71] On some occasions, moreover, reforms have been frankly based on a contemporary exercise of the faculty of *ijtihād*; and, on others, what is really a wholly new rule has been clothed with traditional authority by the expedient of combining two different (and sometimes even incompatible) opinions in a single whole. This is technically known as *talfīq* (patching).

The Muʿtazila

The same conflict between reason and tradition was waged even more bitterly in the realm of theology. As early as the beginning of the second century of the Muslim era we find a tolerably definite group of thinkers known as the Muʿtazila, who dissented from the traditional views and applied the solvent of reason to the dogmas of the Qur'ān. They held that there was an intermediate state between belief and infidelity (and thus between bliss and doom). As the spiritual heirs of the still earlier Qadarīs they upheld the freedom of the human will and denied that God predestined man's evil and unbelief; and they taught that God must of necessity act in accordance with justice and always do what was best for his creatures.[72] The orthodox, on the other hand, denied any intermediate state and held that all man's actions were decreed from eternity on the 'Preserved Tablet'; there could be no necessity upon God even to do justice, and man must unquestioningly accept whatever he did. More, they denied the very basis of human speculation, for they taught that man could not perceive or distinguish between good and evil by the intellect: good and evil derived their nature solely from God's will and could be known only by his commands and prohibitions. There could be no theology or ethics, therefore, apart from revelation.

Yet another subject of debate concerned the nature of the Godhead. The Qur'ān frequently makes use of anthropomorphic expressions: God is visible to some, at least in the next world; he settles himself firmly on his throne; he stretches out his arm, *etc.* Among the Muʿtazilīs all such expressions were spiritualized, and God was conceived as the most impersonal of Spirits. The orthodox, however replied that the Quranic statements must be accepted as they stood (*bi lā kayf*, 'without asking how') and neither explained away nor carried to their logical conclusion.[73]

Again, controversy raged around the question of the relation between the divine attributes (knowing, willing, speaking, *etc.*) and the divine essence – and the kindred dispute as to whether the Qur'ān was created or eternal. The Muʿtazilīs held that God's attributes were not *in* the divine essence (and thus in a sense separable from it), but *were* the divine essence; and the Qur'ān was clearly created, for any other conclusion would involve making the Qur'ān into a second God. To such arguments the orthodox replied that the attributes were neither identical with the essence nor distinct from it ('Not It, nor other than It' – an attitude which bears certain striking resemblances to the Christian doctrine of the Trinity, particularly as developed by John of Damascus and other Greek theologians whose influence on Muslim thought has never received adequate attention). As for the Qur'ān, its inscription and recitation might be created but its meanings were eternal, being none other than that divine speech which was one of God's eternal attributes. In this the influence of the Christian doctrine of the Logos is obvious.

But the Muʿtazilīs were never popular with the masses. For the most part they were regarded as heretics, sometimes persecuted and sometimes protected by constitutional authority. In the event it was an evil day for them when the Caliph al-Ma'mūn tried to enforce their views by law and penalize all non-conformity. This decision was reversed by a subsequent Caliph, but the harm was done: the traditionalist Aḥmad ibn Ḥanbal, who had refused either to recant or even argue but contented himself with repeating Quranic texts and 'true' Traditions, won far greater support. As time went on, moreover, the Muʿtazila retired more and more into barren scholasticism, a fate which D. B. Macdonald says has fallen on all continued efforts of the Muslim mind.[74] But this dictum may no longer be true today.

The philosophers

The place of the Muʿtazilīs as the champions of reason was taken by the philosophers, al-Kindī, al-Fārābī, Ibn Sīnā, Ibn Rushd, and their like. These men seem for the most part to have started from the position of sincere Muslims, but they also whole-heartedly accepted Greek philosophy, with all its contradictory theories, as part of the very form of truth. Their fundamental attitude was simple enough. The Qur'ān was truth; Plato and Aristotle had both expounded the truth: the Qur'ān and philosophy, therefore, whether Platonic or Aristotelian, must all be reconcilable. So to reconcile them they set out, with unconquerable spirit; and it was largely through these men that the philosophy and learning of ancient Greece was preserved and re-introduced into Europe.

The scholastic theologians

But parallel with the later development of Muʿtazilī views there also grew up among the orthodox a party who were no longer content to assert that the statements of the Qur'ān must be accepted as they stood, and that any questioning was *bidʿa* (innovation); instead, they came to use *kalām* (argument) in order to meet the *kalām* of the unorthodox. It was thus that the scholastic theology of Islam was born. The system must, of course, have been of gradual growth; but the chief credit has traditionally been given to al-Ashʿarī (d. *c.* 320 AH/ AD 930). Brought up as a Muʿtazilī and maintaining their views till he was about forty years old, he then swung over to the other side – and opposed at once the rationalism of the Muʿtazila and the gross anthropomorphisms of the more extreme Ḥanbalīs. As developed by his followers, the Ashʿarī system was the application to theology of an extreme atomic metaphysic.[75] To them, space was made up of a multitude of monads each of which has position, not bulk, and is separated from the next by absolute void; and they conceived of time as being similarly composed of a multitude of unrelated time monads. Any idea of causation they utterly rejected. They were compelled, however, to find some explanation of the harmony and apparent connection between one thing and another discernible in nature: and this they found in the will of God, absolutely free and untrammelled by any laws or necessities, which continually creates and annihilates the atoms and their qualities and thus produces all motion and all change. A man sees a beautiful flower; he decides to pick it; he stretches out his hand, plucks it and smells it. But this chain of causation is apparent only. In reality, God at each moment creates and recreates the atoms of the man's mind, of his hand, of the flower and of his nose in such a way as to create the thought, the apparent motion and the result: there is no mutual connection either of space or time except in the mind of God and by the continual exercise of his creative power. On such a basis human free will is neither more nor less than the presence, in the mind of man, of a choice created there by God; there is no order in the universe, and the distinction between miracles and what are normally regarded as the ordinary operations of nature virtually disappears. The sun does not warm, nor water wet: all that can be said is that God creates in a substance a being warmed (if he so wills) when exposed to the sun, and a being wet when submerged in water.

This system seems to have reached tolerably complete form by the beginning of the fifth century AH (eleventh century AD). For a long time it was bitterly opposed by the Ḥanbalīs, while, as a *via media*, it was unpopular with the liberals also. Persecutions broke out, and the Ashʿarī doctors were scattered to the winds. The reaction, however, was not long in coming, and the influence of al-Ghazālī (d. 505 AH/AD 1111) firmly established Ashʿarī views as the dominant school of Sunnī orthodoxy, although the slightly more liberal school of al Mātarīdī still claims its adherents. Essentially, however, the Ashʿarī teaching may be regarded as a vast negative, for it uses reason and logic to demonstrate the barrenness of both. Philosophy cannot even establish a chain of causation, so how can it arrive at any valid conclusion about the nature and attributes of God and the moral duties of man? For any knowledge of such matters man is entirely dependent on divine revelation, whether prophetic, through tradition, or direct, through the mystic's 'inner light'. The profound hold exercised by the former in Islam we have already noticed; and it is to the latter that we must now turn.

The mystics

Mysticism seems to have found some place in Islam from the very first. Muḥammad himself, although in most ways one of the least mystical of men, was strongly drawn at times to solitude and fasting; and it was along the line of asceticism, of renunciation of the world and its evils, that mysticism first made itself felt in the religion he founded. There was much to encourage such an attitude in the influence of Christian hermits scattered about Arabia; in the development of that fear of hell fundamental to primitive Islam; and in the withdrawal of the pious, first from the obvious godlessness of some of the Umayyad Caliphs and then from the very limited piety of the ʿAbbāsids. From an early date, therefore, it must have been a comparatively common sight to see some wandering ascetic surrounded by his disciples, all dressed in the simple woollen garment from which the mystics or Ṣūfis of Islam ultimately derived their name.

But mysticism soon began to develop along more speculative and philosophical lines. In this development it owed much to the Greek church; a good deal to Persian and, indeed, Indian influences; but most of all to Plotinus and the neo-Platonists.[76] It was only by refuge in mysticism that the Muslim philosopher could reconcile some of the teaching of the Qur'ān with the abstractions of Greek philosophy; that the scholastic theologian could find any escape (other than that of blind obedience to tradition) from the utter negation of Ashʿarī metaphysics; and that the ordinary Sunnī Muslim could find any poetry or warmth in his religion. When the scholastic theologians had done their work, the orthodox were left with no 'natural laws', no chain of causation, and no possibility of theology or ethics except in the revealed will of God. They must either be content to rely utterly on the prophetic revelation of the Qur'ān and the Traditions, or they must supplement them by that 'minor inspiration' which, the Ṣūfis asserted, God continuously vouchsafes to those who truly seek him. And to this the true Ṣūfi steadfastly gave himself. He believed that the human soul had in it some spark of the divine, however imprisoned in the world of sense; that the human heart was the mirror, albeit dimmed and blurred, of the Deity. It was the mystic's duty, then, to wean himself from the world of sense; to cleanse this mirror, and direct it to God alone: he would then receive divine enlightenment.

But to the Muslim it was chiefly in ecstasy that the mystic received his revelations. A whole science developed as to how a state of ecstasy could be induced; and a man's piety was judged not by his holiness of life but by the degree and frequency of his ecstatic states, for only in ecstasy did he realize his complete oneness with God. For centuries, however, the mystics were regarded with suspicion by the orthodox. Nor was this strange, for there was much excess. Emphasis on the spirit rather than the letter of the law led many to laxity not only of ritual but of morals. As so often in Islam, there was one law for the enlightened and another for the vulgar. Some, indeed, were not content to claim divine enlightenment; they claimed the very fusion and union of their beings with God. For them the transcendent God of orthodox Islam was deposed, to be replaced by the Only Reality of the pantheist.[77] Perhaps the most famous of these extremists was al-Ḥallāj, who was put to death with great cruelty in 309 AH/AD 919 for claiming 'I am the Truth'.[78] It needed the immense influence of al-Ghazālī to secure the acceptance of the mystic way within the fold of orthodox Islam.

Later, there grew up the great Dervish Orders which are such a feature of Islam today. The Ṣūfī principle of blind obedience of pupil to master became increasingly emphasized, and in course of time the group no longer broke up on the master's death but formed a lasting fraternity. Each Order traces its origin back to some famous saint whose miraculous powers are held to descend, in some degree, to his successors, and is made up both of professional dervishes and of non-professional adherents who visit the monasteries with greater or lesser regularity and take their part in the *dhikr*, or that form of repetition of the name of God adopted by the particular Order to induce a state of ecstasy. Membership of such fraternities was (until recently, at least) exceedingly common in Muslim countries, even, to some extent, among the professional classes.

The vast majority of the common people in all Muslim lands, moreover, believe implicitly not only in the miraculous powers of living holy men (*awliyā'*, heads of Ṣūfī orders, *etc.*), from whose prayers, touch, breath and saliva virtue (or *baraka*) is derived, but also in those of dead saints whose tombs they visit and whose intercession they implore. Under cover of this cult of saints much pre-Islamic animism has been retained in Islam.[79] Stones and trees which were worshipped in pagan days are now commonly connected with some prophet or saint, but the ancient ritual is largely preserved: thus pieces of the clothing of the sick or barren are still attached to the tree in the belief that some of the 'soul-stuff' resident therein will thereby be transferred to the suppliant. Similarly, relics of holy men and charms of all sorts are in constant demand, as protection against the evil-eye, against the *jinn*, and especially against the genie- (or devil-) mate[80] which is believed to dog the footsteps of every mortal. In popular Islam the pure monotheism of the creed has been diluted with a wealth of animistic survivals, some sanctioned by the Prophet and some plainly contrary to his teaching, which still hold multitudes of simple people in the bondage of fear, taboos, and financial exploitation. To gain protection, healing, fertility, *etc.*, the aid is also regularly invoked of a whole hierarchy of saints, led by the Quṭb[81] (or 'Axis', *i.e.* greatest living saint) and his various grades of lieutenants, who periodically hold a sort of mystic parliament, untrammelled by space or time.

The faith and practice of Sunnī Islam

The faith and practice of Islam are governed by the two great branches of Muslim learning – theology and jurisprudence – to both of which some reference has already been made. Muslim theology (usually called '*Tawḥīd*' from its central doctrine of the Unity of the Godhead) defines all that a man should believe, while the law (Sharī'a) prescribes everything that he should do. There is no priesthood and there are no sacraments. Except among the Ṣūfīs, Islam knows exhortation and instruction only from those who consider themselves, or are considered by others, adequately learned in theology or law.

Unlike any other system in the world today, the Sharīʿa embraces every detail of human life, from the prohibition of crime to the use of the toothpick, and from the organization of the State to the most sacred intimacies – or unsavoury aberrations – of family life. It is 'the science of all things, human and divine', and divides all actions into what is obligatory or enjoined, praiseworthy or recommended, permitted or legally indifferent, disliked or deprecated, or positively forbidden. The Muslim may certainly consult his lawyer[82] as to what he may do without incurring any legal penalty; but he may also consult him as a spiritual adviser as to whether acts of which other systems of law take no cognizance are praiseworthy or blame-worthy before God. Until recently the pride and power of the ʿUlamā', or doctors of the law, was enormous; but their influence is, in general, somewhat decreased today. The whole science of law is known as *fiqh*, and formed for centuries the primary study of the pious Muslim.

The articles of faith

In Islam no official redaction of the articles of faith (*ʿaqā'id*) has ever existed, though much has been written on the subject. For our purpose, however, the summary attributed by tradition to the Prophet himself can conveniently be adopted: that a Muslim must believe 'in God, his Angels, his Books, his Messengers, in the Last Day, and . . . in the Decree both of good and evil'.

The importance attached to the doctrine of God can easily be seen from the space allotted to this subject in any Muslim treatise on theology. The fundamental concept is his Unity; and most of the finest passages in the Qur'ān are concerned with this subject. Some of them are very fine indeed; and there can be no doubt that Muḥammad was passionately concerned that men and women should not lavish the worship due to God alone on a plethora of far less worthy objects. Much the same is true of many of his followers. To 'associate anything or anyone with God' is *shirk*, and those who do so are termed *mushriqūn*. This term was originally used by Muḥammed for the idolatrous polytheists of Mecca, but is commonly applied also to Christians because of their belief in the Triune God.

In orthodox Islam, moreover, this concept has been pressed to logical – but unreal – lengths in the doctrines of *mukhālafa* (difference) and *tanzīh* (removal, or 'making transcendent'). By the former, God is declared to be so different from his creatures that it becomes virtually impossible to postulate anything of him. He has styled himself the Merciful, for instance, but this quality need have no connection with the human concept of mercy. The latter, on the other hand, so negates any semblance of impermanence and so emphasizes his self-sufficiency as to deny that he can in any way be affected by the actions or attitude of his creatures. As we have seen, moreover, the God of orthodox Islam maintains literally everything in being, moment by moment, by a continual miracle: even the impression of choice present to the mind of men is his creation. He is the source of both good and evil; his will is supreme, untrammelled by any laws or principles, whatever they may be; whom he will he forgives, and whom he will he punishes.[83] His nature and qualities are partly revealed in his ninety-nine 'most beautiful Names', frequently repeated by the pious as they finger their rosaries.[84] Some of these names are constantly on all Muslim lips, whether in prayer, salutation, bargaining or swearing, while others are regularly used as charms and talismans.

A belief in angels is absolutely enjoined on the Muslim: he who denies them is an infidel. Orthodox Islam acknowledges four archangles (Jibrīl or Gabriel, the messenger of revelation – much confused with the Holy Spirit; Mīkā'īl or Michael, the guardian of the Jews; Isrāfīl, the summoner to resurrection; and Izrā'īl, the messenger of death), and an indefinite number of ordinary angels. They are created of light, do not eat or drink or propagate their species, and are characterized by absolute obedience to the will of God. Two recording angels attend on every man: the one on his right records his good deeds, and the one on his left his sins. There are also two angels called Munkar and Nakīr, who visit every newly-buried corpse in the grave. Making the corpse sit up, these angels examine it in the faith. If the replies are satisfactory it is allowed to sleep in peace, but if it does not confess the apostle they beat it severely, some say until the day of resurrection. Animals are said to hear its cries, although mortals cannot.

Between angels and men there are also a multitude of creatures called *jinn*. These are created of smokeless flame, eat and drink, propagate their species, and are capable of both belief and unbelief. Muḥammad was sent to them as well as to men, and good *jinn* now perform all the religious duties of Muslims.[85] The disbelieving *jinn* – who are often called *'afārīt, shayāṭīn,*[86] *etc.* – were turned out of the first three heavens when Jesus was born, and out of the last four when Muḥammad was born. Sometimes, however, they still go eaves-dropping to the lowest heaven, whence they occasionally pass on information to human magicians; but they are chased away by the angels with shooting stars if observed.[87] Reference has already been made to the *qarīna* or *shayṭān*[88] which is believed to dog every mortal's footsteps and tempt him to evil.

The *jinn* often appear as animals, reptiles, *etc.*, or in human form. Frequently, moreover, a human being will be 'possessed' by one of them – as all poets and soothsayers were held to be; and in such circumstances relief is frequently sought in exorcism, particularly by the incense, dance and sacrifice of the 'Zār' ritual.[89] The devil (Iblīs, or al-Shayṭān) is normally regarded as a fallen angel or *jinn* who disobeyed God's command to the angels to do homage to Adam. He is now the arch-tempter of mankind and the progenitor of the *shayṭāns*, *ʿifrīts*, and all evil *jinn*.

Orthodox Islam is divided as to how many prophets there have been: some say 124,000, and some an indefinite number. The Qur'ān names twenty-eight: most are biblical,[90] while two (Luqmān and Dhū'l-Qarnayn) have been generally identified with Aesop and Alexander the Great respectively. Some 313 of these prophets are named apostles, and the six greatest brought new dispensations: such are Adam, Noah, Abraham, Moses, ʿIsā (Jesus) and Muḥammad.[91]

Among them these prophets brought some 104 divine books. A hundred of these, of minor length, were vouchsafed to Adam, Seth, Enoch and Abraham, but are now lost; while of the four major Scriptures the Law was 'sent down' to Moses, the Psalms to David, the Gospel to Jesus, and the Qur'ān[92] to Muḥammad. All originally corresponded to a heavenly prototype and all comprised the same central message.[93] To the allegation that the Jews subsequently corrupted their Scriptures we have already referred, and the same charge is brought against Christians by way of explanation of the New Testament references to the deity and cross of Christ, and other doctrines denied by Islam.[94]

The last day (the resurrection and the judgment) figures prominently in Muslim thought. The day and hour is a secret to all, but there are to be twenty-five signs of its approach. All men will then be raised; the books kept by the recording angels will be opened; and God as judge will weigh each man's deeds in the balances. Some will be admitted to paradise, where they will recline on soft couches quaffing cups of wine handed to them by the *ḥūrī* (houris), or maidens of paradise, of whom each man may marry as many as he pleases.[95] Others will be consigned to the torments of hell. Almost all,[96] it would seem, will have to enter the fire temporarily, but no true Muslim will remain there for ever. Other Traditions picture a bridge as sharp as a sword over the pit, from which infidels' feet will slip so that they fall into the fire, while the feet of Muslims will stand firm.[97]

Finally, a Muslim is required to believe in God's Decrees. As we have already seen, the orthodox belief is that everything – good or evil

– proceeds directly from the divine will, being irrevocably recorded on the Preserved Tablet. While the Muʿtazila and others have challenged this view, there is much to support it in the Qurʾān – although other passages certainly assume the moral responsibility of mankind. The fatalism to which this cast-iron view of pre-destination logically leads has, in the past, played a large part in the daily lives of millions of Muslims. To this can be partially attributed the lethargy and lack of progress which, until recently, has for centuries characterized Muslim countries.

The Sharīʿa, as we have seen, covers an exceedingly wide field and no systematic division was ever reached. Sunnī Muslims sometimes classify it into obligations regarding worship (*ʿibādāt*), obligations of a civil and personal nature (*muʿāmalāt*) and punishments (*ʿuqūbāt*). Only a very sketchy treatment will be possible here, and we shall confine our attention to the main religious observances; to such fundamental social institutions as marriage, divorce and slavery; and to a few representative crimes.

The 'Five Pillars'

The religious observances of Islam include the 'Five Pillars' (or foundations) of religion: *i.e.* the recital of the creed, prayer, fasting, almsgiving, and the pilgrimage. The creed (*Kalima*) is a simple one: 'There is no God but God, and Muḥammad is the Prophet of God' – but disputes have arisen as to what its proper recital involves. The more exacting require that it be recited aloud at least once; that it be understood with the mind and believed in the heart; that it be recited correctly and professed without hesitation; and that it be held until death. To the majority of Muslims, however, a mere recital of the creed is enough to enrol a new convert in the ranks of Islam; and any more stringent requirement is left to divine omniscience.[98]

Ritual prayer plays a big part in the life of a devout Muslim. He is required to pray five times a day at stated hours, and in this many are most faithful. He may pray alone, in company, or in a mosque; but he must pray in Arabic and must follow a set form of words and a strictly prescribed ritual of stances, genuflexions and prostrations which differs slightly as between the four orthodox schools. Particularly important is the congregational prayer at noon on Fridays, attendance at which is incumbent on all adult male Muslims who live in a sufficiently large community. This service includes a weekly sermon; but the Muslim Friday is not prescribed as a day of rest. Prayer is valueless, however, unless offered in a state of ritual purity,[99] so the law books contain detailed rules concerning the different forms of purification (*wuḍūʾ* and *ghusl*), when each is required and how it must be performed.[100] It may also be remarked that in *popular* Islam there is little connection between prayer and ethics: a man who rises from prayer to cheat will be rewarded for the prayer and punished for the cheating, but the one is commonly regarded as having little or no bearing on the other. But this is by no means universally true.

During the month of Ramaḍān (the ninth month of the Muslim year) all Muslims except the sick, travellers, pregnant women, nursing mothers and young children are required to fast from first dawn until sunset. This involves complete abstinence from all forms of food, drink, smoking or sexual intercourse. As the Muslim year is lunar, the fast sometimes falls at mid-summer, when the long days and the intense heat make complete abstinence, especially from water, a severe ordeal. On the whole, however, it is rigidly observed, especially among the lower classes; and even if the more sophisticated often break their fast in secret, the majority observe it outwardly. The fast is much esteemed as inculcating both self-control and sympathy with the poor and destitute. But it may be observed in passing that the average family spends nearly twice as much in Ramaḍān on the food they consume by night as in any other month on the food they eat by day! It is probably the consequent curtailment of sleep as much as the rigours of fasting which has such a marked effect on the general output of work during Ramaḍān.

The emphasis Muḥammad put on almsgiving is among the best points in the teaching of Islam, although it has inevitably encouraged the indigent in Muslim lands (for whom, it must be added, little other provision was, in the past, normally made). Himself an orphan, the Prophet felt keenly for the destitute and needy. The legal alms enjoined on the Muslim are, however, less than the Jewish tithe, being limited to one-fortieth of money and merchandise, one-tenth or one-twentieth of agricultural produce (the rate depending on the method of irrigation employed), and different rates for cattle, *etc.* These legal alms are known as *zakāt*, and are to be distinguished from *ṣadaqa*, or free-will offerings.

We have already referred to the pilgrimage. The actual ceremonies were taken over from the idolatrous superstitions of pre-Islamic Arabia[101] and retained by the Prophet, with a new significance, possibly to conciliate the people of Mecca. At the same time, however, he destroyed the idols which surrounded the Kaʿba and professed to restore the Black Stone to the position it held in the days of Abraham.[102] The performance of the pilgrimage at least once is enjoined on every adult Muslim, male or female, who can afford it, and its value is emphasized in such Traditions as 'Every step in the direction of the Kaʿba blots out a sin', and 'He who dies on the way to

Mecca is enrolled in the list of martyrs'. As a consequence, thousands assemble in Mecca each year from all over the Muslim world and return to their homes with a greatly heightened sense not only of the international character of Islam but of its essential solidarity.[103]

It is these Five Pillars, and particularly the profession of the creed and the performance of prayer and fasting, which chiefly make up the practice of Islam to the average Muslim. He who acknowledges the Unity and Transcendence of God, pays him his due in prayer and fast, and accepts Muḥammad as the last and greatest of the Prophets, may well, indeed, have to taste the fire, but hopes that he will not, like the infidel, remain in it for ever – through the timely intercession of the Prophet. The most heinous of all sins are *shirk* (polytheism, idolatry, to 'associate' anyone, or anything, with Allāh – a sin of which Muslims commonly accuse Christians), apostasy and scepticism[104] beside which other forms of evil pale into comparative insignificance.

The Jihād

One more religious duty (other than the Five Pillars) deserves notice: the duty of jihād or Holy War. It is incumbent in general on all Muslims who are adult, male and free to answer any legally valid summons to war against the infidels; and he who dies in a jihād is a martyr and assured of paradise. Uncompromising commands from the Qur'ān on this subject are often quoted: 'Slay the polytheists wherever you find them' and 'Make war upon such of those to whom the Scriptures have been given as believe not in God . . . and who forbid not that which God and His Apostle have forbidden, and who profess not the profession of the truth, until they pay tribute out of hand, and they be humbled' (*sūra* 9:5 and 29). But one of the problems in quoting from the Qur'ān is that there may always be an argument about whether an earlier passage has been 'abrogated' by a later one. The jihād, with the fanatical courage it evokes, has been by no means limited to the inception of Islam, and its possible relevance for the future cannot be ignored. The matter is greatly complicated, however, by the question as to when such a summons can be regarded as legally valid. From the earliest times Muslims have divided the world into Dār al-Islām, where Islam reigns supreme, and Dār al-Ḥarb (the Abode of War), where the rule of Islam should be extended, if necessary by war. Polytheists were given the option of conversion or death, while the People of the Books (Jews or Christians) were given, as we have seen, the additional alternative of submission and tribute.[105] In recent years the question has arisen, however, as to whether a country which has once been Dār al-Islam, but has subsequently fallen under a non-Muslim government, is to be regarded as having lapsed into

Dār al-Ḥarb. The majority view seems to be that jihād may be proclaimed only by the lawful Caliph – or presumably, by the Mahdī[106] whom even Sunnī Muslims expect; that it is lawful only in Dār al-Ḥarb; that a once Muslim country does not necessarily lapse into Dār al-Ḥarb as soon as it passes into the hands of infidels, but only 'when all or most of the injunctions of Islam disappear therefrom'; and that it is in all cases essential that there should be 'a possibility of victory for the army of Islam'.[107]

Such is the classical doctrine. But it must be observed that the term *jihād* is often used today without any of these considerations, to connote any struggle (moral, political, physical or terrorist) on behalf of Islam, or what individuals conceive to be its interests. The fact remains, however, that many Muslim countries have signed United Nations Declarations about peoples' liberty to follow, or even change, the religion of their choice.

Family life

Under the general heading of *mu'āmalāt*, or dealings between man and man, the Sharī'a includes provisions corresponding to the modern law of contract and tort (or 'obligations'), in addition to those matters of personal status which are almost the only part of the Sharī'a applied by the courts today in many Muslim lands. This law of personal status includes marriage (*nikāḥ*), divorce (*ṭalāq*), paternity, guardianship, maintenance, wills and inheritance.

Marriage is enjoined on every Muslim, and even the ascetic orders commonly marry. The Prophet is reputed to have said, 'Marry women who will love their husbands and be very prolific, for I wish you to be more numerous than any other people', and again, 'when a man marries he perfects half his religion'. A Muslim may have as many as, but not more than, four legal wives at any one time; and he may also cohabit with as many slave concubines as he may possess. 'Marry such as seem good to you of women, by twos or threes or fours . . . or what your right hand possesses.'[108] Besides Muslim women, he may marry Jewesses or Christians and these may continue to practise their own religion (although, if they do, the spouses will have no mutual rights of inheritance); but a Muslim girl may be given in marriage only to a co-religionist and there must be no intermarriage of any sort with polytheists. Among the Shī'a temporary marriage (*nikāḥ al-mut'a* or enjoyment) is allowed, based partly on the Quranic precept: 'Forbidden to you also are married women, except those who are in your hands as slaves. This is the law of God for you. And it is allowed you, besides this, to seek out wives by means of your wealth, in modest conduct, but not in debauchery. And give them their stipulated hire for what you have enjoyed of them, as God has commanded. But there will be no blame for you if you give them by agreement more than the stipulated sum.'[109] Sunnī Muslims deny the Shīʿī interpretation of this verse and, although most of them admit that Muḥammad at one time countenanced *mutʿa*, maintain that he afterwards forbade it – although it seems in fact to have been first forbidden by the Caliph ʿUmar. It is still practised among Shīʿīs, especially on journeys, when it often approximates to licensed prostitution: *mutʿa* marriage, moreover, may be in excess of four legal wives to which the Shīʿīs, too, are otherwise limited.

In general, however, the Sunnīs and the Shīʿīs concur (except in details) in the rules governing the prohibited degrees of relationship and the dower, maintenance and discipline of wives: for a man who fulfils his own obligations may insist on his wife observing strict *purdah* and may enforce marital obedience even by personal chastisement.[110] When a man has more than one wife he is enjoined to divide his time equally between them and to treat them with impartial justice (except, the classical commentators add, in those matters of the affections which are beyond his control): if he fears he will not be able to do this he should confine himself to one only.[111] This verse is much quoted by modern Muslims to prove that the Prophet virtually enjoined monogamy, since few, they maintain, can behave impartially to a plurality of wives. As a consequence, polygamy has now been forbidden in Tunisia and Turkey, and restricted in a number of other Muslim countries. Muslims also emphasize that Islam has always allowed married women to keep their property.[112]

A Muslim may divorce his wife at any time and for any reason – although in some Muslim countries considerable efforts have been made in recent years to impose restrictions on such unilateral repudiation. When the words of divorce are said only once or twice, the divorce is normally revocable at the option of the husband during a short period known as the *ʿidda*, until the expiration of which the marriage is regarded in such cases as still extant and the husband is responsible for his wife's lodging and maintenance; but thereafter a new marriage contract is required before the parties can come together again. When the words of repudiation are said three times, however, the divorce is immediately irrevocable; and the parties cannot remarry unless the wife has first been properly married to, and divorced by, another man.

The husband's responsibility for maintaining his divorced wife during the *ʿidda* is disputed between the schools. Should it transpire, however, that the wife – however divorced – is pregnant, the husband is responsible for her lodging and maintenance until she gives birth to his child. The children of divorced women remain with their mothers until they reach a certain fixed age,[113] and during this period the divorced wife can claim from their father both money for their support and wages for her suckling and care; but after this age the father has an absolute claim on them. It is divorce rather than polygamy – which is increasingly uncommon – which causes untold suffering to women, and widespread social evil, in Islam today; for it frequently happens that a man will marry a young girl and then, when she has borne him several children and become prematurely aged, divorce her in favour of a younger wife. The divorced wife can then only return to her father or brothers, to be greeted with anything but enthusiasm and often to be married off, if the opportunity occurs, to a second husband, however undesirable. It is not surprising, then, that Muslim women, having little sense of marital security, frequently contrive to put something by as a precaution against divorce, and normally feel more affection for their blood-relatives than their husband. The better type of Muslim father not infrequently attempts to deter a prospective son-in-law from frivolous divorce by stipulating a large dowry for his daughter, the greater part of which is payable only on divorce or at the husband's death (to augment the one-eighth of his estate to which alone his widow will in most cases be entitled).

In this connection it must be remembered that the seclusion of women in orthodox Islam means that a large number of men marry women whom they have never seen; that minors (and in some schools of law virgin daughters of mature age) may be compulsorily married by their fathers; and that in most cases such pressure can be brought to bear on an adult girl – whether virgin, widow or divorcee – as to make that consent to a marriage which the law requires more nominal than real. But much of this has now been changed in some Muslim countries. Women, for their part, can in no circumstances divorce their husbands,[114] and it is only in certain schools and particular contingencies that they can appeal to the courts to annul the marriage. But widespread reforms in this matter, too, have been introduced in one Muslim country after another.

Islam sanctioned slavery and the slave trade, and the unlimited right of concubinage which a Muslim enjoyed with his female slaves has already been mentioned. This extended even to married women captured in war,[115] and opened the door to terrible abuse during the early wars of expansion, when almost any woman in a conquered land could be considered a slave by capture. Stanley Lane-Poole had some strong words to say about this item in Islamic law:

It is not so much in the matter of wives as in that of concubines

> that Muhammad made an irretrievable mistake. . . . The female white slave is kept solely for her master's sensual gratification and is sold when he is tired of her, and so she passes from master to master, a very wreck of womanhood. Kind as the Prophet was himself towards bondswomen, one cannot forget the unutterable brutalities which he suffered his followers to inflict upon conquered nations in the taking of slaves. The Muslim soldier was allowed to do as he pleased with any infidel woman he might meet with on his victorious march. When one thinks of the thousands of women, mothers and daughters, who must have suffered untold shame and dishonour by this licence, one cannot find words to express one's horror.[116]

It must be remembered, however, that this was in an age when the practices of war, all the world over, were distinctly brutal. In general, it should be said, slaves have been well and kindly treated in Muslim lands – including, in many cases, the slave concubine, who was often given no worse treatment than the free wife. Theoretically, of course, the slave had no legal rights: he was a mere chattel, in his master's absolute power. But this was mitigated in practice by the influence of both Quranic injunctions and prophetic maxims extolling kindness to slaves and the virtue of setting them free, and Muḥammad himself set a good example in this respect.

Other provisions

It can only be mentioned in passing that, in matters of diet, pig meat, blood[117] and alcohol are forbidden; that gambling is taboo; and that the law of contract is largely dominated by the prohibition of *ribā*, a term which is commonly translated as 'usury', but which extends to many forms of speculative transactions. Purists, for example, disapprove of insurance policies and such investments as involve a fixed rate of interest, whereas forms of partnership in which both parties stand to lose or gain are permitted. The Sharī'a, therefore, omits any comprehensive theory of contract in favour of a wide range of nominative contracts. But the letter of the law in such matters has been subject to many evasions almost from the first, and is now widely replaced by legislative enactments.

In family life, it is noteworthy that male circumcision is officially described as 'recommended' rather than 'commanded'.[118] It is, however, regularly practised, and is regarded by most Muslims as one of the essentials of their faith.

Another section of the Sharī'a deals with 'punishments' or criminal sanctions. These provide, *inter alia*, for the murderer to be executed by the family of his victim (although the family may accept blood-money instead); for one who causes physical injury to another to be submitted to the like; for the thief to have his right hand cut off; and for the adulterer to be stoned and the fornicator beaten.[119] The severity of these penalties is greatly mitigated, however, by such rigorous rules of evidence that the punishment, in most cases, can very seldom be imposed. But much lawlessness and injustice result from the fact that it is commonly regarded as legitimate for a man to kill his wife or close female relative for unchastity. In the majority of Muslim countries, however, all these (and many other) provisions of the Sharīʿa have been superseded by a modern civil and criminal code, and Sharīʿa courts now confine themselves almost exclusively to questions of personal status, gifts, endowments, inheritance and pre-emption.[120] While it would be regarded as infidelity avowedly to change the Sharīʿa in any particular, those who pay it lip-service as a divinely authoritative system for the Golden Age often quietly put it on one side in this workaday world in favour of a system more suited to modern requirements. In Saʿudi Arabia, however, the Sharīʿa is still largely applied, while elsewhere Islamic fundamentalists clamour for its reimposition.

To many survivals of animistic beliefs and practices in popular, and even orthodox, Islam references have already been made. The Prophet himself not only firmly believed in *jinn* and in the power of the evil-eye, but apparently allowed spells to ward off the latter provided only the names of God and of good angels were used. He is also believed to have said that 'the saliva of some of us cures our sick by the permission of God'. Simple Muslims today firmly believe that a man can utilize the power of demons and *jinn* by means of magic, and the practice of 'counter-magic' to protect from evil of all sorts is exceedingly common. Amulets are worn by animals and men, particularly children; magic cups, many of them made in al-Madīna, are used both for healing and for more sinister purposes; and ceremonies such as the ʿAqīqa[121] sacrifice for new-born children (so called both from the first cutting of the infant's hair and the sacrifice offered on its behalf) are widespread. Some of these survivals can be traced to pre-Islamic Arabia, while others have been adopted from the conquered lands.

Islam today and tomorrow

The enigma

To the detached observer Islam is always something of an enigma. It is not so much its phenomenal expansion in the first century of the

Muslim era, which can largely be explained by the decadence and internal divisions of the surrounding kingdoms; by the tough physique and war-like spirit of the Arab armies, intoxicated as they were by the happy alternatives of fabulous plunder or paradisical delights; and by the military genius of Khālid ibn al-Walīd and others. It is not primarily the splendour of the medieval Caliphate, with its enlightened patronage of learning and its absorption of many alien cultures. The essence of the enigma is the power which the religion of Islam has exercised over its adherents all down the ages and the attraction it has so often exerted over non-Muslims – with the result that it is still, in parts, a missionary religion, and is still winning new converts.

The enigma can, of course, be partially explained. It is easy enough to understand some, at least, of the factors which make Islam such a powerful attraction to 'pagans' – whether in some parts of Africa or elsewhere. They are impressed by the manifest superiority of the Muslim's concept of one true God; for pagans themselves acknowledge, if pressed, the existence of one creator God, although they habitually ignore him in practice and spend their lives trying to propitiate those far more immanent and malignant spirits which so often hold them in a thraldom of fear. Islam, moreover, represents a monotheistic religion which they commonly believe to be indigenous, and certainly not Western, in origin – and this is a powerful attraction to those who are in revolt against colonialism and all its ways. In point of fact Islam, of course, springs from much the same part of the world as Christianity, but it normally reaches pagans in a far more indigenous dress. Again, they are attracted by its world-wide brotherhood, by the vivid sense of belonging to a comparatively closely-knit community, and by the fact that as Muslims they will be welcomed by other Muslims when they leave their villages for work in some big town. This sense of community is reinforced by the fact that Muslims frequently pray together, always fast together, and often enjoy the even closer brotherhood of a Dervish Order. By comparison with Christianity, moreover, the dogmas of Islam appear to be simple and comprehensible to the human mind. Many Muslims boast of a moral code which they believe to be less hypocritical (and much more possible of attainment) than what they regard as the impossible demands of a Christianity professed in theory, but abandoned in practice, in the degenerate West. It is, however, I think, fair to say that many pagans are attracted by the fact that Islam makes ample provision for the polygamy and easy divorce to which they are accustomed.

To the Copts who embrace Islam year by year in Egypt, on the other hand, the motive is almost always the pressure of economic inducements, the desire to divorce a Christian wife, the determination to marry a Muslim girl or, indeed, the desire to escape from the status of what may justly be described as a somewhat second-grade citizen from a minority community. The Muslim himself, moreover, feels a certain superiority not only to pagans, but even to those Arab representatives of ancient Christian churches who have tended to develop minority characteristics under centuries of Muslim dominance. They do not fully share his cultural heritage, steeped as this is in his religion; their ritualistic forms of worship seem little short of idolatry compared with the dignified simplicity of that of the mosque; and their ignorance of the essentials of the Christian gospel is frequently profound. By contrast, the Muslim boasts a doctrine of God which, whatever its ultimate inadequacy, appears comparatively intelligible; a code of ethics whose ample limits are determined by certain express prescriptions; and a conviction that his Prophet has absorbed and retained all that was best in previous revelations.

Yet there is much on the other side. The basic teaching of Islam, however lofty some of its theology and simple its ritual, is at best a somewhat cold and formal religion, as the widespread devotion to the Dervish Orders goes to prove. And its central doctrine of the Unity of the Godhead has been carried to a length which – even to human logic, itself manifestly inadequate in this context – raises almost as many problems as it solves. Again, the finer soul is often repelled by the very laxity of moral standards which attracts others, and especially by the degradation of Muslim womanhood. That the religion still grips the greater part of its adherents, including women, and can still arouse their fanatical devotion, remains an enigma. A partial explanation may, perhaps, be found later in this book.

The crisis

In recent decades, however, Islam has been facing one of the greatest crises of its history. This crisis arises from the very nature of Islam when exposed to the conflicting currents of modern life, and can, perhaps, be summarized under three headings.

Firstly, Islam is essentially a *dominant* creed. It is not so much that Islam has sometimes been imposed at the point of a sword,[122] as that the whole attitude of Muslims to non-Muslims is conceived as that of victor to vanquished, of ruler to ruled. While polytheists were, according to one view, to be given the alternative of conversion or death, the 'People of the Book' could become *dhimmīs* or protected subjects. As such, their persons and property were guaranteed and they might follow their own religion and personal law; but they had to pay tribute, were excluded from full citizenship, and were frequently compelled to show various marks of deference to their Muslim neighbours. In the event their treatment differed widely from age to age and place to place. Sometimes they enjoyed much freedom and even attained high office. At other times they suffered severe persecution. But all this has raised a difficult problem for modern Muslims, many of whom until recently had to live under a Christian or other non-Muslim government. Such a circumstance seems never to have been contemplated by early Islam and has given rise to a number of difficulties, among them (as we have seen) that of knowing where the line should now be drawn between Dār al-Islām and Dār al-Ḥarb and where a modern jihād is obligatory or legitimate.

There can be little doubt that it is the Muslim's instinctive feeling that the practice of his religion cannot properly be reconciled with living under the sovereignty of a non-Muslim government which, almost as much as the growth of nationalism, has led to the strenuous efforts witnessed during the last half century in many parts of the Muslim world to achieve either nominal or complete independence; and by the success of most of these efforts Islam may be said in this respect partially to have weathered the storm. Even when independence has been won, however, a Muslim state must still face the problem of its relations with non-Muslim countries in a world where almost perpetual war or isolation is no longer practicable. An up-to-date example of this problem is provided by the Declaration of Human Rights now accepted by all Muslim states, except Saʿudi Arabia and the Yemen, which are members of the United Nations Organization. Yet the clause which affirms a man's right to change his religion if he so wishes runs directly counter both to the Islamic law of apostasy and to the practice of most of the Muslim states concerned.

Secondly, Islam is essentially a *theocratic* creed. In Islamic theory, as we have seen, church and state are one, and the canon law is the law both of the state and the individual, in every aspect of life. Not only so, but Dār al-Islām is regarded as one and indivisible, united under a single Caliph. In 1923, however, the Ottoman Caliphate (itself of doubtful legality, since the Caliph was not of Qurayshī descent) was abolished; and the rivalries of Muslim powers will probably prevent any speedy revival. Meanwhile, modern states, strongly nationalistic in character, have grown up in many parts of the Muslim world, in most of which parliamentary institutions and responsible governments have been set up on the Western pattern – only to be replaced, in many cases, by military dictatorships. The subjects of such states, moreover, are granted (nominally, at least) equal citizenship without distinction of religion,[123] and a secular state law has to a great extent been substituted for the Sharīʿa. Much of this seems incompatible with historic Islam. Yet again, although Islam is usually declared to be the state religion, the state itself is largely secular in character. Where, in the past, popular literature, holidays and entertainments were almost exclusively religious or semi-religious in character, today the press, radio and cinema are mainly secular. In such circumstances the old cohesion and theocratic structure of Islam has been greatly weakened. It must be remembered, however, that Islam represents a complete system of public and private life as well as a religion, in the narrower sense of that term; and that many who are influenced by secularist tendencies still staunchly support the Muslim social order.

Thirdly, orthodox Islam is essentially a *dogmatic* creed. The Muslim should accept the Qur'ān as the *ipsissima verba* of God, the Traditions as equally inspired in content though not in form, and the whole vast structure of Muslim law and theology, developed by generations of jurists and commentators, as binding on his mind and conscience. There have been, of course, progressive movements in Islam, as we have seen. But for centuries orthodox theology has been dominated by Ash'arism.[124] It is no wonder, then, if the modern student, who is thoroughly up to date in Western thought, finds a fundamental conflict between the teachings of the orthodox and the so-called 'assured results of modern science'. In so far as the interpretations and developments of medieval jurists and theologians are concerned, it would no doubt be possible (and the attempt is in fact being made) for modern Muslims to sweep away this superstructure and insist on the right to go back to the Qur'ān and the Traditions and re-interpret them in terms of modern life. Ultimately, however, the student or reformer is usually faced with a far deeper problem in some explicit dictum of God or his Prophet. This clearly makes the path of reform a slippery one. It must be almost equally difficult for the modern critical mind to accept the whole of the Qur'ān as the *ipsissima verba* of God, or for the enlightened moral conscience to regard the life of the Prophet as the ideal pattern of human conduct. But it is just as difficult to compromise on either of these issues and remain an honest Muslim. Yet it must be remembered that the strength of any system of thought or belief, and its ability to command men's loyalty, are by no means proportionate to its truth or intrinsic spiritual power, and that Islam has many features which still command the allegiance of most of its adherents.

In the more recent past, moreover, other – and in some respects quite contrary – tendencies have become increasingly apparent. There has been a considerable revival of Islam, particularly in the Arab countries, as a political and religious rallying-point against the 'political, economic and cultural imperialism' of the West. This revival is largely the result of purely political factors; in particular of Arab opposition to the 'fragmentation' policy pursued by Britain and France between the wars and to the menace of Zionism and Israel.[125] As a consequence there has been an increasing tendency to identify nationalism with Islam and national culture with Islamic culture; and this has led to more severe restrictions on foreign missions and to discrimination against non-Muslim minorities. The revival, however, has been religious rather than spiritual; it has been marked by a larger number of officials going on pilgrimage and a greater emphasis on using the Sharīʿa as a source of law, but has not been accompanied, in general, by any decrease in official corruption or general rise in moral standards. Still more recently, a new phenomenon, militant 'Islamic fundamentalism', has burst upon the world.

The future

How, then, is the Muslim world reacting to these problems and what does the future hold? To this, only the most sketchy answer can be given. Four different tendencies may be observed.

Firstly, there is a tendency towards *secularism*. The outstanding example of this is provided by Turkey. There, Islam no longer holds the official position it held in the past; the law has been entirely secularized; the Roman alphabet has been introduced; 'Westernism' has been adopted in a wholesale fashion; and monogamy is (officially) enforced by law. True, the mosques are still open and the majority of the population certainly regard themselves as Muslims; but the real religion of many of the élite seems to be Turkish nationalism. Even in Turkey, however, a considerable minority champions the cause of Islamic fundamentalism, but they are outnumbered, for the present, by those who desire to join the European Economic Community. A compromise may, of course, be found in an (uncharacteristic) attempt to keep personal religion distinct from public policy.

Secondly, there has been a recurrent tendency towards *reaction* and *zenophobia*. This directly opposite tendency can be seen in the Wahhābī movement and the early history of the Sanūsī Order (*ṭarīqa*). Both these movements, in their different ways, represent puritanical revivals in which an attempt was made to get back to primitive Islam. The Wahhābīs, in particular, tried to abjure the West and all 'innovation' (*bidʿa*) and find salvation in the Qur'ān and the Traditions of the Prophet. The intrusion of television, air-travel, oil-wealth and the ever-increasing economic problems and pressures of modern life have, however, left some of the once rigidly austere Wahhābī principles somewhat dented. Both reaction and zenophobia have also surfaced in movements such as the Muslim Brotherhood in several Arab lands, the Fedayeen (*al-fidā'īn*) in Iran, and Jamāʿat-i-Islāmī in the Indian sub-continent. The influence of the Brotherhood, now proscribed in

Egypt, has fluctuated considerably, as has that of the Jamāʿat in Pakistan.

Thirdly, there has been a widespread tendency, throughout most of the Muslim world, towards Islamic *modernism*. A classical example of this is provided by movements such as that led by the late Muḥammad ʿAbduh in Egypt, which attempt a synthesis of piety with progress, of Western science with the Muslim faith. The key to any such attempt must necessarily lie along the line of the revival of the right of *ijtihād*[126] and the abandonment, or metamorphosis, of the doctrine of 'agreement'. Like the Wahhābīs and Sanūsīs, these modernists would sweep away many of the accretions of the Middle Ages and seek to reinterpret the original sources of Islam. Unlike the reactionaries, however, they would try to reconcile their reinterpretation with the realities of modern life. The attempt is a bold one and beset, as we have seen, with acute problems; but the movement has already exerted a very widespread influence and continues to expand.

The difference between movements such as the Jamāʿat-i-Islamī and what may be termed Islamic modernism may be illustrated by their attitudes to the legal injunctions of the Qur'ān. The Jamāʿat believes that any attack on polygamy is impious; that insurance and fixed rates of interest should be prohibited; that the severe penal sanctions prescribed in the Qur'ān for theft, adultery and apostasy, and the like, must be reintroduced; and that the control of policy in Pakistan must be reserved for Muslims. The modernists, on the other hand, believe that the Qur'ān itself includes such stringent conditions for polygamy that it should certainly be restricted, and may even be forbidden, by statutory enactments; that the prohibition of 'usury' in the Qur'ān should be interpreted in terms of the exploitation of a brother Muslim's poverty and need rather than interest on investments in banks or companies; that changes in circumstances justify changes in law (as, for example, in regard to slavery and criminal sanctions); and that modern democracy is thoroughly compatible with Islam.

Fourthly, the situation in the Muslim world has recently been radically changed by the irruption of 'Islamic fundamentalism', to which references have already been made. This new phenomenon has been dramatically portrayed (in its specifically Shīʿī form) in the Islamic Revolution in Iran – with minor, but serious, repercussions among the Shīʿīs in Lebanon and Iraq. But Islamic fundamentalism is by no means confined to the Shīʿīs, for a Sunnī variety of what is essentially the same phenomenon has appeared – in a number of forms and with different degrees of success – in Pakistan, in the Sudan, Libya and Egypt. The roots of this movement can be traced back in part, no doubt, to the Muslim Brotherhood in Egypt, the Sudan and the

Levant, to the Fedayeen in Iran, and to the Jamāʿat in the Indian sub-continent. It is clear, however, that the ubiquity and aggression of the current wave of Islamic 'fundamentalism' is what represents the major challenge today to Islamic 'modernism' – and also to the peace of the world.

Yet another, but this time heretical, movement in the Muslim world must be mentioned in passing: that of the Aḥmadiyya. Founded by Mirzā Ghulām Aḥmad Khān towards the close of the last century, the Aḥmadiyya movement has more recently split into two sects, the smaller comparatively orthodox and the larger definitely heterodox. Aḥmadīs all assert that Christ was crucified but later revived in the tomb, escaped, and made his way to Kashmir where he died at the age of 120 years. The more extreme party also believes that Mirzā Ghulām Khān was both the long-expected Mahdī and the Messiah, and even a reincarnation of Krishna as well; but that, instead of world conquest by battle, his mission was peaceable and his holy war was to be waged by propaganda. Most Muslims would feel that the extremists' claim that their founder was a prophet in his own right, albeit 'within the revelation of Islam', amounts to apostasy. Some however would accept the more moderate party, which regards their founder as a reformer (*mujaddid*) rather than a prophet, as still within the Islamic fold.

Such movements as those of the Bābīs and Bahā'īs, however, have clearly ceased to be Muslim. It was in 1844 that Sayyid ʿAlī Muḥammad of Shirāz proclaimed himself to be the *Bāb* or 'Door' to divine truth. In essence this was another extreme development of certain Shīʿī views. But the majority of his followers recognized as his successor Bahā' Allāh (Mirzā Ḥusayn ʿAlī Nūrī), who issued a modified form of his master's teaching and whose followers are called Bahā'īs. This claims to be a universal religion, the wholesale adoption of which would bring world-wide peace. It teaches the duty of doing harm to no one, of loving one another, of bearing injustice without resistance, of being humble, and of devoting oneself to healing the sick. It has no clergy or formalities, and it countenances no austerities. Notice that the common element in all these very different movements is the propagation of what is, in reality, a new religion under the pretext of reforming Islam.

CHAPTER TWO

The twin sciences of Islam: theology and the sacred law

Some comparisons

In any study of Islamic thought, the twin sciences which have dominated Muslim education all down the centuries stand supreme: theology and the sacred law. Islamic theology is encapsulated in *ʿIlm al-Tawḥīd*, the doctrine of the divine Unity, while Islamic law is enshrined in the Sharīʿa, the blueprint of the divine pattern for human life. If *ʿIlm al-Tawḥīd* taught a Muslim what he should believe, it was the Sharīʿa which taught him how he should behave. Essential similarities, but with a distinct difference, can be found in the two great monotheistic religions which preceded Islam: Judaism and Christianity.

The Qur'ān and the Torah (Tawrāt)

The Qur'ān certainly resembles the Torah in the fact that it represents a 'strange combination of precept and prohibition, of religion and ethics' – and, indeed, of history and much else besides. The proportion however of strictly legal material is very much smaller. It is believed by orthodox Muslims to have been written from eternity in Arabic in heaven, and to have been revealed to Muḥammad in instalments as circumstances demanded – at times, at least, in something approaching a state of trance – by the Archangel Gabriel over a period of some twenty years. The word Qur'ān can be translated either 'reading' or 'recitation'. It was certainly regarded by Muḥammad as constituting the divinely inspired book which the Arabs – unlike some of their neighbours – previously lacked. In the words of Professor Arthur Jeffery:

> It is the source from which the Muslim community draws the

> primary prescriptions for the regulation of daily living, and to which its people turn to find nourishment for their devotional life . . . The Qur'ān is the word of Allah. Later Muslim piety, it is true, has made much of the person of the founder, but it was the Book, the Qur'ān, not the person Muḥammad, which was the significant factor in forming the mould in which the Islamic system took shape . . . The Scripture of no other community, not even the Old Testament among the Jews, has had quite the same influence on the life of the community as the Qur'ān has had in Islam.[1]

Unlike many other sacred books, moreover, it

> was not the product of the community in the sense that they decided that this was the collection of writings which had grown up in the community and in which they heard the authentic voice of religious authority, but it was formed by one man and given to the community on *his* authority as a collection of 'revelations' which was to be regulative for their religious life.[2]

There were, indeed, ample precedents in the ancient Near East for the belief that men might be the recipients of divine instructions – whether by means of omens, oracles or dreams. Sometimes these instructions were even believed to represent the communication of the contents of some heavenly tablet; or, again, they might take the form of codes of law which some king claimed to have compiled, under divine inspiration, 'to restore the Law of God'.[3] It was thus that

> the Jews came to believe that the Torah was in written form with God long before the creation of the world, that its prescriptions were in part made known to and observed by Adam and the Patriarchs before it was revealed in its fullness by being brought down to Moses, and that it will be revealed anew when the Messiah comes.[4]

Professor Jeffery argues, moreover, not only that Muḥammad derived from the Jews (whether in Madīna or elsewhere) some such concept of Scripture, but that this explains references in the Qur'ān to the 'Mother of the Book', to a 'preserved tablet', and to 'the entire Book' – which, it would seem, the Prophet thought of as comprising both the revelations given to previous 'Messengers' and also those vouchsafed to him by Gabriel.[5]

Islamic Ḥadīth literature and the Jewish Talmud

A further similarity, but with a difference, between Islam and Judaism may be found in the oral law. The similarity is that in both religions this oral law was accepted as an inspired amplification, and sometimes even amendment, of the written law, while the difference consists in the fact that, in Sunnī or 'orthodox' Islam, the oral law was ascribed exclusively to Muḥammad. Thus, in Judaism, the oral law, which was ultimately committed to writing in the Talmud, emanates from many different authors, and is ascribed to 'Moses' only in the most figurative sense.[6] By contrast the *aḥādīth* (or Traditions) of Islam which, after a period of oral transmission, came to be included in one or more of six recognized books, all derive their authority from the claim that they represent an account of something which Muḥammad himself did, said, or permitted to be said or done. In other words the normative element in the Traditions is the *sunna* or practice of the Prophet which they are alleged to establish. It is true that a few of these Traditions, called *aḥādīth qudsiyya* ('sacred traditions'), are accepted as words spoken to Muḥammad by God himself which, for whatever reason, were not incorporated in the Qur'ān. The authority of the vast majority, however, rests on the belief that *all* that the Prophet of Islam did, said or permitted was divinely inspired in content, although in the *aḥādīth* (in contradistinction to the Qur'ān) this inspiration does not extend to the actual wording.

In point of fact, however, the claim that all those Traditions commonly accepted as authentic really go back to some incident in Muḥammad's life is manifestly without foundation. The word *sunna* originally meant no more than a custom which had been handed down, while in the ancient schools of law it became a technical term for their accepted practice. It was the traditionalists, not the lawyers, who travelled far and wide to seek out stories about the Prophet, while the lawyers of the ancient schools did not always regard even an apparently genuine tradition about the Prophet's practice as necessarily normative.

But al-Shāfi'ī[7], the 'father of Islamic jurisprudence', took a middle line. He sided with the traditionalists in asserting that any authentic Tradition from the Prophet must be accepted as an authoritative source of law, but insisted on much more stringent criteria of authenticity than they did. In time, moreover, this attitude came to be accepted in theory by all the schools. It was still simple enough, however, for them to ignore an alleged Tradition which went against their accepted doctrine and practice by questioning its authenticity or by producing a contrary Tradition which, they maintained, had a greater claim to authority, or was intended to 'abrogate' the Tradition of which they disapproved.

The fact that al-Bukhārī, in compiling the most famous of all the collections of Traditions (*al-Ṣaḥīḥ*), is said to have considered some 600,000 and to have accepted less than 7,000, shows how many spurious traditions were at that time in circulation. Every Tradition accepted as authentic now consists of two distinct parts: the *isnād*, or chain of narrators by which it has been handed down, and the *matn*, or substance of the incident narrated. But while, in course of time, the *isnād* came to be subjected to the most minute scrutiny (*could* the alleged narrators in fact have received the Tradition, the one from the other? Were they men whose probity and memory could be trusted? etc.), this sort of questioning was not extended to the *matn*, which not infrequently provides convincing evidence that the story could not possibly have gone back to Muḥammad. It was obviously easy enough, moreover, for an acceptable *isnād* to be transferred from one Tradition to another, or for an alleged Tradition which had a gap in its chain of narrators (particularly, of course, in the final link with Muḥammad) to be suitably completed.

The composition and text of the Qur'ān[8]

In the traditional view Muḥammad could neither read nor write. This is the sense in which the adjective *ummī* (sūras 7:156 and 158) has been commonly understood, although the term might be regarded as roughly equivalent to the description of Jesus in John 7:15 as *mē memathēkos*, 'unlearned' in any rabbinical school. Richard Bell has made out a strong case for his conviction that Muḥammad himself wrote, and on occasion revised, some of the units (pericopae) of which the Qur'ān is made up. However this may be, some of the 'revelations', we are told, were jotted down by his Companions on 'palm-leaves, leather, and the ribs and shoulder-blades of animals'. For the most part, however, they were committed to memory – a feat that was facilitated by the rhyming and rhythmical prose in which they were composed – and were probably not extensively committed to writing, and certainly not collated as a book, until a few years after his death.

There has been much speculation about the way in which the different units of revelation were arranged in sūras or chapters – in some cases, in Bell's opinion, by Muḥammad himself.[9] Muslims commonly assert that the first Recension of the text of the Qur'ān as a whole was made by Zayd ibn Thābit very soon after the prophet's death – and it is generally accepted that a collection of relevant material must have been made substantially at this date. But it is a mistake to imagine that this was the only collection, for a number of different collections co-existed in early years, some of which attained the status of metropolitan Codices.[10] It was only under the third Caliph, ʿUthmān, that an official Recension was made and sent to the great metropolitan centres, with orders that all other Codices or collections should promptly be destroyed.[11]

A considerable body of variant readings from these Codices were in fact collected by Arthur Jeffery 'from the grammatical, lexical and masoretic literature of later generations which still remembered and discussed them'; and he even discovered and published the only known surviving example of an Arabic work on this subject – the *Codex Book* of Ibn Abī Dāwūd. In addition, until 322 AH/AD 932, the official text was itself purely consonantal and devoid of any diacritical marks, so an enormous number of variant readings and interpretations of this text have been recorded.[12] There were also disputes about such matters as the positioning of the signs used to mark verse endings. So, although it is true that today the Kūfan text of Ḥafs is accepted almost everywhere in the Muslim world, the claim commonly made by Muslims that they have the *ipsissima verba* of what Muḥammad actually said, without any variant readings, rests upon an ignorance of the facts of history.

The Qur'ān and the New Testament

Much of this will represent comparatively familiar ground to students of the Greek New Testament, with its variant readings and its regional textual traditions, represented by the Alexandrian, the Western, the Caesarean and the Byzantine Codices. What is absent is anything comparable to ʿUthmān's attempt to impose an official text and to exclude variants. Even more germane to our subject, Arthur Jeffery has stated that 'Perhaps even in the Prophet's own life-time there were certain members of the community who took an interest in 'collecting' the pronouncements of their Prophet. In this there is nothing unusual. It was precisely this that in the earliest Christian community provided those collections of 'Sayings of Jesus' that we find among the basic material of the Gospels.[13] Thus the discrete units of material which can still be distinguished in the text of the Qur'ān (easily enough, very often, by reason of a change in the prevailing rhyme) correspond to the less clear-cut pericopae (or individual units of tradition) discerned in the Gospels by 'Form-criticism' (see below), while the first major collection of material, attributed to Zayd ibn Thābit in the Caliphate of ʿUmar, may be compared with suggestions about written sources of our Gospels such as a 'proto-Mark', 'proto-Luke' or the 'Logia' ('Sayings') ascribed to Matthew. To the way in which the text of the Qur'ān was committed to memory we must soon revert.

The most obvious difference in the nature of the Qur'ān and the New Testament is not only that the former is a unit, composed by (or, in the Muslim view, 'sent down to') one man, but that it is all represented as the direct speech of God. Fragments of history, legislation, moral teaching and the musings of Muḥammad are uniformly introduced by the imperative '*Qul*' or 'Say'. In consequence it is, strictly speaking, improper to assert that anything in the Qur'ān represents the 'teaching of Muḥammad', since everything is regarded by Muslims as coming directly from Allāh. It is only when we turn to the Traditions that we find material that may properly be cited as teaching ascribed to the Prophet.

The Sharī'a and its sources

The orthodox Muslim view

The sources of Islamic law were not, however, restricted to the Qur'ān and *sunna* alone. There is, in fact, an alleged tradition – itself almost certainly spurious – that Muḥammad sent a man named Mu'ādh to act as a judge in the Yemen, and that he asked him on what he would base his judgments. 'On the Book of God', he replied. Muḥammad commended this answer, but asked him what he would do if he found nothing in the Qur'ān to help him. 'Then I would follow the practice of the Prophet of God', he replied; and was again commended. 'But what would you do if you could find nothing in the *sunna*, either, to guide you?', Muḥammad is then alleged to have asked. 'Why, in that case', Mu'ādh is said to have answered, 'I should follow my own opinion (*ra'y*)' – and Muḥammad is depicted as praising God for giving him such an intelligent emissary.

It is clear, however, that it was not long before Muslims began to feel that an individual opinion about what is right must, of necessity, constitute much too subjective and fallible a source for a law which claims to be firmly based on divine revelation. First, too subjective; so, in place of a general sense of what Islam requires, they insisted on an analogical extension (*qiyās*) of some recognized text to include another situation which could legitimately be held to be covered by the principle (*'illa*) which that text enunciated. Secondly, too fallible; so, in place of the opinion of a single individual, even in analogical reasoning, they gave pride of place to a decision about which a consensus (*ijmā'*) could be claimed, whether in the community as a whole or (much more often) among reputable scholars.

As a result, the four major sources of the law, which came to be recognized by all the surviving orthodox schools (the Ḥanafīs, Mālikīs,

Shāfi'īs and Ḥanbalīs) are now the Qur'ān, *sunna*, *ijmā'*[14] and *qiyās*. It is true that the Ḥanafīs sometimes rejected the view to which *qiyās* would naturally lead in favour of an opinion which they considered 'preferable' (and which they said was based on a more subtle form of analogical reasoning), that the Mālikīs did much the same in favour of what they claimed to represent the 'public interest',[15] and that there are certain other secondary sources of the law which have gained partial acceptance; but this need not detain us here.

A more critical look

This summary of the sources from which the Sharī'a was derived represents an outline of the approach which a Muslim from one of the four Sunnī schools of law would still probably adopt. But the research of Orientalists in recent years has shown conclusively, I think, that the traditional view that Islamic law was derived *directly* from the Qur'ān and *sunna* by Muslim jurists located primarily in Mecca and Madīna, by a process of pure deduction, represents a travesty of what really happened. The fact is that it was the customary law of both Arabia and the newly conquered territories, on the one hand, and the administrative practice of the early Caliphs, on the other, that provided the raw material from which Islamic law was quarried. It was provided, however, only after all the material had been worked through by Muslim scholar-jurists in the light of certain Quranic principles and such Traditions as they knew and accepted. By this process they succeeded, at one and the same time, in systematizing and Islamicizing the law; and the priority in this work came from Iraq, not the Hijāz.[16]

Strange to say, moreover, the law which was thus developed and applied in the early schools departs, on occasion, from what seems to be the clear teaching of the Qur'ān. In some cases such departures were only temporary, and can be explained easily enough by the difficulty of enforcing some prescription or penalty which was previously unknown to the Arabs. In others it may be said to represent not so much a deliberate departure from a Quranic norm as a development, or legal application, of an injunction or prohibition which is expressed in the Qur'ān in embryonic, or purely ethical, terms. But occasionally it represents a clear and long-lasting reversal of Quranic teaching. An example of this can be found in the decisive priority which is typically accorded in Islamic law to oral testimony – together with the virtual rejection of documentary evidence – in spite of the detailed instructions in sūra 2:282 that certain kinds of contracts should be reduced to writing, and how they should be witnessed and proved.[17] It is also relevant to recall in this context that there were, at first, a number of variant versions of the Qur'ān;[18] that it was only under the Caliph ʿAbd al-Mālik[19] that these were officially banned and destroyed; and that instances can be found of legal rules based not only on the *textus receptus* but on one of these variants.

Much the same process of selection seems to have taken place in regard to those elements in Islamic law which were almost certainly derived from Roman, Jewish, Byzantine or other foreign sources. It was not that Muslim legal scholars studied other systems of law and deliberately borrowed principles or precepts from them, but rather that Islamic law was wide open to influences of all sorts during the greater part of the first century of the Hijra. Thus the concept of the *ijmāʿ* of suitably qualified scholars seems to be an echo of the Roman *opinio prudentium*, while the doctrine that 'the child belongs to the marriage bed', the use of legal fictions, etc., can also be traced to Roman law. These were almost certainly brought into Islam by 'the cultured non-Arab converts to Islam who (or whose fathers) had enjoyed a liberal education . . . in Hellenistic rhetoric, which was the normal one in the countries of the Fertile Crescent of the Near East which the Arabs conquered.[20]

Even so, the way in which they were interpreted and applied in the Sharīʿa was distinctively Islamic; as may be seen, for example, in the fact that legal fictions were used in Roman law 'to provide the legal framework for new requirements of current practice with the minimum of innovation',[21] while Muslim lawyers resorted to their *ḥiyal* to enable them to achieve some purpose, which seemed to be forbidden by the Sharīʿa, without actually transgressing the words of the relevant injunction or prohibition. Recourse to such 'devices' was, moreover, no doubt encouraged by the consideration that there were many provisions in the Sharīʿa in regard to which obedience could only be 'blind' (*taʿabbudī*), since no one professed to understand the reason behind them. Examples of borrowings from Jewish or Rabbinic law can also be found in the prohibition (in the Qurʾān itself) of lending money for a fixed rate of interest (*ribā*), which Muḥammad presumably took over from the Jews in Madīna; the penalty of stoning to death for illicit sexual intercourse (which is not in fact Quranic) on the part of anyone who has ever enjoyed a valid marriage;[22] and even the jurisprudential sources (and methods) of *qiyās, istiṣlāḥ*, etc.[23]

From Byzantine law Muslims adopted the office of the 'inspector of the market', which later developed into that of the *muḥtasib*;[24] from the Sassānian administration they borrowed the concept of the investigation of complaints (*naẓar fi'l-maẓālim*), which gave rise to the Court of Complaints, and the office of 'clerk of the courts' (*kātib*), who became an assistant of the *qāḍī*;[25] and from the Canon law of the Eastern Churchs the principle, still retained in the Ithnā ʿAsharī and Ibāḍī law, that adultery constitutes an impediment to marriage.[26] A particularly good example of a distinctively Muslim institution which was originally derived from an alien source, moreover, is provided by the *waqf* system, which was founded on the pious foundations (*piae causae*) of the Eastern Churches but was developed in new ways, and for a variety of different purposes, in Islamic law.[27]

Fragmentation and coherence in Islamic law

Hitherto only a passing reference has been made in this chapter to the four schools of law which still survive in Sunnī Islam (cf. pp. 48f and 17–19 above). But it must never be forgotten that there have been – and still are – far more serious divisions in Islam than these schools which, for all their detailed differences, mutually acknowledge each others' orthodoxy.

The sharp split in the Islamic community caused by the Khārijī secession, with the uprisings to which this led in early Islam, has been summarized in chapter 1 (p. 17 above); and from this secession the Ibāḍī system of law survives until today. Similarly, a brief account has been given in that chapter of the much more serious controversy about the basis and nature of the Islamic community. This gave rise not only to the secession of the Shīʿa as a whole from the much more numerous company of Sunnī, or 'orthodox', Muslims, but also to the fragmentation of several sub-sects of the Shīʿīs which have split off from each other on three major issues. The issues were: the person whom they recognize as their Imām, the status they accord him, and the fact that they regard him as either 'present' with them still today or 'hidden' and represented (whether more, or less, authoritatively) by persons qualified to speak in his name (cf. pp. 14–17f above). We shall have to return to this subject again, and in more detail, in chapter 4, which will be devoted to the way in which Islamic law has developed through the centuries. We will also consider the vicissitudes through which it has passed in countries which have been drawn, by one means or another, into close contact with the Western world; and the degree to which it has been (or may be) resuscitated under the influence of Islamic fundamentalism. In the present context, therefore, we shall confine our attention to principles and generalizations, rather than details.

It has often been remarked that, for all their differences in matters of constitutional theory, the detailed law of the Shīʿīs and Ibāḍīs does not differ very widely from that of the Sunnīs. For this several reasons may be suggested. To begin with, all Muslims accept the same Qurʾān – although it is true that the Shīʿīs complain that a few verses which were particularly favourable to the claims of ʿAlī were deliberately omitted, and the followers of the Āghā Khān believe that he can still speak with the divine voice, and thus introduce radical reforms in their law with a freedom denied to other Muslims. Neither the Shīʿīs nor the Ibāḍīs, moreover, accept the Sunnī books of 'authentic Traditions', since the Shīʿīs reject any tradition whatever that has not been related by or through one of their Imāms, and the Ibāḍīs also have their own collections; but this, too, does not seem to have caused many major differences in practice. Both the Shīʿīs and the Ibāḍīs again, reject the Sunnī *ijmāʿ* and *qiyās*, although both communities, for the most part, accept a sort of consensus of their own and make use of a form of legal reasoning which the Shīʿīs, for example, call *ʿaql*. But the fact remains that the different communities were in sufficiently close touch with each other throughout the formative period of Islamic law for the heterodox groups to take over the law which was being developed in the Sunnī schools with only such modifications as their own political or legal theories seemed to demand.[28]

Yet it is fair, I think, to accept Professor N. J. Coulson's conclusion that, whereas Sunnī political theory 'represents an amalgam of Islamic principles and pre-Islamic practice – rule by the traditional tribal aristocracy subject to the dictates of the religious law' – Ithnā ʿAsharī political theory, on the other hand,

> renounces any connection with pre-Islamic practice and sees the sole source of authority to lie in the founder-Prophet and his attributes as a religious leader . . . Juristically as well as politically, Islam meant a re-orientation and modification of existing practice for the Sunnites, while for the Ithnā ʿAsharites it marked a completely new point of departure.[29]

It is remarkable, however, that, in spite of the debt that the Sharīʿa – particularly in its Sunnī form – owes to the customary law which preceded it, this law has received virtually no official recognition in Islamic jurisprudence. It is true that in many parts of the Muslim world local customary law has not only survived alongside the Sharīʿa, but is regularly applied in its stead, in some spheres of life even by specifically Islamic courts. But the customary law which forms the basis of so much of the Islamic law itself is very seldom acknowledged as such. Instead, it has in most cases been tacitly incorporated in the Sharīʿa under one of the recognized sources of Islamic jurisprudence – occasionally by a verse from the Qurʾān (or the way in which this is interpreted and applied), but more often under the authority of some Tradition or of *ijmāʿ* (particularly, of course, where this is peculiar to some specific area, like the *ijmāʿ* of Madīna in Mālikī law).

The right of ijtihād

I have already referred to the way in which Sharīʿa law was open, in its earliest stages, to the free current of ideas. Throughout this period – and, indeed, until about the middle of the third century of the Hijra (ninth century AD) – any suitably qualified jurist had enjoyed the right of independent reasoning: that is, the liberty to use his own judgment as to what the law ought to be, and to deduce from the original sources the solution to a new problem. But by the beginning of the fourth century of the Hijra (tenth century AD)

> the point had been reached when the scholars of all [the Sunnī] schools felt that all essential questions had been thoroughly discussed and finally settled, and a consensus gradually established itself to the effect that from that time onwards no one might be deemed to have the necessary qualifications for independent reasoning in law, and that all future activity would have to be confined to the explanation, application, and, at the most, interpretation of the doctrine as it had been laid down once and for all. This 'closing of the door of *ijtihād*', as it was called, amounted to a demand for *taqlīd*, a term which . . . now came to mean the unquestioning acceptance of the doctrine of established schools and authorities.[30]

It is true that a number of subsequent scholars have claimed to be *mujtahids* (that is, to have the right to exercise *ijtihād*). But this has usually been confined in practice to comparatively narrow limits, and has never commanded general assent. Even among the Shīʿīs, moreover, who still accord to some of their scholars the title of *mujtahid*, the discretion they exercise in practice is usually far from wide; and in Sunnī or orthodox Islam the author of even the most authoritative treatise has, for centuries, been regarded as a mere *muqallid* (this is, one confined to *taqlīd*). There have, of course, been developments in the law down the centuries, many of which can be found in the books of *fatāwā*, or legal opinions. But the numerous one-time variant opinions in each of the schools have, for the most part, gradually been eliminated in favour of a doctrine which is generally accepted, and the law has become more and more rigid and moribund.

The influence of al-Ashʿarī (on law, ethics and doctrine)

Another factor which has led to rigidity in Islamic law has been the insistence of al-Ashʿarī (who died in the fourth century of the Hijra [tenth century AD]) that man is incapable, of himself, of apprehending the moral quality of human actions without the enlightenment of divine revelation. No doctrine of Natural Law would have been acceptable to him: what man needed was God's direct and explicit revelation. He even went so far as to deny that such qualities as virtue and vice exist of themselves, or have any meaning whatever apart from the divine command or prohibition. God does not command the good because it is intrinsically good, or forbid the evil because it is inherently evil. On the contrary, it is exclusively the divine command or prohibition which makes actions virtuous or vicious. Had the divine revelation been different, then virtue would have become vice, and vice virtue.

As among the Christian Schoolmen,[31] however, there has always been a variety of opinions on this matter within the fold of Islam. The Muʿtazilīs,[32] for instance, took a very different view, for they have always asserted that human acts are either good or bad in themselves, and that God commanded the good because it was good and forbade the evil because it was evil. More, they held that in some cases human reason can perceive, independently of divine revelation, that an act is virtuous or vicious *per se*. In such cases God's revelation merely confirms what man could have apprehended of himself, whereas in other matters he is completely dependent on divine enlightenment. And yet others, such as the Māturīdīs and many Ḥanafī jurists, took up an intermediate position. They agreed with the Muʿtazilīs that human acts are intrinsically good or evil, and that human reason can in some cases discern this. Unlike the Muʿtazilīs, however, they refused – in general – to admit that man had any obligation to do what was right or abstain from what was wrong until this was made plain by a divine command or prohibition. But it was the more extreme view of al-Ashʿarī which predominated in orthodox Islam.

It follows, of course, that the Sharīʿa covers the whole of life, and that there is little difference between law and morality in Islam. It is true that one can at times discern, behind the moral categories of good and evil, a more specifically legal category of valid or invalid. It is morally wrong, for instance, for a man to divorce his wife without adequate reason; but if he pronounces the repudiation in the proper form this constitutes a valid divorce, however sinful it may be. It is also true that a large part of the Sharīʿa could never be enforced by any human court, but must always depend for sanction on the bar of eternity. Many Muslims, for example, classify all human actions in one of five different categories: what is explicitly commanded; what is recommended but not expressly enjoined; what is left legally indifferent; what is reprobated but not explicitly prohibited; and what is expressly forbidden. Clearly, then, it is only the first and last of these categories which could ever be enforced by human courts; and it is only the middle category – what the divine law has left 'legally indifferent' – that represents the proper sphere of human regulations.

Siyāsa sharʿiyya and legislative codes

Very few Muslim governments have tried to enforce the Sharīʿa strictly in the life of the markets, and virtually none of them have been content to leave the maintenance of law and order exclusively to the *qāḍīs'* courts – committed as these are, in theory at least, to the enforcement of the criminal provisions of the Sharīʿa exclusively by those principles of procedure and proof which the Sharīʿa itself prescribes. As a result, both the *qāḍīs* and the legal scholars have commonly conceded that there is a sphere in which the ruler may properly exercise a lawful discretion. This is called *siyāsa sharʿiyya*, and provides the primary foundation for the widespread legislation which has transformed the Muslim world in recent years.

This legislation has commonly been characterized by two main features: first, by the withdrawal of commercial and criminal law – and, in fact, almost everything outside what might be termed 'family law' in the widest connotation of that term – from the scope of the specifically Islamic courts, and its consignment instead to new 'secular' courts to administer under a series of statutory enactments which are largely (although often not exclusively) of alien origin; and secondly, by the introduction of some radical changes even in the sphere of family law itself by one or more of four expedients which, it is claimed, do not deprive it of its basically Islamic character.

One of these is a procedural device which makes no pretension to affect any substantive change in the Islamic law as such, but which radically excludes its application by the courts in specified circumstances. Another (which constitutes far the most widely used expedient of all) represents an eclectic device by means of which the executive or legislature prescribes which opinion of some recognized school or scholar of the past shall be followed in given circumstances; and this principle is often stretched to include opinions drawn from 'heterodox' schools or highly individualistic jurists, or even to cover the resort to *talfīq* (patching), by means of which part of one reputable opinion of the past is so combined with part of another as to produce a result which neither of the authorities concerned would have approved, however respectable the lineage of its component parts may be. A third expedient – to which recourse is normally had only when no authority of the past can be quoted in support – is a new interpretation of some basic text in either the Qurʾān or *sunna*. And the fourth such expedient represents a law or administrative order which is usually based on one of the three devices already mentioned, but which occasionally contents itself with the statement that it is 'not contrary to Islamic law'.

The opponents of these reforms have always been quick to claim that they are contrary to the principle of *ijmāʿ*; that they represent a hotch-potch of provisions which frequently rest on mutually contradictory principles; and that they constitute a thinly veiled cover for what is really a new exercise of the right of *ijtihād* – and an *ijtihād* which rests on singularly inconsistent and unscholarly foundations.[33] More fundamentally still, they assert that the basic nature of the Sharīʿa has been changed; for whereas, in the past, the Sharīʿa represented a God-given blueprint to which both Caliph and slave, sultan and subject were, alike, bound to attempt to conform, it is now the state which legislates as it pleases, and which even presumes to decree which parts of the Sharīʿa are to be applied by the courts, and how this is to be done. This last charge, moreover, is virtually unanswerable – except by a frank admission that times have changed, that parts of the Sharīʿa are no longer suitable for modern life, and that in those parts where a variety of interpretations are possible it is essential for the State to specify which one is to be applied. Even so, the fact remains that, while the Sharīʿa had never, in practice, exercised the monopoly of authority and obedience often ascribed to it in theory, it had certainly provided a canon – to which lip service, at least, was paid by all – against which every man's actions could be measured. In this respect, at least, it had fulfilled a role somewhat similar to that of 'Natural Law'.

The master science?

Whereas, moreover, a failure to observe the Sharīʿa's provisions was in general regarded as human and venial, any questioning of its authority represented rank apostasy and unbelief. Joseph Schacht did not exaggerate when he insisted that 'Islamic law is the epitome of Islamic thought, the most typical manifestation of the Islamic way of life, the core and kernel of Islam itself',[34] nor was Sir Hamilton Gibb indulging in hyperbole when he affirmed that it had always represented the master science in the Muslim world and the most effective agent in holding the social fabric of Islam compact and secure through all the fluctuations of political fortune.[35] It is only natural, of course, that independent states should differ among themselves in the degree to which they have felt this law had to be brought into conformity with the facts of modern life – particularly when some of those states are regarded as 'reactionary' and others as 'revolutionary'. The fact remains, however, that the cement which once bound them together has now become very loose and uneven.

Islamic theology: the doctrine of the divine unity

Traditionally, Muslim education used always to centre on two sciences, not one: on theology and the sacred law. It is fair enough to describe the law as the 'master science', since Islam has always been much more positive, detailed and authoritative about the way of life that the Creator has prescribed for his creatures than about the nature and characteristics of the Creator himself. It is, perhaps, symptomatic in this context that there has always been more concurrence and emphasis in Islam about the five (or six) 'Pillars of Religion'[36] – all of which constitute ways in which men should behave – than about the six 'Articles of Belief'[37] It is also significant that Muslim religious leaders, like Jewish Rabbis, have been primarily lawyers, while it is only among the Ṣūfīs that we find anything approaching an 'ordained' ministry.[38]

Who is a Muslim?

Having said all this, disputes about matters of theology were far from rare. In the fragmentation of Islam between Sunnīs, Shīʿīs and Khawārij, for example, political, theological and legal issues all played their part; and here, as in subsequent disputes, one of the major questions was 'who is a Muslim?' To this the fanatical Shīʿī was wont to reply 'Only he who recognizes the true Imām', while the Khārijī insisted that it was only he whose 'works' went hand in hand with his faith – and this, too, had a political as well as a theological aspect, for it was bound up with people's attitude to the Umayyad dynasty. But if the Khawārij were far too extreme in insisting that any unrepented sin constituted apostasy, was it right to go to the other extreme and hold that faith alone was sufficient for salvation, irrespective of a man's behaviour or his political stance?

One answer to this question was provided by the Murjiʾites – that is, those who deferred or postponed any such judgment until it was pronounced by God himself on the day of judgment. But another early Muslim sect was more exclusively theological in origin – for it turned on the age-old controversy about predestination and free-will. The more puritan wing pointed to a string of Quranic verses

> which proclaim human responsibility and declare that men will be recompensed at the Judgement according to their works and their deserts; man is therefore free to choose for himself, and does so by the power which God has created in him. This was the doctrine of the Qadarites, the 'Abilitarians', as against the absolute Predestinarians.[39]

Controversy with the Muʿtazila

At the beginning of the second century of the Hijra (eighth century AD) a group of Qadarites 'separated themselves' in order to take up a neutral position in regard to whether a Muslim who committed a flagrant sin was a believer or an unbeliever. Such was the origin of the Muʿtazila,[40] to whom passing reference has already been made; and it was among them 'that the beginnings arose of an apologetic or scholastic theology, called in Arabic *Kalām* or "discussion".' This seems to have been primarily aimed at two main purposes: at 'asserting the unity and creatorhood of God against non-Muslim opponents, dualists of various kinds, sceptics, and the Hellenistic philosophy which maintained the eternity of the world'; and at maintaining 'the Qadarite doctrine of human freedom against its Muslim opponents.'[41] Their doctrines found favour with the Caliph al-Maʾmūn, among others, and he established a 'House of Wisdom' in Baghdad about AD 820 in order to organize the production of translations of Greek philosophic works into Arabic.

But it was in their insistence that God must, by his very nature, always do what is intrinsically right and most beneficial for his creatures; that God's attributes must be regarded as *identical* with his divine essence, 'purified from every shadow of createdness or occasionalism',[42] and thus interpreted in a largely negative sense; and that the Qurʾān could not, therefore, be regarded as either 'eternal' or 'uncreated' – that they came into sharp conflict with the 'orthodox'. But it took nearly a century

> before the orthodox realized that reasoned arguments must be met not by slogans but by reasoned arguments on the other side. Early in the fourth century AH (about AD 920) there emerged the beginnings of an 'orthodox *Kalām*', associated with the names of al-Ashʿarī[43] of Baghdad and al-Māturīdī of Samarqand. Methodologically it took over, as was inevitable, many of the bases of the Muʿtazilite *Kalām*, but it rejected the Muʿtazilite claim to establish human reason as the ultimate criterion of religious truth. True, the blessed will not see God in Paradise as a spatially-defined Being, but they will see him nevertheless, in some manner which human reason and experience cannot specify. True, the Koran, as a written book and as recited by human agency, is created, but its quality as the Speech of God is the same as that of the other attributes, existing in his Essence and therefore uncreated. True, there are in the Koran a number of anthropomorphic metaphors, but

> they express actions or attributes of which we, as human beings, can know neither the nature nor the manner, and they are not to be wished away by simple or laborious philological exercises or conceits.[44]

Even this however, went much further than many Muslims were prepared to go. Instead, they were content to accept these mysteries 'without asking "How?" '. But in due course the problem of the relationship between God's 'eternal qualities' and his 'divine essence' was resolved, among orthodox scholars. They resolved the problem by confining themselves to the statement that these qualities were not *identical* with his essence nor separable from it (*lā dhātahu wa lā ghayrahu*). This fact is set out in the creed of al-Nasafī in the words: 'He has qualities [*ṣifāt*] from all eternity [*azalī*] existing in His essence. They are not He, nor are they other than He.'[45]

Controversies with other groups

There were three other groups with which the orthodox felt compelled to contend: the *falāsifa*, or disciples of Hellenistic philosophy, represented especially by Avicenna and Averroes (or Ibn Sīnā and Ibn Rushd); the extreme Ismāʿīlīs, whose doctrine of emanations, when developed along Gnostic lines, enabled them to confer a divine authority on their Imāms by linking them with the Active Intellect of the philosophers; and the Ṣūfīs, or mystics, who aspired to a direct knowledge of God (*kashf*), or even identification with him (*ittiḥād*). The answer to all three was largely provided by the towering figure of al-Ghazālī[46] – but in very different ways. He probed the arguments of the philosophers and ruthlessly refuted both their methods and their conclusions in a scathing work entitled *Tahāfut al-Falāsifa* ('The Collapse of the Philosophers'), for he found their reasoning barren and their deductions both mistaken and misleading.[47] He also carefully examined the doctrine of the Taʿlīmīs, a group of extreme Ismāʿīlīs, and found their teaching eminently unsatisfactory. They would repeat *ad nauseam* formulae they had learnt by rote, but they seemed to know little or nothing else. So his trained mind lost patience with their shallow reasonings and fanciful assertions, and he wrote several books against them.

With the Ṣūfīs, on the other hand, he took an entirely different course. He had himself plumbed the depths of intellectual scepticism, so he started to study the books and teachings of the mystics again (for he had been superficially acquainted with them from his youth) with real avidity. It soon became clear to him that he must be initiated as a mystic himself – live their life and share their ecstatic exercises –

if he was to reach his goal. It was not long before he became convinced that it was the Ṣūfīs who were on the true and only path to an experimental knowledge of God, and accepted the validity of their ecstatic revelations. But he realized that it was both erroneous and dangerous to describe their nearness to God in terms of *ḥulūl* (fusion of being), *ittiḥād* (identification) or *wuṣūl* (union).[48]

The fact is that, while the earliest Muslim mysticism had taken the form of asceticism, largely inspired by the dread of hell, it was soon exposed to many extraneous influences – Christian, Gnostic, Neo-Platonic and Eastern (whether in the form of Buddhism[49] or certain Hindu concepts). With many of its devotees, therefore, an earnest quest for *communion* with God had become transformed into an extravagant doctrine of essential *union* or even *identity* with him (almost after the manner of the Advaita Vedānta). This was accentuated by the practice of using a variety of means to heighten the psychological effect of the continuous invocation (*dhikr*) of the name of God to induce auto-hypnosis or a state of trance, in the course of which they would at times make statements which were exceedingly offensive to orthodox Muslims.

It was thus that in AD 922 an example was made of one of the most notorious theosophists, al-Ḥusayn bin Manṣūr al-Ḥallāj, by putting him to a cruel death for asserting 'I am the Truth'. But there were other Ṣūfīs on whom no shadow of unorthodoxy seems ever to have rested. Such, for example, was al-Junayd, who insisted that no man could be a true Ṣūfī unless he held firmly to the Qur'ān and the *sunna* of the Prophet.[50] So it was, perhaps, al-Ghazālī's major achievement to bring Ṣūfism within the somewhat arid confines of orthodox Islam, and to open up orthodox thought to the acceptance of the Ṣūfism which was truly Islamic.

The love of God

If Judaism is a religion in which the *primary* emphasis falls on the law of God rather than on the love of God, then this is still more true of Islam. For in the Old Testament it is abundantly clear that the law is set in the context of God's covenant with his people, and represents the response which God expects from them to an initiative which he has already taken in sheer grace. Tender passages recur, moreover, in which God is portrayed as a father who teaches his child to walk, a shepherd who carries his lamb in his arms, a lover who woos his beloved, and even a husband who longs for his unfaithful wife to return to him. In Islam, by contrast, the constant reference is to God as sovereign Lord (*Rabb*), and man as his servant or slave (*ʿabd*). It is significant in this context, I think, that 'Love', or 'Loving', finds no place among the seven 'Eternal Attributes' of God (*al-Ṣifāt al-Azaliyya*) to which Muslim theology so often refers.

But this is certainly not to suggest that the concept of the love of God is wholly lacking in Islam. A number of phrases from the Qur'ān itself could be quoted to refute any such assertion. In sūra 2:191, for example, we read that 'Allāh loveth those who do well'; in 2:222 that 'Allāh loveth those who turn continually in penitence, and loveth those who keep themselves pure'; in 3:70 that 'Allāh loveth those who act piously'; and in 5:46 that 'Allāh loveth those who act with fairness'; etc. These verses, it is true, affirm the love of God only for those who in some measure deserve it, and there are far more which assert that God does *not* love those who do not. Against this must be balanced verses like 5:43, which states that 'if anyone repent after his wrong-doing and set things right, Allāh will repent towards him; Allāh is forgiving, compassionate'. In all these verses the Arabic word for 'love' is the verb *yaḥibb*; but a noun for 'love' and an adjective for 'loving' from another root (*wudd* and *wadūd*) are used in 19:96 which states: 'Verily for those who have believed and done works of righteousness will the Merciful appoint love'. The same words appear in both 11:92 and 85:14, which affirm, respectively: 'Verily my Lord is compassionate, loving' and 'He is the Forgiving, the Loving'.[51]

Muslim piety, moreover, largely centres round the constant repetition of the ninety-nine 'Beautiful Names' of God. Far the best known of these are the first two, 'The Compassionate, the Merciful' (*al-Raḥmān al-Raḥīm*), which are coupled together at the head of every sūra except one in the Qur'ān. The two words in Arabic both come from the same root, and when they are conjoined in this way Dr Kenneth Cragg writes that

> the first should probably be regarded rather as a noun than an adjective, with the second qualifying it: 'The Merciful Mercier' or 'the Compassionate Compassionator'. The sequence is not mere repetition. The *Raḥmān* is the One Who is in His character merciful. The *Raḥīm* is He in merciful action. He Who is merciful behaves mercifully. His mercy is of His essence, and also of His deed.[52]

This sounds as though it should convince any Muslim of the unchanging love of God, and prompts the question why this concept is so muted in Islam. Part of the reason may, perhaps, be found in the fact that the last of the above quoted references goes on to describe God as 'The Occupant of the Throne, the Glorious, the Doer of what he intendeth' – which, in Kenneth Cragg's words, represents 'the perpetual condition of all the attributes. They are to be understood finally as characteristics of the Divine will rather than laws of his nature'.[53] Put more starkly, the salient impression one gets from Islamic theology as a whole is that of the sovereign Lord for whose mercy one may certainly hope, but of which one can never be assured.

On this, as on so many subjects, the Traditions record a wide variety of statements which Muḥammad is alleged to have made. In one, for example, he is recorded as stating that the Almighty has said 'My servant does not draw near to Me with anything more loved by Me than the religious duties I have imposed upon him, and My servant continues to draw near to Me with supererogatory works so that I shall love him. . . . Were he to ask [something] of Me, I would surely give it to him; and were he to ask Me for refuge, I would surely grant him it'.[54] Yet, in another, we are told that 'when God resolved to create the human race, He took into His hands a mass of earth, the same whence all mankind were to be formed, and in which they after a manner pre-existed; and having then divided the clod into two equal portions, He threw the one half into hell, saying, "These to eternal fire, and I care not"; and projected the other half into heaven, adding, "and these to Paradise, and I care not".'[55]

I am not, of course, suggesting for a moment that either of these traditions is authentic, but they serve to illustrate two deeply rooted Muslim beliefs: the first, that the faithful worshipper may, indeed, *hope* for God's mercy; and the second that, in the last resort, all depends on the divine decree, and that God is too transcendent to be affected in any way by man's behaviour or destiny. To think of him as being made sad by man's indifference, sin and ultimate damnation, or glad by man's response, obedience and salvation, would derogate from his utter transcendence and self-sufficiency (*tanzīh*). It seems probable, moreover, that this was a concept of God which was absorbed by Islam – as, also, in part at least, by Judaism and Christianity in the Scholastic era – from Aristotelian philosophy, for it is far removed from the language of the Bible. But it certainly looks somewhat less alien in Muslim theology (in which teaching about the love of God was largely ignored, and even al-Juwaynī, Imām al-Ḥaramayn, is reported to have said that, strictly speaking, God can neither love nor be loved)[56] than it does in the religion of the cross.

The transcendence of God

There is, moreover, another basic doctrine of Islam – itself closely connected with the concept of transcendence – which deprives the Quranic testimony to the love and mercy of God of much of its natural import. I refer to the doctrine of *al-mukhālafa*, or the utter difference between God and man. This means, to quote Dr Kenneth Cragg once more, that

> Terms taken from human meanings – and there are of course no others – were said to be used of God with a difference. They did not convey the human connotation but were used in those senses feasible of God. When the further question was pressed: What then do they convey as applied to God? no precise answer was capable of being formulated. Islam here falls back upon a final agnosticism. Terms must be used if there is to be religion at all. But only God knows what they signify. Muslim theology coined the related phrases *Bilā Kaif* and *Bilā Tashbīh*. We use these names 'without knowing how' they apply and without implying any human similarity.[57]

But if we may not conclude that divine compassion and mercy are in some degree analogous, although far superior, to human compassion and mercy, then the 'Beautiful Names' of God – including, of course, *al-Raḥmān al-Raḥīm* – may, indeed, be beautiful sounds in a Muslim's ear, but remain devoid of any intelligible content.

I vividly remember being present one day at a meeting in an Egyptian village, Bilbeis by name. An Egyptian evangelist was speaking to a crowd of men who had just come in from the weekly market. They listened quietly for some ten minutes; but when he began to speak about the love of God a village 'sheikh' rose to his feet and shouted 'Stop! You must not draw any parallel between human love and God's love. God is utterly different' – and the room emptied. There could, on that occasion, be no communication whatever.

It is no matter for surprise, therefore, that the more ardent spirits in the Muslim community have so often turned to the Ṣufis, or mystics of Islam, for a spiritual satisfaction that reaches to the heart. The daily ritual of Islam and the stern demands of the law provide little to quicken the pulse or fire the emotions. The Muslim is normally left to find what spiritual sustenance he can in the somewhat arid pastures of *naql*, or the teachings of tradition, and *ʿaql*, or the deductions of reason. Neither provides any real access to the person or nature of God, except in the form of philosophical abstractions: so many Muslims have turned, all down the ages, to *kashf*, or the direct revelation and knowledge of God which the mystics have always sought and commended.

This is so important that it demands a chapter in its own right. Suffice it to say here that the very chanting of the Qur'ān often serves to arouse a considerable degree of religious emotion in a Muslim audience.

CHAPTER THREE

Islamic mysticism: the most attractive face of Islam?

The origins of Islamic mysticism

We have already seen (cf. pp. 5f above) that Muḥammad himself had, from an early age, shown signs of having a distinctly religious disposition. It is recounted that on a visit to Syria with his uncle, at the age of twelve, he met and conversed with a Christian monk named Baḥīra. In his early manhood, he travelled on the caravan trade of Khadīja – a well-to-do widow, many years his senior, who became his first – and, until her death, his only – wife. He seems to have been impressed, like some of the pre-Islamic poets, by lonely hermits in the desert. Some of these were called Ḥanīfs–Arabs who, though neither Christian nor Jewish, had become profoundly dissatisfied with the polytheism and idol-worship of their Arab contemporaries. Others were Christians, with their night watches and their recital of their sacred books. In D. B. Macdonald's view

> These Christian hermits and the long deserted ruins telling of old forgotten tribes – judged and overthrown by God, as the Arabs held and hold – that lie along the Syrian waste and along the caravan routes were the two things that most stirred the imagination of Muhammad and went to form his faith.[1]

Be that as it may, what is certain is that in early middle life Muḥammad used to spend long hours in meditation, fasting and seeking the face of Allāh ('The God'). From the fact that his own father's name was ʿAbd-Allāh, it is clear that the Arabs already recognized Allāh as a deity – indeed, as the name implies, the supreme deity; but that did not prevent them from squandering their worship on idols. What they needed was a Prophet and a Book of their own.

Some of the earliest sūras in the Qur'ān may well – as many Orientalists believe – properly belong to this period of troubled meditation and wistful seeking. Then, suddenly (if the identification of sūra 96 as the first 'revelation' he received is correct), Muḥammad sensed a voice bidding him:

> Recite in the name of thy Lord who created,
> Created man from clotted blood.
> Recite, for thy Lord is the most generous,
> Who taught by the pen [or 'taught (the use of) the pen'?]
> Taught man what he did not know.[2]

Even so, he remained dubious and perplexed, in spite of Khadīja's encouragement, until he was aroused by the exhortation 'O thou enwrapped in thy mantle, arise and warn'[3] – followed by dire warnings about the Day of Judgment and a vivid description of the torments of hell.

In Muḥammad himself the earlier revelations, to quote Kenneth Cragg,

> were accompanied by intense emotional stress, physical limpness and perspiration, and a state of trance. Though the onset of the experiences subsequently came to occur without the same intensity of degree in these phenomena, they seem always to have been present in some form as the qualifying accompaniment of the 'Qur'anic' state, as distinct from the other, personal deliverances of the Prophet incorporated in the later traditions.[4]

And the predictions of God's wrath and judgment on those who did not receive his mercy were so vivid and repeated that it is scarcely surprising that those Muslims of the first century of the Hijra who took them most to heart may be more accurately described as ascetics than as mystics, characterized primarily by their fear, rather than their love, of God.

Not long into the next century, when the ʿAbbāsids came to power, there was a new wave of asceticism, with men – and women too – rejecting the world and its vanities in a life of poverty and meditation. One of the earliest of these was a saintly woman named Rābiʿa (d. 185 AH/AD 801), to whom asceticism, extreme other-worldliness and an ecstatic devotion which expressed itself in love-poetry, are all ascribed.[5] It is related that on one occasion someone said to her 'I have committed many sins; if I turn in penitence to God, will he turn in mercy to me?' Rābi'a replied 'Nay, but if He shall turn towards thee, thou wilt turn towards Him.'[6]

One of the earliest male devotees was a wanderer of royal blood who drifted from Balkh in Afghanistan to Basra and Mecca, Ibrāhīm ibn Adham by name (d. 161 AH/AD 777).[7] Another, al-Fuḍayl ibn 'Iyāḍ from Khurasan (d. 187 AH/AD 803), was 'a robber converted by a heavenly voice; he cast aside the world, and his utterances show that he lapsed into the passivity of quietism.'[8] A little later another woman saint (for there is no barrier of gender in Islamic mysticism) was the Lady Nafīsa (d. 208 AH/AD 821), 'a contemporary and rival in learning with al-Shāfi'ī and the marvel of her time in piety and the ascetic life.' She was a descendant of al-Ḥasan, the martyred son of 'Alī; and her grave in Cairo is still the site of much visitation, and alleged miracles.[9]

It was about this time that Muslim ascetics and devotees began to wear the robe of coarse wool (ṣūf) from which the mystics of Islam derived their distinctive name of Ṣūfī. The individual surname al-Ṣūfī first appeared, it seems, in connection with Jābir ibn Ḥayyān, 'a Shī'ī alchemist of Kufa, who professed an ascetic doctrine of his own', and with Abū Hāshim, a celebrated mystic, also of Kufa. The term ṣūfī was at first confined to Kufa, but it soon spread to Basra and Baghdad. Previously this coarse woollen garment had been considered 'a foreign and reprehensible fashion of Christian origin' (with which a disciple of Ḥasan al-Baṣrī had been reproached). Soon however it became what it has remained, 'an eminently orthodox Muslim fashion.' In later tradition it was even alleged to be 'Muḥammad's favourite dress for a religious man.'[10]

In this case, therefore, Islamic mysticism's debt to Christianity is clear. So it may be well to pause, at this juncture, for a look at the various extraneous influences to which the Ṣūfīs and Ṣūfism have been exposed (and by which they have, in part, been influenced) over the centuries, before we resume an account of what is, in essence, a distinctively Muslim phenomenon.

Extraneous elements in the development of Islamic mysticism

Christianity

Clearly it was not only the habit of wearing a coarse woollen robe, and the practice of asceticism which Muslim Ṣūfīs owed to the wandering monks (*sa'iḥs*) and Christian hermits, which had aroused Muḥammad's interest and respect. We also find Gospel texts and and apocryphal sayings of Jesus cited in some of the oldest Ṣūfi biographies, while 'the Christian anchorite (*rāhib*) often appears in the role of a teacher giving instruction and advice to wandering Muslim ascetics.'[11] In both Christian and early Muslim mysticism asceticism often went hand in hand with quietism. Another tendency in which some early Muslim mystics were encouraged by their Christian counterparts was their growing emphasis on love. R. A. Nicholson, for example, tells us that a Syrian mystic, Aḥmad al-Ḥawārī, once asked a Christian hermit: 'What is the strongest command that ye find in your Scriptures?' The hermit replied: 'We find none stronger than this: "Love Thy Creator with all thy power and might" '; and that another hermit was asked by some Muslim ascetics 'When is a man most persevering in devotion?' 'When love takes possession of his heart,' was the reply; 'for then he hath no joy or pleasure but in continual devotion.'[12]

At a later date, Nicholson records, some mystics insisted that Muḥammad was 'the Light of God'; that 'he existed before the creation of the world' and is 'adored as the source of all life'; and that 'he is the Perfect Man in whom all the divine attributes are manifested'. A Ṣūfī tradition even attributes to Muḥammad the saying 'He that hath seen me hath seen Allāh'.[13] So there can be no manner of doubt about the source from which *these* ideas were derived.

Greek thought

Al-Fārābī of Turkistan (d. 339 AH/AD 949), who lived and worked in the brilliant circle which gathered around Sayf al-Dawla, the Hamdānid, at Aleppo, was alike master in music, science, philology and philosophy. Aristotle (mediated to him through his Neoplatonist commentators) was his passion. During the reign of Muʿtaṣim a Christian of Emessa in the Lebanon had translated parts of the 'Enneads' of Plotinus into Arabic under the title 'The Theology of Aristotle', on which D. B. Macdonald comments that 'a more unlucky bit of literary mischief and one more far-reaching in its consequences has never been'. He continues:

> The Muslims took it all as solemnly as they took the text of the Qur'ān. These two great masters, Plato and Aristotle, they said, had expounded the truth, which is one. Therefore, there must be some way of bringing them into agreement . . . The more pious added the third element of the Qur'ān, and it must remain a marvel . . . that they got even so far as they did and that the whole movement did not end in simple lunacy. That al-Farabi should have been so incisive a writer, so wide a

> thinker and student; that Ibn Sina should have been so keen and clear a scientist and a logician; that Ibn Rushd should have known – really known – his Aristotle as he did, shows that the human brain, after all, is a sane brain and has the power of unconsciously rejecting and throwing out nonsense and falsehood.
>
> But it is not wonderful that, dealing with such materials and contradictions, they developed a tendency to mysticism. There were many things which they felt compelled to hold which could only be defended and rationalized in that cloudy air and slanting light. Especially, no one but a mystic could bring together the emanations of Plotinus, the ideas of Plato, the spheres of Aristotle and the seven-storied heaven of Muḥammad.[14]

Al-Fārābī, moreover, was not only

> a neo-Platonist, more exactly a Plotinian; although he himself would not have recognized this title. He held, as we have seen, that he was simply retelling the doctrines of Plato and Aristotle. But he was also a devout Muslim. He seems to have taken in earnest all the bizarre details of Muslim cosmography and eschatology; the Pen, the Tablet, the Throne, the Angels in all their ranks and functions mingle picturesquely with the system of Plotinus . . . But to make tenable this position he had to make the great leap of the mystic. Unto us these things are impossible; with God, *i.e.*, on another plane of existence, they are the simplest realities. If the veil were taken from our eyes we would see them. This has always been the refuge of the devout Muslim who has tampered with science.[15]

Under this heading we must include *The Epistles of [Pseudo-] Dionysius the Areopagite* (*cf.* Acts 17:34). They were probably written by a Syrian philosopher-monk of the sixth century AD and not proved to be pseudonymous until 1895 – largely because of their literary dependence on Proclus (AD 411–485). These writings, which include 'The Mystical Theology', exerted an immense influence in Europe as well as the Middle East, on Christians and Muslims alike. They represent an answer to both Gnosticism and Neo-Platonism.[16] Their influence on Muslims, and especially on Ṣūfīs, is due to the emphasis they put on 'the way of negation' as the basis for knowing God: he is far beyond all human understanding, except only by divine illumination.[17]

Gnosticism

The term 'Gnostics' comprises the followers of a variety of religious movements which taught salvation through *gnosis*, or 'knowledge' of God. There is no consensus as to when and how Gnosticism originated, although many think they can discern tinges of its earliest expressions in some of the views to which St Paul and St John addressed themselves in, for example, the Epistle to the Colossians and 1 John. Gnostic teaching was certainly opposed as heretical by the early Fathers.

It comprised a wide variety of views. Central to these was, apparently, 'a dualism which set over against each other the transcendent God and an ignorant and presumptuous demiurge . . . Sparks of divinity, however, have been encapsulated in the bodies of certain pneumatic or spiritual individuals.[18] Matter, Gnostics taught, is essentially evil, and man's only way of escape is by the divine gift of *gnosis*. It was only in 1945 that a number of Coptic codices were found at Nag Hammadi in Upper Egypt. Some of these were non-Gnostic, some non-Christian Gnostic, and some Christian Gnostic – including the apocryphal *Gospel of Thomas* which was probably composed *c.* AD 140 in Syria.[19]

The Mandaean communities in southern Iraq and south-western Iran are today the only surviving remnants of Gnosticism. It is, perhaps, significant that the parents of one of the earliest Ṣūfīs, Maʿrūf al-Kharkhī (d. 200 AH/AD 813), whose tomb in Baghdad is still a place of pilgrimage, were Mandaeans. To Maʿrūf's greater disciple, Sarī al-Saqaṭī (d. 257 AH/AD 870) 'is ascribed, but dubiously, the first use of the word *tawḥīd* to signify the union of the soul with God.'[20] The ancient Ṣūfīs also 'borrowed from the Manichaeans the term *ṣiddīq*, which they apply to their own spiritual adepts.'[21] Apart, moreover, from the emphasis on 'the Gnosis' (Arabic *maʿrifa*) in Ṣūfī teaching, it is perhaps significant that Muḥammad himself *may* have been influenced in his comments on the crucifixion by Cerinthus or Basilides, both of whom were Gnostics (cf. p. 12 above).

Concepts from the East

Long before the conquest of India by Muslims in the eleventh century AD, the teaching of the Buddha exerted a considerable influence in Eastern Persia and Transoxania. There were, apparently, flourishing Buddhist monasteries in Balkh, a city famous for the number of Ṣūfīs who lived there. Reference has already been made to one of the very early Ṣūfīs, Ibrāhīm ibn Adham, who appears in Muslim legend as a prince of Balkh who abandoned his throne and became a wandering *darwīsh* – the story of the Buddha over again. The Ṣūfīs probably 'learned the use of rosaries from Buddhist monks, and . . . it may be safely asserted that the method of Ṣūfism, so far as it is one of ethical self-culture, ascetic meditation, and intellectual abstraction, owes a good deal to Buddhism.[22]

But there was also a strong streak of pantheism in Ṣūfism. One of the earliest of this school was Abū Yazīd (Bāyazīd) al-Bisṭāmī (d. 261 AH/AD 875), who was a Persian whose father had been a follower of Zarathustra. His name has come down to us linked to the saying, 'Beneath my cloak there is naught else than God.'[23] But this is not so much Buddhist thought as the monism – or pantheism – of the Advaita-Vedānta. There is clearly a partial link, for example, between the Ṣūfī concept of *fanā'* (the passing away of individuality) and the Buddhist doctrine of Nirvāṇa, especially in its ethical aspect. When we think of *fanā'*, however, as the ecstatic merging of oneself with God, in the peculiarly Ṣūfī sense of *tawḥīd*, there is a distinct echo of the pure monism of the Vedānta.[24]

From asceticism to ecstasy

We have looked briefly at some of the extraneous sources by which the Ṣūfīs and Ṣūfism were, no doubt, in some degree influenced. Now we must return to the record of how what was, in essence, a distinctively Islamic phenomenon developed, and of the deep and widespread impact it has made, over the centuries, on the thought and practice of Islam as a whole.

Early Ṣūfīs

Reference has already been made to the extreme asceticism of the earliest Ṣūfīs. Al-Fuḍayl ibn 'Iyāḍ is even reputed to have rebuked the great Khalīfa Hārūn al-Rashīd to his face for his luxury and tyranny, although this is chronologically impossible.[25] Together with their asceticism, moreover, many of them practised '*tawakkul*', dependence upon God. In this context, this means that they gave up their previous means of livelihood, and became wandering mendicants. Perhaps the greatest name in early Ṣūfism is that of Junayd (d. 298 AH/AD 910), on whom, Macdonald insists, 'no shadow of heresy has ever fallen.'[26]

One of his pupils was al-Shiblī (d. 334 AH/AD 911), who had asked him to sell him, or give him, 'the pearl of divine knowledge' he was said to possess. To this, Nicholson writes, Junayd replied, 'I cannot sell it, for you have not the price thereof; and if I give it you, you will have gained it cheaply. You do not know its value. Cast yourself headlong, like me, into this ocean, in order that you may win the pearl by waiting patiently.'

When asked what he should do, Junayd first bade him to go and sell sulphur. Then, a year later, he told him to 'Become a dervish and occupy yourself solely with begging.' Next, he told him to go and ask pardon from all those whom he had wronged in the province in which he had previously held an official position – and this took four years. On his return Junayd said to him 'You still have some regard to reputation. Go and be a beggar for one year more.' Every day Shiblī brought the alms that were given him to Junayd, who gave them to the poor and kept Shiblī without food until the next morning. A year later Junayd accepted him as one of his disciples on condition that he should perform the duties of a servant to the others. Then, after a year of such service, Junayd asked him 'What think you of yourself now?' 'I deem myself the meanest of God's creatures', Shiblī replied. 'Now', said the master, 'your faith is firm.'[27]

The *via negativa* however which many of the early Ṣūfīs so wholeheartedly trod (although there were, of course, some who were less sincere) soon changed into a positive search for God and a love relationship with him (as was true of al-Junayd). The concept that the human heart 'is a mirror to image back God and that it is darkened by the things of the body' appears in Abū Sulaymān of Damascus, who died in 215 AH/AD 828. But a more celebrated ascetic, Bishr al-Ḥāfī (bare-foot), who died in 227 AH/AD 841, used to speak of God directly as 'the Beloved' (*ḥabīb*).[28] Another such ascetic, al-Ḥārith al-Muḥāsibī (d. 243 AH/AD 839), was a contemporary of the ultra-conservative Aḥmad ibn Ḥanbal, and 'the only thing in him to which Aḥmad could take exception was that he made use of *kalām* in refuting the Muʿtazilīs[29] (cf. pp. 58f. above). And both Sarī al-Saqaṭī and Bishr were close friends of Aḥmad.

There were, of course, more extreme – and even more dubious – characters among the Ṣūfīs. Dhū'l-Nūn, the Egyptian Ṣūfī who died in 246 AH/AD 861, is described 'as a philosopher and alchemist – in other words, a student of Hellenistic science'. Much of his speculation agrees with the writings of the pseudo-'Dionysius the Areopagite'. He was probably one of the earliest Ṣūfīs through which 'Neoplatonism poured into Islam a large tincture of the same mythical element in which Christianity [at that time] was already steeped.'[30] He is said to have been the first to formulate the doctrine of ecstatic states (*ḥāls, maqāmas*). To him is attributed the saying, 'Music is a divine influence which stirs the heart to seek God: those who listen to it spiritually attain unto God, and those who listen to it sensually fall into unbelief.'[31] To him is also attributed the saying, 'Fear of the Fire, in comparison with fear of being parted from the Beloved, is like a drop of water cast into the mightiest ocean.'[32] He has been described as 'the father of Muslim theosophy.'

Professor A. J. Arberry regards al-Junayd, to whom reference has already been made, as 'by far the most original and penetrating intellect among the Ṣūfīs of this time.' He also attributes to him the responsibility for developing the doctrine of *fanā'*[33] – to which many references will be made in this chapter – 'as an integral part of a well-coordinated theosophy'.[34] Al-Junayd, Arberry writes, describes Ṣūfism (*tāṣawwuf*)

> as meaning that 'God should cause thee to die from thyself and to live in Him'. This 'dying-to-self' is called by al-Junaid *fanā'* (a term reminiscent of the Koranic phrase 'Everything is perishing (*fānin*) except His Face' [55:26]; the 'life-in-Him' is named *baqā'* (continuance). By passing away from self the mystic does not cease to exist, in the true sense of existence, as an individual; rather his individuality, which is an inalienable gift from God, is perfected, transmuted and eternalized through God and in God. At the same time the return to continued existence is a source of trial (*balā'*) and affliction, for man is still apart and veiled from God; and so al-Junaid uses the imagery of the lover yearning after the Beloved, yet taking intense joy in the suffering which this separation causes him. Having enjoyed mystically anew the experience of life-in-God, and being restored to material life – 'after their union with Him, He separates them from Himself (and grants them their individuality again), for He makes them absent (from this world) when they are in union with Him, and makes them present (in this world) when he has separated them from Himself'.[35]

In somewhat the same tradition, but about a century later, was Abū Ṭālib al-Makkī (d. 386 AH/AD 996), who wrote a text-book of Ṣūfism which has survived and is still in use. He wrote and spoke openly on *tawḥīd*, now in the Ṣūfī sense, and got into trouble as a heretic. But his memory has been restored to orthodoxy by the general agreement of Islam. It is significant that when that towering figure, al-Ghazālī, set himself in 488 AH/AD 1095 to seek light in Ṣūfism, among the treatises he studied were the books of four of those mentioned above: Abū Ṭālib, al-Muḥāsibī, al-Junayd and al-Shiblī.[36]

Later Ṣūfīs

But all this time, Macdonald insists, a very different form of Ṣūfism

> had been slowly forcing its way. It was essentially speculative and theological rather than ascetic and devotional. When it gained the upper hand, *zāhid* (ascetic) was no longer a convertible term with Ṣūfī. We pass over [in Christian terms] the boundary between Thomas à Kempis and St Francis to Eckhart and Suso. The roots of this movement cannot be hard to find in the light of what has preceded. They lie partly in the neo-Platonism which is the foundation of the philosophy of Islam. Probably it did not come to the Ṣūfīs along the same channels by which it reached al-Fārābī. It was rather through the Christian mystics and, perhaps, especially through the Pseudo-Dionysius the Areopagite, and his asserted teacher, 'Stephen bar Sudailī with his Syriac 'Book of Hierotheos'.[37]

There was also another influence, through the more extreme doctrine of the Ismāʿīlī branch of the Shīʿīs (cf. pp. 16f above) under the Fāṭimids, with their abstruse speculations.[38] It is, however, important in this context to remember that Nicholson has insisted that 'the vast majority of Ṣūfīs have been, at least nominally, attached to the catholic body of the Muslim community' (that is, the Sunnīs). He explains this fact by the statement that 'Ṣūfism may join hands with free thought – it has often done so – but hardly ever with sectarianism.'[39] And the extreme to which some Ṣūfīs went was, indeed, that of theosophy and pantheism.

The outstanding name among the early Ṣūfī extremists was that of Ḥusayn ibn Manṣūr, better known as al-Ḥallāj (the cotton carder). A pupil of Junayd, he was put to death with great cruelty in 309 AH/AD 922. 'He went along with Junaid so far as seeing in the supreme mystical experience a reunion with God; but he then proceeded further and taught that man may thus be viewed as very God Incarnate, taking as his example not, as one might suppose, Muḥammad, but Jesus. He did not claim Divinity for himself, though the utterance which led to his execution, "I am the Truth" (*ana'l-ḥaqq*) seemed to his judges to have that implication.'[40] So he was executed as a blasphemous heretic by the orthodox, while to the more advanced Ṣūfīs and *darwīshes* of his time, and far beyond it, he became a patron saint. For them he had exemplified in his life and death the spirit of revolt against dogmatic scholasticism and formalism (the Islamic teaching of the *madrasa* network). Years later, however, even al-Ghazālī upheld his basic orthodoxy, although he lamented some of his more incautious statements. There is some mystery about the circumstances of his martyrdom, and Macdonald writes:

His popularity among the people of Baghdad and their reverence for him rose to a perilous degree. He may have had plans of his own as a Persian nationalist; he may have had part in one of the Shīʿite [Ismāʿīlī] conspiracies; he may have been nothing but a rather weak-headed devotee, carried off his feet by a sudden tide of public excitement, the greatest trial and danger that a saint has to meet.[41]

In the history of the more extreme Ṣūfīs, al-Ḥallāj has a somewhat solitary place. His own and his followers' explanation of his times of rapture and his theopathic utterances was in terms of *waḥdat al-shuhūd* (oneness of Witness): that is, God witnessing to himself in the heart of his votary (*ʿābid*). This union with God (*jamʿ*) leads to a unification (*ittiḥād*) which is not a unification of substance. Rather it operates through the act of faith and love (*ʿishq, maḥabba*) which welcomes into the emptiness of oneself the Loving guest (God), 'the essence whose Essence is Love.'[42]

This understanding of the mystical experience was to be sharply criticized by the other main Ṣūfī line of teaching on this subject, that of *waḥdat al-wujūd*, (oneness of Being, or 'the oneness of all existence') which became dominant from the sixth to seventh centuries AH (twelfth to thirteenth centuries AD). By those who espoused this understanding two criticisms of that of *waḥdat al-shuhūd* were commonly raised.

First, they objected to the concept *ʿḥulūl* ('infusion of substance', even 'incarnation').

> Ḥallāj had in fact written, 'Thy Spirit has mingled itself with my spirit as amber mixes with fragrant musk,' and above all 'We are two spirits fused together (*ḥalalna*) in a single body.' But the whole context of the poems and the writings makes it clear that *ḥulūl* here was not to be understood in the sense, which later became current, of 'incarnation' or 'union of substance'. In its most obvious sense the *ḥulūl* of Ḥallāj is to be understood as an *intentional* complete union (in love), in which the intelligence and the will of the subject – all in fact which enables him to say 'I' – are acted upon by Divine Grace.[43]

Secondly, and more frequently, the

> objection aimed at *Ḥallāj* by the *waḥdat al-wujūd*, . . . was to be, as expressed by Ibn ʿArabī, that he maintained in the *jamʿ* and *ittiḥād* a 'duality'. The monism of the 'unity of Being' in fact intends that the *ʿittiḥād* should operate not, indeed, through

> *ḥulūl* but through a total substitution of the divine 'I' for the empirical 'I'. To be one (*aḥad*) with God is to make actual the divine which in man's spirit has emanated from God (emanated, not been created *ex nihilo*). This charge of 'duality' aimed at the 'unity of Witness' reveals the difference in orientation between the two ways: the unification in and through the acts of faith and love (supreme Witness), for the *waḥdat al-shuhūd*; and the re-absorption of the acts of the created being in his first act of existence (conceived as emanating from the Divine Being), for the *waḥdat al wujūd*.[44]

To put al-Ḥallāj's attitude in other words, I shall quote Nicholson:

> According to Ḥallāj, man is essentially divine. God created Adam in His own image. He projected from Himself that image of His eternal love, that He might behold Himself as in a mirror. Hence he bade the angels worship Adam (Qur. 2:32), in whom, as in Jesus, He became incarnate. . . . This doctrine of personal deification, in the peculiar form which was impressed upon it by Ḥallāj . . . survived unadulterated only among his immediate followers. The Ḥulūlīs, i.e. those who believe in incarnation, are repudiated by Ṣūfīs in general quite as vehemently as by orthodox Muslims. But while the former have unhesitatingly condemned the doctrine of *ḥulūl*, they have also done their best to clear Ḥallāj from the suspicion of having taught it . . .
>
> It was not Ḥallāj who cried '*Ana'l-Ḥaqq*', but God Himself, speaking, as it were, by the mouth of the selfless Ḥallāj, just as He spoke to Moses through the medium of the burning Bush (Qur. 20:8–14). This last explanation, which converts *Ana'l-Ḥaqq* into an impersonal monistic axiom, is accepted [today] by most Ṣūfīs as representing the true Ḥallājian teaching.[45]

Ṣūfī monism

Ṣūfī extremists, in their Neo-Platonic monism of the *waḥdat al-wujūd* variety, insisted that 'the human spirit, being a direct emanation from the divine Command, is therefore an emanation from God himself, and could find its highest aim only in the obliteration of its illusory selfhood and absorption into the Eternal Reality'.[46] An outstanding example of Ṣūfī extremism is that of Muḥyī al-Dīn ibn al-ʿArabī. Usually referred to simply as Ibn ʿArabī (to distinguish him from another Ibn al-ʿArabī), he was a Spanish Arab who died in Damascus in 638AH/AD1240. Macdonald describes him as 'the arch-Sufi of the time', who left behind him 'an enormous mass of writings, at least 150 of which have come down to us'. He was a Ẓāhirī literalist in law, but 'his mysticism in theology was of the most rampant and luxurious description . . . So his books are a strange jumble of theosophy and metaphysical paradoxes', tending towards an 'unflinching pantheism . . . All religions to Ibn ʿArabī were practically indifferent; in them all the divine was working and was worshipped. Yet Islam is the more advantageous and Sufism is its true philosophy . . . Nor is there any real difference between good and evil; the essential unity of all things makes such a division impossible.'[47]

The verses which Ṣūfīs like Ibn ʿArabī (and many others) wrote were often couched in terms of human love and carousing: so much so that Ibn ʿArabī even 'found himself obliged to write a commentary on some of his poems in order to refute the scandalous charge that they were designed to celebrate the charms of his mistress'. To quote Nicholson again:

> What kind of symbolism each mystic will prefer depends on his temperament and character. If he be a religious artist, a spiritual poet, his ideas of reality are likely to clothe themselves instinctively in forms of beauty and glowing images of human love. To him the rosy cheek of the beloved represents the divine essence manifested through its attributes; her dark curls signify the One veiled by the Many; when he says, 'Drink wine that it may set you free from yourself,' he means, 'Lose your phenomenal self in the rapture of divine contemplation'. . . . This erotic and baccanalian symbolism is not, of course, peculiar to the mystical poetry of Islam, but nowhere else is it displayed so opulently and in such perfection.[48]

Somewhat similar poetry may be found in the Song of Songs, and there Christians are divided about its interpretation. Does it celebrate the nuptial love which is God's gift to his human creatures, or does it symbolize the relationship between God and Israel, Christ and his church or Christ and the individual Christian? Let us concede that most Ṣūfīs intended such language to describe spiritual ecstasy and nothing more; but when a pantheist does not see 'any real difference between good and evil' it is difficult to exclude the possibility that there may be some more tangible meaning behind 'this erotic and baccanalian symbolism'. Be that as it may, there can be no doubt whatever that some Ṣūfīs had exchanged the austere monotheism of Islam for a vague pantheism or an all-embracing monism. Jalāl al-Dīn al-Rūmī (d. 675AH/AD1276) said:

God is the Sāqī [cupbearer] and the Wine.
He knows what manner of love is mine;

while Ibn ʿArabī had earlier declared:

My heart has become capable of every form: it is a
pasture for gazelles and a convent for Christian monks,
And a temple for idols, and the pilgrim's Kaʿba
and the tables of the Tora and the book of the Qur'ān
I follow the religion of Love, whichever way his camels take.
My religion and my faith is the true religion.[49]

It is, moreover, undeniable that some Ṣūfīs were distinctly casual about the five liturgical prayer-times normally incumbent on all Muslims, since they regarded their own mystic devotions as much more important. Quite a number, too, inclined strongly to antinomianism and libertarianism, on the ground that profound theosophists who enjoy the special favour of God are no longer subject to the rules and negations by which beginners must necessarily be controlled. An extreme example can be found, at a rather later date, in the Bektāshīs and other orders of the 'lawless dervishes'; but individual cases of moral laxity must have been frequent enough at an earlier date. The would-be saint is certainly not immune to the temptations of the body and mind.[50]

The more extreme Ṣūfīs, as we have seen, tended to think in terms of monistic or pantheistic themes. It is when the individual self is 'lost', therefore, that the Universal Self is found. Most Ṣūfīs believed that it was only in ecstasy that the soul can directly communicate with God, while the more extreme thought that in ecstasy they could realize their essential unity with him – even if these times of exaltation were often fleeting. Arabic terms used by Ṣūfīs as, more or less, equivalent to 'ecstasy' are *fanā'* (passing-away), *wajd* (feeling), *samāʿ* (hearing), *dhawq* (taste), *shirb* (drinking), *ghayba* (absence from self), *jadhba* (attraction), *sukr* (intoxication) and *ḥāl* (emotion).[51]

The role of al-Ghazālī

Several references have already been made in this book to al-Ghazālī,[52] whom Macdonald describes as

> the greatest, certainly the most sympathetic figure in the history of Islam, and the only teacher of the after generations ever put by a Muslim on a level with the four great Imāms. The equal of Augustine in philosophical and theological importance . . .

> In his own person he took up the life of his time on all its sides and with all its problems. He lived through them all and drew his theology from his experience . . . When his work was done the revelation of the mystic (*kashf*) was not only a full part but the basal part in the structure of Muslim theology. . . . An ultra-rational basis had to be found and it was found in the ecstasy of the Ṣūfīs. . . . His knowledge and grasp of the problems and objects of philosophy were truer and more vital than in any other Muslim up to his time – perhaps after it, too. Islam has not fully understood him any more than Christendom fully understood Augustine, but until long after him the horizon of Muslims was wider and the air clearer for his work.[53]

Al Ghazālī (d. 505AH/AD1111) had been brought up in a Ṣūfī environment, but had emerged with little personal experience of Ṣūfism as a way of life. He had studied widely: canon law, theology, dialectic, science and the doctrines and practices of the Ṣūfīs; and he ended his student life as the pupil and assistant of al-Juwaynī, 'Imām al-Ḥaramayn'. On al-Juwaynī's death he went to Baghdad, where in 484AH/AD1091 he was appointed to teach in the Niẓāmī Academy and acquired a great reputation in law and theology. But he soon became sick of mind and body, and for two months sank into absolute scepticism, doubting even the evidence of his senses. When he recovered from this he embarked on a wide-ranging and penetrating search for the truth.

He turned first to the scholastic theologians, but they failed to satisfy him. Next, he probed philosophy deeply, over a period of some three years, but found little light. Then he examined the doctrine of the Taʿlīmīs,[54] with their insistence on the need for an infallible teacher; but where was such a teacher to be found? Finally, he turned to the Ṣūfīs and studied their books and teaching with a new earnestness – particularly their claim that, through ecstasy, a man (or woman, for they made no such distinction) could receive direct knowledge of God.

For six months he hesitated; then, at the end of 488AH/AD1095, he took the plunge. He abandoned his position, his reputation, his future and even, temporarily, his family, and he left Baghdad as a *darwīsh* to follow the Ṣūfī path. For two years in Syria he gave himself up to the discipline and religious exercises of the Ṣūfīs. Then he went on a series of pilgrimages. Finally, he returned to his home and family, but not to teaching (although this was forced upon him, temporarily, some ten years later). He was now convinced that the Ṣūfī path was the only way to an empirical knowledge of God. He spent the last few years of his life in Ṭūs with his family, at a *madrasa* (academy of law and theology) for students and in a *khānqāh* (monastery) for Ṣūfīs. It was during his retirement that he wrote the greatest of all his books, *Iḥyā' ʿulūm al-dīn* (Review of the Religious Sciences).

The supreme significance of al-Ghazālī is that he not only combined Ṣūfism and Islamic orthodoxy in his own life and teaching, but that he thereby succeeded – as can be seen in retrospect – in bringing Ṣūfism firmly within the bounds of orthodox Islam. He had himself experienced the ecstasy, as well as the asceticism, on which Ṣūfīs laid such store. He insisted however that the rapture and the revelations (*mukāshafāt*) which they claimed should neither be described by the term *ḥulūl* (fusion of being), which those of the *waḥdat al-shuhūd* persuasion used to use, nor by the terms *ittiḥād* (identification) or *wuṣūl* (union), which those of the dominant *waḥdat al-wujūd* persuasion employed. All of these terms, he insisted, went beyond the proper confines of orthodox Islamic theology in describing experiences of a sense of nearness to God. These experiences, in his case, had brought him back to the faith in which he had been reared, but which he could no longer accept purely on the authority of others. Now, he believed, he had received a personal experience which validated all true prophecy. So back he went to the Qur'ān and the *aḥādīth* of Muḥammad with a fresh confidence. He would have no truck whatever with antinomianism. Ṣūfīs, he believed, had come to a new sense of the love of God, but were in no way exempt from his judgment. On the contrary, privilege involved responsibility.[55]

There are a number of links between Muslim Ṣūfīs and Jewish mystics of the 'Kabbalah' movement.[56] They, too, were much influenced by Neo-Platonism (and the monism, sometimes close to that of the Advaita Vedānta school of Hinduism, which lay behind it). The basic problem which confronted the Kabbalists was, in effect, how to link together two incompatible conceptions of the Deity: the living, dynamic God of the Old Testament, and the static abstraction which philosophers had enthroned in his place. And the same problem confronted Ṣūfīs of the *waḥdat al-wujūd* persuasion, for the Allāh depicted in the Qur'ān can scarcely be interpreted in pantheistic terms or reconciled with any form of philosophical abstraction. Al-Ghazālī's mystical experiences never displaced his fear of God and of the judgment; but they did quicken his love for the one who had, he believed, granted him his favour.

While al-Ghazālī's teaching and influence brought Ṣūfism in general within the bounds of Islamic orthodoxy, and was one factor in the tolerance – and sometimes positive encouragement – of Ṣūfism by Muslim governments, it certainly could not be said that al-Ghazālī's opinions put an end to Ṣūfī extremism. Ibn ʿArabī, to whom reference has already been made in this chapter, outlived al-Ghazālī, while Jalāl al-Dīn al-Rūmī, the great mystic poet whose vast Maṣnavī is read all over the Muslim world, died in 672AH/AD1273, more than a hundred and sixty years after al-Ghazālī. And it was through his poems, Hamilton Gibb has stated, that Ṣūfism:

> spread into the Ottoman Empire and India, the *madrasa*-trained theologians themselves yielded to its fascination, and in spite of a few attempts to stem the tide, the main effort of theological activity in the later centuries was directed to the combination and reconciliation of orthodox Ashʿarite theology with the near-pantheism of Ibn ʿArabī.[57]

Perhaps a few brief quotations from Rūmī's poems, as found in Nicholson's *The Mystics of Islam* will give some idea of the width of his views. In *The Dīvān of Shamsī Tabrīz* Rūmī wrote:

> I have put duality away, I have seen that the two worlds are one;
> One I seek, One I know, One I see, One I call.
> I am intoxicated with Love's cup, the two worlds have passed out of my ken;
> I have no business save carouse and revelry.[58]

Elsewhere he wrote:

> He comes, a moon whose like the sky ne'er saw, awake or dreaming,
> Crowned with eternal flame no flood can lay.
> Lo, from the flagon of Thy love, O Lord, my soul is swimming,
> And ruined all my body's house of clay.
> When first the Giver of the grape my lonely heart befriended,
> Wine fired my bosom and my veins filled up,
> But when His image all mine eye possessed, a voice descended,
> 'Well done, O Sovereign Wine and peerless Cup.[59]

Rūmī's monist theosophy is, perhaps, best summed up in two short quotations:

> O my soul, I searched from end to end: I saw in thee nought save the Beloved;
> Call me not infidel, O my soul, if I say that thou thyself art He.

Or, again:

Ye who in search of God, of God, pursue,
Ye need not search for God for god is you, is you!
Why seek ye something that was missing ne'er?
Save you none is, but you are – where, o, where?[60]

The maqāmāt and aḥwāl of the Ṣūfī path

References have already been made, many times in this chapter, to the Ṣūfī way of life, with its asceticism, renunciation, poverty and ecstasy. We must now look more closely at the technical terms Ṣūfīs use and how they define them. One of the initial difficulties is that different authors give lists, both of the 'stages' on the Ṣūfī path and the mental and psychological 'states' that Ṣūfīs experience, which are far from uniform. So what I can record in this chapter will, of necessity, be fragmented.

The two dominant terms are *maqāmāt* (stages) and *aḥwāl* (states), and the most intriguing question is the relationship, if any, between them. Each *maqām* represents a link in the sequence of 'stages' that constitute the ascetic and ethical discipline of the Ṣūfī path, and on each of these an aspirant embarks by his own volitional decision, under the authoritative guidance of his or her spiritual guide (for there have always been notable female Ṣūfīs). Each *ḥāl*, by contrast, represents a psychological or spiritual 'state' that he may experience; and over these *aḥwāl* (which may, or may not, accompany the 'stages') the aspirant has, in theory, little or no control. Yet in practice the relationship between what he does, and the *ḥāl* that he may then enjoy, is at times undeniably close.

The maqāmāt

The technical term for the path on which a would-be Ṣūfī embarks is '*ṭarīqa*' – a word which before long came to be used for the *particular* 'path' taught and followed by many different groups, and even for the 'brotherhood' of those who followed it. To this we must soon return. The one who embarks on this path regards himself as a 'traveller' (*sālik*), whose goal is to seek a personal knowledge of God. The initial step is his fundamental decision to set out on this quest, properly termed 'repentance' (*tawba*), which itself involves the beginning of a relationship with a *murshid* (guide) – usually referred to as the traveller's *Shaykh* or *Pīr*. This relationship is without parallel in Islam for its intimacy and authority; and it is only under his *shaykh*'s direction that the aspirant is permitted to move on to the next *maqām* in his quest. *Tawba* is, in fact, the term used in Arabic for conversion. It is primarily fear of the day of judgment which, in Islam, is the basic motive. Biographies of eminent Ṣūfīs, however, often mention dreams, or visions of some sort, which have brought home to them their sins and spiritual lethargy and prompted them to amend their ways. But true repentance, Ṣūfīs teach, must include an abandonment of the sins of the past and a determination not to return to them. Needless to say, this repentance may have to be often repeated. As in Christianity, moreover, repentance must include a determination to make such restitution and apology as is possible to any persons whom the convert has wronged.

Repentance is the first and fundamental *maqām* on which all Ṣūfīs agree. But after that the sequence of 'stages' (*maqāmāt*) varies considerably from one authority to another. Nicholson lists the following (from *Kitāb al-Luma'* of al-Sarrāj, a very early authority):[61] abstinence, renunciation, poverty, patience, trust in God, and satisfaction. It is clear from what we have already noted in this chapter that the common ingredients of the life of the *zāhid* (ascetic), the *faqīr* (pauper) and the *darwīsh* (Ṣūfī mendicant) are abstinence, renunciation, poverty, patience and, indeed, trust in God (in so far as that term refers to the *tawakkul* or 'reliance on God' often learnt by Ṣūfīs through begging for their daily needs). These common ingredients characterized the earlier phases of the more positive Ṣūfism which was to follow. But Ṣūfī teachers gradually built up

> a system of asceticism and moral culture which is founded on the fact that there is in man an element of evil – the lower or appetitive soul. This evil self, the seat of passion and lust, is called *nafs*; it may be considered broadly equivalent to 'the flesh', and with its allies, the world and the devil, it constitutes the great obstacle to the attainment of union with God. . . . Mortification of the *nafs* is the chief work of devotion and leads, directly or indirectly, to the contemplative life. All the Sheykhs are agreed that no disciple who neglects this duty will ever learn the rudiments of Ṣūfism. The principle of mortification is that the *nafs* should be weaned from those things to which it is accustomed, that it should be encouraged to resist its passions, that its pride should be broken, and that it should be brought through suffering and tribulation to recognise the vileness of its original nature and the impurity of its actions. . . .

Self-mortification, as advanced Ṣūfīs understand it, is a moral transformation of the inner man. When they say 'Die before ye die', they do not mean to assert that the lower self can be

> essentially destroyed, but that it can and should be purged of its attributes, which are wholly evil.[62]

The Ṣūfī who has 'eradicated self-will' is said, in technical language, to have reached the 'stages' of 'trust in God' (*tawakkul*, in its deeper sense) and of 'acquiescence' or 'satisfaction' (*riḍā*).

The aḥwāl

When we turn to the *aḥwāl*, each of which is regarded as 'the actualisation of a divine encounter' (*wajd*),[63] the same treatise gives a list of ten: meditation, nearness to God, love, fear, hope, longing, intimacy, tranquillity, contemplation and certainty.' Other Ṣūfīs would give a different list of these psychological and spiritual experiences. 'In general, the authors insist upon the "effort" of the soul in its approach to the *maqāmāt*, just as they emphasise the "received" character of every *ḥāl*.'[64] Both the *maqāmāt* and the *aḥwāl* are

> readily called . . . *manāzil*, the traveller's 'halts' along the route, the resting places. *Maqām* evokes the staging posts which continue to remain available – to reach a new *maqām*, does not destroy the preceding *maqām*; the *ḥāl*, on the contrary, is by nature 'instantaneous', there is a succession or alternation of *aḥwāl*, there may be a stabilisation of one or the other, but not a concomitance of several: the heart possessed by a *ḥāl* is seized entirely, even though this *ḥāl* evokes, as it were spontaneously, a second which finally brings it to perfection . . .[65]

But there are many differences between authors. Some, for example, maintain that *ḥāl*, originally 'received by pure grace, can become *maqām* through the zeal of the recipient'. Again, *maḥabba* (love of the soul and of God) is regarded by some as 'the loftiest of the *maqāmāt*', and by others as 'the first of the *aḥwāl*'.[66] When the traveller has completed all the *maqāmāt* to the satisfaction of his *shaykh*, and has experienced such *aḥwāl* as God has bestowed on him, he may be raised 'to the higher planes of consciousness which Ṣūfīs call "the Gnosis" (*maʿrifa*) and "the Truth" (*ḥaqīqa*), where the "seeker (*ṭālib*) becomes the "knower" or the "gnostic" (*ʿārif*)'.[67]

Dhikr and fanāʾ

Little mention has yet been made in this chapter of what are, perhaps, the two outstanding words in the vocabulary of Ṣūfīs: *dhikr* and *fanāʾ*. *Dhikr* (reminding oneself) stands for the continual remembrance of God. In the Qurʾān the command to do this is addressed to all

Muslims: 'Remember (*udhkurū*) Allāh often with much remembrance' (33:41). It is also addressed to Muḥammad individually: 'Remind thyself of (*udhkur*) thy Lord when thou forgettest' (28:24). Among Ṣūfīs the *dhikr* is possibly the most frequent form of prayer, its *muqābal* ('opposite corrective') being *fikr*, (discursive reflection, meditation). In his *Ṭawāsīn* . . . al-Ḥallāj declares that 'the road which passes through "the garden of *dhikr*" and that which takes "the way of fikr" are equally valid.'[68] We must return to *fikr* later. Suffice it to say here that in later years it was *dhikr* which took the higher place.

In the *dhikr* Ṣūfīs continually repeat, both in private and in public sessions, either the name 'Allāh' or some such formula as '*subḥāna'llāh*' ('praise be to Allāh') or '*lā ilāha illa'llāh*' ('there is no god except Allāh'). The repetition continues until the mind becomes conscious of nothing else, and eventually the individual or group concerned falls into a state of trance called *fanā'* ('passing-away,' 'effacement' or 'ecstasy'). L. Gardet has given an excellent description of the different stages in an ideal *dhikr* (with occasional references to somewhat similar phenomena in other religions), a short summary of which I shall now attempt.[69]

There are three main stages in an ideal *dhikr*:

1. *Dhikr* of the *tongue* together with 'intent (*niyya*) of the heart'. At the beginning this requires a continual 'effort', but later it becomes 'effortless'. In this stage of the *dhikr* 'three elements are still present: the subject conscious of his experience, the state of consciousness and the one mentioned: *dhākir*, *dhikr* and *madhkūr*'. Gardet suggests a comparison with the triad of Yoga-Sutra.

2. *Dhikr* of the *heart* (the *qalb*, which is the seat of 'knowledge of divine things'). The Ṣūfī has now 'effaced the trace of the word on his tongue, and finds his heart continually applied to the *dhikr*'. At first, again, this demands 'effort', but later it becomes effortless. In this stage the 'state of consciousness' dissolves into an *acquired* passivity. Gardet suggests a comparison with the stage of 'absorption' (*dhyana*) of Yoga. Al-Ghazālī's analysis in the *Iḥyā* halts at this stage. 'It is in [the disciple's] power to reach this limit, and to make the state lasting by repulsing temptations; but . . . it is not in his power to attract to himself the Mercy of the All-High.'

3. *Dhikr* of the *inmost being* (*sirr*). If the heart was the seat of the 'knowledge of divine things', it is the 'inmost being', 'a substance more subtle than the spirit (*rūḥ*)', that 'will be the place of the "vision" (*mushāhada*) of them.' It is here too that the *tawḥīd* (in its Ṣūfī sense) is said to take place: the 'declaration of divine unity and the unification of the self with the self, and the self with God. The writers often associate this third stage of the *dhikr* with the state of *iḥsān*, spiritual

perfection and beauty.' The 'arrival' of the '*dhikr* of the inmost being' can be known by this, that 'if you leave off the *dhikr* it does not leave you'. The slave of God 'has disappeared (*ghā'ib*) both from the *dhikr* and the very object of the *dhikr*'. So no duality remains. Gardet suggests a comparison with the entry into *samadhi* of Indian Yoga: 'becoming one alone' (cf. the Indian *Kaivalya*) conceived as abolition in God, generally in the line of 'monism of the Being' (*waḥdat al-wujūd*).[70]

The *dhikr* of the tongue is said to be accompanied by 'sounds of voices and rhythms within the periphery of the head', whereas the *dhikr* of the heart 'resembles the buzzing of bees, and is accompanied by luminous and coloured phenomena, at this stage intermittent'. Al-Ghazālī regarded this apparition of 'lights' as 'gleams of truth' released by God's goodwill ('Mercy'), but other authors describe them as intrinsically and obligatorily bound up with the *dhikr* experience. Later writers describe these luminous phenomena as even more brilliant at the stage of '*dhikr* of the inmost being', where 'the fire of the *dhikr* does not go out, and its lights do not flee'. By such authors this 'divine illumination' is not regarded, with al-Ghazālī, as a gift from God's Mercy, but as 'an effect linked to the experience according to the extent to which the *dhikr* of the inmost being has liberated the divine element in the human spirit directly "emanating" from God.'

It is also said that the '*dhikr* of the tongue' effects entry into the world of *jabarūt*, All Power, while the higher stages introduce into the domain of *malakūt*, 'angelic substances'; they may even lead to *lāhūt*, the world of the Divine Essence. Here Gardet suggests a comparison with the 'Pure Land' of the Jodo promised to the disciples of the Japanese *nembutsu*, while in regard to the 'lights' discussed above he suggests comparison with the Buddhist 'objective' illumination, or even the 'uncreated Light of the Thabor' of oriental forms of Christianity.

To al-Ḥallāj the *dhikr* was a *method* of reminding one's self of God, of helping the soul to live in his presence. To al-Ghazālī it was *the* way of the Ṣūfīs, but still a method of preparing the disciple to receive, if the Lord wills, the supreme 'Mercies'. But Ibn ʿAṭā' Allāh no longer speaks of it as a 'preparatory or concomitant method,' but as an 'effective *technique*, up to its consummation: entry into the domain of *lāhūt*.' Later writers 'insist even more on technique – voice, breathing, posture, *etc.*, give themselves up to long disquisitions on the gnostic theme, and never cease to see in the *dhikr* pursued to its last steps a "guarantee" of attainment.'[71]

A grey area

Clearly, we are here in a grey area where comparisons can be made not only with other religions but also with the experiences of those who resort to hallucinogenic drugs – such as LSD, 'sacred mushrooms', Ecstasy (MDMA) or *ḥashīsh*. Only this week I read in *The Times* about a woman who, under the influence of MDMA, 'spoke of an ecstatic encounter with her delphiniums'! Such drugs seem, curiously enough, to induce a sense of 'oneness' with (presumably) whatever is uppermost in one's thoughts or desires.

In the light of the experience recounted by St Paul in 2 Corinthians 12:2–6, for example, I cannot doubt that 'ecstasy' and 'rapture' are sometimes God-given, and therefore both wholesome and inspiring. But to experience a psychological trance (*fanā'*) by deliberately resorting to a technique (the *dhikr*) which is, as some assert, calculated to produce one, is little different from a drug-induced 'trip'. Even to resort to a method which is designed to induce an emotional and psychological condition in the course of which, as al-Ghazālī taught, God *might*, in his mercy, reveal himself, seems to me distinctly dubious.

I should add that early Ṣūfīs discussed the relative virtues of *dhikr* and *fikr* (meditation). Al-Ḥallāj, for example, spoke of the 'garden of *dhikr*' which Muḥammad visited 'without deviating' and of the 'process of *fikr*' which he followed without 'passing beyond', and seems to have given his preference to *fikr*. 'By means of *dhikr* and its rhythmical use of oral prayers the Ṣūfī is almost certain to succeed in attaining subjective spiritual "states" (*aḥwāl*); *fikr* tends to put him within the possibility of experiencing transcendental truths.'[72] But much more emphasis, eventually, was put on *dhikr*.

Somewhat similarly, *fanā'* (passing away, effacement) can be contrasted with *baqā'* (subsistence, survival). In theory, 'the Ṣūfīs generally regard this state of *baqā'* as being more perfect than that of mere *fanā'*, and this is the meaning of their dictum that sobriety (*ṣaḥwa*) supervenes on intoxication (*sukr*).'[73] To those whom I have described as 'the Ṣūfī extremists' this would mean 'the unitive state' whether this is interpreted, with al-Ḥallāj, in terms of 'oneness of Witness' (*waḥdat al-shuhūd*) or, with most of the extremists, in terms of 'oneness of Being' (*waḥdat al-wujūd*). By the former this would imply 'fusion of being' (*ḥulūl*), and by the latter either 'identification' (*ittiḥād*) or 'union' (*wuṣul*). But al-Ghazālī did not approve of any of these terms; they went beyond the bounds of orthodox theology. Yet the experience itself was, he insisted, 'the true basis of all faith and the beginning of prophecy; the *karāmāt* (favours, wonders) of the saints lead to the miracles (*muʿjizāt*) of the prophets.'[74]

The Ṣūfī (or darwīsh) Brotherhoods (ṭarīqāt)

We have already seen that it was the very nature of Ṣūfism for a few disciples to gather round a *shaykh* and to be taught his mystic 'path' (*ṭarīqa*). In early days these small groups would often meet in a corner-chamber (*zāwiya*) of a mosque. Then, in due course, these disciples would proceed to initiate others into the same *ṭarīqa*. It was in this way that there 'grew up a number of "chains" of spiritual affiliation (*silsila*) by which the doctrine taught to the postulant (*murīd*) was authenticated by its transmission through an unbroken series of *shaykhs* back to the original teacher, and behind him (more artificially) through a further series of early Muslim personalities back to one of the Companions of the Prophet, most frequently to ʿAlī.'[75] Unlike the *madrasa* system, these groups were not primarily concerned with matters of doctrine. Rather, they were concerned with their special method of spiritual discipline and the particular formula of invocation (*dhikr*) to be followed by their members in private devotions and their corporate meetings. As we have noted in passing, before long a number of adjuncts – such as music and dancing – had come to be included in such meetings. This was in order to enhance the psychological effect of the continual repetition of the *dhikr* and to hasten the 'absorption of the participants into the Infinite' (or, at least, to induce a temporary unawareness of their distinctive individualities) which was their primary objective.

In the earliest days, we must remember,

> wandering, either solitary or in companies, was the special sign of the true Ṣūfī . . . Next would come a monastery, rather a rest-house; for only in the winter and for rest did they remain fixed in a place for any time. Of such a monastery there is a trace at Damascus in 150 AH and in Khurasan about 200. Then, just as in Europe, begging friars organized themselves. In faith they were rather conservative than anything else; touched with a religious passivism which easily developed into quietism. Their ecstasies went little beyond those, for instance, of Thomas à Kempis, though struck with a warmer oriental flavour . . . As was natural in the case of professional devotees, a constantly prayerful attitude began to assume importance beside and in contrast to the formal use of the five daily prayers, the *ṣalawāt*. This development was in all probability aided by the existence in Syria of the Christian sect of the Euchites, who exalted the duty of prayer above all other religious obligations. These, also, abandoned property and obligations and wandered as poor

> brethren over the country. They were a branch of Hesychasts, the quietistic Greek monks who eventually led to the controversy concerning the uncreated light manifested at the transfiguration on Mount Tabor . . . There is a striking resemblance between the Ṣūfīs seeking by patient introspection to see the actual light of God's presence in their hearts, and the Greek monks in Athos, sitting solitarily in their cells and seeking the divine light of Mount Tabor in contemplation of their navels.[76]

The Growth of Convents

But much was to change. We have already noted the change of emphasis in Ṣūfism 'from asceticism to ecstasy', the revulsion of pious orthodoxy from the excesses of Ṣūfī extremism, and the mediatory role of al-Ghazālī. What we have not yet noted is the fact that it became the policy of Sunnī authorities, 'perhaps only half consciously', to encourage Ṣūfism among the masses as a way of weaning them from Ismāʿīlī propaganda about an infallible Imām and from other heresies. As a result, Sultans, viziers and other prominent Muslims built and endowed convents (still known as *zāwiyas* or *khānqāhs*) for Ṣūfī *shaykhs* and their disciples, while some of the leading *shaykhs* were able to found and maintain their own convents from the gifts that came flooding in.[77]

These convents were large enough to house and support both the initiates and the families of those of them who were married (for, although many Ṣūfīs remained celibate by choice, this was in no way compulsory). They soon became centres of religion and counsel for the whole district around. In some of the semi-nomadic regions a small *zāwiya* would serve as a mosque, school, community centre and deposit store for possessions left behind on tribal migrations – as was the case, for example, with the Sanūsī *zāwiyas* scattered among the tribes of Cyrenaica and Tripolitania. The tribesmen as a whole made no pretension to being Ṣūfī initiates, but they often became ardent champions, in matters both spiritual and temporal, of the Sanūsī leadership and its local representatives. And much the same happened elsewhere.

Among Ṣūfī initiates worldwide, moreover,

> Ṣūfism from the first was a form of Gnosis, the transmission to initiates of a particular doctrine, not necessarily or in principle esoteric, but by which its practitioners were distinguished from the general body of the community. Each Ṣūfī group constituted an *ekklesia*, a 'church', and its organisation was of necessity

hierarchic, the disciple or *murīd* surrendering himself wholly to the will and direction of his *shaykh*. Each new *khānqāh* had as its *shaykh* an initiate who had been a disciple, at first, second or third remove, of some celebrated *shaykh*, and followed his *ṭarīqa* ('path'). Gradually, therefore, as *khānqāhs* were multiplied, they were enrolled as offshoots or daughter-houses of the mother-convent, the original convent of the *shaykh* who had initiated the *ṭarīqa*, and remained under the obedience of the 'prior' of the mother-convent, himself frequently a lineal descendant of the founder. By the thirteenth and fourteenth centuries AD 'regular' Ṣūfism was represented by the convents and 'lodges' of affiliates of a few great *ṭarīqas* (usually translated as 'orders' or 'brotherhoods'), with branches in many different countries. In course of time, as they spread ever more widely, most of the 'orders' were divided into 'sub-orders', founded by eminent *shaykhs* who modified in some respect the original rituals of their parent 'orders'.[78]

The multiplication of brotherhoods

There is not much point in giving a list of more than a very few of these Dervish (*darwīsh*) Orders or Brotherhoods, some of which go back to the sixth century AH (twelfth century AD). The most widely spread of all these *ṭarīqas* is the Qādiriyya, created by ʿAbd al-Qādir al-Jīlānī. He migrated to Baghdad, experienced a Ṣūfī conversion and attracted many followers by his preaching and the miracles he was said to perform. By his death in 561AH/AD1166, converts in many centres recognized his authority, and the Ṣūfīs called themselves Qādirīs after his name. The Order can be found in many lands, and is especially strong in India.[79]

The second of what Professor Arberry considers the four great Orders is the Suhrawardiyya, so named after Shihāb al-Dīn ʿUmar al-Suhrawardī, also of Baghdad. 'A model of orthodox moderation, he enjoyed the confidence and patronage of caliphs and princes, while his lectures and sermons were attended by admiring multitudes.' He died in 632AH/AD1234, and his teaching was carried to India by Bahāʾ al-Dīn Zakarīyāʾ of Multan, where it found immediate acceptance.[80]

The third of these four Orders is the Shādhiliyya. It 'owed its inspiration to a scholar of the Maghrib', Nūr al-Dīn Aḥmad al-Shādhilī (d. 656AH/AD1258), who 'won such a large following in Tunis that the authorities feared his influence, and he found it more prudent to flee to Alexandria.' The Order is strong in Egypt, North Africa, Arabia, Syria and elsewhere.[81]

The fourth great Brotherhood is the Mawlawiyya. It originated in Turkey, and looks back as its founder to Jalāl al-Dīn Rūmī (d. 672AH/AD1273), the great mystical poet of Persia, to whom references have already been made. It owes its name to the fact that he was commonly called Mawlānā (our master), and the Order achieved paramount influence in Turkey under the Ottomans. The most characteristic feature of the ritual of this Order, known in Turkish as the Mevleviya, is the celebrated Whirling Dance.[82]

There are, of course, innumerable other Orders, some of which 'claim to be descended from the celebrated ascetics and *walīs* (saints) Ibrāhīm ibn Adham (d. 161AH/AD777), Sarī al-Saqaṭī (d. 257AH/AD870) and Abū Yazīd al-Bisṭāmī (d. 261AH/AD874), but it may be gravely doubted whether they can show any sound pedigree.'[83] I shall, however, add a few more names. Among the oldest there is the Rifā'īyya, from Aḥmad al-Rifā'ī of Iraq, who is said to have founded the Order in 576AH/AD1180, and who died in 579AH/AD1183; the Chishtiyya, from Mu'īn al-Dīn Chistī from Sīstān (d. 635AH/AD1236); the Naqshbandiyya, from Bahā' al-Dīn Naqshband (d. 791AH/AD1389); the Badawiyya, founded by Aḥmad al-Badawī of Egypt (d. 675AH/AD1276), whose shrine at Tanta in Lower Egypt is still a very popular place of pilgrimage;[84] the Bektāshiyya, to which the Janissaries in the Ottoman Empire were affiliated;[85] and the (Shī'ī) Safavī Order, which established the rule of the Safavid Shāhs in Persia in 1500.[86]

I shall add two modern Orders: the Tijāniyya and the Sanūsiyya. The Tijāniyya which is still of great influence in North and West Africa, was founded by Abū'l-'Abbās Aḥmad al-Tijānī, who died in Fez in 1815. Originally a sub-division of an older Order, it is now distinctly exclusive in the allegiance it claims.[87] The influence of the Sanūsiyya is today chiefly centred in Libya, where its *zāwiyas* are scattered around Cyrenaica and Tripolitania. It was founded by Sīdī Muḥammad al-Sanūsī (d. 1859), whose grandson became King Idrīs of Libya.[88] I knew King Idrīs well during the war and up to the time when Libya was taken over by al-Gadhdhāfī.

The teaching about the Ṣūfī path given to its initiates by each Order, or its sub-Orders, will include its own distinctive prescriptions for the practice of the *dhikr* (posture, breathing, motions of the body, music, dancing, whirling etc.)

Times of decay

It is only the initiates who are, properly speaking, Ṣūfīs, but their influence over the local population, and even over a much wider circle, may be immense. Throughout much of the Muslim world, moreover

– among peasants, artisans, urban dwellers and many of the middle classes – what may be termed the 'folk religion' of Islam now largely prevails, or lies little below the surface. Much of this goes right back to the animistic beliefs and practices of the religion from which they had been converted to Islam. It has been asserted that:

> Animistic practices are almost always a remnant from the days before Muslims came to a people and converted them. One would think Islam would have purged such heretical influences from the lives of the new believers. Such is not the case. More often than not, the initial Muslim missionaries were Ṣūfīs or at least mystically influenced. They were in favour of accommodation and compromise rather than strictly holding to the letter of Islamic law. This was appreciated by the converts. They could retain much of the old and simply add to it that which seemed good and helpful. Cultural and religious conflict was minimized. The resulting expression of Islam mixed with animism is indeed painful to the visiting Saʿudi Arabian diplomat.[89]

Be that as it may, there can be no doubt that Ṣūfism itself has fallen into manifest decay. On the one hand, there has been imposture, charlatanry, exploitation and sensuality; on the other, a strange combination of piety and superstition. ʿAbd al-Wahhāb al-Shaʿrānī (d. 973AH/AD1565) can, perhaps, be taken as an example of the latter. Theologian, canonist and mystic, he had a number of excellent qualities, but he was highly superstitious and inordinately self-satisfied.[90] He lived in a day when the cult of Muslim 'saints' (*awliyā'* [singular *walī*] the 'Friends of God') had gone wild. Of them Nicholson has written:

> The inspiration of the Islamic saints, though verbally distinguished from that of the prophets and inferior in degree, is of the same kind. In consequence of their intimate relation to God, the veil shrouding the supernatural, or, as a Moslem would say, the unseen world, from their perceptions is withdrawn at intervals, and in their fits of ecstasy they rise to the prophetic level. Neither deep learning in divinity, nor devotion to good works, nor asceticism, nor moral purity makes a Mohammedan a saint; he may have all or none of these things, but the only indispensable qualification is that ecstasy and rapture which is the outward sign of 'passing-away' from the

> phenomenal self. Anyone thus enraptured (*majdhūb*) is a *walī* (*waliyya* if the saint is a woman), and when such persons are recognised through their power of working miracles, they are venerated as saints not only after death but also during their lives. . . .
>
> The saints form an invisible hierarchy, on which the order of the world is thought to depend. Its supreme head is entitled the *Quṭb* (Axis). He is the most eminent Ṣūfī of his age, and presides over the meetings regularly held by this august parliament, whose members are not hampered in their attendance by the inconvenient fictions of time and space, but come together from all parts of the earth in the twinkling of an eye, traversing seas and mountains and deserts as easily as common mortals step across the road.[91]

Nor are such fantasies lacking even among some well-educated persons in the present century. Arberry records that when one of the last Ṣūfī authors of the classical tradition, Shaykh Muḥammad Amīn al-Naqshbandī died in 1914, his *Tanwīr al-qulūb* was edited with a biographical note by his 'successor' (*khalīfa*) Shaykh Salāma al-ʿAzzāmī of the Azhar (Cairo: 6th edition, 1929). His biographer records, *inter alia*, that 'for some considerable period of his life, whenever he ate with his disciples, although only a little bread was placed before him this was miraculously adequate for the needs of a large company and still some remained over'; that 'a rival who was appointed Imām of a certain mosque in preference to him was struck down with paralysis the very night of his appointment, and never recovered'; that 'he was seen in the spirit by his disciples when he was absent in the body – on one occasion so far afield as Mecca, although the shaykh was all the time in Cairo'; and that 'all his days he was never seen without a fresh mantle of glittering light that dazzled all beholders.'[92]

Such superstitions have been staunchly resisted by the Wahhābī movement, from the time when the movement was founded by Muḥammad ibn ʿAbd al-Wahhāb, who died in 1787. It emerged into prominence when it was adopted by the family of Saʿūd, and when ʿAbd al-Azzīz ibn Saʿūd captured Mecca and set up his kingdom in Central Arabia. The Wahhābīs are so utterly opposed to superstitions, innovations and the veneration of saints that they even disapprove of the teaching of the Sanūsī Brotherhood, somewhat reformist though they themselves are, because the Wahhābīs oppose Ṣūfism *per se*. It remains to be seen how Islamic fundamentalism, to which my next chapter is addressed, will develop, in both its Sunnī and its Shīʿī manifestations.

I shall close this chapter with a quotation from Kenneth Cragg:

> That the practices of the mystics have encouraged charlatans and rogues is a familiar denunciation. But the scandalous excesses of some should not blind the critic to the force and fervour of restrained and disciplined mysticism . . . Among their humblest devotees one may still find a rare quality of spiritual desire and a sensitivity of soul to God, life and eternity.[93]

It is among such that I myself would locate 'the most acceptable face of Islam'.

CHAPTER FOUR

Islamic fundamentalism: 'Back to the Sharīʿa!'

Introduction

On any count, Islam and its adherents constitute a major factor in the contemporary world. We have already noted how, within a mere decade of the death of their Prophet, Muslim armies had burst out of Arabia and conquered virtually the whole of the Middle East: countries we now know as Jordan, Palestine, Israel, Lebanon, Syria, Iraq, Iran and Egypt. Within a century of the death of Muḥammad, moreover, the Holy War (*jihād*) to which he had commissioned his followers – with its alternative incentives of both victory for Islam and booty for its soldiers, on the one hand, or a martyr's crown, on the other – had successfully swept right across North Africa, through the Iberian peninsula, and into the south of France, in the west; and across central Asia, into northern India, and as far as the confines of China, in the east. It was an empire greater than that of Rome at its zenith.

Since then Islam has suffered a number of major setbacks, but has achieved even greater successes. The Muslim thrust into western Europe was halted by Charles Martel, at the battle of Tours, precisely a hundred years after the death of Muḥammad. It was some centuries later however before the Moors, who had built up a brilliant civilization in the Iberian peninsula, were thrown out of Spain and Portugal. In eastern Europe, it was not till 1453 that Constantinople eventually fell to Muslim assaults. Twice, since then, Muslim armies have penetrated as far as the gates of Vienna. Had they not been thrown back, the history of Europe would have been vastly different. Even so, they left behind some millions of adherents, especially in the Balkans. In India, again, they fought their way southwards, and it was by the sword that they established the Moghul Empire. By contrast, it was chiefly through trade and peaceful penetration that Muslim influence became widespread in Malaysia, Indonesia and the Philippines, as also in East and West Africa.

It must be remembered, too, that it was Muslim scholars who translated the Greek classics into Arabic and passed on the riches of Greek philosophy, mathematics,[1] medicine and much else to a largely barbarous Europe. We all owe them a significant debt. Unhappily, however, it was not long before any close contacts between Christian and Muslim scholars became increasingly rare. By the time of the Crusades, when Christians mistakenly resorted to arms to free their sacred sites from 'Saracen' control – and sank at times to a savagery and moral turpitude worse than that of their opponents – scholarly isolation was virtually complete.

In the last few centuries the position has, however, changed dramatically. The Renaissance, the Reformation and the Industrial Revolution transformed Europe, while much of Africa, the Middle East and the Far East, including most of the Muslim world, remained relatively stagnant. Led by a few pioneers, European traders, missionaries and colonizers (not always in the same order) soon began to penetrate India, Africa and the Far East. There was, regrettably, much exploitation: worst of all in the form of the horrendous slave trade in West Africa. But exploitation was, in general, more than balanced by the message, the education, and the medical aid the missionaries brought – and, later, by the peace, good order and progress experienced under the just and impartial (if foreign and distinctly paternalistic) governments which the colonial powers usually established. One outstanding omission was their failure, in most cases, to develop enlightened self-government at the local level at a considerably earlier date.

More recently, almost inevitable reactions have come to the surface, and the situation has changed once more. From the very beginning there were, of course, many in both Asia and Africa who resented the imposition of foreign rule, however just and benevolent. Nor was this rule always without reproach, by any standard. At first, naturally enough, it was primarily the traditional leaders who must have harboured resentment, although the foreign administrators usually did all they could to preserve the prestige, if not the power, of a positive hierarchy of local dignitaries. But as time wore on, and education became more widespread and effective, it was increasingly from the younger generation that opposition to alien control began to develop. In countries where there is a large (or even significant) Muslim majority, moreover, the conviction that it is inappropriate, at least, for a Muslim community to live under non-Muslim rule has often been virtually a gut reaction.

We have already noted in passing some of the manifestations of this 'gut reaction' in movements such as the Wahhābīs, the Sanūsīs, the Muslim Brotherhood, the Fedayeen (*fidāʾīn*) and the Jamāʿat-i-Islāmī.[2] Today, however, the term 'Islamic fundamentalism' is often used in such a way as virtually to cover all the Islamic protest movements of the past – although it must never be forgotten that Islamic fundamentalism takes many different forms. At the moment the chief menace to peace is the Islamic fundamentalism of Iran and its supporters, which takes a distinctively Shīʿī (indeed Ithnā ʿAsharī) form. But there is also a corresponding Islamic fundamentalism which takes a distinctively Sunnī form, exemplified (with very considerable local variations) in Saʿudi Arabia, Egypt, the Sudan, Pakistan and Libya, for example. There have already been serious clashes between Iran and Saʿudi Arabia, on the one hand, and even between the 'Hezbollah' (*ḥizb Allāh*) variety of Shīʿī fundamentalism and the ʿAmal movement in the Lebanon, and between the supporters of the Islamic Revolution in Iran and those '*Mujāhidīn*' who oppose it.

There is, therefore, always a possibility of violence, whether civil or international, between different varieties of Islamic fundamentalism – to say nothing of the somewhat remote possibility of a more consolidated movement. With both the oil wealth and the religious fanaticism on which these 'fundamentalists', of both the Sunnī and Shīʿī variety, can draw, these different possibilities represent a major menace to the peace of the contemporary world – centred on, but by no means necessarily confined to, the Middle East.

How, then, are we to define this elusive and comprehensive phrase, which takes such different forms and is evoked in such varied contexts? It would be a grave mistake to regard all those Muslims whose attitude to their religion is warm, conservative and at times defensive (or even, in their desire to win converts, offensive) as 'Islamic fundamentalists'. So is there any basic conviction, goal or slogan which characterizes Islamic fundamentalists as such, whether they are Sunnīs or Shīʿīs? I think there is: their constant challenge 'Back to the Sharīʿa!'

If this is true, then clearly any adequate understanding of this contemporary phenomenon demands a brief but reasonably comprehensive review of the different phases through which the Sharīʿa (as understood by Muslims of very varied ethnic origin and religious persuasion) has passed over the centuries, what has happened to it during the last 150 years, and what Islamic fundamentalists want to do about it in the future. This review will, inevitably, involve a certain amount of repetition of material which readers of this book will already have met, in different contexts, in chapters 1 and 2, but which must now be brought together and somewhat expanded.

The Sharī'a before 1850

In general terms it would be true to say that, up until about the middle of the nineteenth century, the Sharī'a law stood supreme, throughout the Muslim world, as the one and only divinely inspired law and, in theory at least, the only written law. Its authority rested on the sources from which it had been derived. Some of it (although not very much) had come from the Qur'ān, which is believed by Muslims to have been written from eternity in Arabic in heaven, and dictated to Muḥammad piece by piece, as occasion demanded, by the Archangel Gabriel. From the first, however, Muslims accepted as another source the *Sunna* (practice) of their Prophet. This was derived from such of the innumerable stories (*aḥādīth*) of what he said, did or had allowed to be said or done in his presence as were later accepted as authentic – since most Muslims came to accept the practice of their Prophet as inspired in its contents, although not (unlike the Qur'ān) in its precise wording. But even so, the Qur'ān and Sunna were not all-inclusive, so from what other source could the law be derived?

The Sunnī, or 'orthodox', Muslims

The answer which was given to this question in the earliest days was simply '*ra'y*', the opinion of a judge or jurisconsult. But it was not long before this was regarded as too subjective a basis for a law which was to be regarded as divinely authoritative. So its place was taken by *qiyās* (analogy): taking some Quranic verse or authoritative tradition, extracting the *'illa* (purpose) which lay behind it, and then deciding whether the principle concerned could legitimately be extended to a different problem.

This was, clearly, a more objective source of law than one man's opinion; but it was still open to question. The original source might, for example, enshrine more than one possible principle; and the way in which this principle (or principles) could be extended to another problem was also debatable. Was there not another, and wholly authoritative, source of law? This they found in a tradition that Muḥammad had once said, 'My people will never agree in error' – the principle, that is, that *ijmā'* (a point on which Muslims as a whole, or their legal scholars in particular, were agreed) was authoritative. But it is an interesting fact that this tradition was clearly not known to the great jurist al-Shāfi'ī when he wrote *Al-Risāla*, since he there argues strongly for the authority of *ijmā'* on other (but rather less obvious) grounds.

Again, whose agreement was required? That of Muslims as a whole could only, in practice, cover basic matters, such as the five times of prayer, rather than detailed points of law. Some said that authoritative agreement should be confined to that of the 'Companions' (that is, contemporaries) of Muḥammad; but most extended it to the agreement of all adequately qualified jurists of any generation. But how could it be known how many such jurists there were (for there was no way of judging whether a scholar had reached the necessary learning other than by the accolade of popular opinion); or, indeed, whether all these qualified jurists had in fact held the same view? So eventually it came to be a matter on which no such qualified jurist (*mujtahid*) was known to have *disagreed* – and even, in point of fact, to something very similar to a majority (rather than strictly unanimous) opinion. Not surprisingly, moreover, suggestions have been made in recent years that a conference of learned Muslims might be called to give an authoritative ruling on some contemporary issue.

Thus the sources of Islamic law to which orthodox (that is Sunnī) Muslims point are chiefly fourfold: the Qur'ān, the Sunna of the Prophet, Consensus and Analogy. There are a few minor sources to which one or another of the Sunnī 'schools' of law, which soon began to emerge, occasionally turn, but these must not delay us now. Customary law (*ʿurf*) is not formally acknowledged as a source of the Sharīʿa, although there can be no doubt that it underlies much of the law included under the four official sources. So much so that Orientalists today insist that the scholar jurists of Islam did not deduce the law at first hand from the Qur'ān and such of the traditions as they knew. Instead, after the phenomenal conquests of early Islam, they worked through the customary law and administrative procedure that confronted them in the light of Islamic teaching – accepting, rejecting or amending it – and thereby both systematized it and Islamicized it.

I have already mentioned the emergent Sunnī law schools. The first stage was for groups of scholars in one locality to draw together – in Kufa, Syria and Madīna, for example – where something approaching a local consensus would emerge. Next, an outstanding scholar would gain a following which spread over more than one area, like al-Shāfiʿī ('the father of Islamic jurisprudence') and Aḥmad ibn Ḥanbal (who was himself more a Traditionalist than a lawyer). Over the years there have been at least six such schools, of which only four have survived – the Ḥanafīs, Mālikīs, Shāfiʿīs and Ḥanbalīs. All accepted the Qur'ān, the Sunna, Consensus and Analogy as the basic sources, but varied among themselves in such matters as which Traditions they accepted and the weight they gave to this source or that. Even more important, in many ways, were the local conditions in which these schools evolved.

Another matter that we should note at this point is that, in the earliest years of Islam, any adequately qualified jurist had what is termed the right of *ijtihād* (that is, going back to the original sources of the law to deduce the answer to any particular problem). But as the schools of law evolved, this liberty of deduction became progressively curtailed, and every subsequent lawyer came to be classed as a *muqallid* (one who was under the duty of *taqlīd*, or following the doctrine which had been accepted by his learned predecessors and had become authoritative in that school). But this is not an example of *stare decisis*; for it was the opinions held by the scholars, not the decisions of the courts, which had to be followed. The process of passing from the more creative stage to the more circumscribed is known as 'the closing of the door of *ijtihād*', but this is not to say that this door has been firmly or finally closed even in Sunnī Islam. There have been a few individuals, down the years, who have claimed to have the right of *ijtihād*; and some of the clauses in recent legislative reforms (to which we shall come later) are based on what is claimed to be *neo-ijtihād*.

There is, however, one other point which should be emphasized before we go into any more detail. The Muslim concept of the Sharīʿa is very much wider than would be covered by any modern definition of law in the West. Whereas we, today, seek legal advice about such matters as the purchase of a house, the drafting of a will or a question of litigation, a Muslim will consult his legal adviser on which conduct would, or would not, be pleasing to God. Much of it could never, in point of fact, be enforced by any human court, but only at the bar of eternity. The Sharīʿa has been aptly described as a 'System of Duties' which covers matters of morality as well as jurisprudence. It is closer to the Jewish concept of Torah than to what we in the West think of as law today. It is all-inclusive and, in theory, omnicompetent: applicable to all, from Caliph to slave.

I have referred up until now only to the four 'schools' of law in orthodox, or Sunnī Islam. This was fair enough, in a sense, since they cover some 90 per cent of the Muslim world. But almost from the beginning there were some who did not conform: the Khawārij and the Shīʿīs. The Khawārij were those (as their name in Arabic signifies) who 'went out' from the body of Islam; and in early days they were certainly wild. But they have survived today only in the Ibāḍīs of Oman, Zanzibar and north Africa, and their law does not in practice differ very much from that of one of the Sunnī schools. The Shīʿīs, on the other hand, demand attention in any survey of Islamic law today.

The Shīʿī[3] Muslims

They started as *ʿshīʿat* ʿAlī – the sect of ʿAlī, the fourth of the Sunnī

Caliphs – but they held very different views from the Sunnīs. The latter believed that the fount of divine revelation had not survived the death of Muḥammad. The Muslim community would, indeed, need a *Khalīfa*, or 'Successor', to lead them in war and maintain the law in time of peace; but he could not speak with the divine voice. The Shīʿīs, on the contrary, could not believe that God had left so vital a matter as the future of the Muslim community to the vagaries of human election. Instead, he must have chosen an *imām*, or leader, who (like all the authentic prophets), was devoid of both sin and error. Such was ʿAlī and, after him, his two sons al-Ḥasan and al-Ḥusayn; and then, one after another, al-Ḥusayn's descendants.

The first major split in the ranks of the Shīʿīs arose from a dispute as to whether Zayd or Muḥammad al-Bāqir, his brother, was to be the fifth Imām. At this point the Zaydīs (mostly to be found now in the Yemen) left what we may regard as the mainstream of the Shīʿīs. The Zaydīs are the least extreme of the Shīʿīs, believing that their successive Imāms must establish themselves by their character and authority; there might even, in some circumstances, be two Imāms at the same time. A more important split arose from a similar dispute about who should be the seventh Imām; Ismāʿīl (or his son, Muḥammad) or Mūsa'l-Kāzim – a point at which the Ismāʿīlīs (or 'Seveners') broke off from those who were to end up as the 'Twelvers'.

The developments among the Ismāʿīlīs are the most fantastic, and in some parts the most secret, in Islamic history. To them the Fāṭimid dynasty in Egypt belonged; and from them came, on one side, the Nizārīs of Alamut (the 'Assassins') and the later community of the Āghā Khān (to say nothing of the Nuṣayrīs, or ʿAlawīs, of Syria, and the Druze of the Lebanon). About them I must confine myself to the bald statements that the Druze are no longer regarded as Muslims; the ʿAlawīs of Syria are highly secretive and largely secular, and include in their number President Asad; while the Imām of the Āghā Khān's community (Karīm Khān, who was educated at the Harvard Law School) is thought to be able to still speak with the divine voice. To them, therefore, law reform is eminently simple.

The Mustaʿlī branch of the Ismāʿīlīs are less colourful, and little need be said of them. Their twenty-first Imām, al-Ṭayyib, disappeared (became *mastūr*, 'hidden') long ago. He is not considered as immortal, so he must long since have been survived by a succession of hidden Imāms. But the community, which has split into several sections, is led by the *Dāʿī Muṭlāq* (plenipotentiary) whom each section (e.g. the Dā'ūdīs, Sulaymānīs, and the like) believes can still speak in the name of the hidden Imām, with what is semi-divine authority.

The main branch of the Shīʿīs accepted a sequence of twelve

Imāms, until the twelfth, Muḥammad ibn al-Ḥasan al-Muntaẓar 'went into hiding in the will of God' in AD 873. For a short time he was in direct contact with his followers, but then that ceased. His community still believe he is alive (over 1,000 years old) and will one day return. In the meantime he is represented by the *mujtahids*, who speak in his name (but not with infallible authority, for it is only the Imām himself who has that). This, in part, explains the ascendancy of the *mujtahids* (or Āyatullahs) in Iran today. I shall revert later to what Islamic fundamentalism in its Shīʿī manifestation has done, or is doing, in Iran.

A fact of which many are not aware is that in Iraq, where power is substantially in the hands of Sunnīs, more than half the population are Shīʿīs, and of the same sub-sect (the 'Twelvers') as those in Iran. They have no doubt resented their political weakness, but it is an interesting point that *most* of them – especially in the south, where they constitute the vast majority – have, apparently, not given any significant welcome to the Iranians.

In Lebanon the population was, until recently, assumed to be fifty per cent Christian and fifty per cent Muslim. This is certainly not true today, when Muslims (together with the Druze) are distinctly in the majority. What has not been realized is that, among the Muslims, the Shīʿīs certainly represent the largest group – although poor and somewhat oppressed. It is among them that the Ḥizb Allāh (party of God) pro-Iranian Islamic fundamentalists (although less in numbers than the much more moderate Shīʿī ʿAmal movement) are to be found. Some readers may not be aware that the constitution of Lebanon (today virtually in abeyance) provides that the President must always be a Maronite Christian, the Prime Minister a Sunnī Muslim, the Speaker of their Parliament a Shīʿī, and the Minister of Defence a Druze. So it is scarcely surprising that it is now in chaos!

Other courts, other laws

So, up until the middle of the eighteenth century, the Sharīʿa reigned supreme, in theory at least, with virtually no other written law. But the specifically Sharīʿa courts, with their *qāḍī* judges, were scarcely ever, in point of fact, the *only* courts. In practice the *wālī* (the local Governor) would have a court of a sort, and so would the *muḥtasib* (the inspector of the markets) and the *shurṭā* (the police). There was also a final court, that of the *Maẓālim* (Complaints), in which the Caliph sometimes sat in person, but usually appointed an official, known as *Ṣāḥib al-Maẓālim*, to act for him. Primarily, as its name implies, it was a court of appeal or review; but it sometimes took cases in first instance, if one of the parties was much more powerful than the other. As such, it emphasized the Caliph's ultimate authority. There was also an informal 'law merchant'.

So the position was that the Sharīʿa was the official law (although, even so, local or tribal customary law often influenced its detailed application). The ruler, however, did not leave matters political – such as 'law and order' – exclusively to courts where the exceedingly strict Islamic rules of procedure were followed, nor did the merchants wholly conform their activities to the Islamic rules about *ribā* (interest) or to the prohibition of contracts regarded as akin to gambling. In point of fact major Muslim jurists, from a very early date, began themselves to invent '*makhārij fī 'l-ḥiyal*' ('ways out by devices') to get around various points of the Sharīʿa. They would defend these *ḥiyal* by saying that, since in many such cases man could not be sure of the reason behind the divine commands, it was sufficient if one followed the letter of such specific commands, even if in a way that defeated their apparent purpose. I could give many examples.

Modern developments since 1850

From about 1850 a very significant change began to take place in regard to the application of the Sharīʿa. It can be seen most clearly, in the earlier years, in the Ottoman Empire, although a somewhat parallel (but inevitably different) development took place in what was then British India.

It is the fact that the Ottoman Empire was both Islamic and independent – although in a growing relationship with Europe – which makes it such a fascinating example.

New codes of law

It was in 1850 that the Tanẓīmāt reforms in the Ottoman Empire (which had begun some eleven years earlier) first impinged on public law in the terms of the Ottoman Commercial Code – followed soon by the Penal Code, 1858, the Code of Commercial Procedure, 1861, and the Code of Maritime Commerce, 1863. All of these were based on European (French) models, together with secular Niẓāmāt courts to apply them – with largely Western rules of procedure and by lawyers trained accordingly. When, however, they came to the law of 'Obligations' (contract, tort, etc.) they hesitated. Should they again turn to French law, or compile a code from Islamic sources, taking a bit from this school of thought and a bit from that? Eventually they decided on the latter, and the Majalla was promulgated by 1876 – to be applied in the Niẓāmāt Courts.

Only the family law of Islam (in the widest sense of family law) was left to the Sharīʿa courts, Islamic procedure and old-style judges and lawyers. So there was a complete dichotomy between the courts, together with their personnel and procedure and, to a large extent, the law they applied. The same happened in Egypt, which had then attained juridical independence. There however the law of Obligations was derived, both for the Mixed and the National Courts, primarily from French sources, combined with about 15 per cent of Islamic principles. When, moreover, the Mixed Courts were abolished in 1948, the mixture of borrowings from European codes in the new law of Obligations was more varied. The inclusion of principles drawn straight from the Sharīʿa however was not greatly increased, in spite of the claims made by Dr al-Sanhūrī. At a later date, I may observe, it was this same Dr Sanhūrī who drafted new codes for both Kuwait and Iraq. In the Iraqi code, moreover, the percentage of material taken from Sharīʿa law was much greater (perhaps fifty per cent of the whole) – a policy facilitated by the fact that Iraq had previously been using the Ottoman Majalla, and had had no experience of French law.

So, for a considerable period, this dichotomy of courts (secular and Sharīʿa) prevailed throughout a large part of the Muslim world, with the law applied in the secular courts, both civil and criminal, containing a large percentage of Western law. No doubt it seems strange, at first sight, that this dichotomy should be accepted by independent Muslim governments. But the explanation, in short, is that they thought that changes had to be made in the law if they were to keep up with the tempo of the modern world, and that it seemed preferable to them at that time to put the Sharīʿa largely on one side, in matters other than personal status, family law and inheritance, rather than to permit any meddling with what they regarded as its immutable provisions.

But even that position could not be sustained for long, since the miserable condition of Muslim wives, under the dominant doctrine of the Ḥanafī school which then prevailed in the Ottoman empire, clamoured for reform. Muslim men would travel to Istanbul, for example, marry a local wife, and sometimes go home without even divorcing her; and she was left with no maintenance or support, and no way of ending the marriage, So, in 1915, the Sultan issued an imperial decree allowing such women to ask the courts to annul their marriages (and another decree allowing the same procedure in regard to wives who had been married, without their consent, to a husband afflicted with a dangerous disease or with insanity) – based on provisions in the Ḥanbalī and Mālikī schools of law; and, indeed, on a 'weaker' view even in the Ḥanafī school. Then, the dyke of strict adherence to the dominant Ḥanafī view once breached, the tide of reform came in very fast indeed, and in 1917 the Ottoman Law of Family Rights was promulgated – covering the whole sphere of family law fairly completely, but not testate and intestate succession – all based on the dominant doctrine of one or another of the four Sunnī schools, or on a variant view in the Ḥanafī school.

After this the vanguard of reform in such matters passed to Sheikh Muḥammad ʿAbduh and to Qāsim Amīn in Egypt, with laws about marriage and divorce in 1920, 1923 and 1929, followed subsequently by similar legislation about inheritance in 1943, and about wills and *awqāf* (charitable and family trusts) in 1946. In point of fact a few of those early reforms were promulgated in the Sudan, where the Grand Qāḍī was then always an Egyptian sheikh, even before they were in Egypt. And, subsequently, similar reforms in family law have been promulgated in Jordan (1951), Syria (1953), Tunisia (1956 and 1959), Morocco (1958) and Iraq (1959 and 1963) – the latter with alternative clauses, in some of its articles, for Sunnīs and Shīʿīs, respectively. Then, too, there was the Muslim Family Law Ordinance of 1961 in Pakistan and the Family Protection Act of 1967 in Iran. In addition, minor but significant reforms have been introduced in Singapore in 1957 and 1968. More recently still, a 'uniform' Law of Marriage Act (allowing for both monogamous and potentially polygamous marriages) has been promulgated in Tanzania in 1971, a radical Family Law (showing Marxist influence) in the Democratic Republic of South Yemen in 1974 and a somewhat similar enactment of the same time in Somalia in 1975. So this 'reform' movement has been widespread in the Muslim world.

Two questions arise: how has it been possible to reform a system of law (the Sharīʿa) believed by Muslims to be divinely revealed, and what has been achieved by these reforms? Unlike the spheres of commerce, crime, contract and tort, for example, Muslims in these countries were determined that their family law must remain distinctively Islamic; but how could that be achieved? Primarily, by four expedients, all of which are noteworthy.

The procedural expedient

Underlying all the reforms I have mentioned in regard to commercial and criminal law and, especially, in the establishment of a system of courts to administer the new codes, was a principle known in Arabic as *takhṣīṣ al-qaḍāʾ*, the right of a Ruler to define and confine the jurisdiction of his courts. This had always been known in Islam to some extent. It was recognized in a geographical sense, in that an individual judge's jurisdiction was confined to a certain area. It had been recognized in a chronological sense, in that a judge might be appointed for a specified period. And it had also been recognized, to some extent, in regard to the type of litigation with which a particular court was authorized to deal. With the advent of the reform movement, however, this principle was given a far wider application; for it was fundamental to the new system that the Sharīʿa courts, for example, were to be restricted to questions of family law, inheritance, gifts and *awqāf*, and that the new secular codes were to be administered by courts staffed by personnel trained in a wholly different way.

But this same principle could be applied, and now was in fact applied, as a means of introducing reforms in the way in which the family law was to be enforced even by the Sharīʿa courts – not by a change in the substantive law, but by insisting that no judicial relief whatever should be available, in any court, for certain specified claims. An easy example is a claim that a deceased person had made an oral legacy to the claimant. Under the classical procedure this could be proved by two eligible witnesses who testified that they heard it. Under the new Egyptian law of 1946, however, no claim to a bequest which was denied by the natural heirs might be upheld by the courts unless the claimant could produce documentary evidence – or, in some cases, even notarial evidence – to support it. But this same expedient had already been widely used in Egypt in regard to a variety of claims in regard to marriage, maintenance, paternity and much else, in a way which, in *effect*, changed the law which was previously being applied.

The eclectic expedient

By far the most fruitful of these expedients, however, was the eclectic principle (technically termed *takhayyur*) by means of which the reformers felt that, far from being bound to the dominant opinion in their own particular school of law, they could borrow freely from all the schools and, indeed, from variant opinions in all the schools, in search of the solution, to one problem after another, which seemed best fitted to modern life. Sometimes they opted for the view held by an eminent jurist of the early years before the Sunnī schools of law had emerged as such. Occasionally they extended their catchment area even wider than that to find a suitable dictum from some other reputable Muslim source. They also quite often indulged in what is technically termed *talfīq* (patching) – namely, combining two such reputable opinions by putting them together as constituent parts of a section or article which none of the jurists concerned would have approved as a composite whole – and which itself, of course, was part of a code or other legislative enactment which might well be built up on the basis of several of these expedients. This basic principle of an eclectic choice between reputable Muslim dicta or opinions of the past has been very widely used – first in a way that only the fanatical adherents of one particular school would oppose, later with much more freedom.

The expedient of re-interpretation

At times, however, even the more elastic forms of this eclectic expedient would not meet the reformers' needs, so they resorted to a re-interpretation of the basic sources of the Sharī'a. Under President Bourguiba of Tunisia, for example, polygamy was not only forbidden but a polygamous contract was treated as void. For this reform the President himself gave two justifications. First, that certain human institutions (such as slavery and polygamy) were appropriate to certain periods in the past, but socially unacceptable to more enlightened modern man (so, just as slavery had been renounced, why should not polygamy be similarly forbidden?). Second, that what is known as the 'Verse of Polygamy' in the Qur'ān allows a Muslim to have as many as four wives at the same time, but – implicitly, at least – on two conditions: that he should treat them all with equal justice (and this, Bourguiba insisted, no one other than a prophet could achieve!) and also be able to support both his existing family and a new wife, with the children she might bear. This was a bold move, equalled only by the Āghā Khān's communities in East Africa; but several other Muslim countries have made certain restrictions on polygamy. As early as 1900, in fact, an Egyptian writer, Qāsim Amīn, wrote a book (whose title in Arabic meant *The Liberation of Women*) in which he upheld a high view of the marriage relationship, denounced polygamy, and maintained that the Qur'ān in effect both allowed it and forbade it.

I must refrain from giving any further examples of the use of this interesting expedient – which represents, of course, what has been termed '*neo-ijtihād*'. But many modern Muslims have argued strongly that contemporary scholars, with all the books from the past now available to them, are in a position in which a reinterpretation of the original sources of the law is not only desirable but responsibly possible.

The expedient of administrative orders

In general, this expedient is basic, of course, to all the legislative reforms which I have been discussing – based, as they almost invariably are, on one or another of the former expedients. Just occasionally, however, a clause or two in some enactment will be justified simply by the statement that it is 'not contrary to Islamic law' – with the obvious implication that Muslims should obey the legislative enactments of their legislature, or the orders of their government, in any matter which is not 'contrary' to the Sharīʿa.

There is one other expedient I should mention, since it is of great importance in the 'Anglo-Muḥammad Law' of the Indian sub-continent which I could not feasibly include in the scope of this chapter. I should add, however, at this point that one of the most effective ways of promoting a reform in this system has been by judicial interpretation of the law, even by a judge who is not a Muslim. If not quashed on appeal, this interpretation of the law then becomes judicially binding under the doctrine of *stare decisis*, which became enshrined many years ago in what was then 'British India'. It has happened on two or three occasions, in the Republic of India, that a judge has given a ruling on a somewhat controversial question of Islamic law which has then become binding as a judicial precedent.

Perhaps I might observe at this point that two of the four visits I have made to India were at the invitation of the Indian Government because they wanted to persuade the Muslim minority (something in excess of eighty millions) to introduce reforms in their personal and family law somewhat similar to those introduced in several countries in the Middle East. Indian Muslims were, however, understandably apprehensive that any change might open the door to the loss of their distinctive law, since one of the 'Directive Principles' of the Indian Constitution declared that the Government should 'work towards' a uniform Code of Personal law for all Indians. During one of my visits I was telling Indian Muslims (at a special conference, and in a number of lectures) that a house which is in good order is much more likely to survive than one which is manifestly leaking. This seemed to be going quite well until, on one occasion, a Supreme Court Judge (himself a Hindu who had been invited to take the chair at one of my lectures) insisted that 'what we want is not the reform of Islamic law, but its abolition'. This was hardly helpful to my enterprise!

Some of the reforms effected

It is clearly impossible to go into any detail, in the course of this chapter, about the reforms effected, by means of one or another of the expedients I have listed above, in all the countries to which reference has been made on p. 105 above. But I think that even a bare summary of the subjects which have been tackled in the course of these reforms will give some indication of what has been achieved. It must always be remembered, however, that the countries concerned differ widely in both the scope and the boldness of the legislation they have introduced.

(a) *Judicial divorce has been made available to ill-used wives.* In many countries today a Muslim's wife has been granted the right to petition for a judicial divorce if he has deserted her, failed to provide her proper maintenance, or treated her with cruelty; if he has been afflicted with insanity or some disease that makes married life dangerous; or, in some countries, if she insists on a divorce in consideration for which she is prepared to return her dower or make some other financial compensation.

(b) *Limitations on a Muslim husband's absolute right to the repudiation (ṭalāq) of his wife.* It has been widely provided today that a *ṭalāq* is invalid if pronounced under compulsion, in blind anger or intoxication, or at a time of calamity, senility or sickness; that the '*triple ṭalāq*' pronounced on a single occasion is to be regarded as a single, and therefore revocable, divorce; and, in some countries, that a husband's divorce is subject to registration and conciliation, or that a husband who insists on divorce must pay his divorced wife some financial compensation (*mutʿa*).

(c) *Restrictions on child marriage and compulsory marriage.* It is often provided today that parties must not marry before prescribed ages; that a girl must not be given in marriage by her father without her consent; and even, rarely, that there must not be an excessive difference between the ages of the parties.

(d) *Restrictions on polygamy.* As we have seen, a polygamous contract of marriage is both criminal and void in Tunisia, and forbidden among the Āghā Khān's communities in East Africa. In a number of other countries a Muslim husband may marry a second wife only with permission of the court, which will determine whether he is in a position both to support his existing dependents and to maintain another wife and her possible children; and also, in some jurisdictions, whether he is capable of treating two or more wives with equal justice.

(e) *Various reforms in the law of testate and intestate succession.* Two examples must suffice. Reforms have been made in some countries to promote the claims of the nuclear family against those of the extended family (the '*aṣaba* or *agnates* of Sunnī law); and provision has been made for 'compulsory bequests' to orphaned grandchildren who would otherwise have been excluded from inheritance.

(f) *The whole system of Waqf endowments* has been abolished in some countries, while in others it has been radically reformed.

A wholly new situation?

The Islamic Revolution of 1979 in Iran, followed by the virtual autocracy of the Āyatullahs which that revolution inaugurated, clearly introduced a wholly new situation in that country; and to that we must soon turn. But the announcement (only a few hours ago, as I write) of the death of General Zia al-Ḥaqq, President of Pakistan, inevitably brings to the fore, in an acute form, a question that has always been present in my mind regarding the aspirations voiced by the Islamic fundamentalists – especially those of Sunnī allegiance. So it may be helpful to turn to this first.

More than twenty years ago I wrote a paper entitled 'Pakistan: An Islamic State?'[4], based largely on a short visit I had paid to that country. It will be remembered that the basic reason why so many of the Muslims of the Indian sub-continent insisted on Partition was their conviction that only in an independent state, that was at least in some sense Islamic, would they be able to ensure the sort of life they desired for themselves and their children. But there is scope for considerable differences of opinion about precisely how Islamic Muḥammed ʿAlī Jinnah, their 'Qāʾid-i-Aʿzam', really wished the new state to be. On one occasion he had said: 'The Muslims demand Pakistan, where they could rule according to their own code of life and according to their own cultural growth, traditions and Islamic laws'.[5] In the same month he told the students of the Islamiyya College of Peshawa that 'The [Muslim] League stood for carving out states in India where Muslims were in numerical majority to rule these under Islamic law.'[6] But on more numerous and more public occasions he emphasized that Pakistan would be a modern, democratic state, with sovereignty resting in the people; and with the members of the new nation having equal rights of citizenship, regardless of their religion, caste or creed. But, however that may be, there can be no room for doubt that two ambitions – the one to be an Islamic state and the other to be a modern, democratic state – are knit together in the aspirations of the people of Pakistan.

This was, indeed, expressed in the Preamble to the Constitution of 1956 – which was largely re-enacted in the Constitution of 1962, and amended in 1963 (largely to reinsert the word 'Islamic' before the words 'Republic of Pakistan'). Under the 'Principles of Policy' (quoting from the amended version) there were, moreover, several strongly Muslim clauses, such as –

> No law shall be repugnant to the teachings and requirements of Islam, as set out in the Holy Qurʾān and Sunnah, and all

existing laws shall be brought into conformity with the Holy Qur'ān and Sunnah.

It is also stated that 'Ribā (usury) should be eliminated'. Other clauses proclaim 'the fundamental human rights (including the rights of equality before the law, of freedom of thought, expression, belief, faith and association' and 'the legitimate interests of the minorities in Pakistan [including their religious and cultural interests])'.

But what are, in fact, 'the teachings and requirements of the Holy Qur'ān and Sunnah'? No mention is made in this clause of either *ijmāʿ* or *qiyās*, from which (as we have seen) so much of the Sharīʿa has in practice been derived; no mention of the different sects and schools into which Muslims, even in Pakistan, are divided; and no mention of the form in which the law (especially as concerns the family law of Muslims) had previously been applied in the sub-continent – nor, of course, of the ways in which the Muslim countries of the Middle East had been trying, for years past, to adapt Islamic family law to the needs of the modern world.

Then came eleven years of General Zia's authoritative rule, first as Chief Military Governor and then as President, with his determination to promote the 'Islamization' of the country. This showed itself to some degree in the spheres of taxation and banking, but most controversially in the criminal law, where he wished to follow Iran in the reapplication of some of the severe physical punishments prescribed in the Sharīʿa for a few specific offences. Flogging was in fact reintroduced fairly widely. Sentences, however, like the amputation of the right hand for theft and stoning for adultery, for example, although sometimes passed locally, seem never actually to have been confirmed by the higher courts.

Finally, in June 1988, President Zia dissolved Parliament and introduced the 'Sharīʿa Bill' under which individual citizens, or groups of citizens, would have the right to request the High Court to strike down any part of the legal codes (as they had been inherited from the British) that did not accord with the Sharīʿa. But the fact is, as we have seen, that the content of the Sharīʿa itself is a matter of dispute, in several particulars, between the different sects and schools of law of which Islam is made up. Again, it seems distinctly doubtful whether the majority of Pakistani Muslims – including the Army officers, who had so much influence at the time (and who would scarcely relish being sentenced to a public flogging for drinking whisky!) – really want to return to all the rigours of the 'prescribed penalties' (*ḥudūd*) of the Sharīʿa. It is also doubtful whether the women of Pakistan would welcome the abolition of the reforms in family law introduced by the Muslim Family Laws Ordinance of 1961 (as a result of the proposals of a Commission set up by the Government of Pakistan in 1955). It is also very questionable what the High Court, or most of the senior judges and lawyers in Pakistan, would make of an attempt to go 'back to the Sharī'a' in its primitive form. I have vivid personal memories of the moderate attitude adopted in 1958 by Mr Justice Muḥammad Sharīf (then Chairman of Pakistan's Law Reform Commission, and himself a very devout Muslim), when he and I were members, under the chairmanship of the Chief Justice of the Sudan (again, a Muslim), of a Panel of Jurists invited by the Government of what was then the Northern Region of Nigeria to advise them on legal matters which concerned Muslims and the Sharī'a.

We must next turn to Iran, where the Islamic Revolution (and Islamic fundamentalism of the Shī'ī variety) has been most extreme. Thousands have been executed by the Revolutionary Courts – most frequently for 'fighting against God and His Apostle' and/or 'spreading corruption in the land'. At first, I thought that these slogans were no more than examples of 'revolutionary justice', with *no* justification in the Sharī'a. Then I found that these two phrases do occur in the Qur'ān (5:33), in a verse applied everywhere else in the Muslim world (so far as I know) only to brigands whose brigandage has involved homicide. It is clear, however, that in Iran's Revolutionary courts these phrases have in fact been applied to anyone hostile to the new regime. Thousands of Bahā'īs, too, have been executed, presumably for what is deemed to be 'apostasy', since they, or their parents – unlike the Armenian Christians, for example – were originally Muslims. Some Iranians convicted of adultery have been stoned to death; the right hands of some thieves have, apparently, been cut off; and thousands have been flogged. These penalties are, indeed, prescribed in the Sharī'a; but the more severe ones were hardly ever actually imposed because of the *exceedingly* stringent evidence specifically demanded (*e.g.* four adult, 'competent', male Muslims as witnesses to the very act of adulterous intercourse, or two such to the very act of stealing by stealth from 'safe custody'). I am, however, *very* dubious whether these strict rules of procedure are always enforced today.

It should be added that the Ḥizb Allāh groups in the Lebanon would wish to extend the Iranian Revolution, with its Islamic fundamentalism, to their own country. And the same goes for some of the groups of the Mujāhidīn of Afghanistan (one of which is named Ḥizb-i-Islāmī); although some of the other groups fighting for a new regime in that country are more moderate.

The Sharī'a still reigns supreme in Sa'udi Arabia, and the *ḥadd* penalties are still exacted. Executions are always by decapitation; but

I remember reading the report of an Arab, who had raped an American woman, being sentenced by the local Governor (a very stern Muslim) to repeated lashings so severe that he in fact died. Even in Saʿudi Arabia, however, the rules of the Sharīʿa previously applied to insurance, and certain other commercial contracts, have been somewhat relaxed. One example of which I have personal knowledge concerns the concessions that have been granted to companies to survey, locate and then extract petroleum.

Under the influence of Islamic fundamentalism the Sharīʿa law was officially imposed, a few years ago, in the Sudan. But its penalties are seldom applied at present even in the Muslim north, while in the southern Sudan the Sharīʿa is fiercely resisted. In Libya, again, some (but by no means all) the *ḥadd* punishments were re-introduced comparatively recently; and I have heard of a thief's hand being amputated by a surgeon under an anaesthetic.

Islamic fundamentalists are very active also in Egypt, although they are at present held under control. It was from one such group that those who assassinated President Saʿdat sprang, and the influence of their less extreme partisans is widespread. Although Egypt has acceded to the United Nations' declaration about the freedom of individual citizens to follow, or change, their religious allegiance, converts from Islam to Christianity are often still persecuted.

The uneasy truce between the Sharīʿa and modern life is, perhaps, most clearly seen in the evolving commercial law in the states of the Gulf Co-operation Council: Bahrein, Kuwait, Oman, Qatar, Saʿudi Arabia and the United Arab Emirates. I can sum up the situation in words written recently by Mr William Ballantyne, after many years of first-hand experience:

> In confronting any legal problem [in the Gulf States], perhaps the first question to be asked is: to what extent, if at all, does the Sharīʿa affect the matter? The answer may vary from 'not at all' in a problem falling within the Commercial Code of Kuwait to 'basically' in a problem in Saʿudi Arabia, while in the other jurisdictions, the answer may be somewhere between these extremes. Overall, we must record and always bear in mind the *uncertainty* engendered by the looming presence of the Sharīʿa which should be one of the factors to be borne in mind in weighing the benefits and risks of any commercial contract . . .

This is a careful, authoritative statement about commercial dealings in the Gulf states. But in this chapter I have been concerned with the nature and application of Islamic law over the centuries and in many different lands. First, I attempted to depict the Sharīʿa as it was until about 1850: very sure of itself, sometimes a little strident, as the only *basic* law, although modified in many places by customary laws and executive interventions. Next, we saw the Sharīʿa, since 1850, in part displaced by modern statute law designed to match the commercial and industrial penetration of the West, and in part modified and softened under the influence of twentieth century human values (especially in so far as women are concerned). Finally, we noted the contemporary emergence of Islamic fundamentalism, which seems to me to be a two-sided phenomenon. On the one hand it is a very understandable revolt against the dominance, and (until recently) the colonialism, of Western powers. On the other, a reaction against what might be termed the Western philosophy of life which, although basically founded upon Christian faith and ethics, has become so engulfed in liberalism and agnosticism that it has largely lost both its cutting edge and its persuasive power. But although, in Iran, the Family Protection Act of 1967 has, presumably, been rescinded, I very much doubt if all the reforms in family law and succession will be widely repudiated elsewhere. The increasing literacy and influence of Muslim women will, I believe, ensure this, except in times of fanatical revolution. It must, after all, be realized that, to go right 'back to the Sharīʿa', would be, *inter alia*, to go back to a very detailed law of slavery, polygamy, arbitrary divorce, male chauvinism and cruel physical punishments – together with the death penalty for those Muslims who renounce Islam or embrace any other religion.

Rampant Islamic fundamentalism – when it comes to power, or even contends for power – is far from an attractive phenomenon. On the contrary, it represents a recurrent menace in the world today, for its fanaticism embodies the very spirit of *jihād*. It has already had, and it may well continue to have, local victories which result in anarchy or autocracy, confusion or bondage. We can be sure, however, that it will never prevail.

PART II

The Christian response: the incarnation, cross and resurrection

Introduction to Part II

As we have seen in Part 1 of this book, the very fount and origin of Islam is the Qur'ān. However much successive generations of Muslims have revered, and even at times tried to imitate, their Prophet (to whom, they believe, the Qur'ān was literally dictated) it is the Book which has always been the *basic* revelation of the God to whom, as Muslims, they have 'yielded their allegiance'.

Not so the Christian – as our Muslim friends discover as soon as they give any serious consideration to the Christian faith. For, to a Christian, God's supreme revelation of himself is not in a book but in a Person. It is to the advent of that Person that the Old Testament as a whole looked forward, and it is with that Person's birth, life, teaching, death and resurrection – and, indeed, with his present exaltation and future reign – that all the books of the New Testament are almost exclusively concerned.

It is scarcely surprising, then, that both the nature of Jesus the Christ and the relationship between him and the Triune God have been central to Christian teaching all down the centuries; or, indeed, that the doctrine of the incarnation has again, during the last two or three decades, become the focal point of Christian debate. It is this relationship between Jesus and the one of whom he spoke as 'my Father' to which the doctrine of the incarnation inherently points, on which the efficacy of his atoning death necessarily depends, and to which his resurrection and exaltation bear unequivocal witness. Sadly, it is these facts (constituting, as they do, the essence of the gospel) which our Muslim friends find so hard to understand. Yet it is to these facts, which mean so much to us, that we as their Christian friends are so eager to bear witness. We can do no other.

It is of primary concern, then, to a Muslim who begins to consider the Christian faith that he should understand what Christians mean when they talk of the 'incarnation'. Why they believe that the one eternal God has uniquely revealed himself, and his message to us, in Jesus the Messiah, and what this implies in regard to the unity of the Godhead in which both Christians and Muslims believe. One point of caution is that Muslims should not recoil in horror when they meet the title 'Son of God' alongside that of 'Word of God'. The two titles are virtually the same, for both basically mean the revelation of God in terms of a human life. Perhaps a simple illustration, inadequate though it is, may help. Just as an Arab might say of a book he had written 'This is *bint fikrī* (the daughter of my thoughts and mind)', so Christians believe that God said of Jesus 'This is my Son whom I love. Listen to him.'

CHAPTER FIVE

The incarnation: background to the contemporary debate

I suppose that the basic, and probably the earliest, Christian confession of faith is the simple statement 'Jesus is Lord' – and that from this no truly Christian theologians of past or present would dissent, however 'orthodox', '*avant garde*' or even 'heterodox' they may be considered. Controversy arises only when one starts to question what, precisely, this confession means, and what it implies in theory and practice. We shall begin to consider this, in general terms, in this chapter. In chapter six, for the convenience of those Christians who are not very familiar with the subject and that of Muslim friends, I shall attempt to outline the christological controversies which led up to the Nicene Creed and the Definition of Chalcedon; those which followed in the next two or three centuries; and those which ensued in the Lutheran and Reformed traditions. I shall then devote chapter seven to a consideration of the incarnation in the context of comparative religion. Finally, in chapter eight, I shall try to draw the subject together and outline my own conclusions.

As a broad generalization, there are always two possible approaches to Christology – or, in terms of the way in which I have introduced the subject, to the confession that 'Jesus is Lord'. One can begin from one's doctrine of God and argue from that to Jesus, adopting a deductive or what may be described as a 'downward' approach. Alternatively, one can start from the Jesus of the Gospels and see whether he leads us to God, following an inductive or 'upward' approach. Obviously enough, both approaches are in fact needed; and in the New Testament – and particularly, perhaps, in the Epistle to the Hebrews – they largely go hand in hand. But the first disciples necessarily began with Jesus, the man they knew so well as teacher and had come to accept as Messiah; and it seems to me that this is the natural starting point for us too.

The upward approach

The Son of Man

What, then, are the basic facts? A great deal has been written in recent years about the titles applied to Jesus in the Gospels, whether by himself or others; but it would go beyond my purpose and my competence to attempt to evaluate the very different theories on this subject advocated by New Testament scholars. I will therefore hazard the dogmatic statement that I myself have no doubt whatever that Jesus repeatedly used the symbolic title 'Son of Man' – or, more accurately, '*The* Son of Man';[1] that he applied it to himself rather than to anyone else (often, perhaps, as an indirect way of saying 'I' or 'me'); and that, in whatever other sense he may have used it, he sometimes invested it with an apocalyptic meaning derived, in part, from Daniel 7.

The suggestion that this title was imported, as it were, by the primitive church, and put by the evangelists almost exclusively into his mouth, seems to me incredible on a number of different grounds – but particularly in view of the fact that it would have appeared so inadequate to them in the light of their Easter faith. It seems, moreover, that there is 'virtually no evidence' for the theory that it was first applied to Jesus by the post-resurrection church.[2] Whereas the phrase, if used by Jesus himself, would have enabled him, in the words of Professor G. B. Caird, 'without actually claiming to be Messiah, to indicate his essential unity with mankind, and above all with the weak and humble, and also his special function as predestined representative of the new Israel and bearer of God's judgment and Kingdom.'[3]

The Messiah

But did Jesus in fact claim to be Messiah? I am myself convinced that Professor C. H. Dodd was right when he wrote, in regard to the trial of Jesus:

> The evangelists, I conclude, John and the Synoptics alike, take the view that Jesus was charged with blasphemy because he spoke and acted in ways which implied that he stood in a special relation with God, so that his words carried divine authority and his actions were instinct with divine power. Unless this could be believed, the implied claim was an affront to the deepest religious sentiments of his people, a profanation

> of sanctities; and this, I suggest, is what the charge of "blasphemy" really stands for, rather than any definable statutory offence . . . Whether or not Jesus had put himself forward as Messiah, the implied claim was messianic at least, perhaps rather messianic plus.[4]

Indeed, I would myself be less cautious. It does seem clear that Jesus did not use the title 'Messiah' of himself in his public teaching. This was largely, I believe, because his Jewish contemporaries would have understood it in terms of those currents in Jewish thought that depicted the Messiah as a national deliverer or conquering king rather than those prophecies about the 'Suffering Servant' by which he himself chiefly interpreted his mission. He sometimes went, however, distinctly further than merely to accept the title tacitly or make messianic claims by implication. At the climax of his ministry, moreover, 'the so-called triumphal entry (Mk. 11) looks uncommonly like a deliberate messianic gesture or demonstration', C. F. D. Moule observes, but

> one so staged as to say, 'If I *am* Messiah, I am not going to fight the Romans. I am going to fight abuse at the heart of Judaism.' And finally, when it is perfectly clear that no violent action is possible, because Jesus is already a prisoner, he is represented, apparently, as acknowledging messiahship before the Sanhedrin (Mark 14:62).

So, he concludes,

> The tenacity of the usage is most plausibly explained . . . if Jesus himself had accepted the royal title, but, during his ministry, had so radically reinterpreted it that it became natural to his followers to use it in this new way.[5]

In view of the statement in Deuteronomy 21:23 that 'a hanged man is accursed by God', moreover, it seems to me almost incredible that Jewish Christians should have used the title unless they 'believed that Jesus believed himself to be Messiah',[6] and there seems to be no substance whatever in the allegation that Jesus refused the title at Caesarea Philippi. Instead, he gave his disciples, in the Marcan account, 'strict orders not to tell anyone about him' (which would suggest that he accepted the title but did not want it to be made public), while he is recorded, in the Matthean account, as having told Peter that his confession 'You are the Messiah, the Son of the living God', had been the result of a revelation from 'my heavenly Father'.[7]

Muslim readers will not need to be reminded that 'Īsā (a name that probably comes from the Syriac Yeshūʿ, which is itself derived from the Hebrew Yeshua) is referred to repeatedly in the Qur'ān as *al-Masīḥ*, in marked contrast with the so-called 'Gospel of Barnabas' (*cf.* Appendix). But as we turn to the contemporary debate in Christendom about the meaning of the title 'Son of God', we must assure our Muslim friends that this expression does not, for a moment, imply that Christians believe that Jesus was Son of God by physical procreation. Christians would regard any such thought with as much horror as does the Qur'ān in sūrā 19:36, which insists: 'It is not for Allāh to take to Himself any offspring; glory to Him!', or sūra 19:93f. which complains: 'They have attributed to the Merciful offspring, when it does not behove the Merciful to take to Himself offspring'. As Kenneth Cragg puts it: 'the terms 'Father' and 'Son' have no physical significance and are used analogically. The divine solicitude for man in ignorance and sin 'begets' or generates the activity of redeeming love which is evident in the historic Christ'.[8]

The Son of God

The addition of the words 'the Son of the living God' in Matthew's account of Peter's confession inevitably raises the question of the use and meaning of the title 'Son of God', or simply 'the Son', when applied or attributed to Jesus in the New Testament. In itself the title need have no deeper significance than that of Messianic King.[9] Some participants in the contemporary debate about Christology point to the impact on the early church of the Hellenistic belief in mythological heroes and 'divine men'; the Roman ascription of 'divinity' to their emperors; and the Old Testament references to Israel's kings, Israel itself as a nation, and even the angels, as God's 'sons'. This, naturally enough, led the church, with its unbounded reverence for the Jesus it believed to be exalted to God's right hand, first to regard him as the 'Son of God' in a theological rather than metaphysical or poetic sense, and then to transform this concept into that of 'God the Son'[10]. But does the evidence in fact support this theory?

The virgin birth

Let us start, by way of illustration, with a point to which I shall not revert except in one or two passing references: namely, the virgin birth or, more precisely, the virginal conception. This is an article of faith included in all the Creeds and constantly repeated by the greater part of Christendom; but it is often questioned today, and even denied, by many who would not regard themselves as *avant garde*. It is, of course, manifestly true that the evidence for the virgin birth – to which unambiguous references in the New Testament are confined to the beginning of the first and third Gospels – is incomparably less strong than that for the resurrection, and that it does not seem to have represented any essential part of the apostolic proclamation. When, however, it is alleged that virgin births are found in many pagan myths and religions, so it was almost inevitable that the Christian church should come to believe that Christ, if divine, must have been born of a virgin – or even that he was divine because he had been born of a virgin – this is wide open to challenge. Pagan mythology, as Dr Alan Richardson rightly insists,

> is full of legends of a supernatural hero born of intercourse between a god and a human woman. But this is scarcely a *virgin* birth, and there is no real parallel to the story of the birth of Christ in pagan literature. The Jewish mind (and Matt. 1 and Luke 1 are intensely Jewish) would have been revolted by the idea of physical intercourse between a divine being and a woman.[11]

Similarly, any idea that the stories of the virgin birth owed their origin to any Gnostic or Manichaean notion that sexual intercourse was in itself sinful or unclean would have been wholly alien to Jewish thought. A much more plausible motive for the invention of such a legend, if legend it were, would have been the insistence of the early church that Jesus had indeed 'come in the flesh': that he was truly 'born of a woman', and not a mere theophany. Nor can it be argued that the church's belief in the sinlessness of Jesus is in any sense 'guaranteed' by the virgin birth, as the Roman Catholic dogma of the Immaculate Conception of Mary herself sufficiently testifies.

The truth is that both Matthew and Luke 'state the fact of Christ's birth of a virgin in a straightforward and unargumentative way; they offer no hints as to why it should have happened thus and they draw no conclusions from it. So-called "theological" objections to the historicity of the Virgin Birth are based upon a reading into the narratives of motives that are not present in them', for the Gospel accounts 'simply relate an historical happening and leave the matter without any form of explanation'.[12] The absence of any mention of the virgin birth by any other New Testament writer, moreover, proves no more than the fact to which I have already referred, that it did *not* form part of the apostolic proclamation. It was something that those who already believed in Jesus were taught, not a ground on which they called others to faith.

Most Muslims will have no difficulty in accepting the virgin birth (or, rather, virginal conception) of Jesus, since the Qur'ān emphatically affirms it. It is only Muslims of a distinctly liberal persuasion who, like their Christian confrères, call it into question. Christians, moreover, do not claim that Jesus was the Son of God because he was born of a virgin. On the contrary, it was because he was Son of God, when that term is properly understood, that he was born in that miraculous way. I have returned to this subject briefly in the Epilogue to this book.

A unique filial consciousness

We must turn to broader issues. It is a fact, I think, that even radical critics commonly acknowledge the profound filial consciousness which characterized the Jesus of the Gospels. We may surmise, moreover, that the secret did not *primarily* lie in a subjective consciousness of his own identity, but in an intimate knowledge of God as his Father. In Father Louis Bouyer's words: 'We must not try to represent to ourselves this consciousness of Jesus, whether messianic or filial, as being essentially, and still less as being primarily, a reflex consciousness of its own identity'. That, he says, has been the common error of Christologies. But

> the difficulties which that starting point cannot avoid accumulating vanish as soon as we recognize that this consciousness of Jesus, like every normal consciousness, was the consciousness of an object before becoming a consciousness of its own subject. The consciousness of Jesus, as the human consciousness of the Son of God, was before all else consciousness *of God*. Jesus was 'the Christ, the Son of the living God', not directly by knowing that he was, but because he knew God *as the Father* . . . What is unique in the consciousness of Jesus of Nazareth is that it was pierced and traversed, from its first awakening, by that intuition, which was to precede, penetrate, and saturate all his states of consciousness, whatever they might be.[13]

And Père Galot makes the same point when he insists that 'When the Son humanly takes consciousness of himself, he does it as a Son, by taking consciousness of his relation to the Father . . .'[14]

Not only did Jesus habitually refer to God as his Father, but it seems clear that it was his practice to address him by the Aramaic term 'Abba'. This was a child's word, C. F. D. Moule comments,

> and it seems to have been used in ordinary family life, but never (so far as our information goes) in direct address to God, except on the lips, first of Jesus, and then of Christians; and

> even Christians soon reverted to the standardised Jewish form 'our Father in heaven' . . . It looks, then, as though it was Jesus himself who first dared to use this very simple, family address in his prayer to God. It is one of the three or four Aramaic words and phrases used in the traditions of the words of Jesus.[15]

When, moreover, we find St Paul using this same Aramaic word, 'gratuitously embedded in the alien texture' of two letters written in Greek to largely Gentile churches, to describe how the Holy Spirit inspires even Greek-speaking Christians to pray, the retention of this term in its original form can, surely, only be regarded as an authentic – and very precious – memory of the historical Jesus himself. And it seems equally clear that it was a consciousness of this unique filial relationship that alone can explain the serene authority with which he habitually spoke and acted. This amazed his contemporaries; and it still strikes us today as at once paradoxical, yet in his case strangely natural, in one who could claim to be 'meek and lowly in heart' and who was, indeed, accepted by his disciples as such.

If Jesus in fact enjoyed such an intimate relationship with his Father, it is surely natural – and even inevitable – that he should sometimes have put it into words in his teachings as well as his prayers. It is hardly surprising, then, that Matthew records that he preceded his invitation, to all who 'labour and are heavy laden', to come to him (the one who was himself 'meek and lowly in heart') for rest and instruction, by the statement that 'All things have been committed to me by my Father. No-one knows who the Son is except the Father, and no-one knows who the Father is except the Son, and those to whom the Son chooses to reveal him'.[16] Such statements are, of course, much more frequent in the Fourth Gospel, where their authenticity has been widely questioned as incongruous with the picture of Jesus we get from the Synoptic records as a whole. But Professor R. V. G. Tasker aptly remarks that

> Though at times the utterances of Jesus in this Gospel sound harsh . . . there is no valid reason for supposing that, when dealing with the Rabbis at Jerusalem, he did not debate with them in rabbinical fashion the nature of his claims; and it may well be just this side of the Lord's ministry that the Galilean disciples knew little about, but with which the fourth Evangelist was more familiar, particularly if, as has already been suggested, he was himself a Jerusalem disciple.[17]

But, however this may be, we too easily forget that to call Jesus the

'Christ' or 'Messiah' after his crucifixion must have been a continual 'scandal' to Jews and that the title could scarcely have survived 'unless his friends had already become convinced that he was Messiah in some unusual and transcendental sense'. In other words, 'it is easier to trace a transcendental conception of the Son to something in Jesus's own life or person' – or, we might add, his teaching – 'than to account for the continued use, after the crucifixion, of the title Messiah, from which it is proposed to evolve a transcendental Sonship.'[18]

Divine authority

Much more could, of course, be written about the Gospel records as a whole. Instead of the time-honoured prophetic formula 'Thus saith the Lord' the Jesus of the Gospels – the Synoptics and John alike – is remembered as habitually introducing his teaching with the arresting words, 'Amen, I say to you'. It was partly for this reason that the people were 'astonished', because 'unlike the doctors of the law, he taught with a note of authority'.[19] It is in this context that Professor A. M. Hunter insists: 'Search Jewish literature and you will look in vain for a man who prefaces his words with "Amen, I say unto you", who dares to address God as Abba, who tells his disciples that he alone knows the Almighty as Father'.[20]

Again, though he taught his disciples always to pray for forgiveness, there is no suggestion in the Gospel records that he himself had any sense of personal sin whatever – even forgiven sin. Instead, his fellowship with his 'Father' seems to have been uniformly close and unbroken, except only at the time of the 'cry of dereliction' on the cross. But side by side with his fellowship (and, no doubt, mediated by it) we find an ever-growing sense of his unique mission – a divine imperative which continually drove him on. When, moreover, the prospect of his own suffering and death came into view, he clearly interpreted this largely, in terms of Isaiah 53, as 'a ransom for many'; as a 'new covenant' sealed by his blood; and as the very essence 'of that for which he had come, and the heart of his mission and authority'.[21] It is obvious, moreover, that any understanding of what he did depends on who he was, and *vice versa*; for soteriology and Christology *cannot* be separated.

But to the end his disciples did not understand. They may have sensed, in some measure, what Professor H. E. W. Turner terms the 'hinterland of his divinity',[22] but what they knew without a semblance of doubt was that he was truly and unquestionably a man. There was much about him that they could not understand, and many of his statements were inexplicable to them at the time. In particular, his predictions of his coming sufferings fell on deaf ears, and when he was in fact crucified all their hopes were dashed to pieces. What is clear beyond any question is that it was his resurrection and exaltation, and this alone, which constituted the 'watershed' in primitive Christology. In a very real sense, indeed, it represented a wholly new beginning.

To our Muslim friends, we must always remember, mentioning the crucifixion of Jesus inevitably raises the problem of the meaning of the statement in the Qur'ān that the Jews 'did not kill him and did not crucify him, but he was counterfeited for them' (sūra 4:156). Further discussion of this verse will be found at pp. 11f above and p. 201 below.

The resurrection

A new beginning for the disciples this certainly proved to be. Far from 'redeeming Israel' in the way they had expected the Messiah would do, he had been betrayed and crucified, had died and been buried, in what must have seemed to them abject failure and disgrace. *But God had raised him from the dead*; and had thereby turned defeat into victory, and vindicated both his person and his work. On the first Easter morning the tomb was found to be empty; and before evening he had himself appeared to several of his disciples, alone or in groups. A number of unforgettable days had followed, in the course of which he had 'presented himself' to them, 'alive after his passion', in a way they subsequently described as 'many infallible proofs'.

He was changed, indeed, for he now lived on a wholly different plane; yet he was unmistakably the same Jesus, whom they had known so well and could confidently identify, although they sometimes failed to recognize him at once. These 'appearances', moreover, could not be written off as visions, however vivid; for he had actually been 'handled' or touched, and on at least one occasion, we are told, he had given concrete evidence of his objective presence by eating a piece of fish. But though the risen Christ was no ghost or phantom, and could invite a finger to explore the print of the nails, he was *very* different from a resuscitated corpse, and was no longer subject to physical limitations.[23]

The ascension and exaltation

Those wonderful days, during which he came in and went out among them (and taught them something of the meaning of his life and, pre-eminently, of his death), had ended, as he had himself made clear by a visible withdrawal from their sight – for, with Michael Ramsay, I certainly accept the ascension as a historical event. Now they knew that he was exalted 'to the right hand of God'. It seems probable, indeed, that from his own point of view his exaltation or ascension had taken place on Easter day; and his disciples subsequently came to see even his crucifixion, in all its apparent shame and weakness, as part of his exaltation. But although he was no longer with them in the visible and objective manner of the 'forty days', yet he had not left them desolate or alone. On the contrary, he had promised that he would come to them in a new way through the ministry of the Holy Spirit, that 'other Paraclete' (helper, counsellor and comforter) whom he would send to them. And on the day of Pentecost they had just this experience. Now their Master and Friend was spiritually available to each one of them, wherever they might happen to be, for he was omnipresent; and now, for the first time, it seemed natural and right to refer to him as the *Lord Jesus*.[24]

Jesus is Lord

It was, indeed, this title, *Kyrios* or Lord, that soon became the most characteristic way of describing, or addressing, the risen Christ. That it was not confined to Gentile Christians, or even Hellenistic Jews, seems evident from the acclamation or prayer *Maranatha* ('Come, our Lord') preserved in its Aramaic form in 1 Corinthians 16:22. It was applied to Jesus in its full meaning, Oscar Cullmann insists, 'only after his death and exaltation',[25] and it implies not only allegiance and obedience, but worship. Its use in Hellenistic and Oriental mystery cults is sufficiently illustrated by St Paul's statement in 1 Corinthians 8:5 and 6 that 'although there may be so-called gods in heaven or on earth – as indeed there are many "gods" and many "lords" – yet for us there is one God, the Father, from whom are all things and for whom we exist, and one Lord, Jesus Christ, through whom are all things and through whom we exist'.

The significance of the title 'Lord' to Jews was even greater, for it was used in the Septuagint to translate the name of God (*Yahweh* or Jehovah) which the Jews hesitated even to pronounce, and for which they commonly substituted *Adonai*. This, Cullmann writes, 'was certainly the characteristic Jewish designation for God in the first century before and the first century after Christ'.[26] That the title should be instinctively – and without hesitation or explanation – used of the risen Christ by Jews who were monotheists through and through is, therefore, of profound significance. It is recorded, indeed, that even on the day of Pentecost St Peter declared that 'God has made this Jesus, whom you crucified, both Lord and Christ.'[27] Coupled with 'Jesus', this is presumably 'the name which is above every name' to which St Paul refers in Philippians 2:9; for he immediately adds that 'at the name of Jesus every knee shall bow, in heaven and on earth and under the earth, and every tongue confess that Jesus Christ is

Lord, to the glory of God the Father'. This constitutes irrefutable evidence that St Paul – or, as many think, the words of a pre-Pauline Christian hymn which he quoted – did not hesitate to transfer to Jesus 'a great monotheistic passage from Isaiah 45:23 in which God is represented as declaring that he must have no rivals'.[28]

No wonder, then, that what seems to have been the earliest baptismal formula was the confession 'Jesus is Lord' – which equally signified that the Lord (with all that that title meant for a Jew) was identified with Jesus. It is clear, moreover, that from a very early date Christians felt perfectly free to address prayer specifically to the 'Lord Jesus'.[29] It is, indeed, often impossible to know whether a prayer which opens simply with the title 'Lord' is directed to the risen Christ or to God the Father; and it seems certain that the early church made no sharp distinction in this respect. They were fully convinced that the Jesus who had been their teacher and master was now exalted to a place of supreme lordship or authority (for surely this is the sense in which the phrase 'at God's right hand' is to be understood?), and that one day he would come again in power as Lord of all.

To suggest, therefore, that the church 'must have allowed his memory gradually to be built up until it attained divine proportions', and the 'departed Master, at first merely invoked by his disciples, eventually becomes a cult deity, acclaimed by his worshippers', simply will not do. The evidence is dead against it, as Moule insists:

> If the deification of Jesus was the end result of an evolutionary process in pious imagination, how was it that a dedicated Jewish monotheist like Paul, at the earliest known stage of Christian literature, was already treating Christ as 'one with God'? Paul does not, it is true, use ontological terms of being or essence; but the implications of what he says are difficult to formulate without it. Whatever explanation is offered for this extraordinary phenomenon, the facile theory of an evolving superstition will not do. It simply does not fit the facts.[30]

The downward approach

Adoptionism

How, then, did the apostolic church now look back on the days of Jesus' earthly ministry; and how did they reconcile their view of the exalted Lord with the monotheism which was as precious to them as to the Judaism from which so many of them had sprung or, indeed, to Islam today? One early answer to this question is provided by what is termed 'Adoptionism'. This is the theory that Jesus was originally not only a true man (a fact which none of those who had 'companied' with him so intimately would have questioned for a moment), but nothing more than a man. Then, at a certain point, he was 'adopted' by God as his 'Son' and raised to divinity or quasi-divinity.

Something like this, for example, was held soon after the fall of Jerusalem by Cerinthus (an Asian Jew who was an early Gnostic teacher), who believed that the purely human Jesus was chosen to be Son of God at his baptism when he was united with 'the aeon Christ', who was himself regarded as above the archangels but not fully divine. Different forms of 'adoptionism' have been expounded by a wide variety of teachers, some of them distinctly heretical and others rather more moderate, down the centuries. It may well be that some echo of such teaching can be heard in verses in the Qur'ān such as sūra 39:6 ('Should Allāh wish to have off-spring, He would choose what He willeth of what He created. Glory be to Him!').

But should we be justified in concluding, with John Knox, that 'the earliest Christology was adoptionist' – as, he asserts, 'we should have expected it to be – but with the moment of adoption not his baptism, but rather his resurrection and exaltation'? The clearest example of this, in Knox's view, is Peter's statement, in Acts 2:36, that 'God has made this Jesus, whom you crucified, both Lord and Messiah'. On this he comments: 'how can this passage be interpreted to mean anything else than that the man Jesus, crucified simply as such, was at the resurrection exalted to his present messianic status?' He admits that it can be clearly shown that

> the author of Luke-Acts had a higher or more advanced, a less simple Christology than the adoptionism I have described. The whole treatment of the earthly life of Jesus in the Gospel section of his work and many an allusion to it in the Acts section indicate beyond question that he did not think of Jesus' messiahship as having been conferred on him only after his human career had ended. Jesus was always 'Son of God'; he was not adopted or installed as such, whether at the resurrection or earlier.

But, he insists, the question 'is not whether the author of Luke-Acts held an adoptionist Christology but whether evidence for the primitive existence of such a Christology is to be found in his work.'[31]

It seems to me, however, that in this argument far too much emphasis is put on the single word 'made' in Acts 2:36. In a very similar passage St Paul states that 'Jesus Christ our Lord' was 'descended from David according to the flesh and designated Son of God in power, according to the Spirit of holiness, by his resurrection from the dead.'[32] But this does not in any way imply that Jesus was not Son of God as well as son of David during his earthly ministry, but simply that he was openly shown and declared to be so by the resurrection.

Again, Dr John Robinson points out that there are many passages in the Epistle to the Hebrews which, taken by themselves, could well be interpreted in an adoptionist sense: for example, that Jesus was 'appointed the heir of all things', has 'become superior to the angels', was 'anointed with the oil of gladness above his fellows', was 'crowned with glory and honour because of the suffering of death', and was 'designated a high priest',[33] etc. Robinson himself however, also calls attention to the fact that this same epistle 'begins with the most stupendous affirmation of Christ, in contrast with all previous and partial revelations of God', as a Son 'who is the effulgence of God's splendour and the stamp of God's very being and sustains the universe by his word of power'.[34] Unless, therefore, we are to regard all the phrases in Hebrews which *could* be interpreted in an adoptionist sense as relics of an earlier view unconsciously preserved by the author – a suggestion which would, I think, stretch our credulity to the limit – it seems clear that the verses concerned should not be taken as evidence for any truly adoptionist Christology.

This is brought into particularly sharp relief by the fact that the author couples in one sentence the statement that it was through the Son whom God '*appointed* heir of all things' that he had previously 'created the world'.[35] What these verses do emphasize, beyond question, is that whatever we are to think of Jesus during his earthly life – and, indeed, of the many New Testament references to his pre-existence, to which we must soon turn – there is a real sense in which the fact that he had been 'made like to his brethren', was 'in every respect tempted as we are', and, above all, had been willing to 'taste death for every one' and 'make propitiation for the sins of the people', had opened up what was clearly a new ministry as our High Priest 'in the power of an endless life'. Before he could assume this he *had*, indeed, to be 'made perfect through suffering' and to enter 'once for all into the Holy Place . . . through his own blood.'[36]

Pre-existence

It is not only in the Epistle to the Hebrews, moreover, that we find references to the pre-existence of Christ. St Paul, for example, refers to it – sometimes by direct statements and sometimes by almost unconscious allusions – in a number of different contexts. The fact that he does this without any argument or explanation demonstrates beyond doubt, as several authors have remarked, that the idea was widespread and well understood in the circles to which he was writing. This leads John Knox to admit that there are

> good reasons for believing that the Church's attribution of a divine pre-existence to Jesus was not, as it has sometimes been thought to be, the final step in a gradual process of pressing back the moment of his 'adoption' to an earlier and earlier time – from resurrection, to transfiguration, to baptism, to birth – until finally it was pushed out of the earthly life entirely and the idea of pre-existence was demanded. Such a process would have required time and could hardly have been completed early enough to account for the general acceptance of the idea in the period of Paul's letters. Rather, we are given grounds for believing – what would also seem inherently probable – that reflection on the resurrection and on the post-resurrection status of Christ led directly and immediately to the affirmation of his pre-existence.[37]

Much the same thesis has recently been discussed in far more detail by C. F. D. Moule in an article published in *Theologia Evangelica*,[38] where he maintains that, although the New Testament writers differ considerably among themselves in their conceptions of how, precisely, the exalted Christ was – and is – experienced by Christians, 'they all seem unanimously to reflect two convictions: first, that the Lord whom they revere and acclaim is continuous with the Jesus of Nazareth who had been crucified: none other than Jesus himself; and secondly, that he is transcendent and divine.' So Moule asks the pertinent question: 'If, subsequently to his death, he is conceived of as an eternally living being, personal but more than individual, one with God and the source of salvation, and if he is still firmly identified with Jesus of Nazareth, then what of his pre-existence? Can "eternal" personality existing after the incarnation be denied existence before it?'[39]

The Logos

Again, the conviction of Christ's pre-existence is at least as prominent in the Fourth Gospel as it is in the Pauline Epistles. Much has been written about the background to John's doctrine of the Logos in Stoic philosophy and, still more, in that of Philo of Alexandria, on the one hand, and in the Jewish belief in the 'Word of the Lord' by which the heavens were made (and which, like the Name of the Lord and the divine Wisdom, is almost personified in the Old Testament), on the other. But if, as is widely assumed, the Prologue to John's Gospel was written after the bulk of its contents, then it seems to me that we can scarcely doubt that a primary factor in the mind of the author must have been those allusions to pre-existence which he had already recorded as made by Jesus himself – however impossible it had been for the disciples to understand them at the time.[40]

In what Dr John Marsh aptly calls 'The Lord's Prayer' in John 17, for example, Jesus is recorded as having prayed: 'and now, Father, glorify thou me in thy own presence with the glory which I had with thee before the world was made.' On this R. H. Lightfoot remarks that 'The Lord . . . now prays that in this final hour He may be glorified at the Father's side with the glory which was His at the Father's side before the world existed', and comments: 'The glory for which the Lord, His work on earth completed, prays here, and to which He refers in 17:24, is the glory of the eternal Word, the glory which is His by nature and right;[41] and Marsh refers to the 'premundial glory of the Son which was his before the world was made and historical time began'.[42]

This is not the place to embark on any discussion of the Logos doctrine, which, no doubt, finds an echo in the Quranic statement, in sūra 4:169, that ʿĪsā was God's 'Word which He cast upon Mary, and a spirit from Him'. We shall return to this verse. But in view of what I have just said it seems to me totally inadequate to interpret Christ's pre-existence, with several of those whose views we shall cite, simply in terms of fore-ordination, or of signifying that he had existed, before his human birth, only in the plan and mind of God. Knox tries to go marginally beyond this when he says that, when we join the church

> in confessing the pre-existence, we are asserting . . . that God, the Father Almighty, Maker of the heavens and the earth, was back of, present in, and acting through the whole event of which the human life of Jesus was the centre. We are saying that *God* was in Christ – not in the resurrection only, but in the whole human career from conception through death . . . To say of the human Jesus, now exalted and transfigured, the 'first fruits' and the guarantor of humanity's redemption, that he had been in process of being created or begotten (in an organic view of reality this distinction loses much of its importance) since time began, and that in God's 'mind' he existed 'before all worlds' – existed as the particular person he was and for the unique destiny he was to fulfil – to say this or something like this is to say all that can be said except in terms of myth or story.[43]

For in his view, to put the matter bluntly: 'We can have the humanity without the pre-existence and we can have the pre-existence without the humanity. There is absolutely no way of having both.'[44] But would not very much the same remark be equally applicable to any *full* belief in Christ's present exaltation, as Professor Geoffrey Lampe recognized?[45]

What Knox, Robinson and a host of other contributors to what I have termed the 'contemporary debate' are determined at any cost to avoid is, of course, any form of Docetism – that is, the idea that Jesus was not really a man, in any full sense of that term, but a divine visitor who merely 'seemed' to be a man. This was, in fact, one of the very earliest heresies in the church. Although it has been repeatedly repudiated and denied in our Creeds and formularies, there can be no doubt that what has been aptly termed 'psychological Docetism' has, all down the centuries, been an ever recurrent phenomenon.

Indeed, as I look back at my own youth and early middle age, I am conscious that I thought of Jesus in such a way that his humanity was very largely swallowed up in his deity. In one sense this is, I think, almost inevitable, for we are now primarily concerned with the exalted Christ – quite apart from our view of his pre-existence, and of the doctrine of the Trinity as such. So, however much we may disagree with some of their conclusions, we owe a real debt to those of our contemporaries who have forced us to think much more radically and seriously of 'the *man* Christ Jesus', and to ponder anew the mystery of how the Word could, in very fact, '*become* flesh'.

The mystery of the incarnation

This mystery is, of course, the fundamental problem of Christology – and it is immediately inherent in the simple confession: 'Jesus is Lord'. It is summed up, in a somewhat more theological form, in the doctrinal statement that he was, and is, *vere deus, vere homo* – truly God and truly man. But how can this be? How, in other words, can Christ be one with us, in our basic humanity, with all that this means, and yet one with God in his essential deity, with all that that implies? Both aspects of this problem are inevitably involved in the 'mystery of the incarnation'. How could Godhead and humanity co-exist in one person – the Jesus of the Gospels? Was he a demi-god, as the Arians used to assert, but as the church firmly denied? Did he in fact have two natures – a human and a divine – in one person, as classical orthodoxy declares? If so, were they strictly parallel, so that sometimes the one might be operative and sometimes the other, in a way which would appear almost schizophrenic? Or was the human nature somehow subsumed in the divine?

All these points, and many others, were the subject of debate – and, indeed, bitter controversy – in past centuries of the church's history.

It was to guard against innumerable exaggerations, deviations and heresies that the Nicene Creed, the Definition of Chalcedon, and other doctrinal statements were drawn up. They have been much criticized, in the contemporary debate, because they are couched in a language which is not very meaningful today; because they are static rather than dynamic, ontological rather than functional; because they present us with a philosophical abstraction, rather than a living person; or because they go too far, whether positively or negatively, in trying to define the indefinable.

Yet it is scarcely adequate, in terms of some devotional comments I have read, to remark: 'How a Person of the Godhead could become a babe, could join, in the most intimate union, His eternal wisdom with the innocence of a child; could unite infinite knowledge with a daily growth in knowledge; is beyond our comprehension. But it is so, and we can only bow and worship.' That we must 'bow and worship' I have no doubt whatever; but surely we must also make some *attempt* to understand, and to avoid making statements which seem merely to cancel one another out? It is partly, I think, the obscurantism in which we so often indulge in this context which has driven some contemporary theologians, as we shall see, to the verge of – or in some cases right into – Unitarianism.

What is *not* open to us, I suggest, is to dismiss the whole subject in the 'no nonsense' manner of C. Edward Barker, a Methodist minister turned psycho-therapist, in *The Church's Neurosis and Twentieth Century Revelations*. In this publication, commended in glowing terms by Canon J. Pearce-Higgins, the author writes of the incarnation:

> This doctrine is considered the foundation stone of Christian belief. The incarnation affirms that the eternal God became man in the person of Jesus. In other words, Jesus was in fact God veiled in human flesh. As the author of Colossians wrote – 'For it is in Christ that the complete being of the Godhead dwells embodied'. This amazing statement implies that Jesus was not only divine by nature, was not only a Son of God, but was God himself in human form.

Then, after quoting part of the Nicene Creed and Paul Tillich's insistence that 'the assertion that "God has become man" is not a paradoxical but a nonsensical statement', Barker continues:

> To attempt to tailor the concept of the incarnation to the needs of our scientific age, with its pragmatic and existential approach to life, is useless. These elaborate theological statements owe

> their origins, not to Jesus, but to the contentious theologians of the early Church. As for St Paul, he was not concerned with the basic contents of Jesus's message. He was almost wholly obsessed with the idea of a 'cosmic catalyst', a divine intervener who would bring together Jews and Gentiles into a harmony of belief, and would act as a salve for guilt.[46]

This summary repudiation, as 'patently unreasonable', 'nonsense'. and 'no longer tenable', of a doctrine which has been accepted by the church all down the centuries, treasured by its greatest saints and explored by its most brilliant thinkers, seems to me sheer arrogance – to say nothing of the positive parody of St Paul's teaching (which was, in any case, substantially shared by St Peter, St John, the author of Hebrews, *etc.*). On such a basis there could, of course, be no such thing as an objective atonement, so it is natural enough that Barker should conclude that:

> This 'reconciliation' by the cross – a cosmic event whereby the 'Incarnate Son of God' bore the sins of the world in his own flesh – is not the good news of Jesus but an artifact of Paul . . . Paul's concentration on *the work of Christ* in dying for us on the cross has had the effect of turning Christianity into a morbid Crossianity. Paul's concentration on sin and its cleansing has led to obsessive traits in Christian believers. It has encouraged moral masochism, false piety and false humility, and not least, a pathetic 'Christian resignation' that is synonymous with defeatism.[47]

One turns with relief from such a complete caricature of both the New Testament and Christian experience to a writer like D. M. Baillie, who certainly cannot be accused of not taking the humanity of our Lord sufficiently seriously. Indeed, he goes so far as to suggest that

> God was continually pressing through into human life in every age, so far as man would allow, and the reason why the Incarnation did not take place earlier is because man was not sufficiently receptive . . . Therefore, when at last God broke through into human life with full revelation and became incarnate, must we not say that in a sense it was because here at last a Man was perfectly receptive?

But Baillie evidently realized that this statement was inadequate, and felt compelled to add:

Yet there is more to be said . . . The divine is always prevenient. And so from the human life of Jesus on earth we are, paradoxically but inevitably, led back to its divine origin and eternal background in heaven, on which it all depended. 'When the fullness of time was come, God sent forth his Son', and He who was 'born of a woman, born under the law', lived as He did because He was Son of God.[48]

CHAPTER SIX

Christology down the centuries

In my last chapter I tried to etch in some of the background to the contemporary debate about the incarnation and to outline part of the New Testament data. So it would, I think, be useful – particularly for those who have a minimal, confused, or somewhat rusty knowledge of the history of Christian doctrine – to interpose a synopsis of the way in which christological thought has developed down the centuries, and to note the constant recurrence, in many different forms, of some of the basic problems with which scholars are still grappling today and to which further references must inevitably be made.

Some readers may, however, find this summary of the controversies of the past too detailed and technical for their taste, and may prefer to concentrate exclusively on the biblical evidence and the contemporary situation. For such it may suffice to say that the classical formulas in which the historic faith of the Christian church has been expressed – such as the 'Nicene Creed' and the 'Definition of Chalcedon' – were the result of the need to express and safeguard, against a number of views which were felt to be deviant or erroneous, two basic truths: first, that Jesus was both God and man; secondly, that he was one person, not two.

Even on this basis there were, of course, different ways in which the 'mystery of the incarnation' could be approached and understood. It is fascinating to note how constantly theories which seem to be new represent little more than a restatement, perhaps with minor variations, of some thesis which has been debated and discarded long ago, or even repeatedly. The purpose of this chapter is to summarize, for those who want it, the way in which these formulas were evolved and debated (usually in the course of controversy, and in a form which was dictated, in part, by the philosophical thought-patterns of the day) from the primary testimony of the New Testament and the living experience of the church. But it would be perfectly possible for some readers to skim or even skip this chapter – for the present at least.

This suggestion may be especially relevant to Muslim readers, since a considerable proportion of the age-long debate about Christology and the Godhead makes stiff, rather than particularly edifying, reading. If, however, they persevere in reading this chapter (whether at this point or, perhaps, later) it may serve to emphasize three important points.

The first is that Christians have certainly not failed to perceive – and to debate among themselves with passion and even unseemly aggression – the possible objections to what eventually became the orthodox teaching on Christology (and, indeed, the Trinity) throughout what is virtually the universal church.

Secondly, most of the disputes and divisions on this subject took place in the centuries before the birth of Muḥammad, who was in intermittent and largely friendly contact, in varying degrees, with members of the Byzantine, Monophysite and Nestorian churches. So it would have been miraculous if he had not got some mistaken impressions from the sectarian differences then current – or surviving from the past – among contemporary Christians.

Thirdly, in the final analysis it is impossible for finite minds to comprehend the infinite, for fallen creatures to plumb the mysteries of their creator. Christians are at one with their Muslim friends in proclaiming the unique unity of the Godhead and refusing to recognize, or associate with him, any other god. But Christians have learnt, both from divine revelation and personal experience, that the unity of the Godhead is far from *simple*, but deeply *satisfying*.

While, however, Muḥammad himself, and early Muslims in general, had considerable contact with Christians – including the hermits of the desert wastes to whom the early ascetics and mystics felt particularly attracted – it was not until the time of the Umayyad dynasty, broadly speaking, that a direct intellectual confrontation between Christians and Muslims developed. The Umayyads were easy going and far from fanatical, and of John of Damascus (*c.* 675–*c.* 749), Macdonald writes that:

> the last great doctor of the Greek Church and the man under whose hands its theology assumed final form, became wazir and held that post until he withdrew from the world and turned to the contemplative life. In his writings and in those of his pupil, Theodorus Abucara (d. AD 826), there are polemical treatises on Islam, cast in the form of discussions between Christians and Muslims. These represent, there can be little

doubt, a characteristic of the time.[1]

In particular, Macdonald insists that the close agreement of the ideas of the *Murji'īs* (*cf.* p. 57 above) and the *Qadarīs* (*cf.* pp. 19 and 57 above) with those formulated and defended by John of Damascus, and by the Greek church generally, can only be so explained. Of the *Qadarīs* I wrote: 'They upheld the freedom of the human will and denied that God predestined man's evil and unbelief', while of the *Murji'īs* I recorded the fact that they refused to follow the more fanatical Shīʿīs (who insisted that only those who recognized the true Imām were genuine Muslims), or the equally fanatical Khawārij (who insisted that any unrepented sin constituted apostasy). Instead, they recognized the Umayyads as their rulers and deferred any such judgments as those of the extremists until they were expressed by God himself on the day of judgment. Like the Muʿtazilīs, who attained such widespread influence later, they could quote verses from the Qur'ān which they alleged supported their views; but orthodox Muslim teaching remained strongly predestinarian. As Macdonald put it:

> The Murji'ite rejection of eternal punishment and emphasis on the goodness of God and His love for His creatures, the Qadarite doctrine of freewill and responsibility, are to be explained in the same way as we have already explained the presence of sentences in the Muslim *fiqh* which seem to be taken bodily from the Roman codes. In this case, also, we are not to think of the Muslim divines as studying the writings of the Greek fathers, but as picking up ideas from them in practical intercourse and controversy. The very form of the tract of John of Damascus is significant, 'When the Saracen says to you such and such, then you will reply. . . .'[2]

So, as we turn to the development of Christology down the centuries, we shall note, from time to time, the way in which verses in the Qur'ān seem to echo (whether in affirmation or denial) the doctrines taught by one or another of the participants in the christological debate.

We have seen how the disciples regarded Jesus, during the days of his ministry, as teacher, prophet and Messiah – but unquestionably as a man among men. So the crucifixion must have shattered all their hopes, for how could one who had been condemned and executed as a criminal be the promised Redeemer of Israel? Instead of being vindicated by God he had, to all appearances, been rejected by him; and it was only the cataclysmic experience of the resurrection which brought them, bewildered and at first doubting, to a wondering and unquenchable joy. Now they were convinced that the 'Lord' Jesus had been 'exalted to the right hand of God' and would one day come again to usher in the Kingdom he had preached. Instinctively, therefore, they began to associate him with God, and sometimes to address him in prayer. At an exceedingly early date, moreover, they came to believe in his pre-existence, in the role he had played in the very creation of the world, and in the fact that all things that exist are 'held together in him' – for it is deeply significant that none of the attacks on St Paul and his teaching during his lifetime seem to have been directed against his Christology, which was, in fact, shared by all the New Testament writers.

Two early heresies

It is scarcely surprising, therefore, that one of the earliest Christian heresies, to which references are made in the New Testament itself, was what came to be known as Docetism; for it was natural enough that Gentile converts, who had never known 'the man, Christ Jesus', should sometimes think of him in terms of a theophany. In its extreme form Docetism was the belief that Jesus had never, in fact, been a man at all; he had, indeed, *seemed* to be a man, but he was really God – or at least a divine being – appearing in human guise. That some such view was propagated by false teachers at a very early date is amply attested by the Johannine epistles. John, for example, propounds two basic tests of whether any doctrine is inspired by the 'Spirit of God' or the spirit of 'Anti-Christ'. The first test is whether the doctrine concerned affirms or denies that Jesus is the Christ 'come in the flesh'.[3] This criterion is also enunciated in the statement in the second letter that 'many deceivers have gone out into the world, men who do not acknowledge Jesus as the Christ coming in the flesh; such a one is the deceiver and the anti-Christ'.[4] In less extreme forms (which do not deny that Jesus had a genuinely human body – or even both body and psyche – but which, in one way or another, deny his full and complete manhood) Docetism, or 'psychological Docetism', has been an ever-recurrent phenomenon which has never ceased to trouble the Christian church.

The second test of false teaching in 1 John is whether it so fails to confess that 'Jesus is the Christ' that it in fact denies 'the Father and the Son'.[5] This test was, presumably, primarily aimed at the Jewish-Christian sect of 'Ebionites' who believed that Jesus was not divine, virgin-born or pre-existent, but was created as one of the archangels on whom, as 'Christ', the Holy Spirit descended at his baptism.[6] It would also cover Gnostic sectaries who, like the followers of Cerinthus, regarded Jesus as having been a mere man until he was united, at his baptism, with the aeon Christ – who left him, according to one form of this teaching, before the passion.[7]

This is, indeed, one of many suggested explanations of the Quranic denial that the Jews 'killed the Messiah, Jesus, son of Mary' (sūra 4:156). Basilides, an Egyptian Gnostic of the second century, is even said to have 'taught that the divine Nous (intelligence) appeared in human form, but at the crucifixion he changed forms with Simon of Cyrene who had carried the cross; the Jews took Simon and nailed him to the cross instead of Jesus who stood by deriding them for their error before ascending to heaven.'[8]

It was against some such perversions of the truth that the reference to Jesus as 'the Son of God . . . who came by water and blood' ('not by water only, but by water and blood')[9] was directed, according to the interpretation of this somewhat obscure allusion first suggested by Tertullian: namely, that the 'water' refers to his baptism, at which the divine voice proclaimed him to be 'My beloved Son', while the 'blood' represents a sort of shorthand symbol for his death on the cross. As in the case of Docetism, this extreme form of Gnostic teaching has long since disappeared. But somewhat similar, although more moderate, doctrines, which may be grouped together under the umbrella of Adoptionism, have reappeared, as we have seen, down the centuries. Some have been more, and some less, heretical and they are sometimes alleged to be the earliest form of Christology.

The nature of God

It was, of course, inevitable that the confession 'Jesus is Lord' should raise theological problems. The apostles not only proclaimed the risen Christ as exalted to God's right hand, but explicitly identified him with Jesus of Nazareth. This was bound to give rise, sooner rather than later, to christological debate. But the major problem of the second and third centuries revolved round the nature of God rather than that of Jesus. This was natural enough, for the unity of the Godhead was as fundamental to Judaism as to Islam today. How, then, could Jewish Christians call Jesus 'Lord', address him in prayer, and somehow identify him with Israel's covenant God, Yahweh? Had they ceased to be monotheists? Or did this mean that there was a previously unsuspected complexity in the divine unity which went far beyond the semi-personification of Wisdom, and the Spirit and Word of the Lord, in the Old Testament? This problem was first apprehended, it seems, in 'binitarian' terms, which concentrated only on the Father and the Son; but later it came to take a trinitarian form.

Monarchianism

How, in either case, was the differentiation within the unity of the Godhead to be understood? Was it in terms of what came to be called 'Monarchianism' – a name derived from the Greek word *monarchia* which emphasizes 'the sole rule of God or one sole originating principle in God', but which was in fact used in reference to two distinct schools of thought? The first, properly known as 'Dynamic Monarchianism', seems to represent a dubious use of the term, for it was applied to men who 'affirmed two entities in the Godhead (the Father and the Son or the Spirit) without any special emphasis either on the unity of the Godhead or on their relation to each other'. They were called Dynamic Monarchians because they held that the divine rested upon the man Jesus as a power (*dynamis*); so their teaching could aptly be described as 'Dynamic Binitarianism'.

The other school of thought was that of 'Modalist Monarchianism', a term applied to those who understood the distinctions in the Godhead as no more than three 'modes' or manifestations of the divine unity. Early Modalists, like Dynamic Monarchians, phrased their doctrine purely in terms of the Father and the Son; but on their premises, as Professor H. E. W. Turner observes, 'three modes would present no more difficulty than two'. It was in fact in a trinitarian form that Sabellius expounded Modalism early in the third century; and the essence of his teaching was that God is by nature a monad, one *hypostasis* or essence with three names or modes of revelation, which Sabellius apparently regarded as successive rather than simultaneous.[10]

Praxeas, another Modalist, exaggerated the idea of the *monarchia*, and

> became leader of the so-called Patripassian Monarchians – i.e. those concerned to maintain the unity of the Godhead even to the point of declaring that God the Father suffered. As Tertullian put it, 'he drove out prophecy and introduced heresy: he put to flight the Paraclete and crucified the Father.' Praxeas conceived of Father and Son as one identical Person . . . Consequently it was the Father who entered the Virgin's womb, thus becoming, so to speak, His own Son who suffered, died and rose again.[11]

Is there, perhaps, an echo of this heresy in the twice repeated statement in the Qur'ān: 'Assuredly they have disbelieved who say that Allāh is the Messiah, son of Mary'? (sūras 5:19 and 76)

The 'Economic Trinity'

Tertullian, who denounced this teaching, was 'himself a defender of the *monarchia*,' but in the much more orthodox form of what came to be termed the 'Economic Trinity'. Economic Trinitarianism held that the Son and the Spirit did not 'have the status of full *Hypostases* but of economies or functional dispensations of the one God extrapolated for the purposes of creation and redemption'.[12] Tertullian's own view, for most of his life, was that

> Father, Son and Spirit are in the one total reality of God. The Son proceeds from this one *substantia* as it is in the Father and thereby receives his own reality, without being separated. Son and Spirit are distinguished through the order of their origin. Tertullian also describes the character of the Son (and the Spirit) by the word *portio*. This does not mean 'part' (*pars*). The Son is not a 'part' of the divine substance, but has a 'share' in it . . . The divine substance is essentially one; the Son is, as it were, an effluence of this one substance . . . [13]

But Economic Trinitarianism reached 'its most sophisticated form in Marcellus of Ancyra, with precisely dated extrapolations and the return of the Godhead into monadic isolation at the conclusion of the economy'.[14] It has, moreover, been espoused in a very modified form, in recent years, by Karl Barth among others, largely because of the misunderstanding to which the use of the term 'Persons' in relation to the Godhead may so easily give rise today. Barth prefers, therefore, to speak of three 'modes of being' in God. But this is not Modalism in the heretical or Sabellian sense. Barth regards this as a grave error. His concept of the doctrine of the Trinity stands for

> real distinctions in God, and, moreover, for the *kind* of distinctions on which orthodox [Christian] belief has always insisted: the three Persons are not *parts* of God, and yet they are not mere attributes, or shifting aspects, relative to our apprehension . . . but are of the eternal being of the God who has revealed Himself to us in Christ and dwells in us by the Holy Spirit.[15]

Tritheism

The opposite pole from Modalism, or from any monist theory of the nature of God, is that of Tritheism, 'in which the plurality of the persons approximates to belief in three Gods' (of which, at a later date, the Cappadocean Fathers were mistakenly accused). Tritheism has *never* been the official doctrine of any church, although Christians are sometimes accused of it by Jews, and particularly by Muslims. It is, for example, denounced in the Qur'ān in sūra 5:77 ('Assuredly, they are deceived who say: "Allāh is one of three".') Some Muslims may, indeed, have been prompted to accuse Christians of tritheism by the verse in the Qur'ān in which God is depicted as asking Jesus 'was it thou who didst say to the people: "Take me and my mother as two gods apart from Allāh"?' (sūra 5:116).

The origin of this strange verse is uncertain. Some have suggested that 'because *Ruh* (Spirit) in Syriac is used in the feminine there was a misidentification of the Holy Spirit with the Virgin', and have pointed out that in the apocryphal *Gospel to the Hebrews* Jesus is made to refer to 'my mother, the Holy Spirit'. Others detect in the words of the Qur'ān 'an echo of the Nestorian protest against the title *theotokos* ('one who gave birth to God) for the virgin – or, indeed, a general protest against the excessive veneration, or even worship, which has been accorded to her. After recording these suggestions, however, J. W. Sweetman adds:

> On the other hand, it may be that a sort of divine family similar to that in pagan myths was in the mind of the Prophet in his protest against [this concept of] the Trinity. We must remember that such notions might have been familiar to Arab paganism and that the Prophet would be right in protesting either against tritheism or such a pagan idea, and that Christians themselves could also protest against such a misreading of the doctrine of the Trinity as that found in the pages of the Qur'ān, or against an incarnation through the conjunction of a god with a woman.'[16]

Any such idea as this would, of course, be unthinkable to Christians. But Tritheism, however conceived, is at best an error into which some Christians may have fallen in their attempts to explain the Trinity.[17]

But 'pluralist' speculations, in their more recondite form, may have opened the door, as it were, to the Arian heresy, which included in a single formula a Father who was fully God, a Son who had the status of a leading creature, and a Spirit who was inferior to the Son.[18] To this we must return soon.

In general terms, however, theologians in the West can be said to have adopted, from Tertullian to Augustine, a firmly monist starting point in their approach to the doctrine of the Trinity, while in the East 'pluralism based on a Platonic interpretation of Christianity became the dominant tradition'.[19] This was developed by Origen, whose trinitarian doctrine was pluralist in framework, and whose special contribution was the doctrine of the eternal generation of the Son by the Father. But although, in his view, all the members of the Trinity were divine, this was, it seems, in a 'graded Trinity' in which the Son mediated the Father to the created world and the Spirit was the first production of the Son.[20]

From what I have already written two points, I think, stand out clearly. First, it was the resurrection, and the consequent conviction that the exalted Lord was somehow one with the Father, that forced the early church to ponder the nature of the Godhead. It is only natural, therefore, that they often spoke in binitarian terms, and that a full trinitarian doctrine should come later. But a strong case can be made for the claim that this was not 'a sort of evolutionary process' but merely a development of what was already inherent, if not explicit, in the New Testament.[21] Secondly, two approaches to the differentiations within the Godhead were possible.

> Monist theologians started from the unity of the Godhead and worked tentatively towards divine plurality . . . Pluralist thinkers, on the other hand, maintained the full co-presence of two (later three) distinct entities within the Godhead and sought a bond of unity strong enough to support their convictions. Unity of derivation from the Father (the Monarchy), harmony of will and finally identity of substance, *Ousia (Homoousios)*, were all laid under contribution.[22]

The Apologists

This digression into some of the developments in trinitarian doctrine during the second and third centuries helps to explain why the great christological controversies of the fourth and fifth centuries tended at first to concentrate on the divine rather than the human problems inherent in the doctrine of the incarnation, and took what I have termed the downward rather than the upward approach (*cf.* pp. 117f above). But the 'Apologists' of the second and third centuries, such as Justin Martyr and Athenagoras, had in a sense paved the way for later controversies by the way in which they tried to express their understanding of the faith in the philosophical language of their educated contemporaries.

In this task they relied greatly on the concept of the Logos, or

'Word' of God. We have already quoted the Quranic echo of this major Christian doctrine in sūra 4:169, which states that ʿĪsā was 'God's Word which he cast upon Mary, and a spirit from him.' Sadly, orthodox Muslims never developed this imagery in the terms of John 1:1 ('In the beginning was the Word, and the Word was with God, and the Word was God'), or of John 1:14 ('The Word became flesh and made his dwelling among us. We have seen his glory, the glory of the One and Only, who came from the Father, full of grace and truth'). Meanwhile the Apologists and their successors worked away, not very adequately, at the full Christian doctrine, as proclaimed by St John.

The contemporary view of God in Hellenistic thought was so abstract and transcendent that he could have no contact with the world except through a mediator. Only the Logos could perform this function. To the Apologists he was a product of the Father's will. Although eternally immanent as a principle in God, in due time he came forth in order to create all things. 'Finite in His own being, since there was a time when He began to be, He forms the natural organ of revelation to the finite', and though 'subordinate to the highest God,' he might 'be called a second God, and ought to be worshipped.'[23]

Irenaeus, Tertullian, Clement and Origen

The Apologists were followed by Irenaeus, Tertullian, Clement and Origen, who all put a major emphasis on the divine Logos. Irenaeus taught that, as Logos, God had always been manifested in the world, first through the prophets, and finally in Christ his Son. 'Through the Word Himself, who had become visible and palpable', he affirmed, 'was the Father shown forth; all saw the Father in the Son: *for the Father is the invisible of the Son, but the Son the visible of the Father*.'[24] So Irenaeus tended 'to construe the Logos not as somehow a portion of the Godhead, much less a second, inferior God, but as God himself breaking forth in revelation'[25] – a view which clearly prepared the way for the Modalist Monarchianism to which reference has already been made.

Tertullian was, it seems, the first person to use the word *trinitas* and to construct the formula 'One substance, three persons', although the reality behind the term *trinitas* is innate in the New Testament and virtually spelt out in verses such as 2 Corinthians 13:14 and 1 Peter 1:2. To Tertullian the Logos was first 'existent in God, as it were . . . in potentiality', and then 'arose out of God as Son by generation before all worlds, being thus projected, or invested with independent being, with a view to the creation of the universe. Thus He had a beginning.'[26] It was this pre-existent Logos or Son who, in the fullness of time, assumed flesh for our salvation – which represents 'the last stage in the coming of the Logos to full personal existence'.

Clement, in turn, concentrated on the Logos doctrine in a way which tended, partially, to 'depersonalise the historic Saviour'. Viewed from below, as Mackintosh puts it, 'He appears as the fullness of the Godhead, concentred in an independent life; from above He is the highest next to the Almighty, the minister of God, mediating all created life, and at a certain distance from the Father as the absolute monad'.[27] But Clement could be strangely self-contradictory. Origen, as we have seen, insisted that, as Son, the Logos proceeds from the Father by an eternal generation. Hence to say that a time was when the Son was not, was an error.[28]

The Arian heresy

By contrast, Arius flatly asserted that, if the Father 'begat' the Son, there *must* have been a time when the Son did not exist. God was a remote and inaccessible being who did not himself create the world except, indirectly, through the Logos, who was at one and the same time a divine and a created being. This was no mere matter of theological hair-splitting, as D. M. Baillie emphasizes, nor was it

> an argument as to whether there was in Jesus a supernatural incarnation of the heavenly pre-existent Logos or Son of God, for the Arians themselves believed that the Logos or Son of God, who had existed from before all ages in glory as a heavenly being above all angels, had come to earth through a virgin birth, lived a supernatural life in a human body, was crucified, rose from the dead, and ascended to heaven, to be worshipped with divine honours. They believed all that. But what availed all that, when they did not believe that this Logos was of one essence with God the Father?

For on this basis 'it is not the eternal God himself that comes to us in Christ for our salvation, but an intermediate being, distinct from God, while God himself is left out, uncondescending, unredemptive.[29]

But this doctrine was just as destructive in the realm of Christology as in that of the Trinity, for the Arians regarded the Son as a sort of demi-god; 'a creature, but not as one of the creatures'. He was a mediator between God and man by being himself neither fully God nor fully man, rather than by being both at one and the same time. They supported their case by pointing to the Gospels, which make it perfectly clear that Jesus grew in wisdom, did not know the date of his second advent, and suffered not only in body but also in soul.

They attributed all this, moreover, to the divine Logos incarnate in him; so this meant that the Logos could change, could be ignorant and could suffer.

God however, – in the dominant philosophical view of the day – was not only transcendent and self-existent, but also immutable, omniscient and impassible. Clearly, then, the Logos could not be fully God. The Arians, moreover, do not seem to have been greatly concerned with the doctrine of redemption, which is an essential element in any adequate Christology. Turner therefore remarks that 'an important control on their Christology was missing', and that Arianism was as defective in its view of the work of Christ as of his person.[30] The Arian heresy was denounced at the Council of Nicaea in AD 325, which promulgated the Nicene Creed.[31]

The Council of Nicaea

This Creed includes the words:

> We believe . . . in one Lord Jesus Christ, the Son of God, begotten from the Father, only-begotten, that is, from the substance of the Father, God from God, light from light, true God from true God, begotten not made, of one substance with the Father, through whom all things came into being, things in heaven and things on earth, who because of us men and because of our salvation came down and became incarnate, becoming man . . . [32]

It is noteworthy that Christ is designated 'Son', rather than Logos; that the two phrases 'the first-born of all creation' and 'begotten of the Father before all ages' (both of which the Arians would have affirmed) were omitted; that 'begotten, not made' and the crucial 'of one substance with the Father' were inserted; and that the addition of 'was made man' to 'was made flesh' ruled out the Arian belief that Jesus had a human body but not a human soul.[33]

Athanasius, the leading opponent of Arius, did not become a bishop until a year after the Council, although he seems to have played a considerable part in it. His principal emphasis – in sharp contrast to the Arians – was on the doctrine of salvation. Man had sinned, and in consequence had become both corrupt and mortal. Repentance alone would not save him; God himself must intervene. So Athanasius insisted that the Son was not merely 'like' the Father, but 'the same in likeness', that 'He did not receive in reward the name of the Son and God, but rather He Himself has made us sons of the Father, and deified men by becoming Himself man'. Indeed, 'the same things are said of the Son which are said of the Father, except His being said to be Father.' Arius, he said, taught pure polytheism; 'for if the Father is not Father everlastingly, and if in time a Son emerges, as the finite progeny of Godhead, and afterwards a Spirit lower still, who can answer for it that this is the end?'[34]

The Council of Nicaea, then, affirmed unequivocally that the divine Son, incarnate in Jesus, was one in essence with the Father. It had also been assumed from the first that he was truly man; and this had been firmly asserted in opposition to Gnostic Docetism.

Two traditions

How were the divine and human united in one person? What was the bond between them, and what emphasis should be given to each? On this a certain division of opinion had begun to appear even before the Arian controversy, and two traditions continued to exist after the Council. Neither tradition, Turner insists, was unorthodox in itself, though both 'were liable to produce equal and opposite exaggerations which were condemned as heretical'. Both, moreover, 'worked within a common framework of the doctrine of God as absolute, impassible and immutable', and both were firmly orthodox in their doctrine of the Trinity. But one tradition, mainly associated with Alexandria, was 'Monist' in tendency, and the other, linked with the Patriarchate of Antioch, was Dualist in inclination. The first has been described as the 'Word-flesh' tradition, with its Christology, in Turner's words,

> firmly anchored in the Godhead both as its starting-point and as the organizing principle within the incarnate Person. The Logos was the ultimate subject even of the incarnate experiences of Christ . . . The emphasis lay upon the unity of the Person of Christ and the description of the tradition as Monist may therefore be equally apt. The Incarnation involved a divine descent into human life or, as Prestige describes it, a divine irruption or inbreaking. Its favourite proof-text was John 1:14; and, though it could recognize that 'flesh' was a piece of biblical shorthand for 'man', it tended to regard the humanity as adjectival or instrumental to the divinity . . . Its doctrine of Redemption was equally centred in God. If the work of Christ was to avail for all men and be transmissible to all it must be centrally and vitally an act of God. In expositions of the doctrine of vicarious victory it is always the divine Logos who is the mighty victor on behalf of men.[35]

By contrast, the second tradition has been called the 'Word-man' tradition;

> but since it emphasized the full co-presence of two simultaneous natures, Godhead and manhood, the label of Dualist may be equally appropriate. While not denying the involvement of God the Logos in the incarnate life it was chiefly concerned to provide adequate living space for the humanity of Christ which was more highly valued and more realistically conceived than in the rival tradition . . . The Incarnation then involved not a substantial union of the Logos with the flesh but a looser conjunction of the divine Logos with a complete humanity . . . Its favourite proof-text was Phil. 2:5–11, where 'being in the form of God' (verse 6) and 'taking the form of a servant' (verse 7) were taken as references to two simultaneous co-present natures within the incarnate Lord . . . In their doctrine of Redemption they assigned a real and sometimes a predominant place to the humanity of Christ.[36]

Two extremes: Apollinarianism and Nestorianism

The Monist tradition, in its most extreme form, gave rise to the 'Apollinarian heresy', named after Apollinarius of Laodicea. In the Nicene Creed the words 'was made man' had been added to 'made flesh' to combat Arian doctrines; but, in spite of this, some degree of Docetism was at that time wide-spread. 'If perfect God were joined to perfect man, they would be two', Apollinarius argued, and a man-God is unthinkable. So at first he denied the entirety of Christ's human nature, acknowledging only that he had a human body. Later he affirmed that his *psyche*, too, was human, but that the place of his human 'spirit' or mind (*pneuma* or *nous*) was taken by the Logos. The result was a 'living unity'. 'But whatever else of humanity Apollinarius believed the Logos to have assumed, Turner emphasizes, the *nous* or directive principle was lacking'. This was vital, since Apollinarius regarded the *nous*, not the body, as the seat of sin.[37] It was in regard to this very truncated (and hopelessly inadequate) view of the incarnation that Gregory of Nazianzus made his famous remark that 'What he did not assume, he did not heal [or redeem]'.

The most extreme form of the Dualist (or Antiochene) school of thought, on the other hand, is represented by the 'Nestorian heresy', which derived its name from Nestorius (d. c. AD 451), although Theodore of Mopsuestia had in fact led the way. For Theodore the integrity of Christ's humanity was just as important as the transcendence of the divine Logos, for it was 'as man that Christ triumphed over sin and death and therefore for redemptive as well as christological reasons he must have both a human soul and will'. In his teaching a clear distinction is drawn between the two natures. After the virgin birth there was a 'conjunction' (*synapheia*) of these two natures, and the divine 'indwelt' the human by God's 'good pleasure' (*eudokia*).[38]

A clash between the two schools was not long delayed. The protagonists were Cyril of Alexandria (d. c. AD 444) and Nestorius, and the occasion was Nestorius' objection to Cyril's use of the term 'Mother of God' of the Virgin Mary. This term was common coin at Alexandria, but somewhat suspect among the Antiochenes, who maintained that 'God the Word' should be sharply distinguished from the man Jesus, who was not deified but 'taken into a unique personal conjunction with the Logos, and after the resurrection lifted up to a share in his universal power'. Another point of difference between the two traditions was 'the christological technique known as *Communicatio idiomatum* whereby attributes or activities proper to one nature are seemingly attributed to the other because of the unity of Person who includes or possesses both.[39]

Nestorius' chief opponent, Cyril, followed Apollinarius in describing the incarnation of the Logos as *kenōsis* ('condescension'); or, in his own words, *krypsis* ('veiling') of the glory of the Logos to make it bearable for men. It also implied *prolepsis* (addition) in the sense of assuming the 'limiting conditions of humanity'. Cyril's major interest, like that of Athanasius, was the doctrine of redemption: humanity imbued with deity through the incarnation. So he insisted that 'if the Word did not suffer for us humanly, He did not accomplish our redemption divinely; if He who suffered for us was mere man and but the organ of deity, we are not in fact redeemed'.[40] The Logos not only assumed, but became, flesh. For Cyril, Christ's human nature was 'impersonal' (*anhypostatos*), since his human nature was 'personal only in the Logos'; and 'as soul and body are one in us, so Godhead and manhood were made the one Christ'. Of the passion Cyril affirmed that 'the impassible Logos suffered in the passible flesh' – or even that 'he suffered impassibly'; while in regard to his apparent ignorance he commented: 'He usefully pretended not to know.'[41]

The dispute between Cyril and Nestorius resulted in the deposition of both of them by the supporters of the other faction at Ephesus in AD 431, although the decision in regard to Cyril was soon reversed. When Cyril died in 444, however, his central thesis was espoused by Eutyches, who was considerably more extreme, but eventually contented himself with affirming: 'I confess our Lord to have become out of two natures before the union. But I confess one nature after the union'. A new Council, described by Leo of Rome as the 'Robber Council', was called at Ephesus in 449, to which Leo sent his 'Dogmatic Epistle'; but it was not until two years later, at the Council of Chalcedon, in 451, that both Eutychianism and Nestorianism were condemned as heretical.

The Council of Chalcedon

This Council primarily 'sought to discover the solution to just *one* disputed question: *how* the confession of the '*one Christ*' may be reconciled with belief in the '*true God and true man*', '*perfect in Godhead, perfect in manhood*'.[42] Eventually, the assembled Fathers promulgated their famous Definition. This began by confessing the Church's belief that 'our Lord Jesus Christ is one and the same Son' – a simple formula in which Alexandrians and Antiochenes could meet[43] – and then continued:

> The Same perfect in Godhead, the Same perfect in manhood, truly God and truly man, the Same [consisting] of a rational soul and a body; *homoousios*[44] with the Father as to his Godhead, and the Same *homoousios* with us as to his manhood; in all things like unto us, sin only excepted; begotten of the Father before ages as to his Godhead, and in the last days, the Same, for us and for our salvation, of Mary the Virgin *Theotokos* as to his manhood.

On this part of the Definition Grillmeier comments:

> Motifs recur from an earlier period, the time of the struggle against Gnostics and docetists. The Arian and Apollinarian denial of the completeness of Christ's human nature is also refuted: Christ has a rational soul and a truly human body. Nothing may be taken away from the human nature of Christ to explain his unity . . . Its chief concern, however, is to express both the distinction and the completeness of Godhead and manhood. To do this, the most disputed word of the fourth century, the *homoousion*, is recalled, this time to be used of both the Godhead and the manhood.[45]

But *how* was both the unity and the distinction of Godhead and manhood in Christ to be understood? At this point the Definition, which could be said to have approximated to the views of Cyril in many respects, in one critical point bowed to the moderating influence of Leo and the Western church,[46] for it continued:

> . . . acknowledged in two natures without confusion, without change, without division, without separation – the difference of the natures being by no means taken away because of the union, and [each] combining in one Person and *hypostasis* – not divided or separated into two Persons, but one and the same Son and only-begotten God, Word, Lord Jesus Christ . . . [47]

On this Turner comments:

> While the paragraph is primarily concerned with the duality of the natures it opens and ends with a strong affirmation of unity. The four negative adverbs are paired off against Monist and Dualist exaggerations. 'Without confusion' is aimed at the use by Eutyches of mixture language; 'without change' directed against Arianism. 'Without division, without separation' excludes Nestorius as currently interpreted.[48]

But the Definition, naturally enough, did not satisfy either the Nestorians or the Monophysites. The Nestorians disliked it because in their eyes a hypostatic or personal union was virtually equivalent to a natural union (that is, one in which 'the ground or possibility of unification lay in the natures themselves'). The Monophysites (who called those who believed in the two natures in the one person of Christ Dyophysites) disliked it because to them a hypostatic or personal union was no substitute for a natural one;[49] and they argued that 'all that is divine in Christ is also human, and all that is human is also divine'. But it may also be criticized as providing – inevitably, no doubt, at that time – a largely abstract, philosophical definition which seems not only negative but strangely remote from the Jesus of the Gospels.

The intrusion of Greek philosophy.

Basic to this definition, in John McIntyre's view,[50] is Aristotelian logic, for it was fundamental to Aristotle's system to make a sharp distinction between 'primary substance' and 'secondary substance'. The examples of 'primary substance' he gives are an individual man or horse. Of these a number of 'secondary substances' can be predicated, such as that both the man and the horse belong to the genus 'animal', and that the man also belongs to the species 'human'. Equally, of course, it may be said that the man or the horse is the subject of suitable 'circumstances, characteristics, qualities and experiences'. But it is impossible to 'predicate' a particular man or horse of, or to say that he 'exists' in, anything or anyone else. Secondary substances, on the other hand, can only exist in, or be predicated of, something else: i.e. some primary substance.

When applied to Christology this meant that neither the divine nor the human nature (*physis*) could exist without a *hypostasis*. This is a word which some writers had identified with *ousia* (substance or essence), some with *physis* (nature) and some even with *prosōpon* (person, or outward appearance), and it is exceedingly difficult to translate. When applied to the Trinity it came to be used of the personal distinctions which exist within the one substance or essence of the Godhead. When applied to Christ it came to be used in the sense that a *physis* (nature), whether human or divine, cannot exist without a *hypostasis* (entity) to which it belongs or adheres: 'no *physis* without a *hypostasis*'; or 'no *physis anhypostatos*.'

This principle was apparently ignored in the Definition of Chalcedon, McIntyre insists, for this affirms the existence of two natures, without confusion and without change, in one person (*prosōpon*) and *hypostasis*. It is preserved, of course, although in very different ways, in Nestorianism, which assigns to the one person both two natures and two *hypostases*, and in Eutychianism, which acknowledges only one nature in Christ 'after the union'. But it is also preserved in the formula by which Leontius of Jerusalem[51] suggested that, instead of leaving the human nature of our Lord without a *hypostasis* (a *physis anhypostatos*), as in the Definition, it should be regarded as having no *hypostasis* of its own, but finding its *hypostasis* in that of the Logos. So, instead of being *anhypostatos*, it is *enhypostatos*.

This suggestion[52] has been criticized on several grounds. First, it is said to come very close to Apollinarianism, although McIntyre points out that 'while Leontius affirms that the Logos takes human nature, Apollinarius speaks more specifically of the *flesh*'; so Leontius' position 'only resembles that of Apollinarius in so far as both of them omit from Christ's person the human ego'. Secondly, W. N. Pittenger (who puts great emphasis on this last point) insists that Leontius still leaves Christ's human nature without any strictly personal centre on which his human experiences can 'home'.[53] Thirdly, McIntyre argues that on this basis the 'particularity and individuality of the man Jesus would be removed. In fact, it would be impossible to differentiate the *man* Jesus from the man Peter or the man John unless, in some way, the human *hypostasis* were retained.' Lastly, he insists, it puts our whole redemption in jeopardy on the principle that 'what Christ did not take, he did not redeem'. But it may be observed in passing that it does not seem to me that some of these arguments are by any means unanswerable.[54]

A different attempt to come to terms with this problem was made by Ephraim of Antioch, who maintained, in conformity with Chalcedonian orthodoxy, that the two natures were not to be divided, since 'two natures does not mean two *hypostases*'. But he then explains that 'while the two natures as such are not confused or compounded, the two *hypostases* are'. So the *hypostasis* of Christ 'is a fusion of the human and the divine *hypostasis*'.

About this McIntyre remarks that, by thus insisting on the presence, in the composite *hypostasis*, of the human *hypostasis*, this theory 'secures the wholeness of the humanity which Jesus Christ took, and firmly avoids the docetic and Apollinarian tendencies of the enhypostatic theory. Jesus Christ is a real man, not simply *humanitas* or the *humanum*'. It also, on the strictly technical side, 'serves to protect Chalcedon from the common charge that it operates with an 'impersonal' view of the human nature of Jesus Christ'.[55] But, however this may be, the major objection to this whole argument is that it is based on a philosophical approach and framework which is alien to us today.

Strengths and weaknesses

The strength of the Nestorian position is that it does at least attempt to give full weight to the fact that, whatever else may be postulated of the Jesus of the Gospels, he was beyond question a man – as all his disciples would have recognized. The strength of the Monophysite view, on the other hand, is that he was also unmistakably one person, not two. The Chalcedonian Definition, by contrast, leaves him very much a philosophical abstraction,[56] admirably though it guards orthodoxy against a number of distortions and aberrations. Curiously enough, the Monophysites and Nestorians come comparatively close together when the former declare that the two natures 'can be distinguished only in theory', and when the latter insist that 'nature' and 'person' are almost equivalent in this context. But the fact remains that the Monophysites end up with a Christ who is not really a man, and the Nestorians with a figure who is not an integrated personality. Always, it would seem, there was an element of falsehood, as well as partial truth, on both sides of the controversy.

This can be seen, yet again, in the dispute between the Monothelites and the Dyothelites in the seventh century as to whether Jesus had one will or two, human and divine. The Monothelites could point to the testimony of the New Testament to Jesus' unswerving obedience to the Father as evidence of a *unity* of will, while the Dyothelites could argue that the voluntary *capacity* is 'inherent in an intelligent being as a function of its nature',[57] and that Jesus must have had a human will. As so often, the New Testament pinpoints the truth, and omits the error, of both sides when it records that Jesus prayed, in the garden of Gethsemane, 'that, if it were possible, this hour might pass him by. "*Abba*, Father", he said, "all things are possible to thee; take this cup away from me. Yet not what I will, but what thou wilt".[58] Here we can certainly discern a human will, but one which was wholly subjected to that of the Father.

Is there anything in Islam that is in any way comparable to this long and involved dispute? The nearest parallel that I can think of (remote though it is) is the controversy in Islam about the relationship between God's divine essence (*al-dhāta'l-ilāhiyya*) and his eternal attributes or qualities (*al-ṣifāta'l-azaliyya*). Were these eternal qualities to be regarded as *identical* with his divine essence, 'purified from every shadow of createdness or occasionalism', and thus interpreted in a largely negative sense? Such was the view of the Muʿtazila who, as a result, insisted that the Qur'ān could not be regarded as 'eternal' or 'uncreated' – an assertion that brought them into sharp conflict with the orthodox. Were it not so, the Muʿtazilīs argued, Muslims would no longer be monotheists, since they would have two Gods: Allāh himself and the Qur'ān – or several other gods, if not only his speech, but also his other attributes, were *not* identical with his essence.

To this 'orthodox' scholars eventually replied that it was true that the Qur'ān, 'as a written book and as recited by human agency, is created, but its quality as the speech of God is the same as that of his other attributes, existing in his essence and therefore uncreated'. But even this concession went much further than many Muslims were prepared to go. For them, divine mysteries were to be accepted *bi lā kayf*: 'without asking "How?".' Eventually, however, orthodox scholars resolved this conundrum by insisting that the eternal attributes of God were not *identical* with his essence *nor separable* from it (*lā dhātahu wa lā ghayrahu'*) – or, in al-Nasafī's words: 'They are not He, nor are they other than He.'[59]

It seems to me that Muslim readers might find this debate between the Muʿtazila and 'orthodox' Muslim scholars a 'lead in' (no more) to the christological debate about the relationship between God and his 'Logos'; or even to the trinitarian concept of the distinction of 'persons' within the unity of substance of the Godhead. It is important, of course, always to distinguish between the seven eternal attributes of God and the ninety-nine 'Beautiful Names' which pious Muslims recite as they finger the beads on their rosaries. Unhappily, Muslims deny any intelligible meaning to these names by their insistence that the radical difference (*mukhālafa*) between God and his human creatures forbids any human comparison or understanding. Happily, Christians can rejoice that the divine character has been displayed to them in the only way that they could begin to understand, in terms of a human life. They long to share this experience with their Muslim friends – together with the knowledge of sins forgiven which results from their Saviour's atoning death. To this, again, Islam has no parallel.

The Reformation

By and large, the Reformers accepted the classical Christology and made no attempt to change it. But it is significant that Luther put a particular emphasis on four points. First, he emphasized the humanity of Christ in his basic approach. 'The Scriptures', he observes,

> begin very gently, and lead us on to Christ as to a man, and then to one who is Lord over all creatures, and after that to one who is God. So do I enter delightfully, and learn to know God. But the philosophers and doctors have insisted on beginning from above; and so they have become fools. We must begin from below, and after that come upwards.

So he emphasized that Jesus 'ate, drank, slept and waked; was weary, sad, joyous; wept, laughed; was hungry, thirsty, cold; sweated, talked, worked, prayed'. Indeed, 'there was no difference between Him and other men save that He was God and without sin'.

Secondly, he insisted that our redemption depends utterly on the deity of Christ, for sinners are guilty, and only God could save us. 'If Deity be wanting in Christ there is no help or deliverance for us against God's anger and judgments,' he wrote; so 'if it could not be held that God [in the person of his Son] died for us, but only a man, then we are lost.' Thirdly, Luther insisted on the vital connection between Christ's person and his work: between the reality of the incarnation and the efficacy of the atonement – as will be apparent from what has already been quoted.

Fourthly, his whole religion was supremely christocentric. 'I have no God, whether in heaven or earth, and I know of none, outside the flesh that lies in the bosom of the Virgin Mary. For elsewhere God is utterly incomprehensible, but comprehensible in the flesh of Christ alone,' he wrote; or, again, 'Wilt thou go surely and meet and grasp God rightly, so finding grace and help in him, be not persuaded to seek him elsewhere than in the Lord Christ. Let thine art and study begin with Christ, and there let it stay and cling.'

But in regard to the details of christological controversy, Luther adopted an essentially experiential and devotional, rather than abstract and philosophical, approach. He apparently accepted the dogma of the 'impersonality' of Christ's human nature, although this seems to have made little difference to him in practice.

> Christ is not called Christ because he has two natures. What is that to me? That he is by nature God and man is for himself. But what gives me comfort and blessing is that he so applies his office and pours forth his love and becomes my Saviour and Redeemer.

Yet Harnack could write of Luther that 'Since Cyril, no teacher has arisen in the Church to whom the mystery of the unity of the two natures in Christ was so deep a consolation'. For unity there certainly was, in Luther's view, since he reacted strongly against the Zwinglian teaching that it is only a figure of speech that we can assert an interchange of qualities between the two natures: 'If I believe that the human nature alone suffered for me,' Luther asserted, 'then is Christ worse than no Saviour to me.[60]

But Lutheran doctrine, as it developed after Luther, became immersed in further dialectical refinements. One dispute was resolved by the Formula of Concord, in 1577; but a further controversy soon ensued, between the theologians of Tübingen and those of Giessen, about whether the incarnate Lord, in the days of his earthly life, actually renounced the use of his divine powers (which both sides agreed that he still possessed), or merely employed them secretly. The theologians of Giessen took the first view, and those of Tübingen the second. The latter maintained that the child Jesus, *qua* man, in secret ruled the universe, and that he later, at times, exhibited omnipotence, omniscience and omnipresence. This controversy was ended by the *decisio Saxonica* in 1624, which basically accepted the view of Giessen (in Pannenberg's words)

> in rejecting a mere concealment (*krypsis*) of the possession and use of the divine attributes of majesty in Jesus' human nature during his earthly life and affirming a real renunciation (*kenōsis*) of their use in the state of humiliation.[61]

But Mackintosh asserts that even the theologians of Giessen saw the 'humiliation' of the incarnate Saviour

> solely in this, that while retaining possession of the Divine qualities conveyed to His humanity by its union with the Logos, He yet made no habitual use of them . . . and only at times did His real powers flash through the veil.[62]

In the light of this, it is not altogether surprising that Lutheran theology was accused of being heir to the Monist traditions of Alexandria – and, indeed, of occasionally showing distinctly Monophysite tendencies.

By contrast, 'Reformed' Christology might be said partially to have retained the traditions of Antioch; and it certainly held rigidly to the Chalcedonian Definition. It understood the *kenōsis*, or humiliation of Christ, in terms of the incarnation itself; and it insisted that the Logos, although he had not divested himself of his essential deity (with all that this entails), had conjoined with himself a manhood that was truly human, of one substance with our own.[63] By contrast with the Lutherans, therefore, they were sometimes accused of having destroyed the unity of Christ's person, and even of Nestorian tendencies.

We must return to the 'Kenotic Theory' in chapter 8 below. Suffice it to say here that any theory which pictures one who was originally God, but who temporarily renounced his deity for the period of his earthly life, only to resume it at his ascension, is totally unacceptable. Even the credal statement that the eternal Son 'came down from heaven' introduces what may be termed 'mythological' imagery which does not adequately convey the essential doctrine of the incarnation: that *God himself, in the 'person' of the Son, actually became truly man without ceasing to be God.*

I think Pannenberg is right, moreover, when he insists that many of our christological problems arise from an attempt to conceive some conjunction of the divine and the human in abstract terms, instead of starting with 'the concrete person of Jesus of Nazareth' and then finding ourselves forced to say, about him and him alone, that he is not only truly man but also truly God.[64] In terms of the classical Christology, what we must take from the Alexandrians is that Jesus Christ himself, and not merely the Logos who assumed manhood in him, was truly God; and what we must take from the Antiochenes is that he himself, as an integrated personality, truly *became* man. And we must also emphasize that there is an essential identity between the pre-existent Logos/Son and the incarnate Lord, both in his state of 'humiliation' and present 'exaltation'.

CHAPTER SEVEN

The incarnation and other religions

In my last chapter I tried to summarize some of the christological controversies which culminated in the Nicene Creed and the Definition of Chalcedon, the continuing disputes in the churches of the East and West about how these statements should be understood and the renewed debates and disagreements which followed the Reformation. Almost inevitably, I think, some of the extravagances, contradictions and seeming quibbles of this age-long attempt to plumb the mystery of the incarnation leave us, today, somewhat dissatisfied and disturbed. It is not only the hair-splitting and *odium theologicum* of those often bitter wars of words which distress us, but the seeming unreality of the philosophical straight-jacket of the classical formulations. Instinctively, we long to get back to the vitality, and apparent simplicity, of the New Testament; to approach its records and statements with an open mind; and to do our utmost to reach at least a tentative understanding of this mystery in a way that satisfies our minds and our hearts. So in the next chapter I shall venture to outline the way in which I myself have come to approach this subject. First, however, let us think about the incarnation in the context of other religions.

A pluralist approach

Today we live in a pluralist society in which we are aware, in a new way, of what other men believe. It is essential, therefore, to try to view the New Testament against the background of other religions. What light, if any, do the 'Mystery religions', some of which preceded the apostolic *kerygma* (and continued for a number of years to vie with it, to some degree, for men's allegiance) throw on the incarnation? Has the history of Mahāyāna Buddhism, perhaps, anything to teach us about the way in which christological thought developed in the Christian church? What, too, of the *avatars* of the gods (or of the 'Ultimate Reality') which occupy so prominent a place in the Hindu classics; or of the austere monotheism of the Qur'ān? Books, monographs and lectures on such subjects follow each other in endless succession today, among the more notorious of which are two books of essays entitled, somewhat provocatively, *The Myth of God Incarnate* and *The Myth of Christian Uniqueness*. These appeared in 1977 and 1988 respectively. So it is to the first of these two books – or, rather, to Professor John Hick's chapter on 'Jesus and the world's religions' in it – that I shall now turn.

The Mystery religions

Hick does not deal in this chapter with the Mystery religions, both Hellenistic and Oriental, which claimed so many adherents around the Mediterranean basin at the beginning of the Christian era – although one of the the other contributors, Dr Frances Young, does allude to them.[1] Of their superficial resemblance to the new faith there can be little question. Basically nature religions and vegetation rites in origin, they mostly centred round a 'saviour god' – with or without a mother, consort or other figure – who died and then came to life again. In their more spiritual and sophisticated form they held out a promise not only of physical renewal and fertility but of future immortality

Two or three of them, moreover, even postulated an interval of about three days between the death and the revival of their saviour-god – a fact which has inevitably been linked with the New Testament witness to the resurrection of Christ on the third day. But Professor B. M. Metzger has emphasized that the evidence for the commemoration of the Hilaria, or the coming back to life of Attis, for example, cannot be traced back beyond the latter half of the second century AD, and in the case of Adonis, too, such references as there are date from the second to the fourth century AD. The categorical affirmation in 1 Corinthians 15, however, that Christ 'was raised to life on the third day' can be confidently dated in the middle of the *first* century. If there was borrowing in this respect, therefore, it seems clear enough which way it went.

Of Osiris, too, Metzger writes that 'after his consort Isis had sought and re-assembled thirteen of the fourteen pieces into which his body had been dismembered by his wicked brother . . . through the help of magic she was enabled to re-animate his corpse'. The contrast between this and the testimony of the apostolic church to the resurrection of

Jesus is obvious. In those Mystery religions which speak of a dying god, moreover, he 'died by compulsion and not by choice', and never in 'self-giving love'. But the fundamental difference between all the Mysteries and the Christian faith is that the former speak of a purely mythological figure who symbolizes the death of nature in winter and its revival at the turn of the year, whereas the primitive church testified to the resurrection 'on the third day' of a historical person whom they had both known and loved.[2]

A Hindu Avatar or a Buddhist Bodhisattva?

Much the same can be said of the *avatars* of Hinduism. To begin with, they represent theophanies or 'descents' of the gods[3] in human guise – in a way to which the only parallel in Christianity would be the most extreme form of Docetism. They are, moreover, acknowledged by all educated Hindus to be purely mythological – that is, in Professor Hick's use of the word myth, 'a story which is told but which is not literally true'. Bishop Lesslie Newbigin, indeed, writes that he has never forgotten the astonishment with which a devout and learned teacher of the Rāmakrishna Mission regarded him when he discovered that Newbigin was prepared to rest his 'whole faith as a Christian upon the substantial historical truth of the record concerning Jesus in the New Testament'. To the Hindu it 'seemed axiomatic that such vital matters of religious truth could not be allowed to depend upon the accidents of history. If the truths which Jesus exemplified and taught are true, then they are true always and everywhere, whether a person called Jesus ever lived or not'.

But there is all the difference in the world between a statement about the nature of God – or a purely mythical *avatar* to illustrate some aspect of that nature – and

> a report that God has, at a certain time and place, acted in a certain way. In the latter case the occurrence is the essence of the message. The care which is taken in the New Testament to place the events recorded in the continuum of secular history is in striking contrast to the indifference which is generally shown with regard to the historicity of the events which Hindu piety loves to remember in connection with the character of the gods. There is no serious attempt to relate them to events in secular history, nor is it felt that there would be any advantage to be gained from trying to do so – even if it could be done.

Their value is that they illustrate truths about God which would remain true whether or not these particular events had ever actually happened.[4]

Professor Hick, however, fails to make any distinction between the purely mythological nature of Hindu *avatars* and the basic historicity of the founder of Buddhism – to say nothing of Christianity. Instead, he insists that

> we should never forget that if the Christian gospel had moved east, into India, instead of west, into the Roman empire, Jesus' religious significance would probably have been expressed by hailing him within Hindu culture as a divine Avatar and within the Mahāyāna Buddhism which was then developing in India as a Bodhisattva, one who has attained to oneness with Ultimate Reality but remains in the human world out of compassion for mankind and to show others the way of life. These would have been the *appropriate* expressions, within these cultures, of the *same* spiritual reality.[5]

Hick's view of Jesus

Professor Hick unequivocally affirms, however, that 'Jesus was a real man who really lived in first century Palestine',[6] and that 'we receive, mainly from the Synoptic Gospels, an impression of a real person with a real message'[7] – although he positively goes to town about 'how fragmentary and ambiguous are the data available to us as we try to look back across nineteen and a half centuries', and 'how large and variable is the contribution of the imagination to our "pictures" of Jesus.'[8] It is, of course, eminently salutary to be reminded how easy it is to construct a Jesus in one's own image, or at least according to one's own preconceived ideas. I have, however, certainly never heard him described as 'a stern lawgiver and implacable judge',[9] and Hick *greatly* exaggerates the paucity of positive evidence we have about the one to whom he refers as 'the largely unknown man of Nazareth'.[10]

He himself, he tells us, sees

> the Nazarene, then, as intensely and overwhelmingly conscious of the reality of God. He was a man of God, living in the unseen presence of God, and addressing God as *abba*, father . . . He was so powerfully God-conscious that his life vibrated, as it were, to the divine life; and as a result his hands could heal the sick, and the 'poor in spirit' were kindled to new life in his presence. If you or I had met him in first-century Palestine we

> would – we may hope – have felt deeply disturbed and challenged by his presence. We would have felt the absolute claim of God confronting us, summoning us to give ourselves wholly to him and to be born again as his children and as agents of his purposes on earth. . . And such is the interaction of body and mind that in deciding to give ourselves to God, in response to his claim mediated through Jesus, we might have found ourselves trembling or in tears, or uttering the strange sounds that are called speaking with tongues . . . [11]

'If this interpretation is at all on the right lines,' he later affirms, 'Jesus cannot have failed to be aware that he was himself far more intensely conscious of God, and that he was far more faithfully obedient to God, than could be said of any contemporaries whom he had met or of whom he had heard.' Indeed,

> he was himself directly and overwhelmingly conscious of the heavenly Father, so he could speak about him with authority, could summon men and women to live as his children, could declare his judgment and his forgiveness, and could heal the sick by his power. Jesus must thus have been conscious of a unique position among his contemporaries, which he may have expressed by accepting the title of Messiah or, alternatively, by applying to himself the image of the heavenly Son of Man – two categories each connoting a human being called to be God's special servant and agent on earth.[12]

The 'deification' of Jesus?

So much for the historic Jesus, as Hick sees him. But then, he believes, the church embarked on a gradual process of deifying him, in a way to which he sees a reasonably close parallel, *mutatis mutandis*, in the deification of Gautama – who, too, 'was a real historical individual who lived in north-east India from about 563 to about 483 BC', but who made no claim to be divine.[13] In the 'earliest Christian preaching, as we have echoes of it in Acts,' he writes, 'Jesus was proclaimed as "a man attested to you by God with mighty works and wonders and signs" (Acts 2:22)', whereas 'some thirty years later the Gospel of Mark could open with the words "The beginning of the gospel of Jesus Christ, the Son of God . . ." And in John's Gospel, written after another thirty or so years' development, this Christian language is attributed to Jesus himself and he is depicted as walking the earth as a consciously divine being'.[14]

This dramatic change, he suggests, must be explained in terms of Jesus' 'tremendous spiritual power',[15] and of 'some kind of experience of seeing Jesus after his death, an appearance or appearances which came to be known as his resurrection'[16] (to which we must soon revert). There were also pressures, that must soon have developed, 'to use titles which would more explicitly present the challenge of Jesus' saving power' – and 'these could only be the highest titles available'.[17] Ideas of divinity embodied in human life were widespread in the ancient world, we are told, so 'there is nothing in the least surprising in the deification of Jesus in that cultural environment'.[18] Within Judaism the King was at times designated, metaphorically, as the 'son' of Yahweh – to say nothing of pagan practice in the Roman empire – so it was natural enough, the argument runs, for this title to be applied to Jesus, once the church came to regard him as the Messiah. Hick, however, thinks it probable that it was 'only with the stories of the virgin birth of Jesus in Matthew's and Luke's Gospels that the Lord's anointed is thought of within Israel as physically (*sic*) God's son'.[19]

Then, as Christian theology 'grew through the centuries, it made the very significant transition from "Son of God" to "God the Son", the Second Person of the Trinity' – although Hick concedes that the 'transposition of the poetic image, Son of God, into the trinitarian concept, God the Son, is already present in the fourth Gospel'.[20] It was in some such way as this, he believes, that we can explain how the church came '*ultimately* to the point of deification'.[21]

Is this theory convincing?

The trouble with this superficially plausible reconstruction is that the evidence, as I see it, does not support it – and actually points in the opposite direction – in point after point.[22] Even in the very sermon recorded in Acts 2 from which Hick quotes what he terms 'echoes of the earliest Christian preaching', for example, Peter refers to Jesus as having been 'raised up' and 'exalted to the right hand of God,' and declares 'Therefore let all Israel be assured of this: God has made this Jesus whom you crucified, both Lord and Christ'.[23] A little later in the same book, moreover, we read that Peter affirms that 'Salvation is found in no-one else, for there is no other name under heaven given to men by which we must be saved' – and we find that the early disciples found it perfectly natural to address prayer to the 'Lord Jesus'.[24] But it is astonishing how some scholars give enormous emphasis to statements in Acts which suit their own thesis, and completely ignore those that do not.

It seems to me, moreover, that this reconstruction flies in the face of the evidence when the stories of the virgin birth are regarded as giving rise to a significant change of attitude. While I myself fully accept these stories as historical, it seems obvious that it is on the person of Jesus, and on his death and resurrection, that the whole emphasis in the apostolic *kerygma* was placed; and it is, perhaps, relevant in this context that no direct reference to the virgin birth is made in John's Gospel, to which Hick attributes so fundamental a role in depicting Jesus, in phraseology which surely represents something of a caricature, as 'walking the earth as a consciously divine being'.[25] It is also relevant to note that the Qur'ān testifies to the virgin birth but *denies* the deity of one so born.

The New Testament witness

Hick deals with the available evidence in a still more cavalier fashion. He gives much prominence to the Fourth Gospel in paving the way for what he terms the ultimate deification of Jesus, and he dates this Gospel – with most, but by no means all, contemporary scholars – in the last decade of the first century. He continually ignores, however, both the evidence of the Pauline epistles some forty years earlier and also that of the letter to the Hebrews – which *must*, I should have thought, be dated before the fall of Jerusalem in AD 70. In 1 Thessalonians, which is often regarded as the earliest of Paul's letters (c. AD 50), for example, we read that the Thessalonians had come to serve 'the living and true God, and to wait expectantly for the appearance from heaven of his Son Jesus, whom he raised from the dead, Jesus our deliverer from the terrors of judgement to come'.[26] For those who regard the Epistle to the Galatians as even earlier, moreover, reference can be made to a number of similar verses – notably, perhaps, the statement that 'God sent his own Son, born of a woman, born under the law, to purchase freedom for the subjects of the law, in order that we might attain the status of sons'.[27]

In the Epistle to the Colossians, again, we read (in reference to God's 'dear Son') that 'He is the image of the invisible God; his is the primacy over all created things. In him everything in heaven and on earth was created . . . And he exists before everything, and all things are held together in him'.[28] The Epistle to the Hebrews, too, speaks in much the same way when it declares that 'When in former times God spoke to our forefathers, he spoke in fragmentary and varied fashion through the prophets. But in this the final age he has spoken to us in the Son whom he has made heir to the whole universe, and through whom he created all orders of existence: the Son who is the effulgence of God's splendour and the stamp of God's very being, and sustains the universe by his word of power'.[29]

To put such an emphasis on John's Gospel, therefore, and completely to ignore the earlier, and almost equally explicit, contribution of Paul and Hebrews – and, indeed, the Petrine and Johannine epistles – to the 'ultimate' deification of Jesus, seems to me to represent a singularly arbitrary selection of evidence. Nor does it take into account verses in the Synoptic Gospels such as 'Everything is entrusted to me by my Father; and no one knows who the Son is but the Father, or who the Father is but the Son, and those to whom the Son may choose to reveal him'.[30] Not only so, but there is Jesus' reply on oath to the High Priest's challenge, 'Are you the Christ, the Son of the Blessed One?' 'I am,' said Jesus. 'And you will see the Son of Man sitting at the right hand of the Mighty One and coming on the clouds of heaven.'[31] Who, moreover, can read the Sermon on the Mount and its sequel without concluding that the one who made such claims must either have spoken with divine authority or else be suffering from monumental megalomania?[32]

When, moreover, Hick suggests a parallel between the development of christological thought in the Christian church and that of the Mahāyāna Buddhist concept of the 'heavenly Buddha', he fails to point out that, whereas the Christian view goes right back to the first generation of Christians, the fact that the Buddhist concept 'began to develop at about the same time as Christianity'[33] – as he puts it – means that this happened some five centuries after Gautama's death.

Experience of the atonement

Hick also asserts that 'There can I think be no doubt that this deification of Jesus came about partly – and perhaps mainly – as a result of the Christian experience of reconciliation with God'. He rightly emphasizes the disciples' 'glorious sense of the divine forgiveness and love' and the fact that the 'early Christian community lived and rejoiced in the knowledge of God's accepting grace'. There was thus, he argues, 'a natural transition in their minds from the experience of reconciliation with God as Jesus' disciples, to the thought of his death as an atoning sacrifice, and from this to the conclusion that in order for Jesus' death to have been a sufficient atonement for human sin he must himself have been divine'.[34]

Now this, as I see it, is an exceedingly important point to which I shall return later, for it is significant that in books and discussions about comparative religion the major emphasis is almost always put on the need for a divine self-revelation, rather than on the equally basic need for an atonement for sin. But when Hick argues that the influence of 'a long tradition of priestly sacrifice', and the thought that 'without the shedding of blood there is no forgiveness of sins',[35] led naturally to 'this deification of Jesus', he omits to note that the Synoptic Gospels record that Jesus himself said that 'the Son of Man did not come to be served but to serve, and to surrender his life as a ransom for many[36] and also, at the Last Supper, that 'this is my blood, the blood of the covenant, shed for many for the forgiveness of sins'.[37] The first of these recorded statements is almost certainly an echo of Isaiah 53, which (as Dr Vincent Taylor has persuasively argued) seems to have dominated Jesus' understanding of his messianic mission and also its interpretation by the early Church[38] – and which was, it would seem, something which the risen Lord specifically explained to his disciples.[39]

The resurrection

But this brings us inevitably to the resurrection, which was almost certainly the basic reason why the disciples began to confess that 'Jesus is Lord', to apply to him references to Yahweh in the Old Testament, and to have no hesitation in worshipping him and addressing him in prayer. Hick rightly remarks that it will be said that 'there is at least one all-important difference between Jesus and Gautama which justifies the ascription of divine attributes to the one and not to the other – namely that Jesus rose from the dead. Does not his resurrection set him apart from all other men and show him to be God incarnate? Such an argument inevitably suggests itself'. But he immediately adds that this argument 'proves difficult to sustain'.[40] To this the obvious reply is that he himself certainly makes exceedingly heavy weather of the way in which he deals both with what he terms 'the resurrection event', and with its nature and implications.

A resuscitated corpse?

First, he asserts that the 'possibilities range from the resuscitation of Jesus' corpse to visions of the Lord in resplendent glory'.[41] But it seems perfectly clear that the records do not point to a resuscitated corpse, and that they go distinctly beyond mere visions. In regard to the first suggestion, there can, I think, be little doubt that St Paul was thinking of the risen Redeemer, as well as the future state of the redeemed, when he made a clear-cut distinction between a 'natural' or 'animal' body and a 'spiritual' body,[42] and this is clearly confirmed by his teaching that 'Christ, once raised from the dead, is never to die again: he is no longer under the dominion of death',[43] and that 'the Lord Jesus Christ . . . will transfigure the body belonging to our humble state, and give it a form like that of his own resplendent body'.[44] It is in this context that Wolfhart Pannenberg writes:

> The notion of the resurrection of the dead that is most obvious on the basis of the analogy of sleeping and waking would be that of a revivification of the corpse in the sense of what has died standing up and walking around. It is, however, absolutely certain that the resurrection of the dead was not understood in this way in the primitive Christian and, in any case, in the oldest, the Pauline, concept. For Paul, resurrection means the new life of a new body, not the return of life into a dead but not yet decayed fleshly body . . . It is self-evident for him that the future body will be a different one from the present body . . . not perishable but imperishable in glory and power, not a fleshly body equipped with a soul but a spiritual body.[45]

Then he adds:

> The explications in 1 Cor. 15:35–56 are not especially concerned with the resurrection of Jesus Christ, but with the resurrection that Christians expect of the future. But Paul must have had the same conception of the resurrected Jesus, for he always and fully thought about Jesus' resurrection and that of Christians in essential parallel. It is particularly significant that Paul understood the resurrection of the dead, and so also the resurrection of Jesus, not as mere resuscitation of a corpse but as radical transformation.[46]

And the way in which the resurrection appearances recorded in the Gospels depict the risen Lord as passing through closed doors – or now appearing and now disappearing – certainly supports this view.

Visionary experiences?

The primary argument against the 'resurrection-event' being understood merely in terms of 'visions of the Lord in resplendent glory', on the other hand, is the evidence that the tomb was in fact empty – and the evidence for this is exceedingly strong. First, there is the positive evidence. Mark's Gospel, in its original form, probably ends with the women's visit to the tomb from which the body had disappeared. Matthew and Luke add rather more details – about which I will content myself, in this context, with stating that I am convinced that the alleged contradictions between the different accounts have been much exaggerated, and that some of the glosses put on the additional material in Matthew are very far fetched. For example, Christopher Evans' remark that 'The guards at the sealed tomb, who are found only in Matthew's version, together with the women, who because of the sealing of the tomb can now come only to visit it and not to anoint the body, become spectators of a divine miracle'. On this particular flight of scholarly fancy I will repeat the comment that I made some years ago.:

> But Matthew tells us that the Chief Priests asked Pilate to set a guard over the tomb on the day *after* the burial, so the women could scarcely have known about this; and there is no conclusive reason why they should not have come to add their 'spices and ointments' (as recorded in Luke 23:56) to those hastily provided by Nicodemus (as recorded in John 19:39) on the Friday evening. Nor is it at all necessary to assume, from this very concise account, that the women had already arrived at the tomb when the earthquake is said to have occurred and the angel to have rolled away the stone. It is intrinsically unlikely, on any showing, that the angel would address the women, in the manner recorded, in the presence of the guards – and there are a number of ways in which the story of the earthquake, and how the angel rolled away the stone, might have become known. It is perfectly possible, moreover, to regard Matthew 28:2–4 as a sort of parenthesis.[47]

And in John's Gospel we have the vivid account of how Mary Magdalene was the first to arrive at the tomb, saw that the stone had been rolled away, and ran to call Peter and 'the disciple whom Jesus loved'; how they set out to the tomb, and in their eagerness began to run; how 'the other disciple', younger than Peter, got there first, stooped down and peered into the tomb, but characteristically did not go in; how Peter, equally characteristically, blundered straight in, followed by his companion; how they both took note of 'the linen cloths lying, and the napkin, which had been on [Jesus'] head, not lying with the linen cloths but rolled up in a place by itself'; and how John (presumably), when he saw this, at once 'believed' in the resurrection. On this story William Temple comments: 'It is most manifestly the record of a personal memory. Nothing else can account for the little details, so vivid, so little like the kind of thing that comes from invention or imagination.'[48]

The fact that the tomb was empty

Then why, it has often been asked, is there no mention of the empty tomb in the earliest tradition about the resurrection to come down to us – in 1 Corinthians 15:3–8? To this the obvious answer is that, while there is no explicit statement that the tomb was empty, there is a most convincing implicit reference to this fact. For what oriental Jew of the first century could possibly have written that 'Christ died for our sins' (physically, of course), that 'he was buried' (again, physically, of course), and that he was then 'raised to life on the third day', if he had not believed that *something* had happened to the body? This would be a most unnatural way of recording a tradition about a purely 'spiritual' survival of Jesus. Surely we must assume that it was the crucified and buried body which was both transformed and 'raised'? There would, moreover, have been no point whatever in saying that this happened 'on the third day' if the reference has been to mere spiritual survival.

This positive evidence is buttressed, moreover, by a considerable amount of what may be termed negative or circumstantial evidence. First, as Paul Althaus puts it: 'In Jerusalem, the place of Jesus' execution and grave, it was proclaimed not long after his death that he had been raised. The situation *demands* that within the circle of the first community one had a reliable testimony for the fact that the grave had been found empty.' This resurrection kerygma, he says, 'could not have been maintained in Jerusalem for a single day, for a single hour, if the emptiness of the tomb had not been established as a fact for all concerned'.[49]

Again, Pannenberg insists that:

> Among the general historical arguments that speak for the trustworthiness of the report about the discovery of Jesus' tomb is, above all, the fact that the early Jewish polemic against the Christian message about Jesus' resurrection, traces of which have already been left in the Gospels, does not offer any suggestion that Jesus' grave had remained untouched. The Jewish polemic would have had to have every interest in the preservation of such a report. However, quite to the contrary, it shared the conviction with its Christian opponents that Jesus' grave was empty. It limited itself to explaining this fact in its own way. . . . [50]

But this explanation of why the tomb was empty – namely, that the disciples came by night and stole the body – is totally unacceptable on both ethical and psychological grounds. And subsequent attempts to explain the emptiness of the tomb on a rationalistic basis – e.g. that of Kirsopp Lake, B. H. Streeter, Venturini, etc. – seem to me equally unconvincing.[51]

The appearances of the risen Lord

The evidence of the empty tomb, however, should never be taken in isolation, but in close connection with the records of the 'appearances' of the risen Lord. For these testify to two quite different facts: the appearances, that it was no resuscitated corpse which appeared to the disciples; the empty tomb, that it was no wholly incorporeal phantom, ghost or vision. The records state that the risen Christ could be clearly seen, recognized with some dawning wonder (for it was so unexpected and it must not be supposed that his transformed body was *exactly* like the body which had been buried). He could invite a finger to explore the print of the nails, and could even eat a piece of fish – not, of course, because a 'spiritual body' had any need of physical food, but presumably in order that his bewildered disciples might have concrete evidence, when his visible presence was withdrawn, that their experience had been no mere vision, but an objective reality.

The implications

But Hick also places great emphasis on the fact that 'it must be doubted whether the resurrection event – whatever its nature – was seen by Jesus' contemporaries as guaranteeing his divinity'.[52] In support of this statement he refers to the account of the raising of Lazarus, of the widow's son at Nain, of Jairus' daughter, etc., and to somewhat similar stories in the Old Testament and even the sub-apostolic age. He significantly fails, however, to make any distinction whatever between such resuscitations to ordinary human life (followed no doubt by another, and final, experience of physical death) – and the resurrection of Jesus, in a spiritual body, to live 'in the power of an endless life'.

It is certainly true, as Hick (quoting George Caird) insists, that no resuscitation of a friend or acquaintance would make us conclude that 'this acquaintance was divine'.[53] This could also be said even about the final resurrection of God's people, to which all Christians look forward one day; for such a resurrection proves the power and love of God, rather than the divinity of those concerned. I would strongly challenge, however, the assertion that Christ's resurrection was *not* 'seen by Jesus' contemporaries as guaranteeing his divinity'. For St Paul specifically states that the one who 'on the human level . . . was born of David's stock' was, 'on the level of the spirit – the Holy Spirit – declared Son of God by a mighty act in that he rose from the dead',[54] and there is ample supporting evidence for the fact that it was the resurrection which prompted them to call him 'Lord' and to feel free – and, indeed, compelled – to worship him.[55]

It is perfectly true, of course, that 'Jesus is not said to have risen in virtue of a divine nature which he himself possessed but to have been raised by God'.[56] Precisely; and we are told that the fact that God did so raise him made it unequivocally clear that he authenticated his claims. Jesus had previously testified to having a unique relationship with his heavenly Father; he had claimed to forgive sins, which all Jews regarded as a divine prerogative; and he had spoken and acted with sublime authority – as is demonstrated by the hostility of the scribes and Pharisees and, supremely, by his crucifixion. If these claims had been false, he would in fact have been guilty of the 'blasphemy' with which he was charged. But would God have raised a blasphemer from the dead? Surely the fact that God did so raise him – and it seems that Jesus had virtually staked his own credibility on the assertion that he would, little though his disciples understood this – could be regarded as a divine authentication of who he was and of the validity of his claims. This, I am convinced, was how the apostolic church saw it. To quote Pannenberg once more:

> Jesus' claim to authority, through which he put himself in God's place, was, as we saw in the discussion of the antitheses in the Sermon on the Mount, blasphemous for Jewish ears. Because of this, Jesus was then also slandered by the Jews before the Roman governor as a rebel. If Jesus really has been raised, this claim has been visibly and unambiguously confirmed by the God of Israel, who was allegedly blasphemed by Jesus . . . That the primitive Christian proclamation in fact understood Jesus' resurrection from the dead as the confirmation of his pre-Easter claim emerges above all in the speeches in Acts.[57]

They also clearly regarded the fact that God had raised him from the dead as authenticating the meaning and significance of his death. This was not that of another martyr, to be interpreted in terms of being 'faithful unto death' and setting a magnificent example. Instead it was, as he himself had said, a 'ransom for many', so that Paul could (and did) base his doctrine of justification by faith on the fact that the raising of Jesus to life proved that he had not 'died for our sins' in vain. Nor was this teaching confined to the Pauline epistles: see also 1 Peter 2:24; 1 John 2:4 and Revelation 1:57, for example.

I have lingered somewhat on the subject of the resurrection because it is so decisive, in my view, not only in the context of 'Jesus and the World Religions' but in regard to the doctrine of the incarnation as a whole. When, therefore, Professor Hick asks: 'Why and how did this [alleged] deification [of Jesus] take place?'[58] The answer – as I see it – is that the decisive point in the experience of the disciples, and in the way in which they regarded Jesus, was the resurrection. This, however, should not be regarded as the time when *they* 'deified' him, but rather when God showed them, and they realized, who he really was and always had been. This does not mean that, even after the resurrection, they looked back on Jesus in the days of his flesh as not having been genuinely human. Instead, it means that they could (and did) believe that, though truly man, he was more than a 'mere' man; that he had come from God in a unique sense; and that now they felt compelled, in a way that they found difficult to explain, to identify him with God. There was nothing in the least 'not literally true'[59] about this conviction, or about the faith of the primitive church that it was through his death alone that they had been 'reconciled to God' and had come to enjoy pardon and peace.

Christianity and other religions

When Hick again turns specifically, towards the end of his papers, to other religions, his conclusions are in part wholly predictable and in part, as I see it, strangely naïve. He dismisses the consistent New Testament witness to the 'doctrine of the incarnation' as basically 'a mythological idea',[60] and the New Testament understanding of the significance of Christ's death as a mistaken deduction from the Jewish sacrificial system. It is then entirely predictable that he would take the view that the life of Jesus was merely 'one point at which the Logos – that is, God-in-relation-to-man – has acted',[61] and should put it on much the same level as 'other particular revelations of the Logos at work in human life – in the Hebrew prophets, in the Buddha, in the *Upanishads* and the *Bhagavad Gita*, in the *Koran*, and so on'.[62] It is almost equally predictable that he would be satisfied with defining 'all salvation' as 'the creating of human animals into children of God'.[63] He is, however, I think, naïve (and perhaps a little disingenuous?) when he suggests that the only alternative (for those who regard Christ alone as 'the effulgence of God's splendour and the stamp of God's very being', and his atoning death as the unique basis for reconciliation between a holy God and sinful men and women), is a wholly 'negative assertion'.[64] They must, as he sees it, assert that 'the Logos has not acted and is not acting anywhere else in human life';[65] that 'the whole religious life of mankind, beyond the stream of Judaic-Christian faith, is thus by implication excluded as lying outside the sphere of salvation';[66] that 'the only doorway to eternal life is Christian faith';[67] and that God 'has decreed that only those born within one particular thread of human life should be saved'.[68] His view is, that the only escape from such a 'negative assertion' is the postulate that 'devout men of other faiths may be Christians without knowing it, or may be anonymous Christians . . . or may have implicit faith and receive baptism by desire, and so on'.[69]

But surely he does not really think that to regard Christ as the unique revelation of God implies that God has wholly 'left himself without witness' in all non-Christian religions; or that to say that 'there is no other name[70] under heaven given among men by which we must be saved' means that all those who have not consciously put their faith in that name are necessarily 'lost'? What about all those Jews in Old Testament days who, convicted of sin, turned to God in repentance and faith, and in suitable cases brought prescribed sacrifices? Surely they were 'saved' – in spite of the fact that they had not been in a position to put their trust in the Christ who had not yet been born? Yet surely it was *through him* that they were accepted and forgiven, for the New Testament explicitly tells us that 'he is the mediator of a new covenant' under which his atoning death brings 'deliverance from sins committed under the former covenant' (Heb. 9:15). So who would dare to say that the same principle may not be applicable to individuals from any culture or religion who, convicted of their sin and need by the Holy Spirit, turn to God – as best they know – in repentance and faith? To deny that there is any 'saving structure' in other religions as such, or to affirm that there is salvation in Christ alone, is not of itself to exclude any repentant sinner – or, indeed, babies, young children, imbeciles, *etc.* – from the scope of that salvation. I emphatically deny that to believe this is an attempt 'to square an inadequate theology with the facts of God's world' or 'an anachronistic clinging to the husk of the old doctrine after its substance has crumbled.'[71]

More recently, however, in an article entitled 'The Non-Absoluteness of Christianity' – in a book, *The Myth of Christian Uniqueness*, of which he is a co-editor – Hick has taken the views he expressed eleven years earlier, in *The Myth of God Incarnate*, to their logical conclusion. After referring to the '*exclusivist*' position which had been adopted in the past by very many Christians (whether in the Roman Catholic version *extra ecclesiam nulla salus*, or in its Protestant version 'outside Christianity there is no salvation', he turns to the '*inclusivist*' position which, he asserts, represents a 'near consensus' among Christians today. This is the view that the benefits of the salvation Jesus came, and died, to bring are not exclusively confined to those who have been in a position to put explicit faith in him.

His argument is that, 'once it is granted that salvation is in fact taking place not only within the Christian but also within the other great religious traditions' – a clause which I myself would wish to word with much more caution – 'it seems arbitrary and unrealistic to go on insisting that the Christ-event is the sole and exclusive source of human salvation.' So we must, he argues, cross the 'theological Rubicon' and adopt the '*pluralist*' position in which 'Christianity is seen in a pluralistic context as *one* of the great world faiths, *one* of the streams of religious life through which human beings can be savingly related to that ultimate Reality Christians know as their heavenly Father.'[72]

But this goes much too far and is a radical departure from biblical teaching. What Jesus himself explicitly said was that 'No one comes to the Father except through me' (John 14:6). He did not say 'through the church', or even 'through Christianity', but through him himself – and, by implication, who he was and the salvation he died to bring. We all admire tolerance and broad-mindedness, and we are rightly suspicious of anything that savours of arrogance. But 'a Christianity which should think of itself as one of the many diverse contributions to the religious life of mankind', Visser't Hooft insisted, 'is a Christianity that has lost its foundation in the New Testament'.[73]

It will have been noticed that this is precisely the sort of Christianity that Professor Hick advocates, in the quotation I have given on p. 175 above, where he has put the revelation of the 'Logos at work in human life' in the life of Jesus much on a level with that 'in the Hebrew prophets, in the Buddha, in the *Upanishads* and the *Bhagavad Gita*, in the *Koran*, and so on'. Now it is with Islam and Christianity that we are primarily concerned in this book, and there is no doubt in my mind that convinced Muslims would react to this bracketing in much the same way as Christians would. Orthodox Muslims, moreover, would wish to make a clear distinction between the three great monotheistic religions – Judaism, Christianity and Islam – and those religions which do not believe in a divine unity which is both personal and all-pervasive. It has recently been suggested, indeed, that Christians should engage in a 'trialogue' with both Jews and Muslims together.

I myself am convinced that dialogue between Christians and those of any other faith is possible and desirable – on the basis of 'reverence for reverence'. I do not believe, however, that the suggested 'trialogue' would be viable for very long. A dialogue between Christians and Jews would soon reveal that they both not only believe in one creator God, but also accept the divine inspiration of the Old Testament. It is on this basis that Christians can share with their Jewish friends their conviction that the Messiah, to whom the Old Testament scriptures continually point, has in fact already come in the person of Jesus of Nazareth. But a dialogue between Christians and Muslims must inevitably take a somewhat different course. They can certainly celebrate their mutual belief in the unity of the Godhead and their conviction that ʿĪsā (Jesus) was the Messiah, as the Qurʾān unequivocally asserts. They can also share, indeed, what their faith means to them in practice. But when it comes to the theological basis on which their spiritual experience rests, the dialogue cannot proceed in the same way as that between Christians and Jews.

The Christian partner can certainly suggest that the Quranic statement that 'they [the Jews] did not kill him [ʿĪsā] and did not crucify him, but he was counterfeited for them' (sūra 4:156) *need* not be so interpreted as to deny that Jesus did in fact die on the cross.[74] The Christian can also gently suggest that the Prophet of Islam, whatever he may have heard about the beliefs of rival Christian churches – and, indeed, doctrines and ideas later dismissed by Christians as heretical – may never have really heard the true gospel or been confronted with the authentic Christ. This is certainly true of most Muslims today; so they cannot be said to have *rejected* him, consciously and deliberately. And it is on those who do reject him that the New Testament pronounces unequivocal perdition. (Jn. 3:16–19). It is our Christian shame that we have failed to bring them the authentic Saviour.

It is inevitable, as Stephen Neill put it, that the Christian faith

> casts the shadow of falsehood, or at least of imperfect truth, on every other system. This Christian claim is naturally offensive to the adherents of every other religious system. It is almost as offensive to modern man, brought up in the atmosphere of relativism, in which tolerance is regarded almost as the highest of the virtues. But we must not suppose that this claim to universal validity is something that can quietly be removed from the Gospel without changing it into something entirely different from what it is. The mission of Jesus was limited to the Jews and did not look immediately beyond them; but his life, his method and his message do not make sense, unless they are interpreted in the light of his own conviction that he was in fact the final and decisive word of God to men . . . For the human sickness there is one specific remedy, and this is it. There is no other.[75]

'The focus of the Gospel', Lesslie Newbigin insists, 'is the word of the cross, and that word is a radical judgment upon all human wisdom, and upon the experience on which that wisdom is founded . . . It is in the presence of the cross that we are compelled to say: 'There is none righteous, no not one.'[76]

CHAPTER EIGHT

The incarnation and personal faith today

The problem posed

A look back

Chapter 5 in this book took the form of a general introduction to the mysteries of the incarnation and atonement and attempted to etch in the background to what I have termed 'the contemporary debate'. Starting from the basic Christian confession, 'Jesus is Lord', we looked first at some of the titles applied to Jesus in the Gospels – Son of Man, Messiah, Son of God, Lord – and at the exceedingly strong evidence there is for the vivid consciousness he had of a unique filial relationship with his heavenly Father, unclouded by any sense of personal sin. We also looked at the evidence for the innate authority which characterized his words and actions, and his constant response to the divine imperative which called him, ever more clearly, to 'give his life a ransom for many'. We saw, too, how his disciples, completely misunderstanding the nature of his mission, were thrown into despair, with all their hopes shattered, by his betrayal and crucifixion. *But God raised him from the dead*, and thereby brought them back – wondering, and at first doubting their very senses – to a living hope and a triumphant joy. Jesus' resurrection and exaltation led them to see him in an entirely new light; and this was why they now felt compelled to call him 'Lord' and began to associate him with God himself in prayer and worship.

How, then, did they now view Jesus' earthly life, during which they must, beyond doubt, have regarded him as a man among men; and how did they explain his new status? One suggestion, which (as we have seen) assumes quite a prominent place in the contemporary debate, can be summed up in the term Adoptionism – that is, the theory that God at some stage 'adopted' him as his Son, and exalted him to a place of lordship and power. We saw that this is regarded by some writers today as the earliest Christology. It is clear, however, that the church of the middle of the first century did not only believe in the exaltation of 'the man, Christ Jesus', but also in his pre-existence, for we find references to this from a very early date – and without any explanation or comment – in several of St Paul's epistles and elsewhere in the New Testament.[1] It would have been natural enough, of course, to reason that a life which the early church believed to be 'eternal' in the sense that it would have no end must equally be eternal in the sense of having no beginning; but I for one have no doubt that the concept can also be traced back to the way in which Jesus himself had sometimes spoken.

Several contemporary writers, however, insist that this concept of 'pre-existence' must be interpreted exclusively in terms of God's foreknowledge, purpose and plan that in the fullness of time a man would be born in whom he could and would uniquely reveal himself. Anything more than that, they maintain, would inevitably compromise the humanity of Jesus and lead to some form of 'psychological Docetism' – or a belief that Jesus was not really human (and certainly not 'a particular man'), but God in human guise.

So, in chapter 6, I attempted to trace, in outline, the history of christological thought down the centuries. Starting with the extremes of Gnostic Docetism, which did not regard Jesus as a real man at all, on the one hand, and those Jewish Ebionites who denied that he was other than a purely human Messiah, on the other, we touched on the Arian, Apollinarian and Nestorian heresies. We discussed the Nicene Creed and the Definition of Chalcedon, and noted the continuing differences between the Alexandrian and Antiochene schools of thought, the controversy between Monophysites and Dyophysites, and the divisions of opinion between Lutheran and Reformed theologians and even within the Lutheran communion.

In part these controversies were based on purely philosophical distinctions; and the protracted disputes about whether the human nature of Christ must be predicated of a human *hypostasis* or entity, or might be predicated of a divine *hypostasis*, do not, *per se*, seem very meaningful today. Broadly speaking, however, it may be said that the Antiochenes held firmly to the view that our Lord was truly man as well as God, but at the expense of depicting him, at times, as a split personality acting first in the one capacity and then in the other. The Alexandrians, on the other hand, emphasized the unity of his person and his essential deity, but at the expense of minimizing his true humanity. The same basic problem has recurred, in somewhat different forms, all down the ages, for how could he be really God and really man –

either alternately or at one and the same time? How could the divine Logos or Son of God – himself, by definition, transcendent, omnipotent and allegedly impassible – become incarnate in a baby or suffer as a man? How could he be omnipresent when lying in his mother's arms? How could he be omniscient, and yet have to learn like other boys? And how could he uphold the universe by his word of power as a sleeping baby – or even as a boy or man?

The issue today

It may have sufficed, at one time, to say that 'the impassible Logos suffered in the passible flesh' or 'usefully pretended not to know'; but such phrases seem little better than quibbles today. It may have been possible then to agree on creeds and definitions which would serve to define the bounds of orthodoxy and exclude unacceptable deviations. But how can Christians of a later age come to any understanding of the Jesus who, we read, shared our nature, grew in wisdom and stature, was in all points tempted as we are, and learned obedience in the school of suffering – and yet, as the church has always believed, was the Word made flesh, the image of the invisible God, the Lord through whom all things were created, and the Saviour who tasted death for every man? To talk of a 'person' in this age of psychology means to think of a real, living personality, with all that this has come to mean, not a philosophical abstraction. So how can the Christian confession that Jesus is Lord be meaningful and relevant for us in the twentieth century?

One of the major ways of attempting to solve the mystery of how the Son or Logos, sharing all the attributes of the Godhead, could be incarnate in the man Jesus, has been through the doctrine of *kenōsis*, or self-emptying. This doctrine is based, in part, on the statement in Philippians 2:5–8 that, 'though he was in the form of God', Christ 'did not count equality with God a thing to be grasped, but emptied himself, taking the form of a slave, being born in the likeness of men. And being found in human form he humbled himself...' In part, however, it may be said to be quite independent of this much-quoted passage and to be inherent in the obvious fact that, when 'the Word became flesh', this must have entailed some limitation of the *manifest* glory of deity, at the very least. As such the concept of *kenōsis* was not unknown to the Fathers; but Pannenberg insists that 'Origen, Athanasius, Gregory of Nyssa, Cyril of Alexandria, Augustine and others who connected Phil. 2:7 to the coming of the Logos in the flesh meant by the term "self-emptying" the assumption of human nature, but not the complete or partial relinquishment of the divine nature or its attributes'.[2]

We have already seen, moreover, how in the seventeenth and eighteenth centuries the theologians of Tübingen under the leadership of Johann Brenz believed that Jesus not only possessed the divine attributes of omnipotence, omniscience and omnipresence from the time of his birth, but actually on occasions used them in a way which was concealed from others, while Martin Chemnitz – who equally believed that Jesus retained all his divine attributes – thought in terms not of concealment (*krypsis*) but a partial refusal to use them. Eventually, however, the doctrine of the theologians of Giessen, which involved a real renunciation (*kenōsis*) of the divine attributes' use during the state of Christ's 'humiliation', triumphed. Turner, indeed, asserts that this distinction between the 'two states' – the state of Christ's humiliation and the state of his exaltation – represents the most distinctive contribution of the Reformation to Christology. But while the Lutherans regarded this *kenōsis* as representing a continual concealment of the divine glory, or renunciation of the use of divine attributes, by the incarnate Lord (so that 'the God-man of this Christology', to quote Pannenberg, 'remained a sort of fabulous being, more like a mythical redeemer than the historical reality of Jesus of Nazareth)',[3] the theologians of the Reformed churches thought in terms of some sort of initial *kenōsis* by the pre-incarnate Son at the time when he became incarnate.[4]

It was this last concept which was the starting point for the remarkable development of the 'Kenotic Theory' in the nineteenth and earlier twentieth centuries. Thus Thomasius, in Germany, taught that at the incarnation the divine Son 'gave up the *relative* attributes of divinity, that is, those which characterize the *relation* of God to the world: omnipotence, omniscience, omnipresence', and 'retained only the *immanent* perfections proper to God independent of his relation to the world: holiness, power, truth and love'.[5] It was in this way, he believed, that we could understand the human life of Jesus without any abandonment of his divine essence or life. In the incarnation the Logos 'exchanged His Divine consciousness for one that was human, or rather Divine-human; and thus became capable of forming the centre of a single personal Life'. In other words, he 'voluntarily contracted His life to the form and dimensions of human existence, submitting to the laws of human growth and preserving His absolute powers only in the measure in which they were essential to His redeeming work; and at the close of His earthly career He resumed once more the glory he had laid aside'.[6] This may be said to represent the classical form of the Kenotic Theory; but there are, of course, numerous variations. Gess, for example, went so far as to interpret the incarnation as 'a transformation of the Logos into a human soul' – which Thomasius regarded as an 'abandonment of his divinity'.[7]

But the Kenotic Theory has been strongly criticized on a number of different grounds. First, it has been repeatedly emphasized that Philippians 2:5–11 should not be regarded as a theological exposition of any such doctrine, but rather as an ethical exhortation to Christian humility based on the example of the humility of Christ himself – and it is significant in this context that the phrase *heanton ekanōsen* in Philippians 2:7, literally translated 'emptied himself' in the RSV, is rendered 'made himself of no reputation' in the AV and 'made himself nothing' in the NEB and NIV. Secondly, the Kenotic Theory, as such, has been criticized as failing to give any explanation of how the divine Son or Logos continued to uphold the universe by his word of power (Heb. 1:3) during his incarnate life. As Temple put it: 'To say that the Infant Jesus was from His cradle exercising providential care over it all is certainly monstrous; but to deny this, and yet to say that the Creative Word was so self-emptied as to have no being except in the Infant Jesus, is to assert that for a certain period the history of the world was let loose from the control of the Creative Word'.[8]

Again, the theory has been criticized as failing to do justice either to the deity of Jesus during the days of his flesh or to the humanity of the exalted Lord. In D. M. Baillie's words: 'Instead of giving us a doctrine of Incarnation in which Jesus Christ is both God and man, the Kenotic Theory appears to me to give us a story of a temporary theophany, in which He who formerly was God changed Himself temporarily into man, or exchanged His divinity for humanity.' If, moreover, the incarnation itself is explained as *kenōsis*, this presumably came to an end with his exaltation. So, in the Kenotic Theory in its extreme form, 'He is God and Man, not simultaneously in a hypostatic union, but *successively* – first divine, then human, then God again.' But this 'seems to leave no room at all for the traditional catholic doctrine of the *permanence* of the manhood of Christ "who, being the eternal Son of God, became man, and so was, and *continueth to be*, God and man in two distinct natures, and one person, *for ever*" '.[9]

We must return to this subject shortly. But at this point I must, I think, begin to attempt to outline the conclusions to which I have myself come, after quite a lot of mental wrestling. They will, of course, inevitably be inadequate, not only because of my own manifest deficiencies as an amateur theologian, but also because no finite mind can hope to plumb the unrevealed secrets of the Godhead or the full mystery of the incarnation. So I will content myself with summarizing my conclusions in the form of two basis principles and a number of tentative propositions.

Two basic principles

The biblical evidence

The first principle that I regard as fundamental is that we must do our utmost to grapple with the biblical evidence as a whole and see where this leads us, rather than put an exclusive – and perhaps exaggerated – emphasis on certain parts of that evidence and explain away, or ignore, anything which may seem to point in a different direction. It is obvious that different New Testament writers had their own distinctive insights and modes of expression; that the way in which any member of the early church wrote, or is reported to have spoken, must have been greatly influenced by the particular context in which he wrote or the audience he was addressing; and that they were all struggling to clothe in words an experience and a mystery they had only very partially apprehended.

But I am myself convinced that Professor Moule is right when he suggests that 'development' is a more appropriate analogy than 'evolution' for the way in which 'descriptions and understandings of Jesus' emerged; for if evolution 'means the genesis of successive new species by mutation and natural selection', development, by contrast, 'will mean something more like the growth, from immaturity to maturity, of a single specimen from within itself'. So he challenges 'the tendency to explain the change from (say) invoking Jesus as a revered Master to the acclamation of him as a divine Lord by the theory that, when the Christian movement spread beyond Palestinian soil, it began to come under the influence of non-Semitic Saviour-cults'; or, indeed, to attempt to explain the change by appeal to the effect of 'lapse of time, which may itself lead to the intensification of terms of adoration'.

Instead, he believes the evidence suggests that 'all the various estimates of Jesus reflected in the New Testament' are, in essence, 'only attempts to describe what was already there from the beginning. They are not successive additions of something new, but only the drawing out and articulating of what is there'. Moreover, 'when once one assumes that the changes are, in the main, changes only in perception', it becomes clear that 'it may not be possible, *a priori*, to arrange such changes in any firm chronological order. In evolution, the more complex species generally belong to a later stage than the more simple; but in development, there is nothing to prevent a profoundly perceptive estimate occurring at an early stage . . .' This is not, of course, to suggest that Moule wants 'to eliminate the chronological factor altogether'. What he does assert unequivocally is that the evidence, as he sees it, 'suggests that Jesus was, *from the beginning*, such a one as appropriately to be described in the ways in which, sooner or later, he did come to be described in the New Testament period – for instance as "Lord" and even, in some sense, as "God".'[10]

If, then, we try to take the biblical evidence as a whole more seriously than do many participants in the contemporary debate, we shall certainly insist that the Word was, in very fact, 'made flesh', and that Jesus was truly man. But we shall not regard his 'total solidarity with all men', in the sense that he was, in himself (or ontologically), *only* human, 'without remainder', as the fundamental criterion by reference to which everything which the New Testament tells us about his earthly life, his pre-existence and his present exaltation must be measured, interpreted or even discarded. Instead, we must do all we possibly can to find a solution to the very real problems inherent in Christology that takes due account of *all* the available evidence. For this virtually our only primary authority is the New Testament – supported, of course, by Christian experience down the centuries. But I see no reason to suppose that the testimony of the New Testament on this subject is either false or misleading. On the contrary, if God did in fact act, uniquely and decisively, in Jesus for the world's salvation – and for this I find the evidence wholly convincing – then it seems to me inherently unlikely that he would have left the basic facts and implications of that action without any reliable records, together with trustworthy teaching about their meaning.

Christology and soteriology

My second fundamental principle is that no understanding of the mystery of the incarnation can be true to the biblical revelation unless it also explains the meaning and significance of the atonement. Any Christology which concentrates on Emmanuel, God with us, at the expense of Jesus, God our Saviour, must surely be defective; for soteriology and Christology are inextricably bound together.

This has, of course, often been emphasized – notably, in recent years, by H. E. W. Turner. But it is significant, I think, that all those who insist on a Christology which regards Christ as exclusively human, even if the locus or agent of a uniquely divine revelatory event, take a subjective rather than objective view of the atonement – or, to be more precise, a view which concentrates on the subjective effect on man of what they would certainly accept as an objective event. Those of us, on the other hand, who regard the atonement as of fundamental importance, not only because of the subjective change it can, should, and does effect in man and his attitude to God, but also, and primarily, because it provides the essential basis on which, alone, a holy God can and does proffer a full and free forgiveness to the repentant sinner

– free to him because the God who proffers it has redeemed him at so great a cost – must necessarily, I believe, find this Christology inadequate.

If, for example, we accept that the biblical doctrine of the atonement clearly includes, among its many different meanings and facets, the fact that Christ died not only on our behalf but in our place, or in any sense as a 'sacrifice for sin', then it would be monstrous to believe that 'God was reconciling the world to himself' in (or by) an entirely innocent and purely human being whom he 'made sin for us', and who thus 'bore our sins in his body on the tree'. The idea would be utterly abhorrent. But that there *is* such an element in the atonement is expressed with his usual trenchancy by Barth in his commentary on the last few verses in 2 Corinthians 5, where he writes about what he terms an '*exchange*'. 'This', he says, 'is what is expressly stated in the verse (21) with which the passage closes. On the one side, the exchange: 'He hath made him to be sin for us (in our place and for our sakc), who kncw no sin . . . And on the other side, the exchange: He does it, He takes our place in Christ, that we (again in the simplest possible form) might be made the righteousness of God (*dikaiosynē theou*) in Him'.

Later, he continues: 'At this point we can and must make the decisive statement: What took place is that the Son of God fulfilled the righteous judgment on us men by Himself taking our place as man and in our place undergoing the judgment under which we had passed'. Elsewhere, moreover, he asserts that 'Jesus Christ for us signifies His activity as our Representative and Substitute . . . If someone gives his life *lytron anti pollōn* (Mk. 10:45), then he necessarily acts in the place and as the representative of the *polloi*, paying on their account but without their co-operation what they cannot pay for themselves.[11] Similarly, Pannenberg writes: 'Paul stressed that Jesus was without sin precisely where he emphasized that Jesus was judged, cursed (Galatians 3:13), treated as a sinner by God in our stead. Only because Jesus was himself without sin can it be said that what he suffered was not the consequence of his own guilt, but that he took his suffering upon himself for our sake'.[12]

This concept of God's 'curse' must, indeed, as Professor F. F. Bruce has persuasively argued, have been one of the earliest elements in Paul's thought. Before the experience on the Damascus road the statement in Deuteronomy 21:23 that 'a hanged man is accursed by God' had, no doubt, sufficed to dismiss as impossible any suggestion of a crucified Messiah. But the resurrection had proved that the crucified Jesus was far from 'accursed' in himself. So 'Sooner rather than later Paul must have reached the conclusion set out in Galatians 3:10–13 –

that Jesus submitted to the death of the cross in order to take upon himself the curse which the law pronounced on all who failed to keep it completely (Deut. 27:26)'[13]

The significance of this for Christology seems to me inescapable. No one who was in himself human '*and no more*' could bear the curse and judgment on our sins or be a 'sacrifice for sin' (for those who favour this translation of 2 Cor. 5:21 and Rom. 8:3); and the 'Son' whom the Father, in his infinite love, sent to be the propitiation or expiation for those sins must have been, in some basic sense (that is, ontologically, rather than functionally), one with the God who was, in him, 'reconciling the world to himself.'

In the light of these two basic principles, it seems to me that we can make the following propositions.

A series of deductions

Before the resurrection

Before the resurrection, the disciples clearly accepted the real manhood of Jesus as axiomatic: indeed, in the Synoptic Gospels, as has often been remarked, this is 'assumed rather than asserted', while in John's Gospel we find the positive assertion that the Word 'became flesh', together with repeated references to his manhood. Jesus' disciples, and many of those who heard his teaching and saw his works of love and power, realized that he was no ordinary man; but certainly did not yet identify him with God – or, still less, a sort of demi-god. There was nothing extraordinary, so far as we know, about his gestation and birth; and although I fully believe in his virginal conception, this (as we have seen) was clearly not part of the basic apostolic *kerygma*. Both Jesus and his apostles called men to faith in him on the basis of his life, death and, supremely, his resurrection, not stories or assertions about his nativity.

He seems in most ways, moreover, outwardly to have been a perfectly normal boy. As John Robinson vividly expresses it, there is something unnatural about the statement in a well-known Christmas hymn 'The little Lord Jesus no crying he makes'; and the line from another Christmas hymn 'Tears and smiles like us he knew' seems to strike a much more authentic note. But I said 'in most ways' deliberately, since the evidence both for his sinlessness and for his unique filial consciousness is exceedingly strong; so his sinlessness must have extended right back to his boyhood, and his filial consciousness, while it must have dawned gradually, seems to have started at a very early age.

Throughout his whole earthly life the Jesus of the Gospels strikes us as an essentially integrated personality, who was accepted everywhere as genuinely human and was the welcome guest of 'tax collectors and sinners'. He grew in body, mind and understanding as other boys grow; he was tempted as we are; he learnt obedience in the school of suffering; and, while he habitually spoke to his heavenly Father in profound tranquillity and confident assurance, he could and did pray to him 'with loud cries and tears' – for in Gethsemane 'anguish and dismay came over him, and he said "My heart is ready to break with grief".' It is clear moreover, that he not only had a human body and 'rational soul', but a human will which shrank from the agony he knew was to be his, although this will was always kept subject to that of his Father.

But we must also make room in our assessment for the more than ordinary knowledge of men's hearts and circumstances which he sometimes showed and the works of love and power which he performed. The former could conceivably be explained in terms of extra-sensory perception, and his 'mighty works' can be attributed, like those of the prophets and apostles, to divine power. But alongside these we must take due account of that innate authority with which he spoke and acted; those claims (explicitly in his words and implicitly in his deeds) which the Jews regarded as blasphemous; and the way in which he moved others to shame and repentance, yet showed no consciousness whatever of personal unworthiness or even the experience of forgiven sins.

After the resurrection

But the watershed, from the point of view of his disciples, was clearly the resurrection. Only after that do we find him regarded as 'Lord' in the full sense of that word, referred to and addressed as the 'Lord Jesus' and instinctively accorded a divine status. But we have already seen that the resurrection could not *of itself* have proved that he was 'Son of God' (Rom. 1:3): it was because of the life he had lived and the claims he had made that the apostolic church insisted that the fact that God had 'raised him from the dead' must be regarded as the divine endorsement both of his Sonship and of the efficacy of his atoning death. Nor was his resurrection a mere resuscitation to terrestrial life, but the beginning of a new life of exaltation in which his spiritual presence was made real to his disciples by the promised Holy Spirit.

It was in the light of his exaltation, I believe, that they remembered words he had spoken during his earthly life which they had been totally unable to understand at the time. I fully agree with Moule that their wide-spread belief, at a very early date, in his pre-existence *could* have been based solely on a logical inference from their experience of the exalted Jesus 'in a dimension transcending the human and the temporal' – a 'divine dimension such that he must always and eternally have existed in it.' The Jesus they had known on earth had retained 'his *personal identity*' after his resurrection and ascension; so must not that personal identity have also existed before his birth at Bethlehem? Where I differ from Moule is when he states that it is difficult 'to conceive of a genuinely human person being conscious of his own pre-existence'. In general terms this is undoubtedly true; but if Jesus, while 'genuinely human', was also God expressing himself in truly human terms (as Moule believes), and if he not only had a vivid consciousness of his relationship to his Father but complete dependence on the Father's power and teaching, might not some intimation of his pre-incarnate life have been revealed to him? For myself, I am content to believe that John 17:5 represents a memory of 'Jesus' *ipsissima vox*'.[14]

It was consequent on his exaltation, too, that an embryonic belief in the Trinity must have begun to emerge. The confession 'Jesus is Lord', with all that the title *kyrios* implies, proves that at a very early date the exalted Saviour was somehow identified with God. This may have come naturally enough to Gentile converts; but in the case of Paul the Pharisee and his like, to whom the unity of the Godhead was absolutely fundamental, it is deeply significant. The Johannine reference to the fact that 'the Word was with God, and the Word was God' (pointing, as it does, to a differentiation existing within a basic identity) – coupled with, or preceded by, the allusions in St Paul's letters and in Hebrews to the one who is the 'image of the invisible God', the 'Son of his love', through whom 'all things were made' and in whom 'all things subsist' – mark the beginning of a theology which was later expanded as a result of the experienced presence of the promised Holy Spirit. The doctrine of the Trinity as such falls outside the scope of this book. I must, however, remark in passing that – while the view that the distinction between Father, Son and (subsequently) Holy Spirit should be understood solely in terms of different 'modes' in which God acted in creation, revelation and redemption[15] (rather than in terms of 'subsisting relations' or 'centres of consciousness' within the unity of the Godhead) does not seem to me to take adequate account, *inter alia*, of the mutual and eternal love of the Father and the Son – the basic truth of the divine unity should restrain us from ever thinking of the 'persons' of the Trinity as in any sense separate individuals (which would, of course, amount to Tri-theism). And this, in turn, should suffice to indicate that while it was, indeed, in the eternal Word or Son that 'God was manifest in the flesh', this does not mean that 'the man, Christ Jesus' was pre-existent as such,[16] or that the eternal Word was not still performing his cosmic functions during the years when he was incarnate in Jesus. But we shall have to return to this point a little later.

God-in-manhood

What I have already said will, I think, explain why I do not believe that any inspirational, rather than incarnational – or functional, rather than ontological – Christology will meet our need. It is true that some of the scholars I have quoted go as far as they possibly can, on their premises, in giving a unique place to Jesus, and that they believe that he was, indeed, the 'human face of God' and the 'exegesis of the Father'; but they insist that that face was in itself purely human and no more. And on this basis I cannot see any justification whatever for according worship even to the exalted Christ, or for ever addressing him in prayer. Few Christians, I think, would be content to explain their 'encounter' with the risen Christ in worship and prayer as being 'encountered by, God, the Spirit who was in Jesus, meeting them with the identical judgment, mercy, forgiveness and love which were at work in Jesus'[17] – for this would be to eliminate the mediation, priesthood and intercession of the one they believe to be still man as well as truly God.[18] I cannot believe that a 'Spirit' or merely 'inspirational' Christology does justice to such a basic statement as 'for you know the grace of our Lord Jesus Christ, that though he was rich, yet for your sakes he became poor, so that by his poverty you might become rich' (2 Cor. 8:9), or to the absolute uniqueness of the one who was not only 'separate from sinners' (Heb. 7:26) but in whom, and for whom, 'all things were created, in heaven and on earth' (Col. 1:16). Nor does it seem in any way adequate for the one almost certainly described as 'the only-begotten God, who is in the bosom of the Father', in John 1:18; to whom the author of the letter to the Hebrews probably attributes – specifically as Son – the title of 'God' (Heb. 1:18 and 9); whom St Paul almost certainly calls 'God' in Romans 9:5;[19] and who is probably referred to as our 'God and Saviour' in Titus 2:13 and 2 Peter 1:1.[20]

Genuinely 'made man'

How, then, can we reconcile this essential deity with full human experience? This is the age-old problem. As we have seen, one way of expressing the testimony of the New Testament to both the true humanity and true deity of Jesus was the doctrine of the 'two natures'. And if, as I certainly believe, Christ was, and is, *vere deus, vere homo*, there is an essential – and virtually unquestionable – truth in saying that he must have had two natures. In Galot's words (as translated by Mascall): 'We cannot appreciate the character of the enterprise unless we recognize the divine transcendence of the person and the wholeness of the human condition in which it is involved; and this is what is expressed by the affirmation of the duality of the natures in Christ.'[21] But this doctrine in its developed form is almost inextricably bound up with the philosophical concept that 'nature' is a 'secondary substance' which must always be predicated of a *hypostasis* (or entity) as a 'primary substance', and the consequent disputes between those whose understanding of the doctrine force them to depict Jesus as almost a split personality and those who regard him as so basically divine that his true humanity, while always asserted, becomes distinctly questionable.

The classical way in which this has been expressed has been by the affirmation that the eternal Son took to himself 'impersonal human nature'; that he became 'man' without becoming 'a particular man'. This means that his human nature was either devoid of a human *hypostasis* ('entity', 'subsistence' or 'primary substance') or found its identity in the Logos/Son: that is, to use the technical terms, that his human nature was *anhypostatos* or *enhypostatos*. Recently, however, it has repeatedly been asserted that any such concept 'totally fails to do justice to the reality and completeness of his humanity'. But we need to get behind the philosophical terms in which the classical doctrine is couched; for the concept of his 'impersonal' human nature should not be thought of as 'human nature in its generality', which would be a purely Platonic idea. The human nature of Jesus was certainly individual, and had distinctive qualities and characteristics. He had a distinctively human will, for example, which he always kept subordinate to that of '*Abba*' (cf. Mk. 14:35–36).

What the doctrine means is that his human nature had no personal subsistence distinct from that of the Logos; for if it had had a distinct 'personal' existence or entity of its own, then he would either have been two 'persons', in the modern understanding of personality, or he would have been no more than a man wholly 'possessed' or 'inspired' by God, as many affirm today. But the concept of his 'impersonal' human nature need not be so understood as to detract in any way from his genuine humanity. The point at issue is simply that 'the human nature formed in and out of Mary did not for a moment exist by and for itself'. In other words, to speak of the 'impersonal' human nature of Christ in any context other than a purely theological and technical one would give a false impression which is very different from the picture of Jesus we get in the Gospels; but in the particular context of denying 'an independently conceived human nature' the term can be used 'without the connotation that some essential constituent of humanity is lacking in Christ'.[22]

But this does little or nothing to elucidate the mystery of how one who was truly God could also be truly man. It is precisely this which so many contemporary theologians dismiss as 'impossible', a 'contradiction in terms' or – at best – a 'myth'. But if the eternal Logos/Son was really incarnate in the man Christ Jesus (which seems to me a much more straightforward way of expressing the essence of the Nicene Creed and the Definition of Chalcedon than the 'descent of a pre-existent divine person into the world'), this must necessarily have involved a very real 'humiliation' or limitation of some sort.

As we have seen, this has very generally been expressed, in recent years, in some variation of the Kenotic Theory. But I have already mentioned some of the objections which have been raised to that theory as such – among them the fact that Philippians 2:7, from which it derives its name, is taken from a passage which should not be regarded as a theological exposition of the incarnation so much as an ethical exhortation to Christian humility. Of this Moule aptly remarks: 'Of course there is no denying that the "pattern" of Phil. 2:5–11 as a whole is the pattern of descent followed by ascent, humiliation followed by exaltation.' But that, he believes, need not prevent one seeing, at the same time, a pattern 'by which height is *equated* with depth, humiliation is *identified* with exaltation'. And he continues:

> Anybody will recognize, for instance, that creative art involves an acceptance, and a positive use, of limitation. A craftsman in wood has to know all about the grain and the capacities of the wood he is working with, and, by accepting them and working within them, he exploits them . . . to the full as a craftsman in wood-carving. So God the creator, when working in humanity, may be expected to express himself most fully, so far as the idiom of that medium goes, by accepting the human range of capacity and exploiting the human medium to the full. This is no more self-emptying than it is complete self-fulfilment in a given medium . . . There is, it must be granted, an "emptying", a *kenōsis*, in respect of *scope*, even if this is in the interests of the "fulfilment", the *plērōsis*, of artistic *skill*. It is possible to recognise a change of "status", even if not of character . . . But it would be a mistake if it were imagined that such language implied a deliberate renunciation of possibilities, as in so-called kenotic theories. Anything so contrived or artificial would simply be inappropriate to the Christian conviction that . . . the incarnation is a positive filling, not a negative emptying;

and, as such, it should, strictly speaking, constitute nothing for surprise, as though it were something incongruous with God's majesty, however much it may be a theme for adoring wonder, as congruous with God's eternal, generous self-giving.[23]

'Two states' of the Logos

Another way of expressing what is, I think, *partially* the same view is to think with Frank Weston (subsequently Bishop of Zanzibar) of the two 'states' of Logos/Son in terms of 'sums of relationships'. He argues, 'the word state in this connection means nothing more than the sum of the relationships of the Logos. On the one hand He lives in universal creative relationships with the whole of His creation, such relations being based upon His own eternal relation to the Father. On the other hand He lives on earth in special, redemptive relationships . . . based upon a new, limited, human relation to His Father. But He himself is one and the same person.'[24] So 'the Person who became incarnate is purely divine. In His eternal essence He is of one substance with the Father, God of God; possessed of all divine powers, prerogatives, and attributes. His Incarnation in no way interfered with His true life in the eternal Godhead, or hindered Him from His divine activities in the universe. He remained true Word of God, "upholding all things by the word of His power".'[25]

But, except in his sinlessness, the manhood he assumed was 'like ours, having the same natural weaknesses and limitations that hinder us', for 'He was content to accept the limitations that are proper to and normal in man. . . . [26]

> He has *as Incarnate* no existence and no activity outside the conditions that manhood imposes upon Him . . . Hence it seems to follow of necessity that as Incarnate the Son has no communion with His Father except through the same medium of manhood. He holds communion with His Father through His human soul. For He is one person; and His manhood is, in the fullest sense, His own nature, although it is assumed. He took it to Himself not as an external organ . . . but as the very true and real nature through and in which He might mediate between God and men. It is not enough that the mediator be in contact with our nature; He must make it really and entirely His own.[27]

Weston insists, moreover, that the sphere in which the eternal Son 'restrains himself' is that of 'His universal activities', while in the sphere of the incarnation 'the self-limited Logos can at every moment exercise only such powers as manhood may mediate'. And he adds:

> I do not mean for a moment that the two spheres can be figured as concentric circles: for that would be to lend to the Incarnate the aid of deity apart from the limitations of humanity. But I do mean that the two spheres touch, meeting in the person of the eternal Son . . . [28]

As incarnate, 'the Son necessarily has a knowledge of Himself, in His relations Godward and manward, that does not belong to His universal life as Logos. The Incarnate is the Son of God existing only under conditions of manhood.' So he 'did not know Himself as God the Son possessed of and exercising unlimited power.' Again, he did not know himself 'as merely a man'; for that he was not. Nor did he know himself 'as divine-human in composite consciousness'. Instead, 'He was conscious of Himself as God-in-manhood' and 'knew Himself as Logos only in the measure that His human soul could mediate that self-knowledge. But all the while in His universal state He was, nay is, the unlimited Logos who wills to be . . . in such special relations of love to the redeemed that, in the sphere in which He meets with them, He is prepared to accept this limited content of self-consciousness.'[29]. So Weston concludes that 'so long as the external limits of the sphere of the Incarnation are as real as those of our manhood, so long will the person who lives within them be as really subject to manhood as we are'[30] – sharing our human experience and human temptations, and providing us with a human example.

All this was written in 1907; but it is significant that seventy years later much of it is echoed in Professor E. L. Mascall's *Theology and the Gospel of Christ*, where he insists that 'the whole of the incarnate life is the life of God-made-man, and Christ's acts are the acts of God-in-manhood. Some of them may show more clearly than others that the personal subject of these acts is not a man but God; none of them, however, are acts of the divine nature acting independently of the human, for any such acts would, like the act by which the divine Word sustains the universe, fall outside the sphere of the incarnate life altogether.'[31]

Weston concludes this part of his book by emphasizing that 'the manhood of Christ is His proper, assumed nature to all eternity. The state of the Incarnation is permanent. 'Jesus Christ the same yesterday, today and for ever.' . . . Thus to all eternity the Incarnate lives in and under the conditions of a glorified humanity, unburdened it is true by the earthly limitations of humanity, yet still in some sense limited . . .'

For there 'remained after the ascension just those limitations that are the measure of the ultimate difference between Godhead and manhood: limitations which we lose sight of perhaps as our eyes are dazzled by the divine glory, but which none the less are real and permanent . . .' This was one of the many reasons why the extreme Kenotic position appeared to Weston untenable.[32]

'The image and likeness of God'

It seems to me, moreover, that we can easily exaggerate the gulf – vast though it certainly is – between God and man. Man, the Bible repeatedly affirms, was made 'in the image and likeness of God'; and that image has never been wholly defaced, in spite of the fall. The insistence of many theologians today 'that humanity and divinity are not only diverse in their metaphysical basis but are also radically incompatible' is, as Mascall remarks, wide open to challenge from the angle both of man and God. When Knox declares that is 'impossible, by definition, that God should become man', he is guilty, Mascall insists, of pushing logical deduction too far; for if there is adequate reason to believe that God did in fact become man in Jesus, then it follows that 'man is what the eternal God could become,' and that 'God, the Creator, *can*, without losing his own identity, become a being of an order radically different from his own. A donkey cannot become man, nor can an angel; but God can'.[33] It is, no doubt, 'peculiarly appropriate' to the Son to become incarnate; and human nature is the 'peculiarly appropriate', or even 'uniquely possible', nature for him to become incarnate in.[34] This seems to be implicit, at least, in Hebrews 2; and Mascall remarks that, 'so far from human nature having an inbuilt metaphysical repugnance to its assumption by God, it is precisely in such assumption that it receives its highest self-expression and fulfilment.[35] He insists, moreover, that 'the total dependence of created human being on the uncreated self-existent deity makes the incarnation of God the Son in human nature not impossible or unfitting, but wholly right and proper. It is indeed supremely wonderful and unpredictable, but that is another matter.'[36] In Psalm 8 David seems to have glimpsed this from afar.

Love is always 'vulnerable'

Now there can be little or no doubt that the noblest quality in human nature is man's ability to love; and the New Testament unequivocally affirms that 'God is love'. But love always involves the risk – indeed, in a fallen world, almost the certainty – of suffering. So this inevitably raises the question of the alleged 'impassibility' of God. It is manifestly inadequate to suggest that it was only the human nature of Jesus which suffered in the garden, on the cross, and when he wept over Jerusalem, for it was the whole person who underwent these experiences. Nor can we confine the concept of divine suffering to the human life of the incarnate Lord who 'learnt obedience in the school of suffering'; for the yearning love of God for his wayward people is clearly revealed in the book of Hosea and in many other parts of the Old Testament, and found its fullest expression when he 'did not spare his own Son but gave him up for us all' (Rom. 8:32) and sent him 'to be the propitiation for our sins' (1 Jn. 4:10).

But the term passibility, Professor Oliver Quick insisted, can be used in three different senses. *External* passibility refers to the relations of one being towards another, or the capacity to be acted on from outside oneself. *Internal* passibility, on the other hand, refers to those fluctuating emotions and moods which a man experiences within himself. And *sensational* passibility denotes the capacity to experience pleasure and pain, joy and sorrow.[37] In the second or 'internal' sense, passibility cannot be postulated of God, who, as the Thirty-Nine Articles of the Church of England put it, is 'without body, parts, or *passions*'; but it was integral to the experience of the incarnate Lord, who had a human soul as well as a human body. In the 'external' and 'sensational' senses, moreover, it is no doubt true that God is impassible in the sense of not being subject to external constraint. Mascall points out that Galot makes a distinction between 'the necessary order of God's being and the free order of his will', and suggests that 'immutability and impassibility belong to the former, but creation and redemption to the latter, in which love and suffering are really and not just verbally implicated. "In God suffering belongs not to the order of necessity and of essence, but to that of free initiative". This involves no imperfection in God; just the opposite. "He is sovereign, and sovereignty consists in acting in the freest manner, and in *not* being imprisoned in an inaccessible altitude" '.[38]

Of course God, as God, cannot suffer physically or die; and this was one reason why he had to become incarnate. But God himself suffers when we sin, and he suffered more than we can begin to understand when, in Christ, he 'reconciled the world to himself'. To take any other view would be to substitute the God of Islam for the God and Father of our Lord Jesus Christ, for Muslims depict Allāh as so utterly transcendent and self-sufficient that he cannot be made sad by man's rebellion, selfishness and sin or glad by his repentance and faith.

In Christian or Jewish terms, however, a God who is incapable of feeling is a philosophical abstraction, not the God of the Bible. To argue that the experience of pain or sorrow is evil in itself,

Quick insists, is without foundation, for neither pain nor pleasure is good or evil *in se*. 'Everything depends upon the cause of the particular pleasure or pain'; so 'it is intrinsically good to have a due sensitiveness in regard to what is intrinsically evil and this sensitiveness directly involves pain'. But the fact remains that God is essentially active, not passive; so in him 'pain or sorrow is never a mere suffering, but rather a moment in the victorious activity of his love which is his joy'.[39]

The Triune God

Even in the 'Essential Trinity' we can, I think, discern a certain element of priority and what may, perhaps, be termed 'subordination'. The Bible almost always speaks in terms of a certain priority residing in, and an initiative being taken by, the Father – or, simply, by 'God'. It is God who 'so loved the world that he sent his only Son'; the Father who 'did not spare his own Son, but delivered him up for us all'; and the Son, 'who is in the bosom of the Father', who has made the Father known. The Son is in no sense a created being, for he partakes fully in the nature of the Godhead: in him, indeed, 'the complete being of God, by God's own choice, came to dwell' Colossians 1:19 (NEB). But the very title Son suggests generation, derivation and a certain subordination together with identity of essence – which is, presumably, the meaning of the concept of the 'eternal generation of the Son'.[40]

Man, on the other hand, is a creature, not the creator; and it is of the very nature of the creature to be dependent on the creator – the God in whose hand is his 'life, and breath and all things.' So when the 'Word became flesh', and the Son became incarnate in 'the man Christ Jesus', I believe that he became what man *should* always have been – utterly dependent on his Father for everything. It is, moreover, in John's Gospel – the Gospel which testifies most explicitly to Jesus' claim to divine Sonship – that we find this utter dependence most consistently and insistently expressed. This can be summed up in what Dodd calls 'the parable of the Apprentice', in John 5:19 f: 'A son can do nothing on his own; he does only what he watches his father doing: what father does, son does; for a father loves his son and shows him all his trade.'[41].

But the same refrain comes again and again: 'I cannot act by myself; I judge as I am bidden'; 'The teaching that I give is not my own; it is the teaching of him who sent me'; 'He who sent me speaks the truth, and what I heard from him I report to the world'; 'I do nothing on my own authority, but in all that I say, I have been taught by my Father'; 'I do not speak on my own authority'; 'The word you hear is not mine: it is the word of the Father who sent me'; 'I love the Father, and do exactly as He commands.'[42] In D. M. MacKinnon's words: 'That which is represented as coming into the world in Jesus, as transcribed in the conditions of his ministry into forms of speaking his Father's words and "doing the will of Him that sent me", is what he eternally is.'[43]

This is a point which Weston, I think, does not adequately emphasize; but, to me, it is *the* secret of the incarnation: that, when God revealed himself as a man among men, the incarnate Son was utterly and completely dependent on his Father. There was nothing in this which was essentially alien to his pre-existent state, and there was nothing which was not utterly 'human', for that is how man *ought* always to have lived. Jesus could still say 'I and my Father are one' (Jn. 10:30), but he had become man, and was living as man should have lived. He had to learn as we have to learn, for this was his Father's will; and his knowledge was limited to what he so learnt except in so far as it pleased his Father to give him some special insight or revelation – as, indeed, he does to *some* degree with others – to teach him what he would not otherwise have known.

It is this which, to me, explains his ignorance about the date of the second advent (and, indeed, a multitude of other things, for he was a real baby, a real boy and a real man) while yet having a unique filial consciousness, a knowledge of men, events and the future which at times went well beyond the ordinary, and the ability to speak, at his Father's prompting, words which were utterly true and authoritative, for his teaching was not his own, but his Father's. There were *many* things that his Father did not tell him, but all that he did tell him was true. This secret also explains both his authority and his vulnerability. His 'self-submission to these conditions,' as Professor MacKinnon has insisted in a broadcast talk, 'is to be seen not as an abdication of divine omnipotence but rather as its only authentic human manifestation.' While, moreover, in the 'Essential Trinity' Father and Son are not to be thought of as having distinct and individual wills, since they are one in the unity of the Godhead, the incarnate Son had a human will as well as a human body and *psyche*, and a truly human shrinking from the agony, physical and spiritual, of the cross. But his human will was wholly subject to that of his Father – at a cost we cannot begin to understand.

Could Jesus have sinned?

To ask whether Jesus could not sin, or, rather, was able not to sin, is essentially to ask the wrong question. For simply to say that he could not sin because he was God would leave us with the impression of a conscious invulnerability which would take the sting out of temptation and erect a barrier between his experience and ours; yet it is clear that if he *had* sinned he would not have been God incarnate, or even the perfect revelation of God.[44] But surely the fact is that he suffered temptation which was as real, poignant and agonizing as any one has ever known, for he was allowed by his Father to drink the cup of temptation and suffering to its dregs. Only one who has been tempted in every way, just as we are, and has learned obedience in the school of suffering, could be our example, inspiration and 'High Priest'. True, Jesus can never have experienced the tendency to slip, once more, down the slippery slope which has so often led us into sin; but it is only the one who never gave way who could plumb the very depths of temptation.

One who fell short at any point, who was human '*and no more*' – man, that is, not only in a positive sharing in human genes, human psyche, and human experience, but also in the negative fact that he was in no real sense God – could never have saved us. 'A Saviour *not quite God* is a bridge broken at the farther end', Bishop Handley Moule once wrote;[45] while a Saviour – and Exemplar – *not quite man* is a bridge broken at the nearer end', as F. F. Bruce once remarked. How Jesus could be both truly God and truly man, 'God-in-manhood', is the mystery of the incarnation; but no one else would suffice.

The cross of Calvary

We have already seen how the Prophet of Islam re-acted to the story of the cross. In the pattern of the Qur'ān prophets were often disregarded, and even persecuted, by the people to whom they ministered; but ultimately they were always vindicated by God. How, then, could the Messiah die on a cross? There were some, like the Ebionites, who believed that the 'aeon Christ' must have left Jesus before the passion; others, with Gnostic or Docetist leanings, insisted that the true Christ *could not* suffer: it must have been a simulacrum, or someone else, who died on the cross. Some such ideas as these may have prompted the Quranic words, 'though they [the Jews] did not kill him and did not crucify him, but he was counterfeited for them' (sūra 4:156).[46] But we are concerned in this context with the Christian message and with personal faith today, and in both these contexts the historical fact that Jesus did die on the cross is of central importance.

It was not solely to reveal our Father-God in the only way that we could begin to understand that the eternal Son was 'made man'. It was also to redeem us from the sin which inevitably alienates us from a holy God. That was why Jesus had to die 'for us men and for our salvation' at Calvary, when 'he bore our sins in his body on the tree'

(1 Pet.2:24). It was only as man that he could die; but, if he had not also been God incarnate, he could not have redeemed us and reconciled us to God. That is why God 'sent his Son, born of a woman, born under law, to redeem those under law, that we might receive the full rights of sons. And because [we] are sons, God sent the Spirit of his Son into our hearts, the Spirit who calls out "*Abba*, Father".' (Gal.4:4–6)

The wonderful fact is that the eternal Son:

> Who, being in very nature God, did not consider equality with God something to be grasped, but made himself nothing, taking the very nature of a servant, being made in human likeness. And being found in appearance as a man, he humbled himself and became obedient to death – even death on a cross! Therefore God exalted him to the highest place and gave him the name that is above every name, that at the name of Jesus every knee should bow, in heaven and on earth and under the earth, and every tongue confess that Jesus Christ is Lord, to the glory of God the Father'.[47]

Resurrection and exaltation

It was at the resurrection that Jesus was vindicated, and 'declared with power to be the Son of God'.[48] It was then, too, that his disciples felt free – indeed compelled – to worship him. After his ascension or exaltation, moreover, they began at times to address their prayers to the Father and at times to the Lord Jesus, and felt free to apply to him some of the great monotheistic passages of the Old Testament. After Pentecost they also experienced the presence and power of the Holy Spirit, as the 'Counsellor' who had been sent to them as their Lord's *alter ego*. They had not yet formulated the doctrine of the Trinity, but Paul could, and did, conclude his second letter to the Corinthians with the words: 'May the grace of the Lord Jesus Christ, and the love of God, and the fellowship of the Holy Spirit be with you all.'

So the exaltation presents no major problem. The Son was always, in some sense, subordinate to the Father, although of the very essence of the Godhead; and he was always the Word or self-revelation of God, in nature and to men. At the incarnation he became Jesus of Nazareth, who lived a truly human life to make the invisible God known to men, and then died a truly human death to reconcile us to the God who loves us so much that he 'sent his Son to be the propitiation for our sins'. During his earthly life he was utterly dependent on his Father, as all men *ought* to be; and he revealed his Father to men to the fullest extent that God can be 'manifest in the flesh'. Then, at the exaltation, he did not cease to be recognizably human, although no longer subject to the limitations of terrestrial life. He is still, today, the 'friend of sinners', our 'elder brother'. As our great High Priest he is still 'touched with the feeling of our infirmities'. It is the fact that he is still man as well as God which makes his intercession for us understandable and meaningful. But he is also the Lord whom we rightly worship and may rightly address in prayer. It is 'in the face of Jesus Christ' that we can now see something of the *shekinah* glory, although only 'darkly, as in a mirror'; but one day we shall 'see him as he is' and at last be 'conformed to his likeness'. Then 'God will be all in all'.

Meanwhile, we confess that 'Jesus is Lord'; the Alpha and Omega, who is the same 'yesterday, today and for ever'. And it is not only his present exaltation, but his sufferings, which speak to our condition. As Edward Shillito wrote, after the first World War:

> If we have never sought, we seek Thee now;
> Thine eyes burn through the dark, our only stars;
> We must have sight of thorn-pricks on Thy brow,
> We must have Thee, O Jesus of the Scars.
>
> The heavens frighten us; they are too calm;
> In all the universe we have no place.
> Our wounds are hurting us; where is the balm?
> Lord Jesus, by Thy Scars, we claim Thy grace.
>
> The other gods were strong; but Thou wast weak;
> They rode, but Thou didst stumble to a throne;
> But to our wounds only God's wounds can speak,
> And not a god has wounds, but Thou alone.

But they must be *God's* wounds, if they are to heal – and that brings us back to the mystery of the incarnation.

Epilogue

I do not intend, in this last chapter, to attempt to outline any detailed dialogue between Christianity and Islam, since the basic dialogue is inherent, I believe, in the two religions about which I have written, and thus, in a sense, in this book as a whole. I shall simply try to suggest this by 'A look back' and then 'A look forward: some points to ponder'.

A look back

Part I is devoted to an objective study of Islam which will, I hope, provide those who are not themselves Muslims with a reasonably adequate introduction to a world religion of major importance whose adherents must today number little less than a billion. The first chapter represents a revised reprint of the chapter I wrote on Islam in *The World's Religions*,[1] and is general in its scope. The second chapter concentrates on the two sciences which have always provided the fundamental element in a traditional Muslim education: theology and the sacred law. It incorporates considerable material from a chapter in *God's Law and God's Love*, now for some years out of print, and a few paragraphs from *The Teaching of Jesus*.[2] Chapter three is devoted to Muslim mysticism, an enormous subject on which I have never previously written more than a few scattered pages, and in it I rely chiefly on standards works. Chapter four is concerned with Islamic fundamentalism and is based, in part, on a lecture I gave comparatively recently on 'Islamic Law Today' – since the common denomination in Islamic fundamentalism, in its various forms, is the clamant summons: 'Back to the Sharīʿa!'

In these chapters I have tried to be both fair and informative – and to refrain, in general, from interjecting specifically Christian comments or comparisons. I realize, of course, that Muslim readers will not always agree with what I have written, but I hope they will not feel that I have either misrepresented the facts or sought in any way to denigrate the faith in which they were nurtured.

In Part II I have not made any attempt to describe or discuss Christianity as a whole. Instead, I have concentrated on those fundamental elements in Christian faith which our Muslim friends find most difficult to understand, appreciate and accept: the incarnation and the atonement. Yet these 'mysteries' (in the biblical sense of 'truths formerly hidden, but now divinely revealed') unquestionably constitute – together with the resurrection and exaltation that crown them both – the very heart of the Christian gospel.

As most readers will be aware, the doctrine of the incarnation has now, for some decades, again become the focus of theological debate in western Europe, Britain and the United States. It was to this debate that I tried to make a layman's contribution when I was invited to give the 'Bishop John Prideaux Memorial Lectures' in the University of Exeter in 1978. These lectures, together with some additional material, were published later in that year as *The Mystery of the Incarnation.* This book has been out of print for some years and so it was suggested to me that four chapters from it should be included, in a considerably revised form,[3] as the Christian component in this present book.

The first of these four chapters is concerned with the factors which led the first disciples, inexorably, to the conviction that Jesus was not only human but also divine. After the resurrection they even began to apply to him some of the great monotheistic passages of the Old Testament, and at times to address him personally in prayer. This process, which took place years before it could have been subject to any external influences, is sometimes described as 'the upward approach'. Inevitably, however, it was not long before the early church began to meditate not only about the relationship of Jesus to God, but also about that of their covenant God to their incarnate Lord – and what this meant in regard to the nature of the Deity. This has been described as 'the downward approach'.

The purpose of chapter six is to summarize the continuing debate, all down the centuries, about two interconnected problems: how Jesus could really be both human and divine, the eternal Word 'made flesh'; and how both he and the Holy Spirit could from eternity have participated in the unity of the Godhead. The Holy Spirit was 'hovering over the waters' at the creation, had inspired the Old Testament prophets, was uniquely present in the ministry of Jesus, and came to the disciples as Jesus' *alter ego* after his ascension. While belief in our Triune God rests firmly on New Testament authority[4] and on the experience of the apostolic church, the term 'Trinity' does not seem to have come into use much before the 'Athanasian Creed' (echoing the earlier Nicene Creed[5]). This summed up orthodox Christian faith in the declaration that 'The Catholic Faith is this: That we worship one God in Trinity, and Trinity in Unity; neither confounding the persons, nor dividing the substance'.[6]

Chapter seven is concerned with the incarnation, atonement and resurrection in the context of other religions. It is not only God's supreme self-revelation in Christ which is unique, but also the redemption Christ died to provide; for revelation and redemption are equally essential and must never be separated. But this gospel would never have been proclaimed to the world (nor completed in itself) had God not raised Jesus from the dead. On the third day the tomb in which the body of the crucified Jesus had been buried was found to be empty, and Jesus himself – with his mortal body transmuted into one which could never die again – began a series of appearances to his disciples. These appearances spread over a period of forty days, during which he explained to them much that they could not previously have understood. In the course of this teaching and intimate fellowship, it is impossible that anyone else could have impersonated him, as some Muslims suggest. Subsequently, after his ascension, he also appeared, in an experience no less real but more visionary, to the apostle Paul. Thus, with the Lord Jesus now exalted to the right hand of God, we have a living Saviour who has not only redeemed us from sin but who both intercedes for us in heaven, and mediates his risen life to us through his Spirit.

In chapter eight I have tried to set out what all this means to us today, expressed in terms of what I myself have come to believe. After a consideration of the 'Kenotic Theory' I have laid down two principles which seem to me to be basic: that we must take the biblical evidence as a whole, and that we must never forget the essential place held by the atonement. Then, finally, I have ventured to make a series of deductions from these two principles, all of which are, I think, of direct relevance to any dialogue between Christians and Muslims.

A look forward: some points to ponder

Divine revelation

To Muslims, as we have seen (pp. 43f above), the basic and most authoritative revelation of God is in a book, not a person. It is the Qur'ān, which they believe was literally dictated to Muḥammad by the Archangel Gabriel, which is their ultimate authority – augmented, to degrees which vary according to their sect and school of thought, by the *aḥādīth* (the Traditions about what Muḥammad himself said, did, or allowed to be said or done in his presence). The official view is that these Traditions are inspired in content, but not (in contrast to the Qur'ān) in wording – except for a very few *aḥādīth qudsiyya* (sayings attributed to God himself) which, for whatever reason, were not included in the Qur'ān. Muslims differ much among themselves, however, about which of the positively innumerable 'Traditions' which soon came into circulation should be accepted as authentic, and about the status they should accord to them. The official Sunnī view is that even a verse in the Qur'ān can be qualified, or even abrogated, by an authentic Tradition, which can be proved to be subsequent in date to the Quranic revelation concerned. But the doctrine of 'abrogation' is itself a matter of dispute, while the arguments about the authenticity and relevance of individual traditions are endemic (pp. 45f above).

To Christians, by contrast, God's supreme revelation of himself is in a person, the Lord Jesus Christ, rather than in a book, however inspired – although it is in an inspired and much revered book that the coming of that person was foreshadowed and predicted in the Hebrew Scriptures; that his life, teaching, death and resurrection are recorded in the Gospels; and that authoritative teaching about the significance of what he said and did are to be found in the remainder of the New Testament. Thus the New Testament, together with the Old Testament, is the only wholly authoritative book which Christians cherish, and it must have been to this corpus (or, at least, to part of it) that the numerous verses in the Qur'ān[7] about the 'Injīl' which was 'given' to 'Īsā (Jesus) must refer.

Muslims, however, find it very difficult to identify the New Testament, or even the Gospels, as the book to which these verses refer. This is partly because sūra 19:31 and other Quranic verses seem to refer to a particular book which was actually 'given', as a whole, to Jesus himself (whether as an infant, as in sūra 19:31, or later); and partly because their basic view of Scripture is that it must consist almost exclusively of the direct speech of God. In the Qur'ān, for example, every sūra except one, whatever its contents – historical, anecdotal, legalistic or hortatory – is introduced by the divine command *'Qul'* ('Say'). So Muslims are apt to classify our Gospels as *sīra*, the word used for any biography of Muḥammad, rather than the Injīl 'sent down' to Jesus.

There can be no valid doubt, however, that the Quranic references to Christians as 'the people of the Injīl', must have pointed to the Greek New Testament (whether in the original or in some translation), numerous manuscripts of which in our possession today go back centuries before the birth of Muḥammad. No suggestion is made in the Qur'ān that the Christians of Muḥammad's time did not possess the genuine Injīl, or parts of it, but revered instead another 'Injīl,' unknown to history.[8] Muḥammad, however, clearly knew much more about the Jewish than the Christian Scriptures, and made many more references to the 'law' of Moses than to the 'gospel' of Christ. As for the comparatively recent suggestion that the so-called 'Gospel of Barnabas' might represent the true Injīl, this fantastic notion must be relegated to an Appendix (pp. 223–234).

Another and much more common Muslim criticism, addressed both to the Jews and Christians, is that they had tampered with their Scriptures (cf. sūra 3:78/72; 5:13/16, 41/45; 2:75/70; 4:44/47ff.) when reading them aloud. The key words in these passages are *ḥarrafa* 'to change' and *lawā* 'to twist'. Passages could be 'changed' simply by altering one radical, which might involve no more than substituting one diacritical mark for another, or by changing the sequence of the radicals; and *lawā* properly means 'to twist', so that to twist a thing with the tongue, in the pretended recitation, would mean much the same as *ḥarrafa*. Most of the passages mentioned above seem, moreover, to have referred to Muḥammad's contact with his 'Jewish contemporaries who knew the Scriptures, presumably in Hebrew, and translated portions for him into Arabic, but deliberately altered words so as to deceive him'.[9]

No similar encounters seem to have taken place between Muḥammad and Christians who translated parts of their Scriptures to him. But the accusation that Christians have actually corrupted the text of their Scriptures is often made by Muslim controversialists – supported, on occasion, by the variety of readings to be found in the footnotes of a scholar's Greek New Testament. The fact remains, however, that no book has ever received such scholarly study, exposure and criticism as the New Testament in general and the Gospels in particular. Experts in what is known as 'lower criticism' (the scrutiny of the numerous Greek manuscripts of the New Testament which we now possess, aided by comparison with several ancient translations) have provided us with a text of the New Testament which in all essentials must correspond *very* closely with the originals, copies of which go back centuries before Muḥammad. Reference has already been made, moreover, to the fact that variations in the text of the Qur'ān began to appear at a very early date (as is inevitable with an ancient Semitic text which is devoid of short vowels and diacritical marks). This situation was summarily remedied by order of the Caliph ʿUthmān when he called in the manuscripts concerned, gave instructions about the establishment of the 'true' text, and commanded that the variants should be destroyed (cf. pp. 46f above).

One other point is inescapable. Muslims have to rely on a single man, Muḥammad, as the sole human intermediary through whom, they believe, the divine message of the Qur'ān was conveyed to man. In the New Testament, by contrast, a number of different authors are involved. God's message, moreover, instead of being 'dictated' verbatim, is distilled through human minds. As with the Old Testament prophets, 'prophecy never had its origin in the will of man, but men spoke from God as they were carried along by the Holy Spirit'[10] The individual authors had their own distinctive style and approach, but the message they brought was divine. As Michael Green has commented on 2 Peter 1:21:

> It is interesting that in this, perhaps the fullest and most explicit biblical reference to the inspiration of its authors, no interest should be displayed in the psychology of inspiration . . . The relative parts played by the human and the divine authors are not mentioned, but only the fact of their co-operation. [The writer] uses a fascinating maritime metaphor (*cf.* Acts 27:15, 17 where the same word, *pheromenē*, is used of a ship carried along by the wind). The prophets raised their sails, so to speak (they were obedient and receptive), and the Holy Spirit filled them and carried their craft along in the direction He wished. Men spoke: God spoke. Any proper doctrine of Scripture will not neglect either part of this truth . . . For revelation was not a matter of passive reception: it meant active co-operation. The fact of God's inspiration did not mean a supression of the normal mental functioning of the human author. The Holy Spirit did not use instruments: He used *men*. God's way is ever one of truth through personality, as was perfectly demonstrated in the incarnation.[11]

The divine unity

We have seen something of the supreme emphasis that Muslims always put on the doctrine of the divine unity. So, too, does Judaism, although ancient Israel as a nation all too often turned to idolatry and pagan practices. It was only after the partial return from exile that Israel's proclivity to lapse into any sort of polytheism seems to have been purged away. There are, however, a number of passages in which the Old Testament writers accorded almost a personal status to God's

'Spirit', 'Wisdom' and 'Word', while the prophets sometimes spoke of the coming Messiah in more than purely human terms. An outstanding example of this can be found in Isaiah 9:6 and 7, where the prophet writes:

> For to us a child is born, to us a son is given, and the government will be on his shoulders. And he will be called Wonderful Counsellor, Mighty God, Everlasting Father, Prince of Peace. Of the increase of his government and peace there will be no end. He will reign on David's throne and over his kingdom, establishing and upholding it with justice and righteousness from that time on and for ever. The zeal of the LORD Almighty will accomplish this.

These factors might, indeed, have prepared the Jews to understand that the unity of the Godhead, on which they rightly insisted, might be more complex than they had thought. But, instead, they focused their attention almost exclusively on the advent of an earthly Davidic kingdom, conceived in somewhat theocratic terms.

This was why, when these predictions began to be fulfilled, the disciples of Jesus stopped short, during his earthly ministry, at recognizing him, progressively, as teacher, prophet and Messiah. Only his resurrection convinced them that he was more than merely human. It was the previously 'doubting Thomas' who, when confronted with the nail-pierced hands and wounded side of Jesus' post-resurrection body, must be credited with the first fully Christian confession, 'My Lord and my God' (Jn. 20:24–28). Then, after the ascension, the disciples came to experience the presence and power of their exalted Lord in his *alter ego*, the Holy Spirit. Even so, it took a long time, as we have seen, before the Christian church was able to express the doctrine of the 'Trinity in unity' in fully credal form, positive and negative, on the basis both of the New Testament revelation and the experience of the Christian church.

So is there, perhaps, some controversy in the history of Islamic theology which might help Muslims to understand this mystery? I think that a 'stepping stone' – no more – can be found in the debate about the relationship between God's divine essence (*dhāt*) and his divine qualities (*ṣifāt*). This arose, it may be remembered,[12] in the context of the debate about whether the Qur'ān was, or was not, created or eternal (*azalī*). The Muʿtazilīs maintained that the Qur'ān could not be eternal, since what is eternal must necessarily be divine, so they would have two Gods and would no longer be monotheists. 'Not so', replied the orthodox; one of God's eternal qualities is that he is a Speaker (*mutakallim*), and the Qur'ān is his eternal speech. 'But God has seven different qualities', the Mu'tazilīs insisted, 'so now you must have a positive plethora of gods.' And the argument ended with the Mu'tazilis maintaining that God's qualities were not *in* his essence, and thus separable from it . . . but that they *were* His essence',[13] whereas the orthodox insisted that God's eternal qualities are 'not He nor are they any other than He'.[14] (*lā dhātahu wa lā ghayrahu'*). This last statement is certainly not the doctrine of the Trinity, but provides a stepping stone for Muslim understanding.

But to return to the 'Trinity in unity': Muslims are right when they insist that the virgin birth (which they accept) does not, of itself, prove that Jesus was the 'Son of God'. They are also right when they ask, 'How can He [God] have a child, when there is for Him no consort?' (sūra 6:10). The virgin mother was uniquely privileged among women, but in *no sense* God's 'consort'. Nor does the divine Sonship of Jesus date from his human birth, but from eternity; and it was openly 'declared' by his resurrection, rather than by his birth (Rom. 1:4). In essential fact Jesus did not *become* the Son of God; on the contrary, the Son of God became Jesus. That is why he could speak to the Father, before his passion, about 'the glory that I had with You before the world began' (Jn. 17:5) – long before Mary came into existence. His birth at Bethlehem was the occasion when the Son of God, one with the Father from all eternity, 'entered into the limitations of time and space by the power of God working through the Virgin Mary and was born as a man', named Jesus. Similarly Jesus is not the Son of God because of his mighty works and wonderful words. On the contrary, he did his mighty works and spoke his wonderful words because he was, and is, the eternal Son of God. 'True, both the manner of Jesus' birth and the nature of his works lend evidence for his Sonship. But neither, alone or together, provide the origin or basis for his Sonship. The distinction is important.'[15]

God and man

We have already seen something of the almost exaggerated transcendence which Muslims attribute to God and the gulf between him and his human creatures. Even the ninety nine 'Beautiful Names' of God which pious Muslims recite as they finger the beads of their rosaries cannot tell them anything positive about the divine nature because of the doctrine of *mukhālafa*, the utter difference between God and man (pp. 63, 156f above). For unless the names *al-Raḥmān al-Raḥīm* point to a divinely exalted form of human mercy and compassion, then to us these names are meaningless jingles. Muslims will continue to use them, but 'without knowing how' they are applicable and 'without implying any similarity'.

This is the *via negativa*, of which no better example could, perhaps, be found than in the thought of such a towering figure as al-Ghazālī, of whom it has been said that he 'heaps negative upon negative in his exposition of the Ashʿarite creed'. But what strikes me most in al-Ghazālī's creed is the exclusively one-sided picture of the relationship between God and man in his insistence that

> Nothing occurs in His kingship and kingdom, little or much, small or great, good or ill, profitable or harmful, faith or unbelief, familiarity or ignorance, success or failure, increase or decrease, obedience or disobedience, except by His decree (*qaḍā'*) and power (*qadar*), His wisdom and will (*mashī'a*). What He has willed has come to be and what He has not willed has not come to be . . . No one can refuse His command and no one can delay His decree . . . [16]

But mankind, unique in God's creation, was made in the divine 'image and likeness' (Gen. 1:1–26f.), and in no other creature could the eternal Word, in God's good time, have 'become flesh and made his dwelling among us' (Jn. 1:14). God had, indeed, designed that mankind should be 'crowned with glory and honour', with 'everything under his feet' (Ps. 8:3–8); although, as a result of the fall, 'at present we do not see everything subject to him'. But, as the author of the letter to the Hebrews goes on to say, 'we see Jesus, who was made a little lower than the angels . . . so that by the grace of God he might taste death for everyone', now 'crowned with glory and honour' because he did in fact suffer that atoning death. (Heb. 2:8) And because our Saviour not only died for us but, raised from death and exalted to the right hand of God, intercedes for us, the 'image and likeness' of God which we lost at the fall is now being progressively renewed in his people, and will be complete on the day when he comes again (Col. 3:10; 1 Cor. 15:49) and we 'see him face to face'.

Nor was the Son of God 'made man' only for the duration of his earthly life, for now there will always be a glorified Man on the throne of the universe. It is in his face that we shall be able to see the God whom 'no man has seen or can see' (1 Tim. 6:16) and the mark of the nails will still be visible in his spiritual body.

Knowing God

'Man's chief end is to glorify God, and to enjoy him for ever,' the Shorter Westminster Catechism reminds us. But we cannot enjoy someone we do not know and knowing God must begin on earth.

A Muslim turns primarily to the Qur'ān for help, but will find that, although he may accept it as a revelation *from* God, it will not take him very far as a revelation *of* God. Hence the exemplary earnestness with which Muslim mystics sought for some personal contact with God himself. Some of them – even most of them, it seems – did this through the 'ecstasy' that they could find through the experience of the *dhikr* (which we have examined at some length in chapter 3), with a result that must have varied greatly from seeker to seeker. Some found themselves led into pantheism, and some into a somewhat sterile monism; while others, like al-Ghazālī, came back to the Qur'ān and the *sunna* of Muḥammad with a new conviction and ardour. As for yet others, who can say what their experience might have been? Be that as it may, we can only observe here that an experience induced by the extreme *dhikr* technique must come very close to that of a drug-induced 'high'.

More promising, it seems to me, would be the *fikr* or contemplative approach (cf. pp. 85, 87 above). Many mystics of all religions – Judaism, Christianity and Islam among them – have sought to know God through plumbing the depths of their own hearts. And 'because man is made in the image of God,' William Temple has observed, 'the attempt to find God through penetrating to the inmost recesses of the self leads in men of all times and races to a similar experience. God truly is the spring of life in our souls; so to seek that spring is to seek Him; and to find it would be to find Him.' He felt compelled, however, to add words of very salutary warning:

> But this can never quite happen. The image of God in man is defaced by sin, that is by self-will. The mind which seeks to reach that image is distorted by sin, and moulded both for good and evil by tradition. The *via negativa* of the mystics cannot be perfectly followed. To rely on a supposedly direct communion with God in detachment from all external aids is to expose the soul to suggestions arising from its distortion as well as to those arising from the God whom it would apprehend. Mediation there must be; imagery there must be. If we do not deliberately avail ourselves of the true Mediator, the 'express image' (Hebrews 1:3), we shall be at the mercy of some unworthy medium and of a distorted image. If we are learning to see God in Christ, let us by all means steep our minds in that revelation, and repose in God so made known to us with complete immediacy of surrender and trust. But let us be sure that the knowledge of God on which we rely is that which reaches us through Jesus, the Word of God made flesh.[17]

In the history of the Christian church there have, of course, been many eminent mystics. Some of them have been 'theocentric', centring their reveries directly on God himself (as mediated through Christ) and others 'christocentric', concentrating their thoughts directly on the Lord Jesus. Now that God has so fully revealed himself in Christ, however, ordinary Christians can enjoy a fellowship with him, and through him with the Father, which they would not normally describe as specifically 'mystical.' Did he not promise: 'He who loves me will be loved by my Father, and I too will love him and show myself to him'; and, again, 'If anyone loves me, he will obey my teaching. My Father will love him, and we will come and make our home with him.'[18]

The vividness of this experience clearly differs greatly from one Christian to another, and can be deeply satisfying. Experiences as authoritative as those described in 2 Corinthians 12:1–4 and Revelation 1:10–20, on the other hand, are probably unique; but many have claimed somewhat similar visions or dreams. It is significant, however, that Christian mystics usually regard these experiences as 'mercies' from God which they certainly do not deserve and by which they do not lay any particular store.

The love of God

As we have seen (pp. 60ff above), it would be wrong to suggest that there is no concept of the love of God in Islam. We noted, indeed, a number of verses in the Qur'ān which declare that Allāh 'loves' those who in any measure deserve it; but there are far more verses which threaten dire judgment on those who do not. True, it is explicitly stated that 'if anyone repent after his wrong doing and set things right, Allāh will repent towards him; Allāh is forgiving, compassionate' (sūra 5:43). But I do not know any verse in the Qur'ān which declares that Allāh loves the unbelieving and the unrepentant, or seeks to woo the unfaithful back to himself. If the sentences from al-Ghazālī's creed which I have quoted above (p. 213) are theologically correct, then any such verses in the Qur'ān, if they exist, would be virtually meaningless; since in Islamic doctrine the fact is that, whether men and women believe or disbelieve, live pure or dissolute lives, repent or remain defiant, depends solely and exclusively on God's own decree (*qaḍā'*), power (*qadar*) and will (*mashī'a*). So I suppose that we should not be as surprised as we are that we do not find 'Loving' or 'Lover' among the seven divine 'attributes' or 'qualities' – which al-Ghazālī lists as 'Living, Knowing, Powerful, a Willer, a Hearer, a Seer and a Speaker.'[19] In Islam, of course, the relationship between God and man (except, that is, for some of the Ṣūfīs) is always that of a Master (*rabb*) and slave (*'abd*).

This is in marked contrast with the Old Testament. There, too, there are explicit statements about the utter sovereignty of God, and solemn warnings of his judgment on those who are wicked or rebellious, for sin is always recognized as such. But there are also tender passages in which God is portrayed as a father who teaches his child to walk, a shepherd who carries his lambs in his arms, a lover who woos his beloved, and even a husband who longs for his unfaithful wife to come back to him. Pictures of the glory that is one day to come are, indeed, centred on God's covenant people, but are clearly to be extended, potentially, to the ends of the earth.

When we turn to the New Testament it is immediately apparent that God loves and cares for all his creatures (including the sparrows!), and his human creatures in particular, just as they are – with all their sin and failure. In the parable of the prodigal son, for example, the father not only welcomed his wayward son when he came home, but was clearly watching, and even longing, for him to repent and come back: he did not simply *cause* him to do so. It was, moreover, a truly divine, as well as human, voice that said, between his tears. 'O Jerusalem, Jerusalem, you who kill the prophets and stone those sent to you, how often I have longed to gather your children together, as a hen gathers her chicks under her wings, but you were not willing! Look, your house is left to you desolate' (Lk. 13:34f). The one who spoke these words had come, indeed, expressly to 'seek and to save what was lost' (Lk. 19:10).

I suppose the best known verses in the whole New Testament are John 3:16f: 'God so loved the world that he gave his one and only Son, that whoever believes in him shall not perish but have eternal life. For God did not send his Son into the world to condemn the world, but to save the world through him'. Again, the apostle Paul insists that 'God demonstrates his own love for us in this: While we are *still sinners*, Christ died for us (Rom. 5:8). But this brings us to our next point.

Salvation

It is a striking fact that, whereas the pages of the New Testament are positively flooded with the concept of salvation, the basic word in Arabic for salvation (*najāh*) occurs only once in the Qur'ān. True, the concept itself is certainly present in Islam, chiefly in the sense of being saved from the torments of hell; but there seems to be very little discussion of salvation in any other sense in books about Islamic theology.

By contrast, there are innumerable references to salvation in the Bible, especially in the New Testament, where the concept of salvation is both rich and many-sided. A simple illustration of this fact is provided by a story about a scholarly bishop who was challenged in a railway train by a fellow passenger with the question: 'Bishop, are you saved?' 'Well,' replied the bishop, 'what precisely do you mean by that question? Is your question whether I *have been* saved, *am being* saved, or *shall be* saved?' (He was quoting the terms in the New Testament Greek for being saved in these three tenses). A Christian, as the bishop probably went on to explain, can *know* that he has been saved from the condemnation of sin if and when he has personally accepted Jesus Christ as his Saviour and Lord. His Saviour because, when Jesus died, he 'bore our sins in his body on the tree' (1 Pet. 2:24); and his Lord because, as the apostle Peter immediately went on to say, 'so that we might die to sins and live for righteousness; by his wounds we are healed' And God can, and does, give us an assurance of this salvation through his Spirit in our hearts.

This is the experience of being saved in the *past* tense, when we thankfully accept God's full and free forgiveness of our sins on the basis of what he himself did for us when our Lord Jesus Christ (God's eternal Son and Word) died, for our sake and in our place, at Calvary. It is also the beginning of being saved in the *present* tense, since we, as forgiven sinners, are 'born again' by God's Spirit to a life set free from the dominion and slavery of sin, although not yet from its presence and temptation. This present tense of salvation means a progressive change of character by the presence of God's Spirit in our hearts. Then, in the *future* tense of salvation, we look forward with humble confidence to the fact that, when we see our Saviour 'face to face' we shall at last be 'like him', free from even the presence and relics of sin.

It is only with considerable trepidation that I venture to describe the position (as far as I can understand it) of a sincere Muslim in this context. He prays repeatedly for the forgiveness of his sins and for the 'mercy' of God. He knows, indeed, that he may have to pass through the 'fire' of God's wrath, but he *hopes* that he will eventually be delivered from this experience of purgation and reach whatever his picture of paradise may happen to be. But he can never (as I understand it) be *sure*: everything ultimately depends on the divine decree. He believes, indeed, that he can gain merit by his obedience to the commands of God, as he sees them, in his acceptance of the dogmas of Islam and in his diligence in performing its prescribed duties of prayer, fasting, almsgiving and pilgrimage. I have, moreover, myself met Muslim students whose fear of God keeps them from the vices in which others indulge, and elderly Muslims whose resignation to the will of God is exemplary.

But none of us, Christians or Muslims, can possibly *earn* salvation. We are all, without exception, sinners, and God is so holy that no sin can ever go into his dazzling presence. Our sin must be purged; but how? In what do Muslims hope? The intercession of even the best of human beings will not suffice for this. Muslims, like the Jews before them, offer animal sacrifices; but, sadly, they do not as yet accept that supreme sacrifice of atonement to which all the Old Testament animal sacrifices were designed to point forward: that of Jesus Christ our Lord, at Calvary.

One point should be added. Salvation will only be complete and world-wide when the Saviour himself comes again in power, as Jesus himself predicted (Mt. 26:63f., Mk. 14:61f.). It is to the eternal Son that the Father has 'entrusted all judgment', precisely because he is also 'The Son of Man' (Jn. 5:22, 27). Matthew devotes a chapter and a half to vivid pictures of this advent (24:36 – 25:46). There is, of course, no echo of this in Islam, except the illusive predictions of a future return of ʿĪsā to which I have referred on p. 12 above. Suffice it to say here than when an inquiry was addressed, in 1942, to the Rector of Al-Azhar University in Cairo about Jesus' bodily ascension to heaven and future bodily return, he replied that 'there is nothing in the Qur'ān, nor in the sacred traditions of the Prophet, which authorizes the correctness of the belief . . . that Jesus was taken up to heaven with his body . . . and would descend therefrom in the latter days . . . Anyone who denies his bodily ascent and his continuance in physical existence in the heavens, and his descent in the latter ages, does not deny a fact that can be established by clear conclusive arguments.'[20]

The cross of Calvary

To Muslims, sadly, the cross is a symbol that they hate, reject and scorn. I vividly remember, years ago, being invited to a party given by 'The School of the King's Sons' in Riyadh, Saʿudi Arabia. I was seated just behind the king, and felt acutely embarrassed when the symbol of the cross was flung down on the floor of the stage in triumphant contempt. The context of this incident was a scene from the Crusades, when the followers of a crucified Lord fought savagely to wrest their sacred sites out of Muslim control and, in the process, sometimes displayed a moral character distinctly inferior to that of their Saracen foes.

But it is not only in the context of the Crusades that Muslims reject the cross of Calvary. It goes much deeper than that. Most Muslims believe that the Qur'ān itself, in a distinctly obscure passage, denies that the prophet ʿĪsā (Jesus) did in fact die on the cross – as the Jews intended and as his own followers believed; instead, another was crucified by mistake in his place, and God 'took Jesus up to himself' (sūra 4:156).[21] The rationale of this is that the Qur'ān regularly reports that earlier prophets had at first encountered resistance, unbelief, antagonism and persecution; but finally the prophets had been vindicated and their opponents put to shame. God had intervened on their behalf. So Jesus, accepted in the Qur'ān as one of the greatest of the prophets (and, indeed, God's 'Word' and a 'Spirit' from him) *could* not have been left to his enemies. Instead, God must have intervened and frustrated their evil purpose. Muḥammad, as himself a prophet – even the 'seal' of the prophets – had a personal interest in the certainty of divine succour. If Messiah 'Īsā had been allowed to die in this cruel and shameful way, then God himself must have failed – which was an impossible thought.

To the Christian, by contrast, the cross is not a shame, but a glory. It is the ultimate measure of the love of God. 'This is love: not that we loved God, but that he loved us and sent his Son as an atoning sacrifice for our sins' (1 Jn. 4:10). Or, as St Paul put it,

> You see, at just the right time, when we were still powerless, Christ died for the ungodly. Very rarely will anyone die for a righteous man, though for a good man someone might possibly dare to die. But God demonstrates his own love for us in this: While we were still sinners, Christ died for us.
>
> Since we have now been justified by his blood, how much more shall we be saved from God's wrath through him! For if, when we were God's enemies, we were reconciled to him through the death of his Son, how much more, having been reconciled, shall we be saved through his life! Not only is this so, but we also rejoice in God through our Lord Jesus Christ, through whom we have now received reconciliation'. (Rom. 5:9–11).

God's love is not limited to those who deserve it. He '*wants* all men to be saved and to come to a knowledge of the truth' (1 Tim. 2:4). And we are explicitly told that he does not '*want* anyone to perish, but everyone to come to repentance' (2 Pet. 3:9). Repentance there must be; for St Paul told the Athenians that God now 'commands all people everywhere to repent. For he has set a day when he will judge the world with justice by the man he has appointed. He has given proof of this to all men by raising him from the dead' (Acts 17:31). It was to call, *not* 'the righteous' but *sinners* to repentance, that the Saviour had come. Those who feel that they cannot (or do not know how to) repent may find release in the fact that 'God exalted him [Jesus] to his own right hand as Prince and Saviour that he might *give* repentance and forgiveness of sins . . .' (Acts 5:31). If we truly *want* to repent, but feel we cannot, we can ask him to give us that essential gift.

It was, of course, only because Jesus was the incarnate Son of God that his death on the cross could, and did, provide a 'full, perfect and sufficient sacrifice . . . for the sins of the whole world'. The death of no mere man could avail. And this reveals, as nothing else could, the nature of the God we worship. As Dr David Rahbar (a Muslim scholar who had written a thesis on '*Al-qaḍā' wa'l-qadar*) wrote in a letter to Muslim and Christian friends to explain why he had become a Christian:

> Allow me to ask you: What is the disposition of God towards his human creatures according to Islam? Is He a merciful God? Is He only an angry God? Or is He both? If He is both, is He so in a capricious way or a judicious way? Is He a Sovereign of strict justice? Or do you wish to dismiss the whole subject of divine disposition by declaring the *bi la kayf* formula,[22] meaning, 'We do not know *how*. God is the transcendent and the incomprehensible. His ways we know not.'
>
> If you choose this last answer (which is implicit in much of Muslim theology), are you not explaining away a whole mass of Qur'anic verses which speak of God's mercy, love, retribution and avenging in various ways? Almost every third verse in the Qur'ān speaks of God as the Lord of Justice who will reward and punish on the Judgement Day . . .
>
> To say, 'We do not know if and how God punishes and rewards and avenges and shows mercy and loves, for His ways transcend our understanding', is to dismiss the entire subject of a divine character. Moreover such a dismissal is only nominal, for in thinking of God as transcendent in the sense of incomprehensible, one evades specifying divine morality and ends up by believing in His inscrutable and unpredictable will . . . Let us think without any bias: To sane human intellect anywhere in the world certainly justice is a necessary attribute of the Sovereign Creator. But what should truly divine justice mean?
>
> Think of the Creator-God in two ways:
>
> (1) The Creator says to Himself: 'I am going to create mankind. On earth they will have sickness, anxiety, fear, social wrongs, infidelities of fortune and fellow-beings, deaths of loved ones, disappointments, toils, and then when they die I shall

reward and punish them strictly. This is my justice.'

(2) Think of the Creator-God then in another way: He says to Himself, 'I am going to create the world that I may have fellowship with man . . . I shall myself go and live a span of earthly human life and disclose directly to men that I am with them in their suffering. In that earthly life I shall suffer literally the *worst* of suffering by dying the worst death of human violence.'

Which of the above justices is superior? That wherein the Creator Himself sits eternally on the Heavenly Throne, from eternity waiting for the Judgement Day when He will sit in judgement on his creatures and reward and punish with stringent equity? Or that justice wherein the Creator Himself is no less a recipient of what He gives to His creatures?

This transcendent justice of God is only another name for His love for men. Only in love does justice transcend itself and become loving sacrifice: giving what is due and then giving more . . .

Mankind has existed for countless generations. In our search for the truly worshipable, we must therefore look in human history for a man who loved, who loved humbly like the poorest, who was perfectly innocent and sinless, who was tortured and humiliated in *literally the worst* manner, and who declared his continued transparent love for those who had inflicted the worst of injuries on him. If we do find such a man, He must be the Creator-God Himself. For if the Creator-God Himself is not that Supremely Suffering and Loving Man, then the Creator-God is provenly inferior to that Man. And this cannot be . . .

Such a man did live on earth nearly two thousand years ago. His name was Jesus . . . When I read the New Testament and discovered how Jesus loved and forgave His killers from the Cross, I could not fail to recognize that the love He had for men is the only kind of love worthy of the Eternal God.

Once more I say: If the innocent Jesus, who forgave and loved His crucifiers from the Cross, was not the Creator-God Himself, then the Creator-God is proven to be inferior to Jesus. And this cannot be.

The Creator-God and Jesus are one and the same being. May all men know that truly divine love.[23]

In 2 Corinthians 13:4 St Paul states that Christ 'was crucified in weakness, yet he lives by God's power' – since it was by the resurrection that he was 'declared to be the Son of God with power' (Rom.

1:4) who now lives, as our great High Priest, to 'intercede for us' (Heb. 7:25) and, as our Saviour, to 'keep us from falling' (Jude 24). Yet, in another sense, it was by voluntarily laying down his life on the cross that both Jesus himself was 'glorified' and God the Father was 'glorified in him' (cf. Jn. 12:23–33) – by being revealed as pre-eminently a God of unfathomable love.

Let me repeat the last verse of a poem I quoted in full at the end of chapter 8:

> The other gods were strong; but Thou wast weak;
>   They rode, but Thou didst stumble to a throne;
> But to our wounds only God's wounds can speak,
>   And not a god has wounds, but Thou alone' –

since, as William Temple put it: 'Only a God in whose perfect Being pain has its place can win and hold our worship; for otherwise the creature would in fortitude surpass the Creator.'[24]

If we ask (as I think we must, and as our Muslim friends certainly will) why an omnipotent creator should ever have allowed sin to enter his fair creation, and his human creatures to experience the fall – and this, in its turn to necessitate such an uniquely costly salvation, which some would embrace with joy but others would reject – there can, I think, be only one basic answer: that it was God's eternal purpose to 'bring many sons to glory' (sons and daughters, *not* mere robots who were only pawns in his hands) for a purpose and a future the wonder of which we can scarcely begin to imagine.

APPENDIX

The so-called 'Gospel of Barnabas'

For some two centuries now, considerable prominence has been given by some Muslims to a so-called 'Gospel of Barnabas'. They seem first to have heard of it towards the middle of the eighteenth century through a reference in George Sale's *Preliminary Discourse* to his translation of *The Koran*, where he wrote:

> The Mohammedans have also a Gospel in Arabic, attributed to St Barnabas, wherein the history of Jesus Christ is related in a manner very different from what we find in the true Gospels, and correspondent to those traditions which Mohammed has followed in his Koran. Of this Gospel the Moriscoes in Africa have a translation in Spanish; and there is in the library of Prince Eugene of Savoy, a manuscript of some antiquity, containing an Italian translation of the same Gospel.[1]

In his preface 'To the Reader', Sale refers only to the Spanish document (which, he says, he had not seen when he made two references to this 'Gospel' in his *Preliminary Discourse* pp. 58 and 106). He proceeds to describe it, and adds that it claims 'to be translated from the Italian, by an Arragonian Moslem, named Mostafa de Arande. There is a preface to it, wherein the discoverer of the original manuscript, who was a Christian monk, called Fra Marino', tells us how he chanced upon it in the library of Pope Sixtus V, purloined it and, through reading it, 'became a convert to Mohammedism'. Sale continues:

> This Gospel of Barnabas contains a complete history of Jesus Christ from His birth to His ascension; and most of the circum-

> stances in the four real Gospels are to be found therein, but many of them turned, and some artfully enough, to favour the Mohammedan system. From the design of the whole, and the frequent interpolations of stories and passages wherein Mohammed is spoken of and foretold by name, as the messenger of God, and the great prophet who was to perfect the dispensation of Jesus, it appears to be a most barefaced forgery. One particular I observe therein induces me to believe it to have been dressed up by a renegade Christian, slightly instructed in his new religion, and not educated a Mohammedan (unless the fault be imputed to the . . . translator, and not the original compiler); I mean the giving to Mohammed the title of Messiah, and that not once or twice only, but in several places; whereas the title of Messiah, or, as the Arabs write it, al-Masīḥ, i.e., Christ, is appropriated to Jesus in the Koran, and is constantly applied by the Mohammedans to Him, and never to their own prophet.[2]

This Spanish manuscript seems now to be lost, but the Italian manuscript from which it was derived was published, together with a translation into English, by Lonsdale and Laura Ragg in 1907. Almost immediately, W. H. Temple Gairdner, the missionary scholar of Cairo, wrote:

> The name (though not the contents) of this strange book had long been known in India, and was not unknown in Egypt, though it was but a name . . . Now, however, an easily accessible edition has been given to the world, and there are many signs that the interest in this book is to be quickened, especially in the Moslem East. Translations are appearing both in India and Egypt, and the wildest talk is being indulged in as to the historical value of the book . . . We believe that when honest men throughout the East know the contents of the book, they will assign its true historical value – which is exactly *nil*.[3]

Repeated attempts have been made to locate or confirm the existence of any ancient version of a 'Gospel of Barnabas', whether in Arabic (as Sale surmized) or any other language, but in vain. 'The Arabic original,' wrote Dr White in his Bampton Lectures in 1784, 'still exists in the East'; but this statement is, he confesses, based only on the authority of Sale's *Preliminary Discourse*, published fifty years earlier. Sale's own knowledge of the Arabic original, as of all else save what appears in his Preface 'To the Reader', is, after all, secondhand, and based on the publications of La Monnoye in 1716 [in *Menagiana*, tom. iv. (Paris, 1715)], and Toland in 1718 [in *Nazarenus* (London, 1718)]. And neither La Monnoye nor Toland had seen an Arabic copy, though the latter initiated that series of challenges to the Moslems to produce one which has been carried on ever since, and always without effect: a circumstance which tends to confirm the general suspicion that the Moslems themselves who boast, under the title of *Barnabas*, the possession of the only true and authentic Gospel, derive their knowledge of the existence of the 'Gospel of Barnabas' solely from Sale's Preface and Preliminary Discourse, of which they are known to possess a translation.[4]

It is true that the 'Galatian Decree' (*Decretum de libris recipiendis et non recipiendis*) mentions an *Evangelium Barnabe* in its index of prohibited and heretical books.[5] This list probably goes back to a Roman synod of AD 382, so it is *possible* that some of the apocryphal stories in the Qur'ān may be indirectly borrowed from this 'Gospel' among the many other apocryphal books which had proliferated. But Montague James, in *The Apocryphal New Testament* which was published in 1924 and described by its publisher as 'the first book to supply the English reader with a comprehensive view of the apocryphal literature connected with the New Testament', regards the existence of a 'Gospel under the name of Barnabas' to be 'most doubtful . . . The extant book under that name (ed. Ragg, 1907) is in Italian, a forgery of the late fifteenth or sixteenth [century], by a renegade from Christianity to Islam.'[6]

Similarly, there are two references in James Hastings' *Encyclopaedia of Religion and Ethics*. The first of these, after a list of some twelve 'Lost and Hostile Gospels', adds:

> Besides these we possess a Muhammadan *Gospel of Barnabas*, based on a Gnostic Docetic Gospel (condemned in *Decret. Gelasii*), now extant in an Italian MS at Vienna . . . The stories of an Arabic original are probably mythical. A wide spirit of tolerance and charity pervades this astonishing production of a Christian mystic who became a Muslim.

The second of these references comes under the heading *Biblical Forgeries*, and reads:

> Probably the most remarkable among these apocrypha is the *Gospel of Barnabas*, which, after it had been occasionally men-

> tioned for some centuries, was edited in Italian and English from a Vienna MS . . . in 1907. Its date is acutely set by the editors for AD 1500–1550 . . . ; and, though the Arabic scribblings on the margin of the MS suggest that Arabic was the original language, the editors are probably right in rejecting this opinion and supposing the Italian to be the original . . . The work, immediately after its appearance in English, was translated into Arabic for use in anti-Christian controversy; but no reference to its existence in Arabic before that date has been found.[7]

About the so-called 'New Testament apocrypha', David Sox writes:

> The collection includes Gospels of Peter, Thomas, and Philip; Acts of John, Paul and Andrew; Epistles of Christ and Abgarus and Lentulus; and Apocalypses of Peter, Thomas and Paul. The gamut of New Testament literature is presented. This apocryphal New Testament is in no way analogous to the Jewish writings [of the Old Testament Apocrypha], for the former was never regarded as acceptable by orthodox Christians; it was produced by and for schismatic or heretical groups, especially the Gnostics. Many of the New Testament apocryphal books served as heretical substitutes for canonical writings.[8]

As has often been remarked, the Johannine statements that 'There were indeed many other signs which Jesus did in the presence of his disciples, which are not recorded in this book' (Jn. 20:30) and 'There is much else that Jesus did. If it were all to be recorded in detail, I suppose the whole world would not hold the books that would be written' (Jn. 21:25) must have seemed to some people positively to have opened the door, or at least to have provided a pretext, for such writings.

These New Testament apocryphal books, none of which have been accepted as authoritative by the Christian church, have all, Sox insists, been 'exposed to regular serious scholarly attention, but not so the extremely spurious grouping known as "modern apocrypha". Of this collection M. S. Enslin has said: "without exception (they) are worthless trash and the rankest forgeries." This assortment includes such books as *The Aquarian Gospel, The Twenty-Ninth Chapter of Acts, The Confessions of Pontius Pilate* and *The Gospel of Josephus*'.[9]

When we turn to the *'Gospel of Barnabas'*, the only text we have is that edited and translated by the Raggs. They were convinced that the paper on which it was written ('a somewhat coarse "cotton-paper" ', with 'a water-mark such as no oriental paper ever bore') dates from 'the second half of the sixteenth century'. The handwriting, they remark, 'cannot, of course, be of greater antiquity than the paper on which it is written, and probability is in favour of its being not very much later'. A fairly close resemblance to it can, they say, be found in a number of Venetian manuscripts of that period, and the most exact parallel they had seen to its orthography was a manuscript dated April 15, 1584. 'Still,' they add, 'there remain certain puzzling peculiarities in the script of *Barnabas* which might conceivably point to a literary fraud.'[10]

The Italian text is replete with a number of Arabic glosses which 'cannot', Professor Margoliouth insists, 'have been composed by any one whose native language was a form of Arabic; the mistakes both of orthography and of grammar being such as to betray the foreigner.' In a footnote to this Ragg observes that 'This fact escaped the notice of Toland, whose erudition was more diffuse than exact, as also of La Monnoye, who describes the "citations Arabes" as "fort bien écrites" (p. lxxi); but the learned Denis (see p. lxxvi) did not fail to observe it.'[11]

When we turn to the subject-matter of *Barnabas*, we can distinguish at once, say the Raggs: (i) an obvious and primary dependence upon the Christian Bible, and especially upon the four Canonical Gospels; (ii) frequent and voluminous insertions of Jewish and Mohammedan matter; and (iii) traces of hagiological and other mediaeval material.[12]

First, then, 'the very obvious dependence of *Barnabas* upon our Canonical Scriptures, more especially upon the four Canonical Gospels, disposes once for all of its claim to be, as it stands, an authentic and independent "evangelium".' 'Of the thirty-nine books commonly enumerated in our Canon of the Old Testament, no fewer than twenty-two are quoted or referred to by *Barnabas*, many of them by name', with occasionally mistakes such as citing 'Proverbs' as 'David' and 'Isaiah' as 'Ezekiel', or vice versa. In general the author's knowledge of the Old Testament is full and accurate, 'showing none of the vagueness and egregious blundering of the Scripture allusions in the Qur'ān'.[13]

Similarly, of the twenty-seven books in our New Testament, 'references direct or indirect' may be found to at least nineteen, including 'The Acts and the Apocalypse, the Epistle to the Hebrews, and the Epistles of St James, St Peter, and St John. And, what is in some ways more important still, there is a fairly frequent dependence upon the writings of that Apostle of the Gentiles, whose "erroneous teaching" it is "Barnabas's" professed purpose to combat.' These frequent references to the epistles of the New Testament 'constitute another of the many conclusive arguments' against the Barnaban authorship of the 'Gospel'.[14]

'But the central document for *Barnabas* is that represented by our four Gospels' – which 'may be shown to form the substratum of the entire document' (the length of which, it may be remarked, exceeds that of the three Synoptic Gospels combined), while 'the distinctively Mohammedan and Talmudic material is introduced as it were parenthetically, and *mostly into discourses put into the mouth of Christ'*.[15]

It may be added that this major dependence on the four canonical Gospels of Christendom is distinguished by a strange type of Diatessaron, or harmony of the Gospels, which Slomp compares with the Tuscan and Venetian Diatessaron texts, which could have been used by a Fra Marino. It is noteworthy, too, that 'the idea of a gospel harmony also meets the Muslim demand that there was one original gospel' – so the suggestion that *Barnabas* may be 'a conscious attempt at imitating a Diatessaron' may well be correct.[16]

While, however, the author of *Barnabas* is very well acquainted with the Bible as a whole and the Gospels in particular, he shows a remarkable ignorance of the geography and circumstances of the Palestine of the Gospels. He seems to think that it was possible to travel by boat to Nazareth,[17] that the arch-enemies Pilate, Herod, and the Chief Priest were often 'hobnobbing together',[18] and he actually depicts Caiaphas begging Pilate 'to procure a decree from the Roman senate making it a capital offence to call Jesus "God" or "Son of God" – and this decree is posted up in the temple, engraved on copper!'[19]

We turn next to the Raggs' category of 'frequent and voluminous insertions of Jewish and Mohammedan matter'. A surprising example of this is that the author of *Barnabas* repeatedly puts into the mouth of Jesus predictions of the coming prophet of Islam. He totally ignores John the Baptist and makes Jesus the fore-runner of Muḥammad, whom he not only names explicitly but refers to as 'the Messiah' – in apparent ignorance, as we have seen, of the fact that the term 'Christ' is the Greek form of Messiah (*al-Masīḥ*). In this, of course, he flatly contradicts the Qur'ān; as he also does when he asserts that the Virgin Mary gave birth to Jesus 'without pain' (in accordance with 'the accepted tradition of Latin mediaeval Christianity').[20] He also spells out, in a typically Muslim fashion, matters about which the Qur'ān is much less explicit. The outstanding example of this is the references made to the passion, which must, I think, be set out in some detail.

In the Qur'ān the relevant passage is, as we have seen, sūra 4:156f., which reads:

> And for their saying 'We killed the Messiah, Jesus, son of Mary,

> the messenger of God', though they did not kill him and did not crucify him, but he was counterfeited for them; verily those who have gone different ways in regard to him are in doubt about him; they have no [revealed] knowledge of him and only follow opinions. Nay, Allāh raised him to Himself. And Allāh is sublime, wise.[21]

By contrast with this strange, somewhat tentative and Docetic passage, the author of *Barnabas* depicts Judas with the soldiers approaching Jesus and God commanding the angels to take Jesus 'out by the window that looketh towards the South' and up to 'the third heaven'. Then

> Judas entered impetuously before all into the chamber whence Jesus had been taken up. And the disciples were sleeping. Whereupon the wonderful God acted wonderfully, insomuch that Judas was so changed in speech and in face to be like Jesus that we believed him to be Jesus. And he, having awakened us, was seeking where the Master was. Whereupon we marvelled, and answered: 'Thou, Lord, art our Master; hast thou now forgotten us?' And he, smiling, said: 'Now are ye foolish, that know not me to be Judas Iscariot!' And as he was saying this the soldiery entered, and laid their hands upon Judas, because he was in every way like to Jesus.[22]

After this Judas was bound, interrogated, and crucified much as in the Gospel accounts, however often he expostulated that he was not Jesus. Judas' only cry from the cross, *Barnabas* records, was: 'God, why hast thou forsaken me, seeing the malefactor hath escaped and I die unjustly?' The voice, face and person of Judas 'were so like to Jesus, that his disciples and believers entirely believed that he was Jesus . . . wherefore some departed from the doctrine of Jesus, believing that Jesus had been a false prophet.' But those who 'stood firm in the doctrine of Jesus' went, with the mother of Jesus, 'to Mount Calvary, and were not only present at the death of Judas, weeping continually, but 'took him down from the cross . . . and buried him in the new sepulchre of Joseph'. Then they 'returned each man to his house,' while 'He who writeth [Barnabas], with John and James his brother, went with the mother of Jesus to Nazareth.'[23]

> Those disciples who did not fear God went by night [and] stole the body of Judas and hid it, spreading a report that Jesus was risen again; whence great confusion arose.' . . . [24] [But] God

who discerneth the heart of men knoweth that between grief at the death of Judas whom we believed to be Jesus our Master, and the desire to see him risen again, we, with the mother of Jesus, were consumed. So the angels that were guardians of Mary ascended to the third heaven, where Jesus was in the company of angels, and recounted all to him.

Wherefore Jesus prayed God that he would give him power to see his mother and his disciples. Then the merciful God commanded his four favourite angels . . . to bear Jesus into his mother's house, and there keep watch over him for three days continually, suffering him only to be seen by them that believed in his doctrine.

Jesus came, surrounded with splendour, . . . saying, 'Fear not, for I am Jesus; and weep not, for I am alive and not dead' . . . Then the Virgin, weeping, said: 'Tell me, my son, wherefore God, having given thee power to raise the dead, suffered thee to die, to the shame of thy kinsfolk and friends, and to the shame of thy doctrine? For everyone that loveth thee hath been as dead.' Jesus replied, embracing his mother: 'Believe me, mother, for verily I say to thee that I have not been dead at all; for God hath reserved me till near the end of the world'.[25]

Such is the nub of this strange, and singularly unconvincing composition, with its massive dependence on biblical material (especially the four canonical Gospels), its mediaeval flavour, and its highly imaginative transformation into a species of Islamic propaganda. 'On some points', indeed, as the Raggs have observed,

Barnabas exhibits quite unmistakable marks of Muslim controversy subsequent to the age of Mohammed, and shows itself, in such sense, antagonistic to the letter of the Qur'ān. The uncompromising determinism of *Surah* xvii, which teaches that 'every man's fate is' irrevocably 'bound about his neck', is here replaced by a remarkably philosophical pleading for the rights of free will on which, together with the law of God, the true doctrine of Predestination is declared to be based . . . Here we may see, if we will, Kadarian or Motazilite doctrine – or the influence of mediaeval Christian speculation.[26]

Similar traces of later doctrinal development, combined also, probably, with Christian sentiment, may be discerned in the mysticism of *Barnabas*, as in its universalistic and ascetic tendencies . . . Once more, our 'Gospel' exhibits a latitudinar-

> ian charity which gives a place side by side with the faithful to virtuous Gentiles who have 'acted up to their lights.' On this point the Qur'ān may be said to give an uncertain sound . . . but in *Surah* iii we are faced by the uncompromising statement that 'whosoever followeth any other religion than Islam, it shall not be accepted of him, and at the last day he shall be of those that perish.'. . . But *Barnabas* declares unhesitatingly that God's saving message is for all . . . and that the virtuous heathen are objects of God's mercy, and will be enlightened at death if not earlier . . . [27]

Sox remarks that

> Father Jomier has commented that the author of *Barnabas* does not rely on the letter of the Koran, contrary to the manner in which he employs New Testament material: 'He is a forger, and would betray himself too quickly if he gave textual references. He is, however, inspired by the Koran – there are more than thirty allusions to its text.'[28] According to Jomier, he uses Muslim sources not as books but as ideas, images. The writer speaks of Islam as one who has learned about it from conversation. He also seems to have been exposed to commentaries on the koranic text – or at least, to popular traditions and developments of what the Koran presents. Nowhere is this more evident than with the account of Judas' substitution. It seems likely that the author read or was told an account like that given by Wahb,[29] which by the sixteenth century had become a popular explanation of the koranic denial of Jesus' death on the cross.[30]

But who was the author of *Barnabas*, and when was it written? It seems clear that the manuscript edited and translated by the Raggs dates from the later part of the sixteenth century; and the Spanish version (now lost) to which Sale and others have referred was, self-confessedly, a translation from the Italian. But who was the author? A strong case has been made out for the suggestion that it was written by the same Fra Marino who said that he chanced upon it in the library of Pope Sixtus V.[31] This Fra Marino was certainly a monk with an extensive knowledge of the Bible (especially the Gospels), well acquainted with mediaeval hagiology (both Christian and Muslim), but with very little knowledge of the text of the Qur'ān. He *may* well have been Father Inquisitor of Venice,[32] have got into trouble with the Holy Office and become jealous of Felice Piretti (later to become

Sixtus V). Whether from conviction or some less worthy motive, he embraced Islam and composed *Barnabas*.

There are many possibilities. Sox suggests that 'Perhaps Fra Marino never lived to see the completed work, and the subsequent Spanish translation (which, according to one source, ended up among the Moriscos in Africa) presented the story of its 'composition' as a kind of explanatory note . . . Fra Marino's scribe/friend/co-author could also have been responsible for the Turkish binding and the Arabic notes.'[33]

Again, as the Raggs put it: 'If we suppose our *Barnabas* to have *originated* with Fra Marino, he may yet have found its nucleus (in Greek or Latin) in the form of the old Gnostic Gospel, and dressed it up beyond casual recognition by the resources of his fertile imagination.'[34] But, in any case, 'what better choice of name for a lost gospel than that of 'Barnabas', already the title of a lost gospel to be found in the Pseudo-Gelasian decree?'[35] The fact that the Barnabas of the New Testament had some differences of opinion with St Paul may have been so inflated, moreover, as to make him appear a suitable author of a distinctly anti-Pauline 'Gospel'.

In this pseudo-Gospel, as in the Qur'ān itself, there is no redemption from sin, no self-revelation of God, no 'empty tomb' and no victorious Saviour. The very heart of the New Testament, on which (for the most part) *Barnabas* relies so heavily for its narrative, is ripped out in favour of figments of imagination that cannot begin to stand against the solid evidence of the true Gospels and Epistles on which the Christian faith rests and from which Christian experience is derived.

Note

David Sox makes passing reference to *Jesus, a Prophet of Islam*, by Muhammad 'Ata ur-Rahim[36]. This goes so far as to describe the so-called *Gospel of Barnabas* as 'the only surviving Gospel written by a disciple of Jesus, that is, by a man who spent most of his time in the actual company of Jesus during the three years in which he was delivering his message'.[37] Wisely enough, 'Ata ur-Rahim does not attempt to give any solid evidence for these unsubstantiated assertions, except to suggest that the true Barnabas, cousin of Mark the evangelist, should 'in all probability' be identified with the Joseph Barsabbas of Acts 1:23, on the grounds that 'there is no other Joseph who accompanied Jesus during his life referred to in the New Testament'![38] Later on, he suggests that Barnabas and the Barabbas of Mark 15:7, Luke 23:18f. and John 18:40, might be identical.

He also asserts, *inter alia*, that 'the Gospel of Barnabas was accepted as a Canonical Gospel in the churches of Alexandria up till 325 AD', and that 'it is known that it was being circulated in the first and second centuries after the birth of Jesus from the writings of Iraneus [Irenaeus] (130–200 AD)'[39] If this were so, it would be exceedingly strange that not a single reference is made to this 'Gospel' by Professor Bruce Metzger, the greatest living authority on the text of the New Testament, in his book *The Canon of the New Testament: its Origin, Development and Significance*, whereas he refers not less than ten times to an *Epistle of Barnabas* and once to a so-called *Acts of Barnabas*.[40] In *Codex Sinaiticus*, Metzger tells us, 'the *Shepherd of Hermes* (with the *Epistle of Barnabas*) stands after the close of the New Testament'.[41] Again, Clement of Alexandria's (*c.* 155 – *c.* 220) *Hypotyposes* 'contained concise comments on all the canonical Scriptures (literally, 'all the testamented Scripture') 'not omitting even the disputed books – that is, the Epistle of Jude and the other Catholic Epistles, and the *Epistle of Barnabas*, and the *Apocalypse of Peter* (although, Metzger adds, 'Clement does not hesitate to criticise an interpretation given by the author of the *Epistle of Barnabas*').[42] Metzger also tells us that Origen (also of Alexandria, *c.* 185 – *c.* 254) 'quotes three times from the *Epistle of Barnabas*' and even calls it a "catholic"epistle'.[43] Clearly, the *Epistle of Barnabas* was a very different document from his alleged Gospel.

Of 'the so-called *Decretum Gelasianum*, which the manuscripts attribute indiscriminately to Popes Damasus, Hormisdas and Gelasius,' Metzger adds that 'according to von Dobschütz it is not a Papal work at all, but a private compilation that was drawn up in Italy (but not in Rome) in the early sixth century'. This Decree gives 'a list of books included in the Old Testament and the New Testament (omitting the Book of Revelation)', and another 'lengthy list of apocryphal works (sixty-two titles) and heretical authors (thirty-five names)'.[44]

But what concerns us in our present context is not whether a Gospel attributed to Barnabas may have existed among the multitude of New Testament apocrypha, but that the only version of such a book which we have today is the so-called *Gospel of Barnabas* in Italian, previously in the Papal Library and now in the National Library in Vienna, which was translated into English by Canon and Mrs Ragg and published by the Oxford Clarendon Press in 1907. This was translated into Arabic in 1908 and is widely distributed in Arab countries, Indonesia and Pakistan, and known even in parts of East and West Africa. ʿAta ur-Rahim asserts that 'Nearly the whole edition of this English translation abruptly and mysteriously disappeared from the market' and that 'only two copies of this translation are known to exist, one in the British Museum, and the other in the Library of

Congress in Washington';[45] but I have had no difficulty in finding one in the Cambridge University Library and another in the Library of Tyndale House, Cambridge. Be that as it may, it is this manuscript and translation on which ʿAta ur-Rahim has based his arguments and which the Begum Aisha Bawani Waqf in Karachi published in English in 1973 and, since then, has repeatedly republished.

But this so-called Gospel, which asserts that it was Judas Iscariot, not Jesus, who died on the cross, *cannot*, in all conscience, be attributed to the Barnabas who was not only the friend and companion of St Paul, but also the friend of Peter and the other apostles. It is true that Paul and he had a 'sharp disagreement' (Acts 15:39) over whether to take John Mark with them on a second missionary journey, and that Barnabas, together with Peter, wavered temporarily about eating with Gentiles in Antioch (Gal. 2:11–13). But Peter, Paul, Barnabas and James all stood together in declaring, at the Council at Jerusalem, that Gentile converts need not be circumcised or observe the ritual requirements of the Mosaic law; and there is no biblical warrant for depicting a 'Pauline church' which led Christianity astray over the doctrine of the Trinity. The basis for trinitarian teaching, although not the *term* 'Trinity', goes right back to the New Testament.[46] It was 'The Christ' himself, not someone else, whom the Old Testament Scriptures had predicted would suffer, and in whose name 'repentance and forgiveness of sins' would be 'preached . . . to all nations, beginning at Jerusalem' (Lk. 24: 45–47) – by Barnabas, Peter, Paul and all the apostles.

It is intrinsically unlikely, moreover, that the Barnabas of the first century should have predicted by name the coming of Muḥammad[47] and should (contrary to the Qur'ān as well as the Bible) have referred to him, rather than Jesus, as the Messiah. It is very strange that orthodox Muslims should accept a book which flatly, and repeatedly, contradicts the clear Quranic statement 'O Mary, Allāh giveth thee tidings of a word from Himself whose name is the Messiah, Jesus, son of Mary . . .' (sūra 3:40). The Qur'ān never gives this title to Muḥammad.

Notes

Chapter 1: An introduction to Islam

[1] Islam, the correct term for the religion of Muḥammad, is the infinitive of the Arabic verb for 'to submit' (i.e. to the will of God, as Muslims understand it); while 'Muslim', the correct name for those who follow that religion, is the present participle of the same verb.

[2] S. M. Zwemer, *A Factual Survey of the Muslim World* (New York: Loizeaux Brothers, 1946), p. 5.

[3] See below, pp. 101f.

[4] R. A. Nicholson, *Literary History of the Arabs* (New York: Cambridge Univ. Press, 1969).

[5] Some scholars think considerably later, *e.g. c.* AD 580.

[6] According to orthodox theory they were outstanding members of the tribe, but this has been seriously questioned by Western scholars (*cf.* sūra 43:30, *etc.*). *Note:* The references to the Qur'ān in this book adopt the verse numberings used, *e.g.*, in Bell's translation, from which the translations are usually, but not invariably, taken. *Cf. The Qur'ān* (translated, with a critical re-arrangement of the Surahs), Richard Bell (Edinburgh: 1937 and 1960), Vols 1 and 2.

[7] *Cf.* sūra 93:6ff.

[8] So called because it affirmed that there was only one nature in the Person of Christ. *Cf.* chapter 6 below for the Monophysites, the Orthodox (Byzantines) and the Nestorians.

[9] Mecca, too was a considerable market for foreign merchants, while the number of Ethiopic loan-words in the Qur'ān is also significant. There were, however, Arab monotheists (named Ḥanīfs) at the time, who were neither Jews nor Christians.

[10] Sūra 96:1–5. According to one Tradition Muḥammad replied, 'I am no reader.' Another Tradition, however, makes him reply, 'What am I to recite (or read)?' *Cf.* Isaiah 40:6 ('A voice says, "Cry!" And I said, "What shall I Cry?" ').

[11] Sūra 74:1. This is sometimes regarded as the first revelation of all.

[12] Officially, of course, these too are regarded as part of the divine revelation vouchsafed to him as Prophet.

[13] Although by no means chronologically arranged (almost the opposite), a large measure of agreement has been reached regarding the date of the different sūras or their component parts.

[14] For the next three chapters, it seems best to give dates AH as well as AD. Dates given in AH can roughly be converted into AD by adding 622 and deducting 3 for each century (to represent the difference between lunar and solar years).

[15] This is reflected in the new emphasis in his revelations on obedience to the Prophet (*cf.* sūra 3:29, 126; 4:17, 18, *etc.*) and on how he should be treated (*cf.* sūra 24:63; 33:53; 49:2–5; 58:13, 14, *etc.*).

[16] *Cf.* sūra 10:94; 28:52, 53, *etc.*; 42:11.

[17] One example of this inaccuracy is, perhaps, the depicting of Haman as a minister of Pharaoh (sūra 40:38). But other examples of apparent confusion could be quoted.

[18] Sūra 12:103. *Cf.* also sūra. 69:43–46.

[19] *Cf.* sūra 2:70,73,169; 3:72; 4:48; 5:16, 45; 6:91, *etc.* It is not clear whether Muḥammad believed that the Jews had actually tampered with their manuscripts or only falsified their reading or statement of the text.

[20] His religion, he now affirmed, was that of Abraham, who was neither Jew nor Christian (sūra 2:129; 3:60, 89).

[21] Sūra 2:136–145.

[22] *Cf.* sūra 22:27–30, *etc.*

[23] *E.g.* C. S. Hurgronje, *Muhammadanism* (New York: Putnam, 1937).

[24] *Cf.* R. Bell, *Introduction to the Qur'ān* (Edinburgh: 1953), where Weil and Sprenger are cited in support of these two views.

[25] D. B. Macdonald, *Aspects of Islam* (New York: Macmillan, 1911), p. 72.

[26] See Tor Andrae, *Mohammad: the Man and his Faith* (New York: Harper and Row, 1960), pp. 260, 264–269. For the Ebionites, *cf.* pp. 140f. below.

[27] D. S. Margoliouth, *Mohammed* (Glasgow: Blackie, 1939), pp. 85ff. Also an article on Muḥammad by the same author in *Encyclopedia of Religion and Ethics*, ed. J. Hastings (New York: Scribners, 1908). For another explanation see Fr. Buhl's article on Muḥammad in the *Encyclopedia of Islam* (New York: Humanities, 1960–1969), p. 645.

[28] This demand was later met by the assertion that the very style of the Qur'ān was inimitable (sūra 17:90) and by alleged angelic aid at the battles of Badr (sūra 3:11, 120, 121; 8:17) and elsewhere (sūra 9:25, 26; 33:9, 10, *etc.*). Later, Tradition added a plethora of apocryphal miracles of every kind, many of which find a place in the most 'canonical' collections.

[29] His opponents alleged that 'tales of the ancients' were dictated to him morning and evening (sūra 25:5, 6; *cf.* 16:105; 44:13). It is, however, clear that he was quite unable to read the Hebrew Old Testament (which is probably the true explanation of the adjective *ummī* – sometimes rendered 'illiterate' – applied to him in sūra 7:156) and completely misunderstood the very nature of the Injīl (New Testament) which he conceived as a book 'sent

down' to 'Īsā (Jesus: *cf.* sūra 5:50; 57:27, *etc.*) and to be 'observed' like the Law (*cf.* sūra 5:70, 72).

[30] R. Osborn, *Islam under the Arabs*, p. 21.

[31] Bell, *op. cit.*, p. 35. It is in this context that we can best understand the problem of the so called 'Satanic verses'. Al-Ṭabarī writes that Sūra 53:19–23 in their original form included a reference to three goddesses of the Meccans as 'exalted females' whose 'intercession is to be hoped for'. But subsequently Muḥammad recalled this as suggested by Satan rather than revealed by Gabriel, and substitued a strictly monotheistic reference to them.

[32] In *e.g.*, sūra 12:103: see A. Jeffery in *The Muslim World*, October 1954, p. 256.

[33] Macdonald, *Aspects of Islam*, p. 80.

[34] Sūra 33:49.

[35] Sūra 33:51.

[36] Sūra 33:36–38.

[37] Sūra 66:1–5.

[38] Sūra 33:53 (*cf.* 33:32, 33)

[39] Sūra 33:30.

[40] Sūra 33:53.

[41] But see A. Jeffery in *The Muslim World*, October 1954, p. 256; and R. Bell. *op. cit.*, pp. 31–36.

[42] *Cf.* sūra 39:31.

[43] *Cf.* sūra 18:110; 40:57; 41:5; 47:21; 48:2.

[44] *Cf.* sūra 33:21. The ethical influence of this doctrine has been lamentable.

[45] D. G. Hogarth, *A History of Arabia* (London: OUP, 1922), p. 52.

[46] Contrast the Qur'ān, of which the most extreme form of verbal inspiration is asserted. It was written from eternity on the Preserved Tablet (sūra 85:22), whence it was sent down to the lowest heaven on the Night of Power (*Laylat al-Qadr*; sūra 97:1), to be revealed to the Prophet piecemeal as need arose (sūra 17:107; 25:34). Others, however, interpret sūra 97:1 as meaning that the first revelation was vouchsafed to the Prophet on the Night of Power.

[47] The two most famous collections among the 'orthodox' are those of al-Bukhārī (d. 257 AH/AD 870) and Muslim (d. 261 AH/AD 874). The former, especially, is accorded a reverence almost equal to that of the Qur'ān.

[48] A Tradition depicts Muḥammad himself as having said, 'What I have commanded to believers outside the Qur'ān is equal in quality to the Qur'ān itself, or even greater.' This is obviously spurious, but illuminating.

[49] The deterioration in his attitude to Christianity at al-Madīna may be explained as a reflection of his attitude to the Jews, as caused by the change in his own fortunes, or as representing his reaction to Monophysite as opposed to Nestorian theology. For Quranic references, *cf.* 2:59; 57:27 (favourable); 5:21, 56–58; 9:29–32 (unfavourable).

[50] *Cf.* sūra 4:169, *etc.*

[51] For details, Muḥammad's source was chiefly apocryphal stories.

[52] Sūra 4:156 (probably, in Dr Bell's opinion, a reference to the Docetic assertion that only a simulacrum of Jesus was crucified). Other verses such as 3:48 and 19:34, seem to suggest that he did die. See also pp. 140f, 201

below, and Epilogue p. 218f.

[53] *Cf.* sūra 5:116 with 4:169 and 5:77–79; also sūra 19:36; 19:91; 112:3.

[54] *E.g.* those of Cerinthus, who believed that 'the Christ' descended on a wholly human Jesus at his baptism and withdrew from him before the crucifixion (*cf.* A. R. C. Leaney in *Dictionary of Christian Theology* ed. Richardson (London: 1969), p. 136. Basilides, another gnostic thinker, believed that 'The Ungenerated Father sent his firstborn Mind (Christ) to free those who believe in him from the power of those who made the world. He did not suffer, but Simon of Cyrene was crucified instead' (*ibid.*, p. 135). This is even closer to the Muslim view.

[55] Some think that sūra 61:6 rests on a confusion between 'Paraklytos' and 'Periklutos', a possible Greek equivalent for 'Aḥmad'. But see also Epilogue. An eschatological figure who will restore Islam in its purity and power.

[56] J. T.. Addison, *The Christian Approach to the Muslims* (New York: AMS Press, 1942), p. 18.

[57] When beaten they retired, like true Bedouin, into the desert to recuperate. On one view they originated in those Arabs who opposed the predominance of the tribe of Quraysh: on another in the early Qur'ān readers. Both theories may be in part correct.

[58] Who probably adopted this 'heresy' largely from racial particularism.

[59] On conversion to Islam these Persians were attached to Arab tribes in the subordinate position of the pre-Islamic client (originally either a stranger attached to the tribe or an ex-slave).

[60] For the origin of this name, see below (pp. 101f.). The Arabic is Ithnā ʿAshariyya.

[61] The seventh in their line of Imāms, whence the term 'Seveners'.

[62] The twelfth in their line of Imāms, whence their name.

[63] See below, p. 53.

[64] A group which flourished at Baṣra in the middle of the fourth century AH (tenth century AD) and endeavoured to construct a universal system of religious philosophy. Their encyclopaedic 'Epistles' (fifty in number) exercised a widespread influence.

[65] This is by far the most numerous school.

[66] *Cf.* article on 'Uṣūl' by J. Schacht in *Encyclopaedia of Islam.*

[67] Strictest of all were the Ẓāhiris, a school of complete literalists which has since disappeared; next the Ḥanbalīs; then the Shāfiʿīs; then the Mālikīs.

[68] 'My people will never agree upon an error,' the Prophet was (ultimately) alleged to have said.

[69] *Istiḥsān. Cf.* the Mālikī *istiṣlāḥ, etc.*

[70] 'The disagreement of my people is a mercy from God' is the traditional saying of the Prophet quoted in this context.

[71] Space forbids a fuller treatment here of this very interesting phenomenon.

[72] Partly for this reason they called themselves the 'people of Unity and Justice'. The 'Unity' refers to the controversy, mentioned below, concerning the divine attributes.

[73] The view here attributed to the 'orthodox' was in fact a *via media* between the Muʿtazila on the one hand and the extreme literalists or 'anthropomorph-

ists', of whom there were many, on the other.

[74] *Cf.* D. B. Macdonald, *Development of Muslim Theology, Jurisprudence and Constitutional History* (New York: Scribners, 1903), pp. 158–159.

[75] *Cf. ibid.*, pp. 202ff., on which this section is largely based.

[76] Probably reaching Islam largely through a Christian from Emessa (in Lebanon).

[77] Even the central dogma of Islam, the divine Unity, was interpreted by the Ṣūfīs as denying any reality outside God.

[78] This is the reason traditionally given for his execution, although the real reason may well have been political.

[79] As also, of course, in much popular Christianity. *Cf.* S. M. Zwemer, *The Influence of Animism on Islam* (New York: Macmillan, 1920), *passim.*

[80] The *qarīn* or *qarīna* (see sūra 41:24; sūra 50:22, 26, *etc.*). This mate is regarded as malignant, jealous, the cause of physical and moral ill, of hatred between spouses, barrenness, miscarriage, *etc.*, except when frustrated by religion or magic.

[81] His two favourite haunts, it seems, are the Kaʿba at Mecca and one of the city gates in Cairo, on which shreds of the clothing of petitioners can always be found. Elsewhere the Ghawth (Succourer) is regarded as the chief, and the term Quṭb used for the next grade in the hierarchy.

[82] In most Muslim countries there is also an official called the 'Muftı' whose function it is to give legal opinions (*fatāwī*) to individual applicants, to the government, or to the judges of the Sharīʿā courts (the 'Qāḍīs').

[83] The Muslim God can best be understood in the desert. Its vastness, majesty, ruthlessness and mystery – and the resultant sense of the utter insignificance of man – call forth man's worship and submission, but scarcely prompt his love or suggest God's.

[84] In popular Islam the rosary is regularly used (1) as an aid to prayer, (2) as a talisman to indicate whether some proposed action is propitious (*istikhāra*), and (3) as a magical agency for healing.

[85] See sūra 72:1, 5, 6 and elsewhere, as well as many Traditions.

[86] Singular, *ʿifrīt, shayṭān.*

[87] Sūra 72:8, 9, *etc.*

[88] Devil-mate; see footnote 80 above.

[89] This is purely animistic in origin but is now practised throughout a great part of the Muslim world, particularly among women. Pamphlets have been written against it, however, by the learned.

[90] Including Sulaymān (Solomon), who is credited with having attained an extraordinary power over the *jinn* and animals. He is thus virtually regarded as the patron saint of 'white' magic.

[91] Islam has come to believe in the impeccability (*ʿiṣma*) of all prophets – but against the plain teaching of the Qur'ān.

[92] Not only bibliolatry but bibliomancy flourishes in popular Islam. The Qur'ān must be touched only by the ritually pure; certain chapters are of special power against sickness and demons; and extracts are used for every sort of charm.

[93] *Cf.* sūra 26:192–97; 3:75–79; 6:92; 35:28; 46:11, *etc.*

[94] *Cf.* sūra 2:141; 3:64. Also *cf.* 5:116, 117.

[95] These are distinguished from such mortal women as shall attain paradise (whose position and marital delights are shrouded in obscurity) by most commentators although some suggest that virtuous wives become houris hereafter. For the *ḥūr* see sūra 44:54; 55:56–58, 70–76; 56:22–23, 34–39. *Cf.* also sūra 2:23; 3:13; 4:60. But it is only fair to add that the sensual delights of paradise are interpreted in metaphorical terms by more spiritually-minded Muslims.

[96] Except martyrs, and some others.

[97] Muslim eschatology is a curious hodge-podge of Jewish, Christian and animistic legends and folklore.

[98] The creed – the shortest in the world – is repeated by many Muslims several times a day, in every sort of context.

[99] Muslim prayer – at least in its prescribed form – seems to partake more of the nature of a continual acknowledgement of God's sovereignty than of communion with him. This is shown (*inter alia*) by the insistence on ritual purity and the use of Arabic, an unknown tongue to three-quarters of the Muslim world.

[100] The basic idea, it seems, is not the virtue of physical cleanliness, but the need for cleansing from demon pollution. This has been brought out by Wensinck and Goldziher. The fact that the passing of the hands over one's sandals may often be substituted for washing the feet supports this view. To a similar pre-occupation with demons may be traced the use of some object as a *sutra* (that which covers or protects) to mark off the place of prayer ('It protects from the demons'); certain regulations about the position of the fingers and the covering of the back of the head during prayer, and about the exact times of prayer; and parts of the ritual followed in the special prayers for rain, *etc.* See S. M. Zwemer, *op. cit.*, pp. 43–65.

[101] Including the sacrifice (sūra 22:27–38), which is also offered at the same time by Muslims who are not performing the pilgrimage. This is the Feast of Sacrifice (*ʿīd al-aḍḥā*), substituted for the Jewish Day of Atonement, but without the same significance.

[102] It is still, however, kissed and rubbed, as in the pagan ritual. Similarly, the practice of pilgrims being shaved and cutting their nails at the end of the pilgrimage rites, and the custom of burying the hair and nail clippings in sacred soil (see Burton, *Pilgrimage*, Vol. II, p. 205), are obvious survivals of animism, where hair and nails are regarded as especially charged with 'soul-stuff' and as channels of spiritual communion, on the one hand, or deadly means of enemy attack, on the other. Such superstitions still survive in Muslim (and other) lands quite apart from the pilgrimage ritual.

[103] But often, it has been widely remarked, with little moral uplift.

[104] *E.g.* a man can be forgiven for breaking the divine law, but scarcely for denying or doubting its validity in the least particular.

[105] And similar treatment was also in practice given to Hindus in India, and others whom Muslims would officially regard as polytheists.

[106] A 'rightly guided' eschatological figure.

[107] *Cf. Dictionary of Islam*, ed. T. P. Hughes (London: W. H. Allen, 1935),

'Dār al-Ḥarb'.

[108] Sūra 4:3.

[109] Sūra 4:28. It is noteworthy that one early reading included the phrase 'for a fixed term'.

[110] Sūra 4:38.

[111] Sūra 4:3.

[112] Any other rule would, of course, be farcical in view of the husband's unfettered freedom of divorce.

[113] This age varies considerably as between school and school. The Ḥanafī rule is seven for a boy and nine for a girl (or, according to a variant view, nine and eleven respectively), while the Shī'īs say weaning for a boy and seven for a girl. The other schools are more generous to the mother.

[114] Although sometimes husbands expressly delegate to their wives the right to divorce themselves in certain contingencies.

[115] Muḥammad quieted the consciences of those who hesitated to violate women captives whose husbands were still alive by the divine revelation already quoted on p. 31 (sūra 4:28). In other words, captivity annuls marriage.

[116] Preface to S. Lane-Poole, *Selections from the Koran*.

[117] Animals must be slaughtered by cutting their jugular vein, after pronouncing the name of God.

[118] Except by the Shāfi'īs, who regard it as 'commanded' for both boys and girls. Female circumcision – whether in the more or less extreme form – is practised in many Muslim lands. The more extreme form is horrendous.

[119] The distinction is whether the guilty party has ever enjoyed a valid married life.

[120] *Shuf'a*: the right of a co-owner compulsorily to take over a third party's purchase of another co-owner's share in jointly-held land. It is sometimes extended to a neighbour's right over adjacent property.

[121] In many respects this should probably be regarded as Jewish rather than animistic in origin, but there has been much accretion.

[122] The mass conversion of subject peoples was much more commonly the result of sustained social and economic pressure.

[123] It should be observed, however, that the 'freedom of religion' guaranteed by the Constitution of many modern Muslim states is usually limited in practice to freedom for non-Muslims to worship in their own way. Any attempt to propagate another religion is severely restricted, and often no provision whatever is made for a Muslim to change his faith. This is not true of Pakistan, where both preaching and change of faith are allowed, provided only that Islam, the Qur'ān or Muḥammad are in no way attacked.

[124] *Cf.* p. 53.

[125] Coupled, of course, with a general upsurge of pan-Arabism.

[126] See pp. 19, 53 and 100.

Chapter 2: The twin sciences of Islam

[1] A. Jeffery, *The Qur'ān as Scripture* (New York: Russell E. Moore, 1952), pp. 3–5.

[2] *Ibid.*, p. 6.

[3] *Ibid.*, p. 14.

[4] *Ibid.*, p. 14.

[5] *Ibid.*, pp. 15ff.

[6] I say 'figurative' in regard to specific later interpretations; but that the Jews did in fact believe that an oral as well as a written law was revealed to Moses on Sinai there can be no doubt.

[7] Born AD 767.

[8] For this section and the next I am indebted to Hodder and Stoughton for permission to reproduce material from my book *The Teaching of Jesus* (London: Hodder and Stoughton, 1983), pp. 12–14.

[9] R. Bell, *Introduction to the Qur'ān* (Edinburgh: 1953), pp. 17ff, 82ff.

[10] A. Jeffery, *op. cit.*, pp. 92ff.

[11] *Ibid.*, p. 95.

[12] *Ibid.*, pp. 97f.

[13] *Ibid.*, p. 92.

[14] Which is now accepted chiefly on the basis of an alleged Tradition (which was not known, it seems, when al-Shāfi'ī wrote about *ijmā'* in *al-Risāla*) that Muḥammad had once said: 'My community will never agree in error.'

[15] These two sources are termed *istiḥsān* and *istiṣlāḥ*, respectively.

[16] For this whole subject cf. the magisterial work of Joseph Schacht in *Origins of Muhammadan Jurisprudence* (and elsewhere).

[17] *Cf.* J. Schacht, *op. cit.*, pp. 224 ff.; and Schacht, *Introduction to Islamic Law* (Oxford: Clarendon Press, 1964), pp. 10ff., 18f., etc.

[18] *Cf.* A. Jeffery, *op. cit.*, pp. 3, 89–103; Schacht, *Introduction*, p. 18.

[19] 65–86 AH/AD 684–705.

[20] *Cf.* Schacht, *op. cit.*, p. 20; p. 21; p. 78ff. Legal fictions are doctrines or statements *assumed* to be true: e.g. that a child born to a married woman is a 'child of the marriage bed', and thus legitimate.

[21] Schacht, *op. cit.*, pp. 79f.

[22] This last clause represents Islamic law. The Mosaic law prescribed stoning, for both parties, only in cases of intercourse with another man's wife (*cf.* Lv. 20:10).

[23] Schacht, *op. cit.*, pp. 21, 37f.

[24] *Ibid.*, p. 25.

[25] *Ibid.*, pp. 51, 21.

[26] *Ibid.*, p. 21.

[27] *Ibid.*, p. 19.

[28] *Ibid.*, p. 16.

[29] N. J. Coulson, *A History of Islamic Law* (Edinburgh: 1964), p. 118.

[30] Schacht, *op. cit.*, pp. 70f.

[31] For Duns Scotus, for example, a thing is good not because it corresponds to the nature of God (or, analogically, to nature of man) but 'because God so

wills', and William of Occam was equally emphatic; whereas other Schoolmen, including Thomas Aquinas, found the basis for natural law not *primarily* in the will of God, but in his divine essence and reason. *Cf.* H. A. Rommen, *The Natural Law*, trans. T. R. Hanley (London: 1947), pp. 57ff.; 45ff.

[32] *Cf.* pp. 19f. above.

[33] See pp. 106f. below.

[34] J. Schacht, *op. cit.*, p. 1.

[35] H. Gibb, *Mohammedanism* (London: 1953), pp. 9–11.

[36] *Cf.* pp. 25–28 above.

[37] *Cf.* pp. 28–30.

[38] One reason why both Judaism and Islam have had much more to say about what God commands men to do than what he himself is like, was the result of the Aristotelian philosophy which prevailed during the Scholastic period. This affected Christian thought, too; and it was primarily the incarnation which saved Christian doctrine from the narrow confines of the *via negativa*.

[39] H. Gibb, in *The Concise Encyclopedia of Living Faiths*, pp. 183f.

[40] *Cf.* p. 54 above.

[41] *Cf.* Gibb, *Encyclopedia*, p. 184.

[42] *Ibid.*,

[43] *Cf.* p. 54 above.

[44] Gibb, *Encyclopedia*, p. 185.

[45] *Cf.* D. B. Macdonald, *Muslim Theology, Jurisprudence and Constitutional Theory*, (New York: 1903), p. 309.

[46] Died in AD 1111

[47] *Cf.* Macdonald, *op. cit.*, pp. 216–224; Gibb *Encyclopedia*, pp. 187 ff.

[48] *Cf.* Macdonald, *op. cit.*, pp. 224–228.

[49] *Cf.* the partial resemblance between the Ṣūfī concept of *al-fanā'* and that of *Nirvāna*.

[50] *Cf.* Gibb, *Encyclopedia*, p. 190.

[51] The translation of all these verses has been taken from *The Qur'ān*, trans. Richard Bell (Edinburgh: T. and T. Clark, 1937).

[52] K. Cragg, *The Call of the Minaret* (New York: OUP, 1956), p. 40.

[53] *Ibid.*, p. 42.

[54] An-Nawawi's *Forty Hadiths*, trans. E. Ibrahim and D. Johnson-Davies (Damascus: The Holy Koran Publishing House, 2nd ed., 1977), p. 118 (from al-Bukhārī's *al-Saṇīḥ*).

[55] Hughes' *Dictionary of Islam* (London: W. H. Allen & Co., 1895), p. 148 (from *Mishkātu'l-Maṣābīḥ, Bābu'l-Qadr*).

[56] A. S. Tritton, *Muslim Theology* (London: Luzac, 1947), pp. 9 and 185.

[57] K. Cragg, *op. cit.*, p. 55.

Chapter 3: Islamic mysticism

For convenience of reference, I have confined my frequent references to five authors to one only of their books. These are, A. J. Arberry, *Sufism: an account of the mystics of Islam* (London: 1950); K. Cragg, *The Call of the Minaret* (New York: OUP, 1965); H. A. R. Gibb, 'Islam' in *The Concise Encyclopedia of Living Faiths*, ed. R. C. Zaehner (London: 1977); D. B. Macdonald, *Muslim Theology, Jurisprudence and Constitutional Theory* (New York: 1903); R. A. Nicholson, *The Mystics of Islam* (London: 1914).

[1] Macdonald, *op. cit.*, p. 125.
[2] *Cf.* The Qur'an, trans. R. Bell (Edinburgh: 1937), Vol. II, p. 667.
[3] This is the usual translation of the first line of sūra 74. But Bell remarks that the word *mudaththir* might, possibly, simply mean 'something like [thou] laggard' (Bell, *op. cit.*, p. 617).
[4] Cragg, *op. cit.*, p. 78.
[5] *Cf.* Macdonald, *op. cit.*, p. 173.
[6] *Cf.* Nicholson, op. cit., p. 31; Arberry, *op. cit.*, pp. 42f.
[7] *Cf.* Macdonald, *op. cit.*, p. 174; Arberry, *op. cit.*, pp. 36ff.
[8] *Cf.* Macdonald, *op. cit.*, p. 175; Arberry, *op. cit.*, pp. 41f.
[9] *Cf.* Macdonald, *op. cit.*, p. 173.
[10] *Cf.* Louis Massignon, 'Ṣūfism' in *Encyclopedia of Islam* (London: 1939) Vol. 4 II p. 681f.
[11] *Cf.* Nicholson, op. cit., p. 10.
[12] *Ibid.*, p. 11.
[13] *Ibid.*, pp. 82f.; Arberry, *op. cit.*, pp. 100ff.
[14] Macdonald, *op. cit.*, pp. 163f.
[15] *Ibid.*, pp. 164f.
[16] *Cf.* G. D. Dragas, 'Pseudo-Dionysius the Areopagite' in *New Dictionary of Theology* (Leicester: IVP, 1988), pp. 542ff.
[17] *Cf.* G. L. Bray 'Apophatic Theology', in *New Dictionary of Theology*, p. 39.
[18] *Cf.* E. M. Yamauchi, 'Gnosticism', in *New Dictionary of Theology*, p. 273.
[19] *Loc. cit.*
[20] Macdonald, *op. cit.*, p. 175.
[21] Nicholson, *op. cit.*, p. 14.
[22] *Ibid.*, pp. 16f; *cf.* Arberry, *op. cit.*, pp. 36ff.
[23] Macdonald, *op. cit.*, pp. 182f; *cf.* Arberry, *op. cit.*, pp. 54f.
[24] Nicholson, *op. cit.*, pp. 17f. *Cf.* N. Anderson, *God's Law and God's Love* (London: 1980), pp. 11f.; 97.
[25] *Cf.* Macdonald, *op. cit.*, p. 175.
[26] *Ibid.*, p. 176. But *cf.* Arberry, *op. cit.*, pp. 56–59.
[27] *Cf.* Nicholson, *op. cit.*, pp. 34f.
[28] *Cf.* Macdonald, *op. cit.*, p. 175.
[29] *Cf.* ibid., pp. 175f. But *cf.* Arberry, *op. cit.*, p. 46.
[30] Nicholson, *op. cit.*, p. 13; Arberry, *op. cit.*, pp. 52ff., 61.
[31] Nicholson, *op. cit.*, p. 65.
[32] *Ibid.*, p. 116.

[33] Literally 'passing away'. It is to this that the words 'ecstasy', 'rapture', 'fainting' and 'trance' commonly refer.

[34] Arberry, *op. cit.*, p. 56.

[35] *Ibid.*, pp. 58f.

[36] Macdonald, *op. cit.*, pp. 176f.

[37] *Ibid.*, pp. 180f.

[38] *Cf. ibid.*, p. 182.

[39] *Cf.* Nicholson, *op. cit.*, pp. 88f.

[40] Arberry, *op. cit.*, pp. 59f.

[41] *Cf.* Macdonald, *op. cit.*, p. 134.

[42] L. Massignon [L. Gardet], in *Encyclopedia of Islam*, (London: 1971), Vol. 3, p. 102.

[43] *Loc. cit.*

[44] *Loc. cit.*

[45] Nicholson, *op. cit.*, pp. 150ff.

[46] Gibb, *op. cit.*, p. 193.

[47] *Cf.* Macdonald, *op. cit.*, pp. 261ff. But *cf.* also Arberry, *op. cit.* pp. 61, 97–104, 110f., 119; who considers Ibn Arabī 'the greatest mystical genius of the Arabs' (p. 97) and remarks that 'his system can be regarded as more monistic than pantheistic' (p. 101).

[48] Nicholson, *op. cit.*, pp., 102ff. He considers Ibn ʿArabi 'the greatest theosophist the Arabs have produced'.

[49] Ibid., p. 105.

[50] *Cf. ibid.*, p. 95.

[51] *Cf.* Nicholson, *op. cit.*, p. 59. But see also al-Junaiydī's definition of *fanā'* on p. 73 above.

[52] See index.

[53] Macdonald, *op. cit.*, p. 215; *cf.* W. Montgomery-Watt, in *Encyclopedia of Islam* (London: 1965) Vol. 2, pp. 1038–1041.

[54] A sect of the Shīʿīs.

[55] *Cf.* Macdonald, *op. cit.*, pp. 215–240.

[56] *Cf.* R. J. Zwi Werblowsky, in *Concise Encyclopedia of Living Faiths*, ed. J. R. C. Zaehner (London: 1977), pp. 26–31; *cf.* also N. Anderson, *op. cit.*, pp. 63ff., 138ff.

[57] Gibb, *op. cit.*, p. 193.

[58] Nicholson, *op. cit.*, p. 96.

[59] *Ibid.*, p. 106f.

[60] *Ibid.*, p. 119.

[61] *Cf. ibid.*, pp. 28ff.; Arberry, *op. cit.*, pp. 67f., 79.

[62] Nicholson, *op. cit.*, pp. 39f.

[63] L. Gardet, in *Encyclopaedia of Islam* (London: 1971), Vol. 2, p. 83.

[64] *Ibid.*, pp. 83f.

[65] *Loc. cit.*

[66] *Idem.*

[67] Nicholson, *op. cit.*, p. 29.

[68] L. Gardet, in *Encyclopaedia of Islam* (London: 1965), Vol. 2, pp. 223.

[69] *Ibid.*, pp. 223–226.

[70] For *waḥdat al-wujūd cf.* pp. 75f above.

[71] Gardet, *op. cit.*, pp. 223–226. I can only hope that this bare summary will prompt readers to consult Gardet's excellent article in full.

[72] *Cf.* L. Gardet, 'Fikr' in *Encyclopaedia of Islam* (London: 1965), Vol. 2, pp. 891f. For comparison, *cf.* the appeal of 'Transcendental Meditation' today.

[73] *Cf.* F. Rahman, 'Baqā' in *Encyclopaedia of Islam* (London: 1958), Vol. 1, p. 951.

[74] *Cf.* Macdonald, *op. cit.*, p. 228.

[75] Gibb, 'Islam' in *Concise Encyclopaedia of Living Faiths*, ed. R. C. Zaehner (London: 1977), p. 191.

[76] Macdonald, *op. cit.*, pp. 177f.

[77] *Cf.* Gibb, *op. cit.*, pp. 190f.

[78] *Ibid.*, pp. 191f.

[79] *Cf.* Arberry, *op. cit.*, p. 85; Gibb, *op. cit.*, p. 192; Macdonald, *op. cit.*, p. 267; Cragg, *op. cit.*, p. 136.

[80] *Cf.* Arberry, *op. cit.*, pp. 85f.; Gibb, *op cit.*, p. 192; Cragg, *op. cit.*, p. 136.

[81] *Cf.* Arberry, *op cit.*, pp. 86f.; Gibb, *op. cit.*, p. 192; Cragg, *op. cit.*, p. 136; Macdonald, *op. cit.*, p. 267.

[82] *Cf.* Arberry, *op. cit.*, pp. 88f.; Gibb, *op cit.*, p. 192; Macdonald, *op. cit.*, p. 167; Cragg, *op. cit.*, p. 136.

[83] Macdonald, *op. cit.*, p. 268.

[84] *Cf. ibid.*, p. 267.

[85] *Cf.* Gibb, *op. cit.*, p. 192.

[86] *Cf. ibid.*, p. 192.

[87] *Cf.* Arberry, *op. cit.*, pp. 128f.; Gibb, *op. cit.*, p. 192; J. S. Trimingham, *Islam in West Africa* (Oxford: 1959), pp. 91f.; J. N. D. Anderson, *Islamic Law in Africa* (London: 1953 and 1967), p. 378; D. S. Margoliouth, in *Encyclopaedia of Islam* (London: 1929), Vol. 4, II, pp. 745ff.

[88] *Cf.* Arberry, *op. cit.*, p. 129; Gibb, *op. cit.*, p. 192; *Encyclopaedia of Islam* (London: 1934) Vol. 4, I, pp. 154f.

[89] P. Parshall, *Bridges to Islam* (Grand Rapids: 1953), p. 72.

[90] *Cf.* Arberry, *op. cit.*, pp. 123–128; Macdonald, *op. cit.*, pp. 179–283.

[91] Nicholson, *op. cit.*, pp. 122–124.

[92] *Cf.* Arberry, *op. cit.*, pp. 129f.

[93] *Cf.* Cragg, *op. cit.*, p. 136.

Chapter 4: Islamic fundamentalism

[1] In mathematics, the Arabs passed on to Western Europe their own fusion of principles derived from both Greek and Hindu sources.

[2] *Cf.* pp. 40f above.

[3] For the Shīʿīs, *cf.* pp. 14–17 and pp. 51f above.

[4] Published in *Law, Justice and Equity*: Essays in tribute to G. W. Keeton (London: 1967).

[5] Speech delivered at the Frontier Muslim League Conference at Peshawar,

on 21 Nov. 1945. Quoted by Khurshid Aḥmad in *An Analysis of the Munir Report*, p. 132.

[6] *Ibid.*, p. 133.

Chapter 5: The incarnation

[1] *Cf.* C. F. D. Moule, *The Origin of Christology* (C.U.P., 1977), pp. 13–22.

[2] *Ibid.*, p. 20.

[3] Commentary on St. Luke's Gospel (The Pelican Gospel Commentaries, 1963), p. 94.

[4] C. H. Dodd, 'The Historic Problem of the Death of Jesus', in *More New Testament Studies* (Manchester University Press, 1968).

[5] Moule, *op. cit.*, pp. 33f.

[6] *Cf.* O. Cullmann, *The Christology of the New Testament* (London: SCM Press, 1959), p. 8.

[7] Mk. 8:30 and Mt. 16:17.

[8] K. Cragg, *The Call of the Minaret* (New York: OUP, 1965), p. 315.

[9] *Cf.* 2 Sa. 7:14 and Ps. 2:2 and 7.

[10] E.g. *The Myth of God Incarnate* (London: SCM Press, 1977), pp. 100ff.

[11] *A Dictionary of Christian Theology*, ed. A. Richardson (London: SCM Press, 1969), pp. 357f.

[12] A. Richardson, *An Introduction to the Theology of the New Testament* (London: SCM Press, 1958), pp. 171ff.

[13] L. Bouyer, *Le Fils éternel* (Paris: Cerf, 1974), p. 510 as quoted by Mascall, *Theology and the Gospel of Christ* (London: SPCK, 1977), pp. 137 and 150.

[14] Galot, *La Conscience de Jésus* (Gembloux, Duculot, and Paris: Lethielleux, 1971), pp. 179f. as quoted by Mascall, *op. cit.*, p. 167.

[15] C. F. D. Moule, *The Phenomenon of the New Testament* (London: SCM Press, 1967), pp. 65ff.

[16] Lk. 10:22; Mt. 11:27. This represents one of those 'Q' passages which are often regarded as among the earliest strands in the traditions. But *cf.* also the inescapable implication in the parable of the wicked husbandmen.

[17] R. V. G. Tasker, *The Nature and Purpose of the Gospels* (London: SCM Press, 1957), pp. 96f.

[18] *Cf.* C. F. D. Moule, 'Incarnation: paradox that will not go away' in T.H.E.S., 23 Dec. 1977.

[19] Mk. 1:22 NEB.

[20] A. M. Hunter, *Bible and Gospel* (London: SCM Press, 1969), p. 133.

[21] A. M. Ramsey, *God, Christ and the World* (London: SCM Press, 1969), p. 89.

[22] H. E. W. Turner, *Jesus the Christ* (London: Mowbray's, 1976), *passim.*

[23] See below, pp. 169f, etc.

[24] It will be found on analysis that the fairly frequent use of the word 'Lord' in regard to Jesus before the resurrection, particularly in the AV, is almost always either in the vocative (where *kyrie* simply meant 'Sir') or in the *narrative*

passages in Luke (where it must have come naturally to the author's pen).

[25] O. Cullmann, *The Christology of the New Testament*, p. 203. *Cf.* also Moule, *The Origin of Christology* pp. 35ff., and 148ff. for the use of this term.

[26] Cullmann, *op. cit.* p. 200.

[27] Acts 2:36.

[28] C. F. D. Moule, *Origin*, p. 41f.

[29] *Cf.* Acts 7:59.

[30] Moule, 'Incarnation: paradox that will not go away', in T.H.E.S., 23 Dec., 1977.

[31] J. Knox, *The Humanity and Divinity of Christ* (C.U.P., 1967), pp. 7–9.

[32] Rom. 1:3 RSV.

[33] Heb. 1:2; 1:4; 1:9; 2:9; and 5:10.

[34] J. Robinson, *The Human Face of God* (London: SCM Press, 1973), p. 155.

[35] Heb. 1:2.

[36] *Cf.* Heb. 2:17; 4:2; 9:2; 2:17; 7:16; 2:10; and 9:12.

[37] Knox, *op. cit.*, p. 11.

[38] C. F. D. Moule, Theologia Evangelica, Vol. VIII, No. 3, Sept., 1975.

[39] *Cf.* also C. F. D. Moule, *Origin*, pp. 136ff. *Pace* Dr. Young, *The Myth of God Incarnate*, pp. 21 and 35.

[40] Even on the most critical view, these allusions must clearly be taken as evidence for the author's own conviction about the pre-existence of Jesus.

[41] R. H. Lightfoot, *St. John's Gospel* (OUP, 1956), pp. 297ff.

[42] J. Marsh, *St. John* (The Pelican New Testament Commentaries, 1968), p. 559. At pp. 549–552 Marsh discusses the critical arguments relevant to John 17 as a whole.

[43] Knox, *op. cit.*, pp. 107f.

[44] *Ibid.*, p. 106.

[45] Cf. G. Lampe, *God as Spirit* (Oxford: 1977), *passim*, but particularly chapter 6.

[46] Barker, 1975, pp. 4ff.

[47] *Ibid.*, pp. 54f.

[48] D. M. Baillie, *God was in Christ* (London: Faber and Faber, 1961), pp. 149f.

Chapter 6: Christology down the centuries

[1] D. B. Macdonald, *The Development of Muslim Theology, Jurisprudence and Constitutional Theory* (New York: 1903), pp. 131f.

[2] Macdonald, *op. cit.*, p. 132.

[3] 1 Jn. 4:2f. *Cf.* J. R. W. Stott, *The Epistles of John* (London: 1964), pp. 155f.

[4] 2 Jn. 7. *Cf.* Stott, *op. cit.*, pp. 208–210.

[5] 1 Jn. 2:22. *Cf.* Stott *op. cit.*, pp. 110–112.

[6] A. Grillmeier, *Christ in Christian Tradition*, trans. John Bowden (London: Mowbrays, 1975), p. 76f.

[7] *Cf.* G. L. Carey, *The New International Dictionary of the Christian Church*

(Exeter: The Paternoster Press, 1974), p. 207.

[8] G. Parrinder, *Jesus in the Qur'ān* (London: 1965), p. 110.

[9] 1 Jn. 5:5f. Cf. Stott, *op. cit.*, pp. 178f.

[10] *Cf.* H. E. W. Turner, in *A Dictionary of Christian Theology*, ed. Alan Richardson (London: 1969), pp. 223, 220f., and 299.

[11] See J. G. G. Norman, in *The New International Dictionary of the Christian Church*, ed. J. D. Douglas (Exeter: 1974), p. 796.

[12] Turner, in Richardson, *op. cit.*, pp. 334 and 345.

[13] *Cf.* Grillmeier, *op. cit.*, p. 119.

[14] Turner, in Richardson, *op. cit.*, p. 345.

[15] *Cf.* D. M. Baillie, *God was in Christ* (London: Faber and Faber, 1961), pp. 135ff.

[16] J. W. Sweetman, *Islam and Christian Theology* (London: 1945), Vol. 1, Part 1, p. 32.

[17] *Cf.* G. L. Bray, in *New Dictionary of Theology* (Leicester: IVP, 1988), p. 694.

[18] *Cf.* Turner, in Richardson, *op. cit.*, p. 351.

[19] *Ibid.*, p. 346.

[20] *Cf.* R. P. C. Hanson, in *A Dictionary of Christian Theology*, p. 245. But it should be noted, in this context, that Origen also believed in the eternal creation of the world (or, perhaps, in a succession of worlds) by the eternally-generated Logos.

[21] For the difference between 'evolution' and 'development' in Christology, see C. F. D. Moule, *The Origin of Christology* (London: SCM Press, 1959), pp. 1–3; for the development of the doctrine of the Trinity, see Arthur W. Wainwright, *The Trinity in the New Testament* (London: SPCK, 1962), *passim*.

[22] Turner, in Richardson, *op. cit.*, p. 345.

[23] H. R. Mackintosh, *The Doctrine of the Person of Christ* (Edinburgh: T. and T. Clark, 1912), p. 141.

[24] *Ibid.*, p. 145.

[25] *Ibid.*, p. 147.

[26] *Ibid.*, p. 154.

[27] *Ibid.*, pp. 162f.

[28] *Ibid.*, p. 165.

[29] D. M. Baillie, *op. cit.*, p. 70.

[30] H. E. W. Turner, *Jesus the Christ* (London: 1976), pp. 32 ff.

[31] Which differs somewhat from the 'Nicene Creed' recited in the Communion Service in the Church of England. This is often called the 'Niceno-Constantinople Creed', in the belief that it was promulgated by the Council of Constantinople in AD 381. But this is doubtful.

[32] Grillmeier, *op. cit.*, p. 267.

[33] *Cf.* Mackintosh, *op. cit.*, pp. 181f.

[34] *Cf. ibid.*, pp. 183ff.

[35] Turner, *op. cit.*, p. 37.

[36] *Ibid.*, pp. 37ff.

[37] *Cf.* Mackintosh, *op. cit.*, pp. 198f.; Turner, in Richardson, *A Dictionary of Christian Theology*, p. 56 and *Jesus the Christ*, pp. 40ff. *Cf.* also Baillie, *op. cit.*,

p. 88; G. T. D. Angel, in *The New International Dictionary of the Christian Church*, p. 56; and Grillmeier, *op. cit.*, pp. 330ff.

[38] Turner, *op. cit.*, pp. 47f.

[39] *Ibid.*, pp. 49f.

[40] Mackintosh, *op. cit.*, p. 207.

[41] *Ibid.*, pp. 205f.; Turner, *op. cit.*, pp. 44f.

[42] Grillmeier, *op. cit.*, pp. 544f.

[43] *Ibid.*, p. 546.

[44] *I.e.* 'consubstantial.'

[45] Grillmeier, *op. cit.*, p. 547.

[46] *Cf.* Mackintosh, *op. cit.*, p. 213; Turner, *op. cit.*, pp. 54f., who notes that the phrase 'perfect God' and 'perfect man' was 'a characteristically Dualist expression'.

[47] Translation according to *Christology of the Later Fathers*, ed. E. R. Hardy (1954), p. 573.

[48] Turner, *op. cit.*, p. 55.

[49] Turner, in Richardson, *A Dictionary of Christian Theology*, p. 58.

[50] J. McIntyre, *The Shape of Christology* (London: SCM, 1966), pp. 82–100. But *cf.* in this context, C. Stead, *Divine Substance* (Oxford: Clarendon Press, 1977), especially pp. 113ff.

[51] *Not* Byzantium. *Cf.* Mascall, *Theology and the Gospel of Christ*, p. 242, note 109.

[52] Which would seem to be the only reasonable explanation of what Cyril must have meant by the phrase 'impersonal human nature'. *Cf.* p. 155 below.

[53] *Cf.* W. N. Pittenger, *The Word Incarnate* (Nisbet, 1959), pp. 100–103.

[54] See, in part, chapter 8 below.

[55] *Cf.* J. McIntyre, *op. cit.*, pp. 82–100.

[56] Expressed, moreover, in terms of a philosophical framework in which we do not normally think today.

[57] *Cf.* W. Pannenberg, *Jesus – God and Man* (London: SCM Press, 1968), p. 293.

[58] Mk. 14:35f. NEB.

[59] For a somewhat fuller account of this debate, see pp. 20, 58f above.

[60] Mackintosh, *op. cit.*, pp. 230–234.

[61] Pannenberg, *op. cit.*, pp. 308f.

[62] Mackintosh, *op. cit.*, pp. 238–242.

[63] *Ibid.*, p. 243.

[64] Pannenberg, *op. cit.*, p. 284.

Chapter 7: The incarnation and other religions

[1] F. Young, *The Myth of God Incarnate* (London: SCM Press, 1977), p. 102ff.

[2] *Cf.* B. M. Metzger, *Historical and Literary Studies* (Leiden: 1968), pp. 19f.

[3] Or, in the view of more sophisticated Hindus, of the 'Ultimate Reality'.

[4] *Cf.* Newbigin, *The Finality of Christ* (London: 1969), pp. 50ff.
[5] J. Hick, *The Myth of God Incarnate*, p. 176. My italics.
[6] *Ibid.*, p. 168.
[7] *Ibid.*, p. 172.
[8] *Ibid.*, p. 167.
[9] *Ibid.* Hick does not reveal the source of this description.
[10] *Ibid.*, p. 168. Contrast the remarks of A. N. Sherwin White in *Roman Society and Roman Law in the New Testament* (Oxford: Clarendon, 1963), pp. 187ff.
[11] Hick, *op. cit.*, p. 172.
[12] *Ibid.*, p. 173.
[13] *Ibid.*, pp. 168ff.
[14] *Ibid.*, p. 173.
[15] *Ibid.*, p. 173.
[16] *Ibid.*, p. 170.
[17] *Ibid.*, p. 174.
[18] *Ibid.* See also Frances Young's account of philosophers, Emperors and 'divine men' to whom a miraculous birth, or some sort of 'divinity', was attributed (*Ibid.*, pp. 93ff.).
[19] *Ibid.*, p. 175.
[20] *Ibid.*, p. 175.
[21] *Ibid.*, p. 173. My italics.
[22] This point has been recently emphasized in an article in *The Times Higher Education Supplement* (23 Dec 1977) by Professor C. F. D. Moule.
[23] Acts 2:31–36.
[24] Acts 4:12 and 7:59.
[25] J. Hick, *op. cit.*, p. 173.
[26] 1 Thes. 1:9f NEB.
[27] Gal. 4:4 and 5 NEB.
[28] Col. 1:15–17 NEB.
[29] Heb. 1:1–3 NEB.
[30] Lk. 10:22. *Cf.* Mt. 11:27 NEB.
[31] Mk. 14:61f.
[32] *Cf.* Mt. 5:21–48; 7:21–29.
[33] Hick, *op. cit.*, pp. 168f.
[34] *Ibid.*, p. 176.
[35] *Ibid.*, p. 176.
[36] Mk. 10:45 NEB.
[37] Mt. 26:28 NEB.
[38] *Cf.* Lk. 22:37; 1 Pet. 2:24f; *etc.*
[39] *Cf.* Lk. 24:25–27, 44–48.
[40] Hick, *op. cit.*, p. 170.
[41] *Ibid.*, p. 170.
[42] 1 Cor. 15:42, 44–54.
[43] Rom. 6:9 NEB.
[44] Phil. 3:21f NEB.
[45] W. Pannenberg, *Jesus – God and Man* (London: SCM Press, 1968), p. 75.
[46] *Ibid.*, p. 76.

[47] *Cf.* N. Anderson, *A Lawyer among the Theologians* (London: Hodder & Stoughton, 1973), pp. 144f. – together with footnotes. In this book I have attempted to discuss this whole matter in much greater detail than is feasible here.

[48] *Cf.* John 20:1–10, and W. Temple, *Readings in St John's Gospel* (London: Macmillan, 1949), p. 376.

[49] P. Althaus, *Die wahrheit des Kirchlichen Osterglambeus*, pp. 22ff. – as quoted by Pannenberg, *op. cit.*, p. 100.

[50] Pannenberg, *op. cit.*, p. 101.

[51] *Cf.* N. Anderson, *op. cit.*, pp. 120ff.

[52] Hick, *op. cit.*, p. 170.

[53] *Ibid.*, p. 171.

[54] Rom. 1:3 NEB.

[55] *Cf.*, *inter alia*, John 20:24–29.

[56] Hick, *op. cit.*, p. 171.

[57] Pannenberg, *op. cit.*, pp. 67f. Pannenberg cites 'Acts 2:36; 3:15; 5:30f. *et al.*'

[58] Hick, *op. cit.*, p. 173.

[59] *Ibid.*, p. 178.

[60] *Ibid.*, p. 178.

[61] *Ibid.*, p. 181.

[62] *Ibid.*, p. 181.

[63] *Ibid.*, p. 181.

[64] *Ibid.*, p. 181.

[65] *Ibid.*, p. 181.

[66] *Ibid.*, p. 179.

[67] *Ibid.*, p. 180.

[68] *Ibid.*, p. 180.

[69] *Ibid.*, p. 180.

[70] The 'name' to which reference is made in this statement is, of course, that of Jesus. But 'name' in the Bible stands for the person concerned: that is, who and what he is.

[71] Hick, *op. cit.*, p. 180. I have discussed this question in some detail in chapter 5 of *Christianity and World Religions* (Leicester: IVP, 1984).

[72] *The Myth of Christian Uniqueness* (London: 1988), pp. 22f.

[73] V. Hooft, *No Other Name* (London: 1960), p. 117.

[74] *Cf.* G. Parrinder, *Jesus in the Qur'ān* (London: 1960), pp. 108–119.

[75] S. Neill, *Christian Faith and Other Faiths* (London: 1961), pp. 16f.

[76] L. Newbigin, *The Finality of Christ* (London: 1969), p. 57.

Chapter 8: The incarnation and personal faith today

[1] *Cf.* Jn. 1:1–14; Heb. 1:2–3, 10–12; 1 Jn. 1:1–3 – among others.

[2] W. Pannenberg, *Jesus – God and Man* (London: SCM Press, 1968), p. 308 – citing F. Loofs.

[3] *Ibid.*, p. 309.

[4] H. R. Mackintosh, *The Doctrine of the Person of Christ* (Edinburgh: T. and T. Clark, 1912), p. 243.

[5] *Cf.* Pannenberg, *op. cit.*, p. 310.

[6] Mackintosh, *op. cit.*, p. 266.

[7] Pannenberg, *op. cit.*, p. 310.

[8] W. Temple, *Christus Veritas*, pp. 142f. For this point, see pp. 192ff below.

[9] *Cf.* D. M. Baillie, *God was in Christ* (London: Faber and Faber, 1961), pp. 96f., with the final quotation taken from the *Westminster Shorter Catechism* (his italics).

[10] C. F. D. Moule, *The Origin of Christology* (London: SCM Press, 1959), pp. 1–4.

[11] K. Barth, *Church Dogmatics* IV, ed. G. W. Bromiley and T. F. Torrance (Edinburgh: T. and T. Clark, 1960), Pt. 1, pp. 75 and 222f. *Cf.* Richard Hooker, *Works*, Vol. ii, p. 606, 'We care for no knowledge in this world but this, that man hath sinned and God hath suffered; that God hath made Himself the sin of men, and that men are made the righteousness of God.'

[12] Pannenberg, *op. cit.*, p. 355.

[13] F. F. Bruce, *The Epistle to the Romans* (London: Tyndale Press, 1963), pp. 36f.

[14] For Moule's views on these points, *cf.* (*inter alia*) *The Origin of Christology*, pp. 138f.

[15] To lump together 'Modalism', the concept of the 'Economic Trinity' and other similar concepts (see chapter 6 above).

[16] *Cf.* E. L. Mascall, *Theology and the Gospel of Christ* (London: SPCK, 1977), pp. 180f.

[17] *Cf.* G. W. F. Lampe, 'The Holy Spirit and the person of Christ' in *Christ, Faith and History*, p. 130.

[18] Lampe has discussed this subject much more fully in *God as Spirit* (Oxford: Clarendon Press, 1977), pp. 164ff.

[19] *Cf.* B. M. Metzger, *Christ and Spirit in the New Testament* (C.U.P., 1973), pp. 95–112.

[20] All the New Testament passages in which Jesus is probably, or possibly, referred to as 'God' are discussed in some detail in Arthur W. Wainwright, *The Trinity in the New Testament* (London: SPCK, 1975), pp. 53–74. *Cf.* also O. Cullman, *The Theology of the New Testament* (London: SCM Press, 1957), pp. 307–314.

[21] Galot, *Vers une nouvelle christologie* (Gembloux, Duculot; and Paris, Lethielleux, 1971), p. 48 – quoted in Mascall, *Theology and the Gospel of Christ* (London: SPCK, 1977), p. 174.

[22] Cf. G. P. Berkouwer, *The Person of Jesus* (Grand Rapids Michigan: Eerdmans, 1954), pp. 306, 310f, and 321. For an eminently lucid discussion, see H. E. W. Turner, *Jesus the Christ* (London: 1974), pp. 60ff.

[23] C. F. D. Moule, 'The Manhood of Jesus in the New Testament' in *Christ, Faith and History*, pp. 98f.

[24] F. Weston, *The One Christ*, (London: Longmans, Green & Co., 1907), p. 147. *Cf.* also Mackintosh, *op. cit.*, pp. 241–245, especially the quotation from

Calvin on p. 244.

[25] Weston, *op. cit.*, pp. 135f.

[26] *Ibid.*, p. 138.

[27] *Ibid.*, pp. 140f. My italics.

[28] *Ibid.*, pp. 145–147.

[29] *Ibid.*, p. 152f.

[30] *Ibid.*, p. 168.

[31] Mascall, *op. cit.*, pp. 180f.

[32] Weston, *op. cit.*, pp. 174–177.

[33] Mascall, *op. cit.*, pp. 130f.

[34] *Ibid.*, p. 149.

[35] *Ibid.*, p. 167.

[36] *Ibid.*, p. 181.

[37] I have taken these references from some as yet unpublished lectures given in Oxford, for the loan of which I am indebted to Professor Donald MacKinnon.

[38] *Cf.* Mascall, *op. cit.*, pp. 182f.

[39] Oliver Quick, *loc. cit.*

[40] As Professor Tasker put it, in his comment on John 14:28: 'The words "greater than I" were frequently appealed to by the Arians to support their doctrine of the creaturely subordination of the Son to the Father. They do not, however, mean that the Father is greater in power or divinity, but . . . that He that is begotten is secondary to Him who begets.' *The Gospel according to St. John* (London: Tyndale Press, 1960), p. 173.

[41] *Cf.* C. H. Dodd, 'A Hidden Parable in the Fourth Gospel', in *More New Testament Studies* (Manchester University press, 1968), pp. 30ff.

[42] Jn. 5:30; 7:16; 8:26 and 28; 12:49; 14:24 and 31 (NEB).

[43] D. M. MacKinnon, 'The Relation of the Doctrines of the Incarnation and the Trinity', in *Creation, Christ and Culture*, ed. R. J. McKinney (1976), p. 97.

[44] It is here, moreover, that we find the answer to the common question: 'Could Jesus have come down from the cross?' Like the question about whether he could sin, this is ill-conceived. Instead of the answer being either 'No, being man, he could not' *or* 'Yes, being God, he could', the answer is 'No, *being who he was*, he could not have done so, because it would have been contrary to his character, his nature, his love for mankind, and his obedience to his Father's will'. It would also, of course, as Weston puts it, have been to act outside the limitations of the humanity he had assumed.

[45] Prefatory Note to Sir R. Anderson, *The Lord from Heaven* (1910).

[46] See pp. 11f, 140f above and pp. 218f, 229 below.

[47] Phil. 2:5–11.

[48] Rom. 1:4.

Epilogue

[1] By courtesy of the publishers, IVP.

[2] By courtesy of the publishers, William Collins and Hodder and Stoughton, respectively.

[3] By courtesy of the publishers, Hodder and Stoughton. Other chapters, which analyzed the views of several active contributors to 'the contemporary debate', have not been included in this book.

[4] *Cf.* Mt. 28:19; Jn. 14:25f.; 15:26f.; 16:15; 2 Cor. 13:14; Eph. 3:14–17.

[5] Which said of the Spirit: 'Who with the Father and Son together is worshipped and glorified.' *Cf.* A. V. Wainwright, *The Trinity in the New Testament* (London: 1962) p. 6; *Dictionary of the Christian Church* ed. J. D. Douglas (Exeter: 1974), p. 707.

[6] Wainwright, *op. cit.*, p. 81.

[7] Sūra 57:27; 5:50f.; 70f.; 110. *Cf.* also 7:156; 31:2, 58; 48:29; 9:112.

[8] Unless the reference is to the apocryphal '*Gospel of Thomas*'. Three third-century Oxyrhynchus papyri contain fragments of a Greek version of this book, compiled *c.* 140, of which the Coptic is a more gnosticized translation. It consists of some 120 'secret words' of 'the living Jesus', many very close to synoptic parallels, others more obviously syncretistic. *Cf. Dictionary of the Christian Church*, ed. J. D. Douglas (Exeter: 1904), p. 971.

[9] *Cf.* A. Jeffery, *The Qur'ān as Scripture* (New York: 1952), pp. 72f.

[10] 2 Pet. 1:21.

[11] Michael Green, *2 Peter and Jude* (London: IVP, 1968; 2nd edn. Leicester, IVP, 1984), pp. 91f.

[12] *Cf.* pp. 63, 156f above.

[13] D. B. Macdonald, *Muslim Theology, Jurisprudence and Constitutional Theory* (New York: 1903), p. 136.

[14] *Ibid.*, p. 309.

[15] E. Hahn, *Jesus as the Son of God* (Toronto: 1989). In the sentences preceding this quotation I have ventured to convey the author's sequence of thoughts in virtually his own words, but with very minor changes to fit the context.

[16] J. W. Sweetman, *Islam and Christian Theology* (London: 1967): Part II, Vol. II, p. 22.

[17] W. Temple, *Readings of St John's Gospel* (London: 1942), pp. 92f.

[18] Jn. 14:21 and 14:23.

[19] *Cf.* Macdonald, *op. cit.* p. 304.

[20] *Islamic Review*, September, 1961, pp. 11ff. For this whole subject see G. Parrinder, *Jesus in the Qur'ān* (London: 1969), pp. 122–125.

[21] *Cf.* chapter 1, pp. 11 above. Muslims often suggest that Judas Iscariot was crucified, by mistake, instead of ʿĪsā, while Dr Bell (as noted) plausibly suggests that we find here an echo of 'the Docetic assertion that only a simulacrum of Jesus was crucified' (*cf.* R. Bell, *The Qur'ān* (Edinburgh: 1937 and 1960), Vol. I, p. 89.

[22] *Cf.* pp. 63, 156f above.

[23] He gave me his permission to quote this in *God's Law and God's Love* (1960).

[24] W. Temple, *Readings in St John's Gospel* (London: 1942) pp. 92f. – quoting Edward Shillito, 'Jesus of the Scars'.

Appendix: The so-called 'Gospel of Barnabas'

[1] George Sale, *The Preliminary Discourse*, p. 58.
[2] *Ibid.*, p. X.
[3] W. H. Gairdner, *The Gospel of Barnabas* (Cairo: 1907).
[4] L. and L. Ragg, *The Gospel of Barnabas* (Oxford: 1907), p. xvi.
[5] *Cf.* The New International Dictionary of the Christian Church, ed. J. D. Douglas (Grand Rapids, 1974), p. 289.
[6] *Cf.* David Sox, *The Gospel of Barnabas* – a mine of information on this subject – p. 10.
[7] J. Hastings, *Encyclopaedia of Religion and Ethics* (Edinburgh: 1917), Vol. 6, p. 351 and Vol. 9, p. 483.
[8] Sox, *op. cit.*, pp. 14f.
[9] *Ibid.*, p. 15. *Cf.* M. S. Euslin, *The Interpreter's Dictionary* and E. J. Goodspeed, *Strange New Gospels*.
[10] Raggs, *op. cit.*, pp. xiv and xv.
[11] *Cf. ibid.*, p. xlix (footnote)
[12] *Ibid.*, p. xvii.
[13] Raggs, *loc. cit.*
[14] *Ibid.*, p. xviii.
[15] *Ibid.*, pp. xviii and xix, my emphasis.
[16] Sox, *op. cit.*, pp. 35f. These references to Slomp come from his *Islamochristiana*.
[17] Raggs, *op. cit.*, p. xxi.
[18] Sox, *op. cit.*, p. 31.
[19] *Ibid.*, p. 31.
[20] Ragg, *op. cit.*, p. xxv.
[21] R. Bell, *The Koran* (Edinburgh: 1960), p. 89.
[22] Ragg, *op. cit.*, p. 471.
[23] *Ibid.*, p. 481.
[24] Ragg, *loc. cit.*
[25] *Ibid.*, pp. 483 and 485.
[26] *Ibid.*, p. xxxiii, xxxiv.
[27] *Ibid.*, pp. xxxiv, xxxv.
[28] Jomier, *Mélanges*.
[29] An eighth-century Arabian storyteller.
[30] Sox, *op. cit.*, pp. 69f.
[31] *Cf. ibid.*, chapter 4 (pp. 49–72)
[32] *Ibid.*, pp. 65 and 67.
[33] *Ibid.*, p. 70.
[34] Raggs, *op. cit.*, p. xlvi (footnote)
[36] Sox, *op. cit.*, p. 12.

[37] ʿAta ur-Rahim, *Jesus, a Prophet of Islam* (London: 1979), p. 39.
[38] *Ibid.*, p. 52.
[39] *Ibid.*, p. 39.
[40] Metzger, *The Canon of the New Testament: its Origin, Development and Significance* (Oxford: 1987), pp. 65, 134, 140, 174, 188 *et. al.*
[41] *Ibid.*, p. 65.
[42] *Ibid.*, p. 134.
[43] *Ibid.*, pp. 140 and 188.
[44] *Ibid.*, p. 188.
[45] ʿAta ur-Rahim, *op. cit.*, p. 42.
[46] *Cf.* Mat. 28:18–20; Jn. 14:15–17, 25, 26; Acts 1:4 and 5; 1 Pet. 1:1 and 2; 1 Jn. 3:21–24; Jude 20–21; Rev. 1:4–6 and 22:16–19 – quite apart from the Pauline epistles.
[47] This so-called Gospel even alleges that the name 'Mohammed' was written on the left thumb-nail of Adam before the creation of Eve!

Glossary of Arabic words and names

ʿabd, slave
al-ʿAbbās, uncle of the Prophet
ʿAbbāsids, his relatives and later Caliphs
ʿAbd al-ʿAzīz ibn Saʿūd, first king of Saʿūdī Arabia
ʿAbd al-Mālik, Caliph
ʿAbd al-Qādir al-Jīlānī, eminent mystic
ʿābid, votary (in context)
Abū Bakr, first Caliph
Abū Ḥanīfa, traditional founder of the Ḥanafī school of Sunnī law
Abū Yazīd (Bāyazīd) al-Bisṭāmī, early mystic
Abū Sulaymān of Damascus, early ascetic
Abū Ṭālib al-Makkī, wrote text on Ṣūfism
Abū Ṭālib, uncle of the Prophet
Abū Hāshim, celebrated mystic
ʿafārīt (plural of *ʿifrīt*), demons, evil *jinn (q.v.)*
Āghā Khān, Ismāʿīlī leader
aḥad, one (with God)
aḥādīth (plural of *ḥadīth*), sayings, etc., attributed to the Prophet
aḥādīth qudsiyya, those few sayings outside the Qurʾān attributed to God himself
Aḥmad, variant of Muḥammad
Aḥmad ibn Ḥanbal, great Traditionalist and lawyer
Aḥmad al-Badawī, Egyptian mystic
Aḥmad al-Ḥawārī, Syrian mystic
Aḥmadiyya, a sect which claims to be Islamic, but Muslims largely repudiate this
aḥwāl (plural of *ḥāl*, *q.v.*), states of mind, often ecstatic (Ṣūfī)
ʿĀʾisha, wife of the Prophet

Allāh, God
Alamūt, stronghold of Ismāʿīlīs
ʿAlawīs (ʿAlawites), extreme sub-sect of Ismāʿīlīs, no longer really Muslims
ʿAlī, Caliph and relative of Prophet
ʿAlī Zayn al-ʿAbidīn, son of al-Ḥusayn, great-grandson of the Prophet
ʿAmal, Shīʿī party in Lebanon
Ana'l-Ḥaqq, extreme mystic claim to unity with God
ʿaqīda (plural *ʿaqā'id*), article of faith
ʿaqīqa, sacrifice for new-born child
ʿārif, Ṣūfī term for gnostic
ʿaṣaba, agnates, those descended from the same male ancestor
Asad, President of Syria
al-Ashʿarī, eminent theologian
Ashʿarī(s) (Ashʿarites), disciple(s) and teaching of al-Ashʿarī
awliyā', plural of *walī, q.v.*
awqāf, plural of *waqf, q.v.*
Āyatullāh(s), eminent Shīʿī theologian(s)
azalī, eternal
al-Azhar, famous Muslim Universty in Cairo

Bābīs, followers of Sayyid ʿAlī Muḥammad of Shirāz, who in 1844 proclaimed himself to be the Bāb (Door) to divine truth. No longer regarded as Muslims
Badr, battle of
al-Badawiyya, Ṣūfī brotherhood founded by Aḥmad al-Badawī (*q.v.*)
Baghdād
Bahā' Allāh, Mirza Ḥusayn ʿAlī Nūrī, who led a major split from the Bābīs (*q.v.*)
Bahā'al-Dīn, Naqshband, founder of the Naqshbandiyya Ṣūfī brotherhood
Bahā'īs, followers of Bahā' Allāh (*q.v.*)
Bahrein (Baḥrayn), state in Persian Gulf
Baḥīra, Christian monk met by Muḥammad
balā', trial and affliction
baqā', survival (Ṣūfī term)
baraka, blessing
Baṣra
Bektāshīs, members of Bektashiyya Ṣūfī Order
bidʿa, innovation
bi lā kayf, 'without asking how'
bi lā tashbīh 'without (human) similarity'

Bilbeis, market town in Egypt
Bishr al-Ḥāfi, the 'bare foot' ascetic
bint fikrī, lit. 'daughter of my mind'
al-Bukhārī, the great Traditionalist

Chistiyya, Ṣūfī order founded by Mūʿīn al-Dīn Chistī

Dāʿī Muṭlaq, plenipotentiary
Dār al-Islām, the part of the world where Islam prevails
Dār al-Ḥarb, the part of the world where Islam does not prevail as yet
darwīsh, dervish
Dāʾūdīs, sub-division of the Ismāʿīlī Shīʿīs
dhikr, lit. 'remembrance', Ṣūfī religious exercise
dhākir, the one who so 'remembers'; *madhkūr*, the one so remembered
dhāt, being, essence, himself, person
al-dhāta'l-ilāhiyya, the divine being
dhawq, taste
dhimmī(s), Christians and Jews who live in a Muslim state
Dhu'l-Nūn, Egyptian Ṣūfī
Dhū'l-Qarnayn, probably Alexander the Great
Dīwān of Shamsī Tabrīz, poem by al-Rūmī
Durzī (pl. *Durūz*), Druze

falāsifa, philosophers
fanāʾ, passing away, extinction of individual existence (Ṣūfī term)
al-Fārābī, great Muslim philosopher
al-Faqīh, title given to the ultimate legal authority in Iran
faqīr, poor, mendicant Ṣūfī
Fāṭima, daughter of Muḥammad
Fāṭimid(s), those of Faṭimid dynasty in Egypt, etc.
fatwa (pl. *fatawa* or *fatāwī*), legal opinion(s)
fikr, thought, meditation
fiqh, jurisprudence
al-Fuḍayl ibn ʿIyāḍ, early mystic

ghāʾib, 'absent', in a state of trance
al-Ghawth, 'the Succourer', greatest living saint
ghayba, 'absence', (Ṣūfī term for state of trance)
ghayr, other than
al-Ghazālī, great Muslim theologian and mystic
Ghulām Aḥmad Khān, founder of Aḥmadiyya (*q.v.*)
ghusl, ablution of whole body (one form of ritual purification)

al-Ḥabīb, 'the Beloved' (Ṣūfī term for God)
ḥadd (pl. *ḥudūd*), prescribed penalty
ḥadīth (pl. *aḥādīth, q.v.*), Tradition
Ḥafs (Kūfan text of), most widely accepted text of the Qur'ān
al-Ḥākim, one of the Fāṭimids of Egypt worshipped as God by the Druze of Lebanon
ḥāl (pl. *āḥwāl*), state, often ecstatic among Ṣūfīs
ḥalalna, 'we are fused together' (mystic experience)
al-Ḥallāj, al-Ḥusayn-ibn Mansūr, famous mystic
Hamam, depicted in Qur'ān as a minister of Pharaoh
Ḥanīf(s), pre-Islamic Arab monotheists
Ḥanafī(s), the largest of the four Sunnī schools of law today. See Abū Ḥanīfa.
Ḥanbal, Aḥmad ibn, traditional founder of fourth surviving Sunnī law school
al-Ḥaqīqa, 'the Truth' (God)
Hārith al-Muḥāsibī, see under al-Muḥāsibī
ḥarrafa, to change, alter
ḥarīm, a man's wives and concubines
al-Ḥārith al-Muḥāsibī, Ṣūfī ascetic
al-Ḥasan, eldest son of the Caliph ʿAlī
Ḥasan al Baṣrī, celebrated ascetic
al-Hāshim, family from which Muḥammad himself sprang
Hāshimīs, group of Shīʿis
ḥashīsh, narcotic
al-Hijāz, a province of Arabia
al-Hijra, flight of Muḥammad to al-Madina, from which years of Hijra (AH) begin
al-Ḥīra, Nestorian stronghold at gates of Syrian desert
ḥiyal (sing. *ḥīla*), artifices, legal fictions
Ḥizb Allāh, the 'Party of God'
Ḥizb-i-Islamī, the 'Party of Islam'
Ḥulūlīs, Ṣūfīs who 'believe in incarnation'
ḥūr, the maidens of Paradise
al-Ḥusayn, son of the Caliph ʿAlī

ʿibādāt, obligations regarding worship
Ibāḍī(s), survivors from the *Khawārij* (*q.v.*)
Iblīs, Satan
ʿīd al-aḍḥā, the Feast of Sacrifice
ʿidda, wife's period of waiting after widowhood or divorce
Ibn Abī Dāwūd, author of *Codex Book*
Ibn ʿArabī, Muḥyī al-Dīn Ibn ʿArabī, Ṣūfī extremist

Ibn ʿAṭāʾ Allāh, mystic extremist
Ibn Rushd ('Averoes'), great philosopher
Ibn Sīnā ('Avicenna'), great philosopher
Ibrāhīm ibn Adham, early mystic ascetic
Idrīs, formerly King of Libya
iḥsān, state of spiritual perfection
Iḥyā, famous book written by al-Ghazālī
ijmāʿ, consensus
ijtihād, right to go back to original sources of the law
Ikhwān al-Ṣafāʾ, somewhat shadowy figures
ʿilla, underlying principle
ʿilm al-tawḥīd, theology, the doctrine of the divine unity
Imām, leader
Injīl, Gospel, New Testament
ʿĪsā, Jesus
Islām, the religion of Muslims
ʿiṣma, sinlessness, infallibility
Ismāʿīl, son of Jaʿfar-al Ṣādiq, Shīʿī Imām
Ismāʿīlī(s), those who trace the Imamate through Ismāʿīl
isnād, chain of witnesses to a Tradition
ʿishq, passionate love, a term used by Ṣūfīs
istikhāra, use of rosary to make propitious decision
istiṣlāḥ, method of legal reasoning peculiar to Shāfiʿīs and Ithnā ʿAsharīs
Ithnā ʿAsharī(s) (-iyya), 'Twelvers', the largest group of Shīʿīs
ittiḥād, identification with God, term used by Ṣūfī extremists
Izrāʾīl, the messenger of death

jabarūt, omnipotence, 'All Power' (a Ṣūfī term)
Jābir ibn Ḥayyān, a Shīʿī alchemist and ascetic
jadhba, attraction (used by Ṣūfīs of emotional state)
Jaʿfar al-Ṣādiq, Shīʿī Imām
Jalāl al-Dīn al-Rūmī. See under al-Rūmī
jamʿ, union with God (a Ṣūfī term)
Jamāʿat-i-Islāmī, a Pakistani political party
Jibrīl, the (arch)angel Gabriel
jihād, 'holy' war
al-Jīlānī, see under ʿAbd al-Qādir
jinn, demons (but not necessarily evil)
jizya, poll tax for non-Muslims
al-Junayd, outstanding Ṣūfī
al-Juwaynī, Imām al-Ḥaramayn, a great Muslim theologian

Kaʿba, shrine at Mecca containing a black meteorite
kalām, reason, argument, discussion
kalima, Muslim creed
karāmāt, favours, wonders
Karīm Khān, Imām of the Āghā Khān's community
kashf, direct knowledge of God (Ṣūfī)
kātib, clerk of the courts
Kaysānīs, group of Shīʿīs
Khadīja, wife of Muḥammad
Khālid ibn al-Walīd, Muslim general
Khalīfa, Caliph
khānqāh, monastery for Ṣūfīs
Khārijī(s) (pl. Khawārij) 'seceders', Muslim sect
kharajū, 'they went out'
al-Kindī, philosopher
Kitāb al-Lumaʿ, book written by al-Sarrāj (an early Ṣūfī)
Kūfa, early Ṣūfī centre
Khurāsān, province

lā dhātahu wa lā ghayrahu, 'not identical with nor different from'; ('not He, nor are they any other than He')
lāhūt, the world of the divine essence
lā ilāha illā Allāh, 'there is no god except Allāh'
laylat al-qadr, The Night of Power
lawā, to twist
Libya, Cyrenaica and Tripolitania
Luqmān, Aesop(?)

al-Madīna, the place of Muḥammad's *hijra*
madrasa, school
maḥabba, love
al-Mahdī, the 'Guided One'
Majalla, Ottoman code of the law of 'obligations'
majdhūb, enraptured
al-makhārij fī'l-ḥiyal, 'ways out by devices'
malakūt, domain of 'angelic substances'
Mālik ibn Anas, the traditional founder of the Mālikī school of Sunnī law
Mālikī(s), the doctrine and followers of the Mālikī school of Sunnī law
al-Maʾmūn, a Caliph of Muʿtazilī persuasions
manāzil, 'halting places' in Ṣūfī experience
maqām(āt), stages along the Ṣūfī path

maʿrifa, Gnosis (Ṣūfī term)
mashīʾa, will
al-Masīḥ, the Messiah
Maʿrūf al-Kharkhī, early Ṣūfī
Maṣnavī, vast poem of al-Rūmī
maʿṣūm, infallible, impeccable
mastūr, 'hidden' (Shīʿī imāms)
al-Māturīdī(s), great theologian and his followers
matn, subject matter of a Tradition
mawālī, Persian 'clients'
mawlānā, 'our Master' (al-Rūmī)
al-Mawlawiyya, Ṣūfī brotherhood
Maẓālim, Court of complaints
Mīkāʾīl, archangel Michael, guardian of the Jews
Mirzā Ghulām Aḥmad Khān, founder of the Aḥmadiyya
Mirzā Ḥusayn ʿAlī Nūrī, founder of the Bahāʾīs
Muʿādh, judge (of very dubious historicity)
muʿāmalāt, obligations of a civil and personal nature
Muʿāwiya, governor of Syria
Muḥammad ʿAbduh, Egyptian jurist
Muḥammad ʿAlī Jinnah, Pakistani leader
Muḥammad Amīn al-Naqshbandī, Ṣūfī author
Muḥammad al-Bāqir, Shīʿī Imām
Muḥammad ibn ʿAbd al-Wahhāb, founder of Wahhābī movement
Muḥammad ibn al-Ḥanafiyya, regarded as Imām by *some* Shīʿīs
Muḥammad ibn al-Ḥasan al-Muntaẓar, 'hidden' Imām of 'Twelver' Shīʿīs
Muḥammad Sharīf, Mr Justice, Pakistanī judge
Muḥarram, month of Muslim year
al-Muḥāsibī (Ḥārith al-Muḥāsibī), early Ṣūfī author
Muḥyī al-Dīn ibn al-ʿArabī, see under Ibn ʿArabī.
muḥtasib, inspector of markets
Muʿīn al-Dīn Chistī, founder of Chistiyya Order
mujaddid, reformer, one view of Mirzā Ghulām, founder of Aḥmadiyya
mujāhidīn (mujāhidūn), supporters of 'Islamic Revolution' in Irān
muʿjizāt, miracles
mujtahid(s), those qualified to go back to the original sources of the law
mukāshafāt, revelations (Ṣūfī)
mukhālafa, difference (theological doctrine)
Munkar, angel who questions the dead
muqābal, opposite, corrective
muqallid(s), those bound by *taqlīd* (authority of predecessors)

murīd, postulant, disciple
Murji'īs (Murji'ites), those who postponed judgment
Mūsa'l-Kāzim, an Imam of the 'Twelver' Shī'īs
mushāhada, 'vision'
mushriqūn, those guilty of *shirq* (q.v.)
Muslim(s), those who 'surrender' to the God of Islam
Musta'lī(s), branch of the Ismā'īlī Shī'īs
mut'a, temporary marriage (in Shī'ī law); financial compensation to divorced wife (in some Sunnī schools)
mutakallim, 'Speaker' (an attribute of God)
Mu'tasim, a Caliph

Nafīsa, 'The Lady Nafisa', a very early female Ṣūfī
nafs, 'the flesh', the lower and appetitive self
Nag Hammadī, site in Upper Egypt of recent discovery of early documents
najāh, salvation
Nakīr, one of the two angels who question the dead
naql, the study and teaching of tradition
al-Naqshbandī, Bahā' al-Dīn, founder of Ṣūfī Order
Naqshbandiyya, the Order he founded
al-Nasafī, author of a creed
naẓar fī'l-māẓālim, investigation of complaints
nikāḥ, marriage
nikāḥ al-mut'a, temporary marriage among Shī'īs
niyya, intent
Naẓāmī Academy, in Baghdād
Niẓāmāt, secular courts in Ottoman Empire
Nizārīs of Alamut, the 'Assassins' (properly Ḥashāshīyūn, *ḥashīsh* smokers)
Nuṣayrīs, 'Alawīs of Syria who deify 'Alī

qaḍā', the divine decree
qadar, power, both divine and human (latter in sense of free will)
Qadarīs, 'Abilitarians', those who believed in man's free will
Qadhdhāfī, Colonel, ruler of Libya
qāḍī(s), judge, judges
Qā'id-i-A'zam, supreme leader
Qādirī(s), followers of the Qādiriyya Order (*q.v.*)
Qādiriyya, Ṣūfī Order named after 'Abd al-Qādir al-Jīlānī
qarīn, qarīna, evil genie-mate, who dogs men's footsteps
Qarmaṭī(s), Qarmathians (or Karmathians) of Iraq
qalb, heart

Qāsim Amīn, Egyptian reformer
Qatar, one of the Gulf states
qiyās, analogical extension of a recognized text
qul, 'say!', as in Qur'ān
Qur'ān, the Koran
Quraysh, the Arab tribe from which Muḥammad sprang
Quṭb, 'Axis', 'greatest living saint' (Ṣūfī)

Rabb, sovereign Lord
Rābi'a, early female Ṣūfī
Rahbar, Dr David, learned Muslim
al-Raḥmān al-Raḥīm, the Compassionate and Merciful
rāhib, anchorite
Ramaḍān, the month of fasting
ra'y, opinion
ribā, usury, a concept extended to many forms of speculative transactions
riḍa, satisfaction
al-Rifā'i, Aḥmad al-Rifā'ī, founder of a Ṣūfī Order
Rifā'iyya, the Order he founded
al-Risāla, book written by al-Shāfi'ī
al-Riyāḍ, Riyadh, capital of Sa'ūdī Arabia
rūḥ, spirit
al-Rūmī, Jalāl al-Dīn, great mystical poet of Persia

ṣadaqa, free-will offerings
Sa'dat, former President of Egypt
Ṣafavids, Shāhs of Persia
Ṣafaviyya, Ṣūfī Order
Ṣāḥib-al-Maẓālim, presided over the Maẓālim (Complaints) Court
al-Ṣaḥīḥ, al-Bukhārī's famous collection of Traditions
ṣaḥwa, awakening, sobriety
sā'iḥs, wandering monks
Salāma al-'Azzamī, a shaykh of the Azhar
al-ṣalawāt, the five daily prayers
sālik, traveller (a Ṣūfī term)
samā', hearing (in the Ṣūfī sense)
Samarqand, home of al-Māturīdī, the theologian
al-Sanhūrī, Egyptian jurist
al-Sanūsī, Sīdī Muḥammad al-Sanūsī, founder of a Ṣūfī Order
Sanūsī(s), followers of the Ṣūfī Order (Sanūsiyya), centred on Libya
Sarī al-Saqaṭī, a leading Ṣūfī
al-Sarrāj, author of early Ṣūfī book, *Kitāb al-Luma'*

al-Sāqī, cupbearer
Sayf al-Dawla, the Hamdānid of Aleppo
Sayyid ʿAlī Muḥammad of Shirāz, proclaimed himself to be the Bāb
Saʿūdī Arabia
al-Shādhilī, Nūr al-Dīn Aḥmad, a scholar from the Maghrib
al-Shādhiliyya, Ṣūfī Order inspired by al-Shādhilī
al-Shāfiʿī (Shāfiʿīs), founder of a Sunnī school of law, and his followers
al-Sharīʿa, Islamic law
al-shayṭān, Satan
shayāṭīn, devils
shaykh, sheikh, man of learning, old man
Shīʿa, Shīʿī(s), those who believe in a series of divinely appointed Imāms
Shīʿat ʿAlī, the first phase of the Shīʿa
al-Shiblī, famous Ṣūfī
Shihāb al-Dīn ʿUmar al-Suhrawardī, Ṣūfī after whom a Ṣūfī Order was named (*q.v.*)
shirb, drinking
shirk, the association of anything, or anyone else, with God
al-Suhrawardiyya, the Ṣūfī Order named for Shihāb al-Dīn al-Suhrawardī
shufʿa, a special right of a co-owner of land
shurṭā, police
ṣiddīq, honest, strictly veracious, used by early Ṣūfīs of their spiritual adepts
Sīdī Muḥammad al-Sanūsī, grandfather of King Idris of Libya
al-Ṣifāt al-azaliyya, God's eternal qualities
silsila, chain of spiritual affiliation (Ṣūfī)
sīra, term used for a life of Muḥammad
sirr, 'inmost being' (Ṣūfī term)
siyāsa sharʿiyya, sphere of lawful discretion in legislation
subḥāna'llāh, 'praise be to God' (one of the phrases used in the *dhikr*)
ṣūf, wool
Ṣūfī(s), Muslim mystics
sukr, intoxication (used of ecstasy by Ṣūfīs)
Sulaymān, Solomon
Sulaymānīs, sub-sect of the Ismāʿīlī Shīʿis
Sulṭān, title of Ottoman rulers
al-*sunna*, the practice of the Prophet, established by the *aḥādīth* (*q.v.*)
Sunnī(s), orthodox Muslims, their schools of law, teaching and practices
sūra, chapter of the Qur'ān

sutra, what covers or protects; what marks off the place of prayer

taʿabbudī, 'blind' obedience
al-Ṭabarī, Muslim author, (note 31)
Tahāfut al-Falāsifa, 'The Collapse of the Philosophers', written by al-Ghazālī (*q.v.*)
takhayyur, an eclectic principle used in legislation based on the *Sharīʿa*
takhṣīṣ al-qaḍāʾ, limitation of jurisdiction
ṭalāq, divorce
ṭālib, pupil, seeker (Ṣūfī term)
talfīq, 'patching', combining two different opinions in a new enactment
Ṭalḥa, a leading Companion of Muḥammad, who rose in revolt aganst ʿAlī
Taʿlīmīs, a group of extreme Ismāʿīlī Shīʿīs
Ṭanṭā, a town in Lower Egypt, with a shrine of al-Badawī
tanzīh, removal, making transcendent (theological doctrine)
Tanẓīmāt, reforms in Ottoman Empire
taqlīd, acceptance of the rulings of earlier authorities
ṭarīqa, Ṣūfī path, Ṣūfī Order
taṣawwuf, the practice of Ṣūfism
tawakkul, dependence on God, sometimes mendicancy
al-Ṭawāsīn, book written by al-Ḥallāj (*q.v.*)
tawba, repentance
tawḥīd, unity of Godhead; theology; merging of oneself with God (Ṣūfī)
tawrāt, Torah, the Jewish law
al-Ṭayyib, 'hidden' Imām of one branch of Ismāʿīlīs
al-Tijānī (Abū'l-ʿAbbās Aḥmad), founder of a Ṣūfī Order
al-Tijāniyya, the offshoot (of an older Order) which al-Tijānī founded
Ṭūs, the home of al-Ghazālī

udhkur(ū), remember, remind yourself; one of the bases of the *dhikr* (*q.v.*)
ʿUmān, Oman
ʿUmar ibn al-Khaṭṭāb, second of the 'Rightly Guided' Caliphs
Umayya(ds), the dynasty which succeeded the Rightly Guided Caliphs
ʿUthmān, Third of the Rightly Guided Caliphs, of Ummayed stock
ummī, illiterate (as Muslims claim that Muḥammad was)
ʿuqūbāt, punishments, criminal sanctions
ʿurf, custom, customary law

wadd, wadūd, love
wuḍū', ritual purification
waḥdat al-shuhūd, oneness of Witness (Ṣūfī)
waḥdat al-wujūd, oneness of Being (Ṣūfī)
Wahhābī(s), prevalent doctrine of central Arabia
wajd, feeling, ecstasy (Sufi term)
wālī, local governor
walī(s), awliyā', saints
waqf, wuqūf, pious (or family) foundation
wazīr, minister
wuṣūl, attainment, union (Ṣūfī)

yaḥibb, 'he loves'
Yazīd I, son of Muʿāwiya

Zia al-Ḥaqq, former President of Pakistan
zāhid, ascetic
Ẓāhirī(s), a school of complete literalists
zakāt, legally enforceable alms
zār, a ritual to exorcise a *jinn (q.v.)*
Zaydī(s), the least extreme of the Shīʿīs
Zayd ibn Thābit, made first recension of the Qur'ān
zāwiya, small mosque with religious centre
al-Zubayr, leading Companion of Muḥammad who rose in revolt against ʿAlī

Index

al-ʿAbbās 15
ʿAbbāsids 15, 17, 22, 66
ʿAbd al-ʿAzīz ibn Saʿūd 93
ʿAbd al-Mālik, Caliph 50
ʿAbd al-Qādir al-Jīlāni 90
ʿAbd al-Wahhāb al-Shaʿrani 92
Abū Bakr 13
Abū Hāshim 67
Abū Ḥanīfa 17–18
Abū Sulaymān of Damascus 72
Abū Ṭālib 4
Abū Ṭālib al-Makki 73
Abū Yazīd (Bāyazīd) al-Bisṭami 71, 91
Abū'l-ʿAbbas Aḥmad al-Tijānī 91
Addison, J. T. 12
Adonis 162
Adoptionism 127–129, 141, 181–182
Advaita Vedanta 60, 71, 80
Aesop 27
Āghā Khān communities 17, 52, 101, 107, 109
aḥādīth, see Traditions
aḥādīth qudsiyya (sayings of God outside the Qur'an) 45, 208
Aḥmad al-Badawī 91
Aḥmad al-Ḥawārī 68
Aḥmad al-Rifāʿī 91
Aḥmad ibn Ḥanbal 10, 18, 20, 72, 99
Aḥmadiyya 42
ʿĀʾisha 14
Aisha Bawani Waqf 234
Alamūt, Grand Master of 17
ʿAlawis (ʿAlawites) 4, 101
Alexander the Great 27
Alexandrians 152
ʿAlī 6, 13–14, 16–17, 51, 67, 88, 100–101
ʿAlī Zayn al-ʿAbidīn 15
Almsgiving 29
Althaus, Paul 172
ʿAmal 97, 102
An-Nawawi 243
Anderson, J. N. D. 205–206
Anglo-Muhammad Law 108
anhypostatos 151, 193
Animism 24, 35, 92, 239–241
Apocrypha, New Testament 225–226
Apollinarius, Apollinarianism 150–152, 154–155, 182
Apologists, the 145–146
Arberry, A. J. 73, 90, 93
ʿārif 84
Aristotle, Aristotelianism 21, 62, 68–69, 153–154, 243
Arius, Arianism 132, 144, 147–150, 152–153, 182, 254
Asad, President 101
Ascension, *see* Jesus, ascension
al-Ashʿarī 21, 53–55, 58
Ashʿarī(s) 21–23, 213
Assassins, *see* Nizārīs of Alamūt
ʿAṭāʾur-Raḥīm, Muḥammad 232–234
Athanasian Creed 207
Athanasius 148, 151, 183
Athenagoras 145
Athos, Mount, monks of 89
Atonement, *see* Christ, work of; Jesus, atonement

Attis 162
Augustine of Hippo 78–79, 144, 183
Avatars 162–163
Averroes 59
Avicenna 59
awliyā' see walī
Āyatullāh 16, 102

Bābīs 42
Badawiyya 91
Badr, battle of 236
Bahā' al-Dīn, Naqshband 91
Bahā' al-Dīn Zakarīyā' 90
Bahā'Allāh (Mirza Ḥusayn 'Alī Nūrī) 42
Bahā'īs 42, 112
Baḥīra 5, 65
Baillie, D. M. 134–135, 147, 185
Ballantyne, William 113
Barker, C. Edward 133–134
Barnabas, Gospel of 120, 209, 223–234
Barth, Karl 143, 188
Basilides 70, 141, 238
Bektāshīs (Bektashiyya) 78, 91
Bell, Richard 8, 46
Berbers 14
Bhagavad Gita 175, 177
Bibliolatry 239
Bibliomancy 239
Bishr al-Ḥāfī 72
Book of Hierotheos 74
Bourguiba, President, of Tunisia 107
Bouyer, Louis 122
Brenz, Johann 184
Bruce, F. F. 188–189, 201
Buddha, Gautama 165, 168–169, 175, 177
Buddhism 60, 71–72, 162, 164
al-Bukhārī 46, 237, 243
Byzantine Church 138, 235
Byzantines 5, 12

Caird, G. B. 118, 173
Caliphate, the 13
Caliphs, 'Rightly Guided' 14–15
Cappadocean Fathers 144
Carmel, Battle of the 14
Cerinthus 70, 128, 141, 238
Chalcedon, Council of 152
Chalcedon, Definition of 117, 133, 137, 152–155, 159, 161, 182, 194
Chemnitz, Martin 184
Chistiyya 91
Christ, work of 134, 148–150, 154, 157–158, 168–169, 175–176, 220; *see also* Jesus, atonement
Christianity
  claims of 178–179; dialogue with Islam 178, 205, 207; dialogue with Jews 177–178; and other religions 175–179
Christians in Qu'rān (people of the Injīl) 209
Christological controversies, *see* Adoptionism; Apollinarius, Apollinarianism; Arius, Arianism; Dyothelites; Monophysites; Nestorius, Nestorianism
Christological controversies and Islam 156
Christological heresies, *see* Cerinthus; Docetism; Eutyches, Eutychianism; Gnosticism
Christology 137–159
  Alexandrian 86, 149–150, 159, 182
  Antiochene 149–150, 159, 182, 250
  and Aristotelian logic 153–154
  and atonement 187–189, 207
  'downward' 117, 127–132, 145, 206
  dualist, *see* Christology, Antiochine
  evolution and development 145, 249
  incarnational (ontological) 192
  inspirational (functional) 192
  Logos 130
  Lutheran 117, 157–159, 182, 184
  monist, *see* Christology, Alexandrian
  and New Testament 167, 186–187, 207
  Reformation 157, 161
  Reformed 117, 159, 182, 184
  and resurrection 189–192
  Spirit, *see* Christology, inspirational
  two natures 192–193
  'upward' 117–127, 206
  Western 153
  'word-flesh', *see* Christology, Alexandrian
  'word-man', *see* Christology, Antiochine
  see also Christological controversies; *enhypostatos*; *homoousios*; *Hypostasis*; Jesus, titles; *kenōsis*; *Kenotic Theory; anhypostatos*
Circumcision, female 241

Circumcision, male 34
Clement of Alexandria 146–147, 233
Collyridians 11
Communicatio idiomatum 151
Concubinage 33–34
Copts 36–38
Coulson, N. J. 52
Cragg, Kenneth 61–63, 66, 94, 120
Cullmann, Oscar 126
Cyril of Alexandria 151–153, 158, 183, 250

Dār al-Ḥarb 30–31, 38
Dār al-Islām 30, 38
darwīsh (dervish) 74, 79, 83
Dā'ūdīs 101
Decisio Saxonica 1624 158
Demon pollution, cleansing from 240
Demons, *see jinn*
Dervish Brotherhoods or Orders 4, 23–24, 90–91
Devil, *see* Iblīs
Devil-mate, *see qarīn*
dhikr (Sufi religious exercise) 24, 60, 84–86, 88, 91, 214
Dhū al-Nūn 72
Dhū'l-Qarnayn 27
Divorce 31–33, 105, 108–109, 114
Docetism 12, 132, 140–141, 149–150, 152, 182, 201; psychological 132, 140, 182
Dodd, C. H. 118–119, 199
Drugs, hallucinogenic 87
Druze 4, 17, 101–102
Dualism 153
Duns Scotus 242–243
Dyophysites 153, 182
Dyothelites 155

Ebionites 140, 182, 201
Eckhart 74
enhypostasis 154–155
enhypostatos 193
Enslin, M. S. 226
Ephesus, Council of 151
Ephraim of Antioch 155
Euchites 88
Eugene of Savoy, Prince 223
Eutyches, Eutychianism 54, 151–153
Evans, Christopher 171

Family law 104–105, 111–112; *see also* divorce; marriage; polygamy; slavery

fanā' (extinction of individual existence) 73, 78, 84–85, 87, 243, 245
al-Faqīh 16
al-Fārābī 21, 68–69, 74
Fasting 29
fatāwā, fatāwī (legal opinions) 53, 239
Fāṭima 5
Fāṭimids 17, 74, 101
Feast of Sacrifice 240
Fedayeen 40, 42, 97
fikr (thought, meditation) 85, 87, 214
Five Pillars of Islam 28–30, 57
Food laws 34
Formula of Concord 158
Fra Marino 223, 228, 231–232
Francis of Assisi 74
Friends of God (Islamic saints) 92–93
al-Fuḍayl ibn'Iyāḍ 67, 71
Fundamentalism, Islamic 40–42, 51, 93, 114, 205
  Shī'ī 97, 112
  Sunnī 97

Gabriel, archangel 5, 26, 43–44, 98
al-Gadhdhāfī 91
Galatian Decree (*Decret. Gelasii.*) 225, 232
Galot, Père J. 122, 193, 198
Gambling 34
Gardet, L. 85–86
Gess 184
al-Ghazālī 22–23, 59–60, 73–74, 78–80, 85–87, 89, 213–215
Gibb, Hamilton 56, 81
Giessen, theologians of 158, 184
Gnosticism 12, 60, 69–71, 121, 141, 152, 201
God
  in Christianity, nature of 210–212, 216, 220–222, *see also* Trinity; impassibility of 197–199;
  in Islam 20, 25–26, 30, 37, 141, 220–222
    99 Beautiful Names of 26, 61, 63, 156, 212; attributes, 20, 58–59, 61, 156, 211–212, 215; essence 20, 58–59, 86, 156, 211–212; identification with, *see ittiḥād*; knowledge of 59, 63, 213–214: love of 60–62, 75, 84, 215, 219; transcendence of 25–26, 62–63

156, 212, 215; union with 60, 70, 73, 75–76, 80, 87, *see also wahdat al-shuhūd, wahdat al-wujūd*; unity of (*'Ilm al-Tawhīd*) 43, 57–64, 210–212, 239
in Judaism, nature of 210–211
Green, Michael 210
Gregory of Nazianus 150
Gregory of Nyssa 183
Grillmeier, A. 152

Ḥafs 47
al-Ḥākim 17
al-Ḥallāj, al-Ḥusayn bin Manṣūr 23, 60, 74–76, 85–87
Ḥanafī(s) 17–19, 48–49, 99, 104–105, 241
Ḥanbalis 18, 21–22, 49, 99, 104, 238
Ḥanīfs 235
al-Ḥārith al-Muḥasibī 72–73
Harnack, A. 158
al-Ḥasan 15–16, 67, 102
Ḥasan al-Baṣrī 67
Hāshimīs 4, 15
Hastings, James 225
Hebrews, Gospel to the 144
Hesychasts 89
Hick, John 162–169, 173, 175–177
Hijāz 49
Hilaria, the 162
Hinduism 60, 162–164, 175, 177, 240, 250
Hishām, Caliph 16
Ḥizb Allāh (Hezbollah) 97, 102, 112
Hogarth, D. G. 10
Holy Spirit 12, 26, 126, 143–145, 191, 202, 206, 210–211
Holy War, *see* Jihād
Homoousios 145, 152
Hooker, Richard 253
Houris (Arabic *ḥūr*) 240
ḥulūl (fusion of being) 60, 75–76, 80, 87
Ḥulūlīs 76
Hunter, A. M. 124
al-Ḥusayn 15–16, 101
Hypostasis 143, 153–155, 182, 193

Ibāḍīs 12, 14, 50–52, 100
Iblīs 27
Ibn Abī Dāwūd 47
Ibn 'Arabī 75, 77–78, 80–81, 245
Ibn 'Aṭā' Allāh 86
Ibn Rushd 21, 59, 69
Ibn Sīnā 21, 59, 69
Ibrāhīm ibn Adham 67, 71, 91
Idrīs, King of Libya 91
ijma' (consensus) 18, 48–49, 52, 56, 98
ijtihād (right to go back to sources) 16, 19, 41, 53, 56, 100
ijtihād, neo- 100, 107
Ikhwān al-Ṣafā 17
'illa (underlying principle) 48, 98
Imām 15–16, 51, 57, 59; 'hidden' 16, 101–102
Incarnation, *see* Jesus, incarnation
Injīl (New Testament) 208–209, 236–237
Injīl, people of (Christians) 209
Interest, *see ribā*
Iran, Islamic Revolution 1979 110, 112
Irenaeus 146, 233
'Īsā, *see* Jesus, in Islam
Isis 162
Islam
and angels 25–26; articles of faith ('aqā' id) 25–28, 57; and Christianity 25, 30, 36, 60, 96; civil and personal obligations (*mu'āmalāt*) 28; contemporary crisis of 37–40; creed (*Kalima*) 28; development 3–4, 12–24; divine books 27; eschatology 12, 27; faith and practice 24–35; and freedom of religion 241; and freewill 230; and God's Decrees 27–28; and Greek philosophy 20, 58–59, 62, 96; and Judaism 27, 43–45, 60; and last judgment 27; law in, *see* Sharī'a; and Logos 175; and mysticism, *see* Mysticism, Islamic; nature of 37–40; origin of term 235; origins 4–12; and other religions 231; revival of 39–40; scholastic theologians 21–22; study of 205; and Talmud 45; theology (*tawḥīd*) 24, 57–64, 205; today and tomorrow 3, 35–42; Traditions 4; and Trinity 25; view of Bible 208–209; worship (*'ibādāt*) 28
Islam in Algeria 16; Arabia 18, 90; Central Arabia 18; Cyrenaica 91; East Africa 15–16, 18, 107, 109; Egypt 18, 41, 90–91, 97, 101, 104–106, 113; Gulf states 113;

India 16, 90, 108; Indian subcontinent 40, 42, 108; Iran 16, 40–42, 97, 102, 105, 110, 112, 114; Iraq 16, 41, 102, 104–105; Jordan 105; Kuwait 104, 113; Lebanon 16, 41, 97, 101–102, 112; Levant 42; Libya 41, 91, 97, 113; Morocco 105; North Africa 90, 100; North and West Africa 18, 91; Northern India 17; Oman 100, 113; Ottoman Empire 17, 91, 103–104; Pakistan 41, 97, 105, 110–112; Persia 91; Sa'udi Arabia 35, 38, 97, 112–113; Singapore 105; Somalia 105; South-East Asia 18; Sudan 18, 41, 97, 105, 113; Syria 16–17, 90, 101, 105; Tanzania 105; Tripolitania 16, 91; Tunisia 32, 105, 107, 109; Turkey 32, 91; Yemen 16, 38, 101, 105; Zanzibar 100
Ismā'īl 16, 101
Ismā'īlis ('Seveners') 16, 59, 74, 89
Isrāfīl, archangel 26
Ithnā 'Asharī ('Ashariyya) ('Twelvers') 50, 52, 97, 238
ittiḥād (identification with God) 59–60, 76, 80, 87
'Izrā'īl, Archangel 26

Jābir ibn Ḥayyān 67
Ja'far al-Sādiq 16
Jalāl al-Dīn al-Rūmī 77, 81–82, 91
Jamā'at-i-Islāmī 40–42, 97
James, Montague 225
Janissaries 91
Jeffrey, Arthur 8, 43–44, 47
Jesus
  ascension 125–126, 211, 218
  atonement 134, 168–169, 181, 187–189, 206–207, 213, 219
  consciousness of God as father 122–123
  death 166–167, 174–175, 179, 201–202, 216, 220–221, 237, 254; in Kashmir (Aḥmadiyyas belief) 42
  deification 167–169, 173–175
  dependence on Father 199–200
  divine authority 124
  divinity 185, 206, *see also* Jesus, titles
  eternal generation 145, *see also* Jesus, pre-existence
  exaltation 125–126, 132, 145, 166, 181–182, 185, 190–191, 196–197, 202, 206, 213, 219
  filial consciousness 124, 164–165, 189
  glorified humanity 196
  in *Gospel of Barnabas* 223–224, 229–230
  humanity 185, 192–195, 206
  impersonal human nature (*anhypostatos*) 151, 155, 193–194, 250
  incarnation 132–135, 149, 159, 169, 175, 181, 185, 194–197, 201, 203, 206–207, 220; and atonement 187–189; and other religions 117, 161–179; and personal faith today 181–203
  in Islam 11, 27, 119–120, 125, 178, 200–201, 207–208, 218–219, 224, 228–229, 234–235, 237, 254–255 ascension 218; death 11–12, 27, 70, 78, 125, 201, 218–219, 255; Messiah (Masīḥ 224, 234; pre existence 219; second coming 218
  prayer in John 17 131
  pre-existence 129–131, 135, 182, 184, 19
  resurrection 125, 145, 162, 166–167, 169–175, 181, 189–190, 202, 206–207, 219, 221; and empty tomb 172–173; implications of 173–175; theories of 169–171
  second coming 218
  and sin 200–201
  titles
    Alpha and Omega 203; Christ 167–168; God 192, 253; God and Saviour 192; High Priest 203, 221; Logos, *see* Logos, *see also* Jesus, titles, Word; Lord 128, 165–166, 174, 181, 186–187, 190, 192, 202, 211, 247–248; Messiah 118–119, 124, 128, 165–166, 178, 181, 188, 201; Saviour 222; Son of God 120, 135 147, 165–166, 174, 181, 188, 190, 192, 196, 202, 212–213; Son of Man 118, 165, 168–169, 181; Word 130–131, 146, 189, 191–192, 206, 211
  two natures 206; *see also* virgin birth
'Jesus is Lord' 117, 126–127, 141, 169, 203

Jibrīl (Gabriel), archangel 26
Jihād (Holy War) 30–31, 38, 95, 114
jinn 6, 26–27, 35
Jinnah, Muḥammed 'Alī 110
John of Damascus 20, 138–139
Jomier, Father 231
Judaism 241–243
Judas Iscariot, crucifixion of 229–230, 234, 255
al-Junayd 60, 71–74, 245
Justin Martyr 145
al-Juwaynī, Imām al-Ḥaramayn 62, 79

Ka'ba, pilgrimage of 6–7, 17, 29
kalām (apologetic or scholastic theology) 21, 58, 72
Karīm Khān 101
Kaysānīs 15
Kenōsis 151, 158–159, 183–185, 194
Kenotic Theory 159, 183–185, 194, 207
Khadīja 5–6, 65–66
Khalīfa Hārūn al-Rashīd 71
khānqāh 80, 89–90
Kharījī(s) 14, 17, 51
Khawārij 57, 100, 139
al-Kindī 21
Knox, John 128, 130–132, 197
Koran, see Qur'ān
krypsis 151, 158, 184

La Monnoye 225, 227
Lake, Kirsopp 173
Lampe, Geoffrey 132
Lane-Poole, Stanley 33–34
Last Supper 169
Law, *see* Sharī'a
Law courts 102–103
Leo of Rome 152–153
Leontius of Jerusalem 154
Lightfoot, R. H. 131
Logos 130, 145–151, 154, 156, 159, 175, 183, 185, 193; in human life, 175, 177; and Islam 20, 131, 146, 177; and Old Testament 177; 'two states' of 195–197
Luqmān 27

Macdonald, D. B. 8, 20, 65, 68–69, 73–76, 78–79, 138–139
McIntyre, John 153–155
MacKinnon, D. M. 200, 254
Mackintosh, H. R. 147, 158–159
madrasa 74, 79, 88
Mahdī 12, 16, 31, 42
Mālik ibn Anas 18
Malīkī(s) 17–18, 48–49, 99, 104, 238
al-Ma'mūn, Caliph 20, 58
Man, nature of 213
Mandaeans 70
Manichaeans 70
Manichaeanism 121
Marcellus of Ancyra 143
Margoliouth, Prof. 227
Marriage 31–32, 105; child 109; temporary 31–32
Marriage customs 241
Marsh, John 131
Martel, Charles 3, 95
Martyrs 240
Ma'rūf al-Kharkhī 70
Mary the Virgin Theotokos 152
Mascall, E. L. 193, 196–198
mashī'a (wisdom and will of God) 213, 215
al-Mātarīdī 22, 58
Mātarīdīs 54
Mawlānā 91
al-Mawlawiyya 91
Mecca 30, 235
Metzger, B. M. 162, 233
Mikā'il (Michael), archangel 26
Mirzā Ghulām Aḥmad Khān 42
Modalism 142–143, 253
Monarchia (Monarchy) 143, 145
Monarchianism 142; Dynamic 142; Modalist 142, 146; Patripassian 142; and Qur'an 142–143
Monism 80, 144–145, 153
Monophysite Church 138
Monophysites 5, 12, 153, 155, 182, 235, 237
Monothelites 155
Mosaic law 242
Moule, C. F. D. 119, 122, 127, 130, 186–187, 190–193
Moule, Handley 201
Mu'ādh 48
Mu'āwiya 14–15
Muftī 239
Muḥammad
  character of 7–10; and Christianity 5, 11–12, 12, 138, 237;

death 7; early life 4–5; and Hijra 6; illiteracy (*ummi*) 236; inspiration of 45; and Jews 5, 7; as light of God 68; as Messiah, in *Gospel of Barnabas* 224, 228, 234; and mysticism 22, 65–66; and New Testament 209; obedience to 236; and Old Testament 7, 209, 236–237; and Qur'an 5, 9–10; religion of 65–66, 236; revelations to 5, 210
Muḥammad son of Ismāʿīl 101
Muḥammad ʿAbduh 41, 105
Muḥammad al-Bāqir 16, 101
Muḥammad ʿAṭāʾ ur Rahim 232–234
Muḥammad, Companions of 13, 99
Muḥammad ibn ʿAbd al-Wahhāb 93
Muḥammad ibn al-Hasan al-Muntazar 16, 101–102
Muḥammad ibn al-Hanafiyya 16
Muḥammad, son of ʿAlī 15
al-Muḥāsibī 72–73
Muḥyi al-Dīn ibn al-ʿArabī (ibn ʿArabī) 76
Muʿīn al-Dīn Chistī 91
mujāhidīn 97
mujtahid(s) (those qualified to go back to law sources) 53, 99, 102
mukhalafa (difference) 25, 63
Munkar 26
Murjiʾīs (Murjiʾites) 57, 139
Mūsa'l-Kāẓim 16, 101
Muslim Brotherhood 40–41, 97
Muslim (d.261) 237
Mustaʿlīs 101
Muʿtasim 68
Muʿtazilīs (Muʿtazila) 19–22, 28, 54, 58–59, 156, 211–212, 239
mystery religions 161–163
Mysticism, Christian 214
Mysticism, Islamic 22–24, 65–94, 205, 214; and Christianity 67–68; ecstasy 23, 72, 78, 87; external influences on 60, 62–71; and Greek church 23, origins 65–67; *see also* Sufī(s), Sufism

Nafīsa, Lady 67
Nakīr 26
Naqshbandiyya 91
al-Nasafī 59, 156
Neill, Stephen 178
Neo-Platonism 23, 60, 69, 72, 74, 76, 80
Nestorian Church 138
Nestorianism 54, 144, 150–153, 155, 159, 182, 237
Nestorius, Nestorians 5, 12, 54, 144, 150–153, 155, 159, 182, 235, 237
Newbigin, J. E. L. 163, 178–179
Nicaea, Council of 148–149
Nicene Creed 117, 133, 137, 148, 150, 161, 182, 194, 207, 249
Niceno-Constantinople Creed 249
Nicholson, R. A. 4, 68, 71, 76–77, 81–83, 92–93
Night of Power (*Laylat al-Qadr*) 237
Nirvana 243
Niẓāmāt courts 103
Nizārīs of Alamut (Assassins) 101
nous 150
Nūr al-Dīn Aḥmad al-Shādhilī 90
Nuṣayrīs (ʿAlawīs) 17, 101

Old Testament 175–176, 208, 210, 216
Origen 145–147, 183, 233, 249
Orthodox (Byzantines) 235
Osborn, R. 8
Osiris 162
Ottoman Caliphate 38
Ousia 145, 154

Pannenberg, Wolfart 158–159, 170, 172, 174, 183–184, 188
Pantheism 72
Passibility 198
Passion Play of 10th of Muharram 15
Pearce-Higgins, Canon J. 133
Philo of Alexandria 130
Physis 154
Physis anhypostasis 154
Physis enhypostasis 154
Pilgrimage 6–7, 29–30, 40, 240
Pittenger, W. N. 154
Plato, Platonism 21, 68–69, 145
Plerōsis 194
Plotinus 23, 68–69
Pluralism 161
Pneuma 150
Polygamy 32–33, 41, 107, 109, 114
Portio 143
Praxeas 142
Prayer, Islamic 28–29, 78, 88, 240
Predestination and freewill 57

Pre-existence, *see* Jesus, pre-existence
Proclus 69
Prolepsis 151
Prosōpon 154
Pseudo-Dionysius the Areopagite 69, 72, 74
Psychē 150
purdah 32

qaḍā' (decree of God) 213, 215
qadar (power of God) 213, 215
Qadarīs, Qadarites (Abilitarians) 19, 57–58, 139
qāḍī(s) 50, 55, 102, 239
Qādirīs (Qādiriyya) 90
Qā'id-i-A'zam 110
qarīn, qarīna (devil-mate) 24, 26, 239
Qarmaṭians 17
Qāsim Amīn 105, 107
Qiyās (analogical deductions) 18, 48–50, 52, 98
Quick, O. 198–199
Qur'ān
  composition and text 13, 46–47, 49–50, 209–210; and Greek philosophy 23; inspiration of 6, 39, 47, 98, 208, 214, 237; and Muḥammad 5, 9–10; nature 20, 43–44, 58, 156, 211–212, 236; and New Testament 47–48, 209; style 8; and Talmud 8; and Torah 43–44
Quraysh 4, 6–7, 13, 238
Quṭb (Axis) 24, 93, 239

Rābi'a 66
Ragg, Lonsdale and Laura 224–228, 230–233
Rahbar, David 220–221
Ramaḍān 29
Ramakrishna Mission 162
Ramsay, Michael 125
Repentance 219–220
Revelation, divine, in Christianity and Islam 207–210
ribā (interest, usury) 34, 41, 50, 103, 111
Richardson, Alan 121
Rifā'iyya 91
Robber Council (Ephesus 449) 152
Robinson, John A. T. 129, 132, 189
Rosary, in Islam 239
Rūmī, *see* Jalāl al-Dīn al-Rūmi

Sabellius 142
Sacrifice, animal 241
Safavi Order 91
al-Ṣaḥīḥ, of al-Bukhārī 46
Sāhib al-Maẓālim 102
Sale, George 223–225
Salvation 216–218; in Islam 216–218; in New Testament 216–217; in non-Christian religions 176–177
al-Sanhūrī, Dr 104
Sanūsī Brotherhood 40, 93
Sanūsīs 97
Sarī al-Saqaṭī 70, 72, 91
al-Sarrāj 83
Satanic verses 237
Sayf al-Dawla (the Hamdānid) 68
Sayyid 'Alī Muḥammad of Shirāz 42
Schacht, Joseph 56
Scripture, inspiration of 210
secularism and Islam 40
'Seveners', *see* Ismā'īlīs
al-Shādhiliyya 90
al-Shāfi'ī 18, 45, 67, 98–99, 242
Shāfi'īs 18, 49, 99, 238
Sharī'a 18, 24–25, 43, 205; and Byzantine law 50; and commercial law 113; and Eastern Churches 50–51; extent of 28; and Jewish law 50; law of contract 34; and lawful discretion (*Siyāsa shar'iyya*) 55; and legislative codes 55–56; and Natural Law 54, 56; nature of 54–55; before 1850 98–103, 114; since 1850 103–109, 114; punishments (*'uqūbāt*) 28, 34–35, 41, 111–112; reforms 105–109, 114; and Roman law 50; schools of 99; and secular courts 38–39, 55, 104; sources 48–56, 99; and Torah 100: and Western law 100
Sharīf, Mr Justice Muḥammad 112
Shaykh Muhammad Amīn al-Naqshhbandi 93
Shaykh Salāma al-'Azzāmī of the Azhar 93
shaykh (man of learning) 82, 84, 88–90
al-shayṭān (Satan) 26–27
Shī'a 4, 14–17, 51
al-Shiblī 72–73
Shihāb al-Dīn 'Umar al-Suhrawardī 90

Shī'ī(s) 12, 17, 32, 41, 51–52, 57, 100–102, 139
Shillito, Edward 203, 222
shirk (polytheism, idolatry) 25, 30
Sīdī Muḥammad al-Sanūsī 91
Simon of Cyrene 238
Sixtus V, Pope 223, 231
Slavery 33–34, 41, 107, 114
Sox, David 226, 231–232
Spirit of God 211
Stephen bar Sudaili 74
Stoic philosophy 130
Streeter, B. H. 173
Substance, *see Ousia, Homoousios*
Substantia 143
Succession, laws of 109, 114
Succession, Wars of 13
Ṣūfī, origin of term 23, 67
Ṣūfī Brotherhoods 88–91
Ṣūfī convents 89–90
Ṣūfī monism 76–78
Ṣūfī mysticism
  and Buddhism 72, 86;
  higher planes of consciousness 84;
    and Jewish Kabbalah 80; states and stages 72, 82, 84–85, *see also fanā'*; and Yoga 85–86
Ṣūfī(s) 23, 25, 57, 59–60, 63, 67, 71, 73–76, 215, 239; repentance and self-mortification 83–84; *see also* Dervish Brotherhoods
Suhrawardiyya 90
Sulaymān (Solomon) 239
Sulaymānīs 101
Synapheia 151
sunna 45, 48–49, 98, 214
Sunnī(s) 12, 16–19, 32, 41, 51–52, 57, 74, 98–100; *see also* Ḥanafīs, Mālikīs, Shafi'īs, Hanbalīs
Suso 74
Sweetman, J. W. 144

al-Ṭabarī 237
talfīq (patching) 19, 55, 106
Ṭalḥa 14
Ta'līmīs 59
tanzīh 25–26, 62
Tanẓīmāt reforms 103
taqlīd 19, 53, 100
ṭarīqa 82, 88, 90
ṭalib 84
Tasker, R. V. G. 123
tawakkul 83–84
Taylor, Vincent 169
al-Ṭayyib 101
Temple, William 171, 185, 214, 222
Temple Gairdner, W. H. 224
Tertullian 141–144, 146
The Mystical Theology 69
The Myth of Christian Uniqueness 162, 176–177
The Myth of God Incarnate 162, 176
The Theology of Aristotle 68
Theodore of Mopsuestia 150
Theodorus Abucara 138
theotokos (God-bearer) 144, 152
Thomas Aquinas 243
Thomas, Gospel of 70, 255
Thomas à Kempis 74
Thomasius 184
Tijāniyya 91
Tillich, Paul 133
Toland, M 225, 227
Traditions, Islamic (*aḥādīth*) 10–11, 18, 20, 23, 39, 45–46, 48, 52, 62, 80, 98–99, 208
Trinity
  doctrine of 20, 132, 143, 146–147, 191, 199–200, 202, 206–207, 211–212, 234; Economic 143, 253; Essential 199–200; 'graded' (Origen) 145; and Islam 144
Tritheism 143–144, 191; and Qur'ān 144
Tübingen, theologians of 158, 184
Turner, H. E. W. 124, 142, 148–150, 153, 184, 187
'Twelvers' 16, 101

'Umar ibn al-Khaṭṭāb 13, 32
Umayyads 13, 15, 22, 138–139
Unitarianism 133
Upanishads 175, 177
Usury, *See ribā*
'Uthmān, Caliph 13–14, 17, 47

Venturini 173
Via negativa 72, 213–214
Virgin Birth (virginal conception) of Jesus 120–121, 151, 165, 189; and Islam 11, 121–122, 167, 212
Virgin Mary 11, 144, 151, 157, 212; in *Gospel of Barnabas* 228–230
Visser't Hooft, W. A. 177

von Dobschütz 233

Wahb 231
waḥdat al-shuhūd (oneness of Witness) 75–76, 80, 87
waḥdat al-wujūd (oneness of Being) 75–76, 80, 86–87
Wahhābīs 18, 40–41, 93, 97
walī 24, 92–93
wālī 102
Westminster Catechism, Shorter 213, 253
Weston, Frank 195–197
White, Dr 224
William of Occam 243
Wisdom of God 130, 141, 211
Women in Islam 33, 37, 104–105
Word, *see* Jesus, titles

Yazīd, I. 15
Young, Francis 162

Ẓāhirīs 76, 238
Żar ritual 27
Zarathustra 71
zāwiya 88–89
Zayd 6, 16, 101
Zayd ibn Thābit 46–47
Zaydīs 16, 101
Zia al-Ḥaqq, General 110–111
Zionism, and Islam 40
al-Zubayr 14
Zwemer, S. M. 3
Zwingli, H. 158